ST. EDMUND OF
ABINGDON

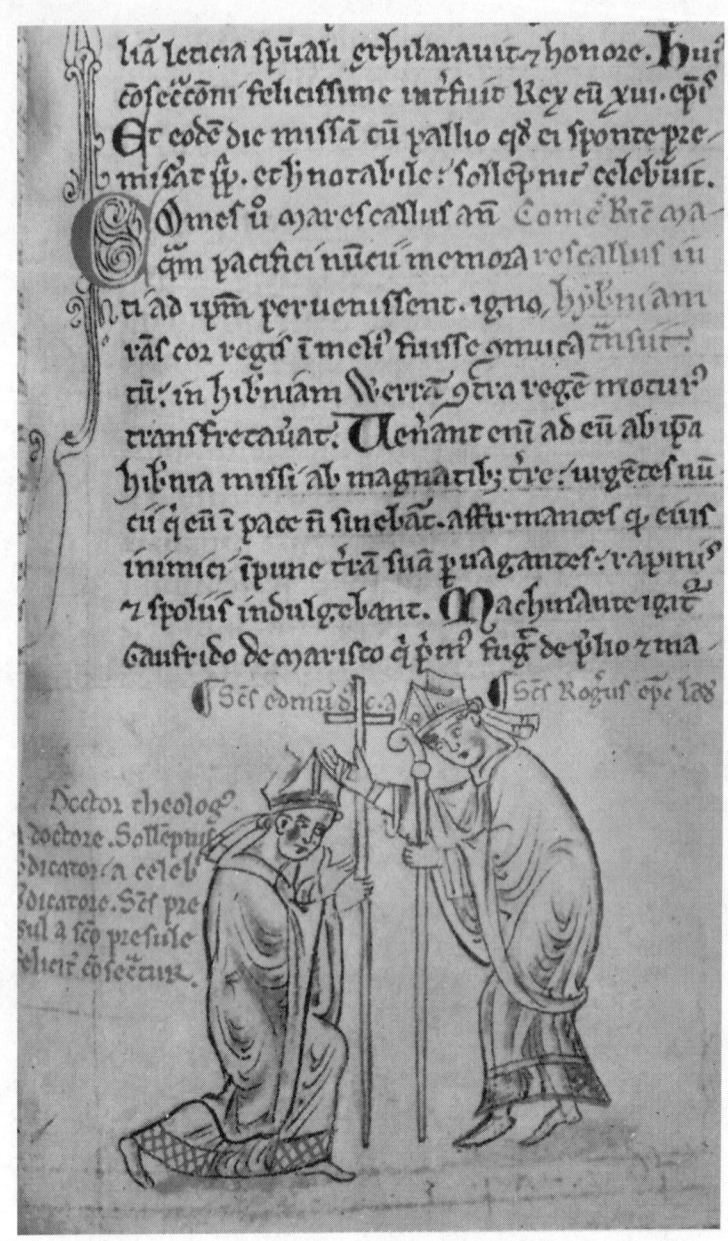

The consecration of Archbishop Edmund drawn by Matthew Paris in the margin of the *Historia Anglorum* (B.M. Royal MS. 14 C vii, fo. 122ʳ), cf. p. 89

ST. EDMUND OF ABINGDON

A Study in Hagiography and History

BY

C. H. LAWRENCE

OXFORD
AT THE CLARENDON PRESS

OXFORD
UNIVERSITY PRESS

Great Clarendon Street, Oxford OX2 6DP

Oxford University Press is a department of the University of Oxford.
It furthers the University's objective of excellence in research, scholarship,
and education by publishing worldwide in

Oxford New York

Athens Auckland Bangkok Bogotá Buenos Aires Calcutta
Cape Town Chennai Dar es Salaam Delhi Florence Hong Kong Istanbul
Karachi Kuala Lumpur Madrid Melbourne Mexico City Mumbai
Nairobi Paris São Paulo Singapore Taipei Tokyo Toronto Warsaw

with associated companies in Berlin Ibadan

Oxford is a registered trade mark of Oxford University Press
in the UK and in certain other countries

Published in the United States
by Oxford University Press Inc., New York

© Oxford University Press 1960

The moral rights of the author have been asserted

Database right Oxford University Press (maker)

Special edition for Sandpiper Books Ltd., 2000

All rights reserved. No part of this publication may be reproduced,
stored in a retrieval system, or transmitted, in any form or by any means,
without the prior permission in writing of Oxford University Press,
or as expressly permitted by law, or under terms agreed with the appropriate
reprographics rights organization. Enquiries concerning reproduction
outside the scope of the above should be sent to the Rights Department,
Oxford University Press, at the address above

You must not circulate this book in any other binding or cover
and you must impose this same condition on any acquirer

British Library Cataloguing in Publication Data

Data available

ISBN 0-19-821275-5

1 3 5 7 9 10 8 6 4 2

Printed in Great Britain
on acid-free paper by
Biddles Ltd., Guildford and King's Lynn

PREFACE

My interest in Edmund of Abingdon was first aroused by a series of lectures on the early Secular Masters of Oxford given by Fr. Daniel Callus ten years ago. I should like to thank him for this and for the enlightenment gained from him in subsequent discussions. I am very grateful to Sir Maurice Powicke, who initiated me into research and who has pursued me with many kindnesses. I should also like to thank Professor C. R. Cheney, Mr. W. A. Pantin, and Dr. C. H. Talbot for valuable criticism and help. I owe much to the unwearied interest and encouragement of Mr. A. B. Emden, who, with characteristic generosity, made over to me his collection of photostats when I embarked on the history of St. Edmund. He has also been kind enough to read the book in proof. The staff of the Clarendon Press has displayed much learning and great forbearance in preparing my texts for publication. Many others have given help with specific points and I have tried to discharge my debt to them in the notes. A grant from the Central Research Fund of London University enabled me to purchase microfilms of foreign manuscripts. My wife was manœuvred into compiling the index, and Mrs. Curran was very kind in permitting St. Edmund to impound a room of her flat for a period of several months.

Bedford College   C. H. L.

CONTENTS

The consecration of Archbishop Edmund — *frontispiece*

ABBREVIATIONS — ix

INTRODUCTION — 1

PART ONE

I. The *Quadrilogus* and the canonization process — 7
II. The Life by Eustace of Faversham — 30
III. The Pontigny Life and the Anonymous A — 47
IV. The Anonymous B — 61
V. The Anonymous C — 64
VI. The Life by Matthew Paris — 70
VII. A Comparative Synopsis — 100

PART TWO

I. The family of St. Edmund — 106
II. Oxford, Paris, and Salisbury — 110
III. The Canterbury election and politics — 124
IV. The *familia* of Archbishop Edmund — 138
V. Archbishop Edmund — 155

PART THREE

I. Text of the *Quadrilogus* — 187
II. Text of the *Vita S. Edmundi auctore Eustachio* — 203
III. Text of the *Vita S. Edmundi auctore Matthaeo Parisiensi* — 222

APPENDIXES

A. Letters of postulation — 290
B. The *acta* of St. Edmund — 303
C. Some documents relating to St. Edmund's family — 315
D. Two documents relating to Eustace of Faversham — 318
E. Muniments in the Trésor of Sens cathedral — 320
F. Manuscripts cited — 326

INDEX — 329

ABBREVIATIONS

AA. SS.	The *Acta Sanctorum* of the Bollandists.
AFH	*Archivum Franciscanum Historicum.*
Anal. Boll.	*Analecta Bollandiana.*
Ann. Mon.	*Annales Monastici*, ed. H. R. Luard (RS 1864–9), vols. i–iv.
Auvray	*Les Registres de Grégoire IX*, ed. L. Auvray (École française de Rome, 1896–1910).
Arch. Cant.	*Archaeologia Cantiana*
ASOC	*Analecta Sacri Ordinis Cisterciensis*
Berger	*Les Registres d'Innocent IV*, ed. E. Berger (École française de Rome, 1884–1921).
BHL	*Bibliotheca Hagiographica Latina* of the Bollandists (Brussels, 1898–9).
CChR	*Calendar of Charter Rolls.*
CCR	*Calendar of Close Rolls.*
CPL	*Calendar of Papal Letters.*
CPR	*Calendar of Patent Rolls.*
Canivez, *Statuta*	*Statuta Capitulorum Generalium Ordinis Cisterciensis*, ed. J. Canivez (Louvain, 1933–6).
Chron. Maiora	The *Chronica Majora* of Matthew Paris, ed. H. R. Luard (RS 1872–84).
CS	Camden Society.
CYS	Canterbury and York Society.
Denifle Chart.	*Chartularium Universitatis Parisiensis*, ed. H. Denifle and A. Chatelain (Paris, 1889–).
EETS	Early English Text Society
EHR	*English Historical Review*
Flores	*Rogeri de Wendover Flores Historiarum*, ed. H. O. Coxe, 5 vols. (Eng. Hist. Soc. 1841–4).
Fontanini	G. Fontanini, *Codex Constitutionum quas Summi Pontifices ediderunt in solemni canonizatione sanctorum* (Rome, 1792).

Abbreviations

Gervase	The *Gesta Regum* of Gervase of Canterbury, ed. W. Stubbs (RS 1880), 2 vols.
Hist. Angl.	The *Historia Anglorum* of Matthew Paris, ed. F. Madden (RS 1886–9), 3 vols.
Materials	*Materials for the History of Thomas Becket*, ed. J. C. Robertson & J. B. Sheppard (RS 1875–83), 7 vols.
MD. Thes.	E. Martène and U. Durand, *Thesaurus Novus Anecdotorum* (Paris, 1717).
MGH. SS.	*Monumenta Germaniae Historica, Scriptores.*
MOFPH	*Monumenta Ordinis Fratrum Praedicatorum Historica.*
OHS	Oxford Historical Society.
PL	J. P. Migne, *Patrologiae cursus completus, series latina* (Paris, 1844–55).
Potthast	A. Potthast, *Regesta Pontificum Romanorum 1198–1304* (Berlin, 1874–5).
Recueil	Bouquet etc. *Recueil des historiens des Gaules et de la France.*
RS	Rolls Series
TBGAS	*Transactions of the Bristol and Gloucester Archaeological Society.*
TRHS	*Transactions of the Royal Historical Society.*
Wallace	W. Wallace, *St. Edmund of Canterbury* (1893).
Wilkins	*Concilia Magnae Britanniae et Hiberniae* of David Wilkins (1737).

INTRODUCTION

CANONIZATION might do strange things with a man's reputation. Its object was not to benefit the dead, but to edify the living, and this lesson was taken to heart by the medieval hagiographer, who dipped his pen in prodigies and portents. Edmund of Abingdon, as transmitted to history through the work of his biographers, is hardly more than a lay figure draped in the religious sentiment of his age. But, although his character is hard to detach from the masses of hagiographical convention, his public life is of much interest to the historian of the thirteenth century. For St. Edmund is not only the first Oxford master to have been officially canonized, he is also the first member of the nascent university about whom anything considerable is known. He is the most conspicuous figure in the obscure company of Masters who were teaching Arts at Oxford in the last decade of the twelfth century and, if Roger Bacon is to be believed, he played a part in bringing the New Logic into the Oxford schools. He made his mark as a theologian also, though he never achieved the fame of Langton or Grosseteste. His *quaestiones* and glosses have, with one exception, disappeared, but there remains the *Speculum Ecclesie*, a work which was widely read in the Middle Ages and on which his reputation as a master of the spiritual life rested. As archbishop he was known as a stern upholder of the pastoral ideal and the champion of sacerdotal immunities, though in the latter role he was more moderate than some would have wished. But above all, it was his leadership during the war of Richard the Marshal which impressed his contemporaries. He was remembered as the intrepid archbishop who forced on the king a change of council and saved England from civil war.

Although St. Edmund's public life is not as well documented as could be desired, there is, in place of record, a plethora of literary materials, all of which took their origin from the canonization proceedings of the years 1244–6. There are on the one hand the records deposited by the commission, and on the other the different Lives, written before and after 1246, which drew on these records. The need for a critical examination of this material has long been obvious. No serious attempt has yet been made to establish the relationship of the various Lives one to another, or to the original records of the Process. Efforts to assign the Lives to authors have generally been unfortunate and ascriptions to this writer or that, often on trivial grounds, have only resulted in confusion. Yet the working out of the hagiographical tradition is an essential preliminary to placing Edmund in his proper place in the history of the thirteenth century. The absence of this kind of preliminary work on the materials for the Life of Thomas Becket[1] is the reason why no modern character study of Becket carries complete conviction.

It is perhaps understandable that the Lives of St. Edmund have not received much critical attention. The hagiographical tradition is complex and would-be students may have doubted whether the reward would justify the effort. For the picture of Edmund's personality painted by the Lives is not a specially attractive one. In place of a portrait they offer us an ascetical programme. They were more interested in the archbishop's private macerations than in public events, about which they are often unhelpful, if not actually misleading.

The object of this study is to trace the development of the hagiographical tradition and to apply the results of this investigation to some aspects of St. Edmund's career. Three texts are printed below, of which one, the *Quadrilogus*, is a collection of depositions made by four witnesses in the course of the canonization process, the second is the earliest Life of St. Edmund, a rather jejune work by the archbishop's chaplain, Eustace of Faversham, and the third is the Life by Matthew Paris. An attempt has been made to show how these three texts are interrelated and so to trace the early growth of the tradition. Since the relationship between these texts is a complex

[1] A notable exception to this is the study by E. Walberg, *La Tradition hagiographique de saint Thomas Becket avant la fin du xiie siècle* (Paris, 1929).

Introduction

one, it will be helpful to set it down immediately, in diagrammatic form. It can be represented as in Fig. 1.

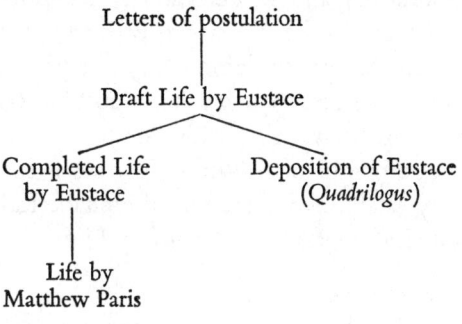

FIG. 1

As can be seen, the starting-point, the material that is which Eustace used, was the letters of postulation. Texts of the relevant letters have been included in an appendix. Of these three texts, the Life by Eustace and the *Quadrilogus* have never been published, although the latter has been used and quoted by modern writers from Anthony Wood onwards. The Life by Matthew Paris, for long unidentified, was published by Dom Wilfrid Wallace as an appendix to his biography of St. Edmund.[1] But Wallace believed it to be the work of Eustace, and his text was in no sense a critical one.

Although, from a critical point of view, these three texts have a unity of their own, they form only a part of the literary materials for the Life of Edmund of Abingdon. The *Quadrilogus* and the other records left by the Process were a quarry which attracted other workers, and four other Latin Lives of St. Edmund are extant. An attempt has been made to show how all these stand in relation to one another and to the original deposit of documents, and so to reconstruct the complete hagiographical tradition, as far as it can be known from the surviving sources. The results of this investigation are shown diagrammatically in Fig. 2. Part of the reconstruction must, in

[1] *St. Edmund of Canterbury* (1893), pp. 543-88.

the nature of the case, remain tentative. The official dossier of miracles, compiled by the papal commissioners in England, which underlies X and its derivatives, has unfortunately disappeared. Thus it has been easier to prove the existence of the missing source X than to demonstrate the precise form that it took, and for this reason it has been possible only to suggest the relationship between this source and the Anonymous B. Since the authorship of the other Lives has in no case been satisfactorily established, a system of alphabetical reference has been adopted, except for the Pontigny Life.

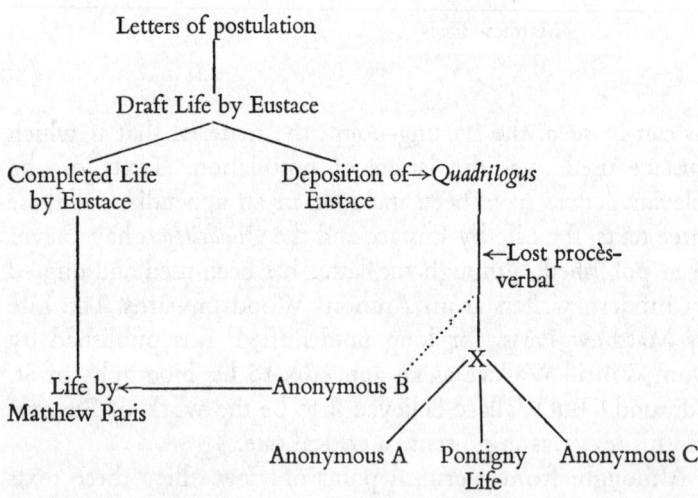

FIG. 2

The canonization of 1246 aroused great interest in the shrine of St. Edmund at Pontigny. Henry III sent a chasuble of white samite and a chalice for the first celebration of the feast,[1] and allocated twenty marks annually from the farm of Canterbury to maintain four candles burning perpetually round the shrine.[2] In November 1254 he made a personal pilgrimage to Pontigny,

[1] CCR 1242–7, p. 497.
[2] CChR 1226–57, p. 369; CPR 1242–58, p. 89; the grant was renewed by *inspeximus* in 1285: CPR 1281–92, p. 196.

on his way back from Gascony.[1] The flow of English pilgrims seems, however, to have dwindled towards the end of the thirteenth century[2] and to have been virtually brought to an end by the outbreak of hostilities between England and France. Outside Salisbury and Abingdon[3] the cultus was not a popular one in the later Middle Ages.[4] Nevertheless, the Lives of St. Edmund were still copied and read. Archbishop Arundel, when harassed by the anti-clerical Parliament of 1404, is said to have sought comfort from reading the Life of St. Edmund, and the continuing interest is attested by the late manuscripts.

Of the modern biographers of St. Edmund, Dean Hook did as well as any.[5] His careful study was based on the text of the Pontigny Life published by the Maurists. The portrait of Edmund that he presented was not an unsympathetic one, despite occasionally fanciful embellishments and the whiggish facetiousness with which he handled the hagiographical anecdotes. The most ambitious work on St. Edmund that has been attempted is the biography of Dom Wilfrid Wallace, which appeared in 1893. It is obviously a work of piety, but it is, despite its hagiographical tone, a scholarly book. Its obvious weakness lies in the fact that the author made no serious effort to subject the literary sources to criticism. Nevertheless, Wallace included a valuable collection of documents in the appendixes, and his texts of the Life by Matthew Paris, and of the Anonymous writers B and C, are the only ones which have hitherto been printed.

[1] *CPR 1242-58*, pp. 326, 384.
[2] Letters of protection for the king's greater tenants going to Pontigny are to be found on the Patent Rolls *passim*, but these cease towards the end of Edward I's reign.
[3] At Salisbury there was an altar dedicated to St. Edmund in the north transept of the cathedral, and in 1270 Bishop William de la Wyle dedicated to him his new collegiate church: C. Wordsworth, *Ceremonies and Processions of the Cathedral Church of Salisbury* (1901), pp. 78, 121.
[4] Thus only one church dedicated in his name has been traced: F. Arnold-Forster, *Studies in Church Dedications*, i (1899), p. 362.
[5] W. F. Hook, *Lives of the Archbishops of Canterbury*, iii (1865), pp. 128-227.

The biography published a few years later by the Baroness de Paravicini is chiefly valuable for an introductory chapter in which she discusses the manuscript sources.[1] She displayed the same unfortunate eagerness as Wallace to attach the names of Robert of Abingdon and Robert Bacon to extant Lives of St. Edmund, and her efforts to do so are open to the same criticism. On the other hand, to her belongs the credit of having first suggested that the Life of the Julius manuscript was the work of Matthew Paris. She pointed out that the Julius Life uses the authorities whom Matthew cites in the *Chronica Maiora*, and she also drew attention to the stylistic similarities between the Life and Matthew's chronicles. She noticed the difficulty that the Julius Life contains what purports to be an eye-witness account of the funeral procession to Pontigny, but this she explained as a borrowing from the Pontigny Life.

A more recent study which deserves mention is the chapter on St. Edmund in A. B. Emden's history of St. Edmund Hall.[2] Mr. Emden was of course primarily interested in the connexion of Edmund's scholastic life with the early history of the Hall, and he wrote mainly about this part of Edmund's career and the subsequent cultus. Within these limits, his account is the best that we have. A number of other studies have appeared in France and England, but they have been hagiographical rather than historical in intention, and they cannot be said to have contributed anything to the subject.[3]

[1] F. de Paravicini, *St. Edmund of Abingdon* (1898), pp. xiii–xlii.
[2] *An Oxford Hall in Medieval Times* (1927), pp. 81–104.
[3] The hagiological essay by L. F. Massé, *Life of St. Edmund of Canterbury* (transl. G. White, 1874), contains a note on the archives of Sens and Auxerre, but is otherwise devoid of interest. B. Ward, *St. Edmund, Archbishop of Canterbury* (1903), contains translated excerpts from the literary sources. He discusses the manuscript sources in an appendix, pp. 235–45, but is content to summarize the views of Wallace and Paravicini. M. R. Newbolt, *Edmund Rich, Archbishop and Saint* (1928), is a popular sketch based on the three earlier books mentioned.

PART ONE

I

THE *QUADRILOGUS* AND THE CANONIZATION PROCESS

HAGIOGRAPHY is biography designed to serve the cultus of the saints. This meant that, from the twelfth century onwards, biographers wrote either to promote the canonization process or to celebrate its success. In either case they often drew their material from it. This is so in the case of St. Edmund, and a systematic edition of his *Vitae* must rest upon a study of the materials left by the Process, for this is the starting point of the hagiographical tradition. The materials which have survived are only a fragment of the whole, but enough remains to make a reconstruction of the Process possible. For this we have to thank the monks of Pontigny who carefully guarded the documents which they regarded as *pièces justificatives* for the cultus of the saint, title-deeds, as it were, for the most lucrative of all their properties.

These records fall into two classes. In the first are the original documents deposited at Pontigny by the canonization commission. They comprise letters of postulation from English prelates and Oxford University, letters written by the commissioners in the course of their work, papal bulls, letters of indulgence, and a parchment roll of six membranes, containing part of the procès-verbal of the inquiry.[1] This collection passed at the Revolution into the family of the last abbot of Pontigny. In 1854 it was presented to Sens cathedral, where it is still preserved in the Treasury.

In the second class is the copy of these and other records which the monks wrote up in the thirteenth century into a

[1] See the list of the Sens archives on pp. 320-5.

large *Liber Memorandorum*. This contained a Life of St. Edmund, an account of the canonization process composed by Archbishop Albert of Armagh, transcripts from many original letters of postulation, and a record of miracles worked at the shrine. This book, which I call the *Liber Sancti Edmundi*, is now MS. 123 (ancien Pontigny 165) of Auxerre public library.[1] It forms a codex of 158 folios in a medieval leather binding. The contents are as follows:

fos. 1–56^v Life of St. Edmund.
fos. 57–59^v Sermon of Archbishop Albert on the translation of St. Edmund.
fos. 59^v–83^v Albert's *Historia Canonizationis*.
fos. 83^v–96   Account of the translation.
fos. 96–104^v The promise of St. Thomas to Pontigny.
fos. 104^v–12^v Miracles of St. Edmund.
fos. 113–54^v Additional miracles (in a different hand from the foregoing).
fo. 158   Gospel and collect for the feast of St. Edmund (in a sixteenth-century hand).

The contents of this manuscript were published by the Maurists, Martène and Durand, in their great *Thesaurus*.[2]

The Benedictines of St. Maur seem to have displayed a continuous interest in the Pontigny archives. In August 1662 Papebroch and Henschenius visited the abbey on their way back from Rome, and Papebroch noted a manuscript which, from his description, is evidently the *Liber Sancti Edmundi*.[3] A transcript was made of it by Dom George Viole about this time, in preparation for his monumental history of the town and diocese of Auxerre.[4] It was from this transcript, and not

---

[1] See *Catalogue général des MSS des bibliothèques publiques de France*, tome vi (Paris, 1887), p. 48.

[2] *Thesaurus Novus Anecdotorum*, iii (Paris, 1717), cols. 1751 ff.

[3] 'Ostensus item codex ms. est totus de vita, translatione, canonizatione, miraculis S. Edmundi et totus postea, curante P. le Blanq, descriptus'; see the extracts from Papebroch's diary edited by F. Halkin in *Anal. Boll.* lxv (1947), pp. 94–96.

[4] See Tassin's notes on Viole in *Histoire littéraire de la congrégation de St. Maur* (Brussels, 1770), pp. 69–72.

The Quadrilogus and the Canonization Process

from the original, that Martène printed his text. He found it among Viole's papers which were preserved at the abbey or St. Germain at Auxerre. He stayed at St. Germain for four weeks in the autumn of 1708, in order to work on Viole's materials. During his stay he made an excursion to Pontigny to celebrate the feast of St. Edmund, his patron saint, and he was allowed to inspect 'deux beaux cartulaires qui me donnèrent de grandes lumières'.[1] He evidently had no time to check Viole's transcript against the original.

In addition to these sources for the Process, there is the document printed here, to which I have given the title of *Quadrilogus*. The only copy of it known to exist is to be found in MS. 154 of Corpus Christi College, Oxford. This is a small volume containing Sicard of Cremona's commentary on the *Decretum*[2] (fos. 6 ff.), and a number of shorter items written in different hands of the thirteenth and fourteenth centuries. Part of a monastic letter book (fos. 386–93), transcripts of charters, and fragments of manorial accounts on the end papers show that the book was the property of the Augustinian priory of Llanthony by Gloucester.[3] The *Quadrilogus* (fos. 375^b–85^b), which is without title, is written in double column in a rather clumsy book hand of the mid-thirteenth century. It consists of depositions concerning the Life of St. Edmund made by four members of his *familia*. This document was known to Anthony Wood[4] and has been freely used by modern writers on St. Edmund,[5] but it has never been published *in extenso*. It can be

---

[1] E. Martène and U. Durand, *Voyage littéraire* (Paris, 1717), p. 57.

[2] Cf. Gabriel Le Bras in *Bodleian Quarterly Record*, v (1927), p. 191.

[3] N. R. Ker, *Mediaeval Libraries of Great Britain* (RHS 1941), p. 62. In the fourteenth-century library catalogue of Llanthony, reference to a life of St. Edmund has been inserted slightly later beside a book containing the Life of St. Thomas: BM Harl. MS. 460, fo. 81^v; cf. T. W. Williams, 'Gloucestershire Mediaeval Libraries', *TBGAS* xxxi (1908), pp. 141ff. This can hardly be the *Quadrilogus*, however.

[4] *A Survey of the Antiquities of the City of Oxford*, ed. A. Clark (OHS 1890), ii. 100 and n. 5.

[5] Thus W. Wallace, op. cit., pp. 9 and *passim*; F. de Paravicini, op. cit., pp. xvi, &c.

rightly understood only in its context in the process of canonization, and to this we must first turn.

From an early period, the cultus of a new saint was officially inaugurated by the solemn translation of the relics which was carried out by the bishop. During the twelfth century, however, canonization by means of a solemn papal judgement was becoming increasingly common. This prepared the way for the papal reservation of the exclusive right to canonize, which was firmly established during the first two decades of the thirteenth century.[1] It has been shown that the formal reservation of this right to the papacy coincided with the reception of the decretal *Audivimus* of Alexander III by the canonists during the pontificate of Innocent III.[2] In this process of centralization England played an important part. Edward the Confessor was the first English saint whose canonization by the pope can be certainly established. But thereafter, for England at least, the Holy See was the only official source of canonization, and episcopal canonization may be said to have lapsed.[3]

With the growth of papal control came the establishment of the papal Process. By the time of Urban II the commission of inquiry was regarded as the regular preliminary to canonization. An embarrassing flood of petitions in the following century necessitated more discrimination and a more careful formulation of procedure.[4] The evolution of procedure can be traced from the surviving records of a number of causes which were submitted to Rome between 1200 and 1240.[5] From these

[1] E. W. Kemp, *Canonization and Authority in the Western Church* (1948); the official history of canonization is that of Benedict XIV, *De Servorum Dei Beatificatione et Beatorum Canonizatione* (Bologna, 1734–8). On the development of the Process see the evidence reviewed by L. Hertling, 'Materiali per la storia del processo di canonizzazione', *Gregorianum*, xvi (Rome, 1935), pp. 170–95.

[2] S. Kuttner, 'La Réserve papale du droit de canonisation', *Revue historique de droit français et étranger*, xvii (1938), pp. 172–228.

[3] This does not exclude the occasional authorization of an existing cult by a local bishop.

[4] See Alexander III's reasons for postponing the canonization of St. Bernard of Clairvaux: Fontanini, no. 15, discussed by Hertling, op. cit., p. 189.

[5] See the notes on processes conducted between 1218 and 1240 by M. Bihl,

it can be seen that Innocent III gave clearer definition to the conditions which a candidate for canonization must satisfy, and imposed stricter rules of evidence. Those who promoted a person for canonization must establish two facts: that he had lived a life of heroic virtue, and that he had performed miracles after his death. Neither one would serve without the other.[1] At the same time, Innocent demanded a more rigorous scrutiny of the evidence. The written testimonials of an earlier age were no longer regarded as adequate. In 1201 the promoters of the cause of St. Gilbert of Sempringham had their dossier set aside. Instead of reports of miracles supplied by prelates at second hand, they were required to take down directly the depositions made by sworn witnesses. There was to be no writing up of the evidence. Moreover, selected witnesses were to be dispatched to the papal Curia to give their testimony to the pope in person.[2] That this was no isolated case appears from the act canonizing St. Wulfstan of Worcester in 1203.[3] Here, too, depositions were taken from witnesses on oath, and the pope was certified of the facts *non solum testimoniis, sed et testibus*. This insistence on the *ipsissima verba* of the witnesses is reflected in the preface to the Miracles of St. Laurence of Dublin, canonized by Honorius III in 1225. The writer states that he is reproducing evidence given at the inquiry, and that the inquisitors had transmitted to the Curia the simple unvarnished speech of the witnesses.[4] The rules governing the commission

---

'De canonizatione Sancti Francisci', *Archivum Franciscanum Historicum*, xxi (1928).

[1] See the canonization of the Empress Kunegunde in 1200: 'ad hoc tamen, ut ipse sanctus apud homines habeatur in Ecclesia militante, duo sunt necessaria, virtus morum et virtus signorum, videlicet merita et miracula. . . . Non enim aut merita sine miraculis, aut miracula sine meritis plene sufficiunt': Fontanini, no. 29, pp. 37–38. Similar words are used in the act canonizing St. Homobonus of Cremona in 1199: ibid., p. 34.

[2] R. Foreville, *Le Livre de saint Gilbert de Sempringham* (Paris, 1943), pp. xxxv–xli.

[3] Fontanini, no. 30, pp. 40–41.

[4] 'verba simplicia pro maiori parte posita testium iuratorum': 'Vie et miracles de S. Laurent', *Anal. Boll.* xxxiii (1914), pp. 129 ff.

of inquiry were further tightened by Honorius III. The decretal *Venerabili* of 1225 ordered another inquiry in the case of Abbot Maurice of Quimper on the ground that the first examiners of the cause had omitted to question witnesses individually and that circumstances of alleged miracles had not been stated with sufficient clarity.[1]

The growing rigour of the rules of evidence is reflected in the care taken to authenticate cures by obtaining the opinion of the neighbourhood. Thus in the course of the inquiry into the miracles of St. Gilbert, a subsidiary commission visited the parishes where a witness, Ralph of Attenborough, had resided, to obtain evidence of his previous illness.[2] In the case of St. Hugh of Lincoln, which was conducted by Stephen Langton in 1219, subsidiary commissions were dispatched to the villages of Cheshunt and Alconbury to take evidence of miraculous cures.[3] A further development, designed to ensure a searching inquiry, was the sending of a form of questionnaire along with the rescript appointing the commissioners. When directing an inquiry into the life and miracles of John Buoni of Mantua in 1251, the pope added to the commission a short formulary (*brevem formam*) according to which the witnesses were to be examined. They were to be asked *quomodo sciant*; *quo tempore*; *quo mense*; *quo die*; *quibus presentibus*; *quo loco*; *ad cuius invocationem*; *quibus verbis interpositis*, &c. These questions were to be put for each item (*circa singula capitula*).[4] This last looks like a reference to the *capitula* or articles for inquiry which were submitted by the promoters of the cause.[5] It is probable that

[1] c. 52, X. ii. 20, *De Test. et Attest*. The case is discussed by Foreville, op. cit., p. xl.

[2] Foreville, op. cit., pp. 65–67. In the case of St. Wulfstan, Archbishop Hubert Walter made two visits to Worcester to examine the evidence of miraculous cures: R. R. Darlington, *The Vita Wulfstani of William of Malmesbury* (CS 3rd ser. xl 1928), p. xlvii.

[3] BM Cotton Roll xiii. 27, m. 1 and m. 3. This contains the procès-verbal. The report on the two miracles is printed in *Giraldi Cambrensis Opera*, ed. J. F. Dimock (RS 1877) vii. 188–92.

[4] *AA.SS*. Oct. ix. 768 ff.

[5] On the *capitula generalia* see M. R. Toynbee, *St. Louis of Toulouse and the*

The Quadrilogus *and the Canonization Process* 13

this obvious device for keeping witnesses to the point already existed, at least embryonically, in the thirteenth century.

The thirteenth-century popes insisted on evidence of *mores* as well as evidence of miracles because, as the canonists explained, the Devil could work miracles, a fact which could be plainly seen from the feats of Simon Magus and Moses' daughter.[1] On the other hand, miracles could not be dispensed with. It was possible to be deceived about a man's life. Miracles provided the divine seal of authenticity without which an exemplary life might be only a public façade concealing secret laxity. In consequence, the evidence bearing on the life of the alleged saint was gradually subjected to the same critical scrutiny as the evidence of miracles. The two types of testimony were always kept distinct in the thirteenth century. It is possible to discern a considerable advance in criticism between the Process of St. Hugh of Lincoln in 1219 and that of St. Dominic in 1233. In the former case, the critical attention of the commissioners seems to have been focused wholly on miracles, and a short summary of the saint's life was placed at the head of the report.[2] The depositions taken in the Process of St. Dominic, however, show that the witnesses of the saint's virtue were being as closely controlled as the witnesses of miracles. Each witness is introduced by a stereotyped formula, stating his identity and office and the duration of his acquaintance with St. Dominic. The pressure of the questioners is often evident, and is sometimes recorded by the notary with some such phrase as 'Interrogatus quomodo scit hoc, respondit', &c. The fact that most of the depositions make identical points in the same order strongly suggests that the commissioners were following a list

---

Process of Canonization in the Fourteenth Century (1929), pp. 164–9. Her account of the development of the Process, pp. 133–45, is valuable but, approaching it from the standpoint of a later period, she exaggerates the degree of haphazard in the Process of the thirteenth century.

[1] Thus Bernard of Parma, *Glossa Ordinaria in Decretales* (Venice, 1504), fo. 122; cf. *Innocentii quarti super libros quinque Decretalium* (Frankfurt, 1570) in lib. iii, tit. xlv.

[2] BM Cotton Roll xiii. 27, m. 1.

of *capitula* submitted by the promoters.[1] Witnesses are clearly being discouraged from straying into the thaumaturgical. The documents of this Process are of special interest because of its nearness in time to that of St. Edmund.

During the forty years preceding the Process of St. Edmund, the procedure of the papal inquiry was acquiring a common form and the rules of evidence were becoming increasingly rigorous. It was no uncommon thing during this period for the report of a first inquiry to be set aside on grounds of irregularity or inadequacy. In this respect the Process of St. Edmund may be regarded as a typical one, and the claim of Albert of Armagh that few saints since St. Peter had endured such an intensive scrutiny before elevation to the altars,[2] was a rhetorical flourish rather than an exact statement of fact.

St. Edmund died at Soisy on 16 November 1240. He had declared it his wish to be buried at Pontigny. After the body had been embalmed, therefore, the clerks set off with the remains of their archbishop. The procession met with impressive demonstrations of popular devotion all along the route.[3] At the village of Trainel enthusiasm became so intense that the abbot of Pontigny began to fear for the safety of his precious freight and decided to take a strong line with the thaumaturge. The saint was invoked and ordered in virtue of obedience (he was a confrater of Pontigny) to desist from his miracles until the procession reached home. Thereafter progress was better. In these propitious circumstances no time was lost in petitioning for a papal commission of inquiry. The earliest dated letter of postulation was dispatched in December 1240, by the abbot of

[1] *Acta Canonizationis S. Dominici*, ed. A. Walz, *MOFPH* xvi (1935). Hostiensis, commenting on the decretal *Venerabili fratre*, lays down rules which commissioners must follow in interrogating witnesses testifying to a man's sanctity of life: *Summa Aurea Henrici cardinalis Hostiensis* (Lyons, 1548), fo. 188.

[2] *MD. Thes.* iii, cols. 1833, 1851.

[3] The statements on this subject in the *Vitae* are supported by the testimony of witnesses recorded in the fragment of the procès-verbal: Trésor of Sens cathedral, muniment no. 26. The Pontigny writer speaks of the archbishop's largesse to poor people whom he encountered on the road from Pontigny to Soisy.

The Quadrilogus and the Canonization Process

Provins where St. Edmund's entrails were buried.[1] But the main initiative came from Pontigny. The Cistercian General Chapter of 1241 discussed the *negotium Pontigniacense* and, in the absence of the abbot of Cîteaux who was in an imperial prison, deputed Abbot Bruno of La Ferté to write a letter of postulation to the pope.[2] The Cistercians were most active promoters of the cause throughout and found a willing agent at the Curia in the English Cistercian cardinal, John of Toledo.[3]

The course of the Process is described by Albert of Cologne, archbishop of Armagh, in his *Historia Canonizationis*, the sole text of which survives in the *Liber Sancti Edmundi*.[4] As head of the papal commission of inquiry, Albert was able to write a first-hand account of the proceedings and to include a selection of the letters which passed through his hands. This account can be supplemented from the documents kept at Sens cathedral. According to Albert, it was the occurrence of miracles at Pontigny which induced the prelates of France to assemble and draft letters petitioning for an inquiry. These letters, which he quotes, are undated, but an *inspeximus* of some of them survives at Sens.[5] It is dated 1242. Similar letters were sent by the prelates of England. Letters are extant from Walter Gray, archbishop of York, the bishops of Bangor, Bath, Chichester, Dunblane,[6] Ely,[7] Exeter, and Salisbury, the abbots of Abingdon, Eynsham, Reading, and Westminster, the prior of Merton, and the university of Oxford. A textual comparison shows that,

[1] MD. *Thes.* iii, col. 1897.

[2] Canivez, *Statuta*, ii. 233. The abbot's letter is dated *tempore capituli generalis*, 1241: Sens cath. mun. no. 7; MD. *Thes.* iii, col. 1898.

[3] MD. *Thes.* iii, col. 1849. On Cardinal John of the title of S. Lorenzo in Lucina, see Matthew Paris, *Chron. Maiora*, iv. 354, 578–9; v. 306.

[4] MD. *Thes.* iii, cols. 1831–58.

[5] Sens cath. mun. no. 15: from Bourges, Tours, Meaux, Nevers, Senlis, and Auxerre.

[6] The letter of Clement, the Dominican bishop of Dunblane, is extant only in a transcript in the draft Life: Trinity College Cambridge MS. R.5.40, fo. 59.

[7] The letters from Oxford, the bishops of Bath, Ely (the only extant text), Salisbury, and Abingdon abbey are copied in a mid-thirteenth-century hand in BM Add. MS. 46352, fos. 48–50ᵛ. Thomas Hearne transcribed them from this manuscript into Bodleian Rawlinson MS. B. 254, fos. 86–90ᵛ.

Oxford apart, these letters are not entirely independent productions. The writers borrow phrases from one another freely, a fact which suggests that a circular was being sent round to which all were invited to contribute a petition. The fact that the letters were gathered in this snowball fashion gains added probability from the survival of a copy of five of them in one of the St. Augustine's cartularies.[1] Something of the same sort seems to have been done in the case of St. Gilbert of Sempringham. There, Archbishop Hubert Walter ordered a preliminary inquiry and sent a report of it to his suffragans, asking them to contribute letters of their own.[2] All the letters sent in St. Edmund's cause are undated, with the exception of the Merton letter which is dated 27 February 1242.[3] The Oxford letter is addressed to Pope Gregory IX and must therefore be dated prior to the end of September 1241.[4] Having these points in view, it will be fairly safe to place all the English letters between the summer of 1241 and the early months of 1242.[5]

The Process may be said to have begun with the preliminary inquiry into *fama* made by Bernard de Sully, bishop of Auxerre, in whose diocese Pontigny lay. The bishop made this inquiry on his own initiative and reported his findings to the pope.[6] It was not unusual for a long interval to elapse between the postulations and the setting up of a papal inquiry. In this case, the vacancy of the Holy See for nearly two years made delay inevitable. Mandates for an inquiry were issued by Innocent IV on 23 April 1244. Two commissions were appointed, one in France consisting of Albert, archbishop of Armagh, the bishop of Senlis, and the dean of Paris,[7] and one in England consisting of the bishops of London and Lincoln.[8] The letters repeat the

[1] See n. 7 on p. 15.
[2] Foreville, op. cit., p. xxxvi.
[3] Sens cath. mun. no. 9; *MD. Thes.* iii, cols. 1899–1900, where it is incorrectly dated 1241.
[4] Gregory IX died on 21 Aug. 1241.
[5] Wallace, op. cit., p. 396, unaccountably places them in 1244–5.
[6] *MD. Thes.* iii, col. 1837.   [7] Berger, no. 622; *MD. Thes.* iii, cols. 1841–2.
[8] Sens cath. mun. no. 19; Berger, no. 619.

The Quadrilogus *and the Canonization Process* 17

formulas used by Innocent III in defining the marks of sanctity, and request that the commissioners should send to the Curia not only depositions, but also four, or three, or at least two witnesses, who have been the subject of cures.

In the absence of the bishop of Senlis, Archbishop Albert and the dean of Paris opened the inquiry at Pontigny on 17 July 1244.[1] The brief narrative of the opening of the proceedings suggests that the commissioners followed a formulary supplied by the pope. Witnesses were summoned through their ordinaries, and depositions were taken which were dispatched under the commissioners' seals to the pope. The same was done by the English commissioners.[2] According to Albert, a number of witnesses were sent to the pope together with the dossier of this inquiry.

Innocent's response was cautious. He apparently found the dossier too prolix and the miracles insufficiently attested. Another inquiry was ordered in France, again under the presidency of Archbishop Albert, and in England under St. Edmund's former chancellor, Richard Wych, now bishop of Chichester, who was assisted by the prior of Canon's Ashby and the Dominican master Robert Bacon.[3] The papal mandates for this second inquiry seem to have escaped registration, and although Albert quotes from them, he does not mention the date. The French commission submitted its returns in May 1245, but those from England were not dispatched until November.[4] The replies show the commissioners attempting to meet the pope's demand for good evidence of only four or five miracles, the essential thing being *pluritas testium*. Neither reply makes any mention of the dispatch of witnesses to the Curia. This dossier reached the pope at Lyons. Its examination was delegated to a committee of seven *sapientes*, consisting of the three cardinals, Hugh of S. Sabina, John of the title of S. Lorenzo

[1] *MD. Thes.* iii, col. 1902.
[2] The reply from England, undated, is in Sens cath. mun. no. 21.
[3] *MD. Thes.* iii, col. 1844.
[4] Sens cath. mun. nos. 23, 25; *MD. Thes.* iii, col. 1845, 1913–14, where, however, the reply from the English commission is undated.

in Lucina, and William of the title of The Twelve Apostles, the bishops of Lincoln and Cambrai, the canonist Vincentius Hispanus, and the theologian Alexander of Hales.[1] It was the duty of this committee to make a report to the pope in consistory. In these arrangements we can see foreshadowed the shape of the Canonization Process of later times. It is interesting to observe that three members of this committee were among the most distinguished theologians of their generation, and that two of them were Englishmen.

The report of the committee was favourable, but Innocent was still unwilling to pronounce sentence. Albert voices the suspicion of the promoters of the cause that the pope's delay was prompted by the opposition of the English court and the church of Canterbury. Although this is not improbable, the chief reason for the delay seems to have been the healthy scepticism of the Curia in face of this plethora of miracles. An unnamed cardinal in conversation with Albert expressed doubts on this subject and confided that he had some difficulty in swallowing the story that St. Martin of Tours had resurrected three people. This seemingly gratuitous confession probably represents a garbled version of the cardinal's comments on the Life of St. Edmund by Eustace of Faversham, which contains a rather unlikely comparison between the two saints. The cardinal's scepticism was no greater than that which Sulpicius Severus met with in his own time.[2] At any rate the Curia was not yet satisfied, and it was objected that the witnesses who had been the subject of cures had not been presented for inspection at the right time. At this point, the English cardinal, John of Toledo, took the initiative and sent to France and England to obtain witnesses. Albert says that the bearer of this commission was 'the sole faithful Achates, who carried the whole burden of the business, the *secretarius* of the blessed father Edmund, whom we mentioned at the beginning.'[3] As

[1] *MD. Thes.* iii, col. 1847.
[2] See H. Delehaye, 'S. Martin et Sulpice Sévère', *Anal. Boll.* xxxviii (1920), pp. 73 ff.   [3] *MD. Thes.* iii, cols. 1849–50.

the letters show, this was Eustace of Faversham. He was sent with letters to the bishop of Lincoln,[1] the abbot of Bayham,[2] and Archdeacon Simon Langton,[3] requiring the production of two or three persons who had been the subject of cures, together with suitable witnesses. Similar letters were evidently sent to the abbot of Provins.[4] The letters are dated at Lyons on 9 April 1246. Langton's reply and report is dated 6 June 1246. It throws an interesting light on the background of a papal inquiry. It appears that he found his commission very difficult to execute. On receiving the letters, he had set off with Eustace for the district where the necessary proof could be obtained. This involved a journey of six days from Canterbury. The necessary witnesses were presented to him by the clergy, and the whole neighbourhood supported their testimony to St. Edmund's miracles. But when he urged a number of them to undertake the journey to the Curia, there was an ugly scene, and anti-clerical sentiments were expressed in very strong language. Even the offer to pay expenses failed to overcome 'the effective excuses and canonical impediments' which the people raised against going. It was no light matter for the peasant farmer to be absent from home during the harvest, and the witnesses were not surprisingly angered by this example of clerical insouciance. In the end a small but, it was hoped, convincing party of witnesses was cajoled into going.[5]

On arrival at Lyons, the witnesses were summoned to the houses of the individual cardinals and examined, and were finally examined in the pope's presence. This closed the inquiry. In face of the accumulated evidence, canonization could not be delayed longer with decency. On Sunday, 16 December 1246, a full consistory met in Lyons cathedral. Cardinal Hugh of S. Sabina delivered an address on the merits and miracles of

[1] *MD. Thes.* iii, col. 1912; Sens cath. mun. no. 27.
[2] Ibid., no. 28.
[3] *MD. Thes.* iii, col. 1914; Sens cath. mun. no. 29: this is only Langton's reply.
[4] His reply is in Sens cath. mun. no. 30.
[5] Ibid., no. 29. *MD. Thes.* iii, col. 1914.

the saint, stating that the pope had taken counsel of the cardinals on the previous Saturday and that they had urged him to delay no longer.[1] After the cardinal had finished, the pope pronounced sentence and declared Saint Edmund to be inscribed in the catalogue of the saints. The bull *Novum matris ecclesie*, in which this sentence was promulgated, was issued on 11 January 1247.[2]

Apart from mandates and letters of postulation, the only surviving original record of all these proceedings is the fragment of a procès-verbal, now muniment no. 26 in the Trésor of Sens cathedral. This is a parchment roll of six membranes, each measuring $8\frac{1}{2}$ by 20 inches. The early part of the roll, containing the opening of the inquiry, is missing. The depositions are written on both sides in a small and heavily abbreviated cursive hand. The haste of the writing and the rather chaotic insertions and deletions, with notes on the interrogation of witnesses, show that the document is the original draft made by the notary while the proceedings were going on. It is a record of miracles, all of which, with one exception, were performed after the saint's death. The witnesses appear from their names to be all Burgundian peasants. Most of the entries vary between three and five lines, though some are longer. The brevity of the entries and the copious notes of interrogations indicate that the commissioners were keeping a firm hand on the witnesses.

Although the roll is an undated fragment, having neither beginning nor end, it is evidently a record of the first inquiry held at Pontigny in July 1244. This much is clear from the number of miracles and the variation in the number of witnesses for each. Thus Robin de Cortiniaco, who was partially

---

[1] On the two public consistories preceding canonization, as well as the committee deputed to examine the report, cf. the early-fourteenth-century procedure in Ordo Romanus XIV in Mabillon, *Museum Italicum*, ii (1689), pp. 418–24. On the part played by the cardinals see J. B. Sägmüller, *Die Thätigkeit und Stellung der Kardinäle bis Papst Bonifaz VIII* (Freiburg, 1896), pp. 49–51.

[2] Potthast, 12392; bulls, addressed to the church of Lyons and to the English baronage, are in Sens cath. mun, nos. 31 and 32.

cured of lameness at the tomb of St. Edmund, is supported by only one witness (m. 1), but Bernard of Perrons is able to produce three (m. 1), whereas the testimony of Margaret of Ligny (?Leginaco) concerning the cure of her daughter is unsupported (m. 6). The testimony of Anclina of Beoli concerning her son is also unsupported, and the notary has written in the margin *querantur testes* (m. 2). In the light of this document, it is easy to understand the pope's discontent with the plethora of ill-attested miracles and his demand for fewer miracles and more witnesses.

Besides evidence of miracles, the papal commission had to submit evidence of the saint's virtuous life. The *Quadrilogus* evidently relates to this stage of the inquiry. It contains depositions made by four witnesses, of whom one had been a close acquaintance of the archbishop, and the other three had been members of his *familia*. These are Richard of Dunstable, a Dominican friar, Stephen, a subdeacon, and Robert, formerly a Canon Regular but now a Cistercian postulant, both former chamberlains of the archbishop, and Eustace the monk of Christ Church, the archbishop's chaplain. The only surviving text is the copy, which lacks heading or preface, in the Corpus Christi manuscript. If these four depositions are compared with the surviving acta of other inquiries of the same period, certain marked differences become apparent.

In the first place, it is clear that not all of the depositions are of the same character. The first, made by Richard of Dunstable, is not oral testimony at all, but a letter written from the Dominican house at Paris. The writer closes with an attestation made in the presence of Friar John of Montmirail[1] and others, and states that he is appending the conventual seal of the Paris priory. Unfortunately the letter is undated and has evidently been altered in order to give it more of the customary form of a deposition, the address and salutation being omitted. This

---

[1] A Dominican John of Montmirail appears in the *familia* of the bishop of Paris in 1249; see *Cartulaire de l'Église Notre-Dame de Paris*, ed. M. Guérard (Coll. de docs. inédits, Paris, 1850), i. 159.

omission made it necessary to supply the identity of the writer in some other way and accounts for the clumsy and ungrammatical phrase in the first sentence: 'set secundum quod ego sum Ricardus de Dunstapel de ordine Fratrum Predicatorum . . . .' This was obviously inserted as an afterthought. Richard states that he had known St. Edmund for nearly ten years before entering the Dominican Order. He appears again in the Oxford letter of postulation where the university mention him as one of their informants on the life of St. Edmund. The letter (1241) describes him as prior of the Dominican house at Oxford. This exhausts our knowledge of him. But we may suppose that the friars would not have elected a tiro to be head of one of the most important *studia* of the Order and that Richard must have assumed the habit some years before 1241. This, and the acquaintance of ten years which he mentions, indicates that he was associated with St. Edmund when the latter was canon of Salisbury. In fact he speaks of Edmund's unwillingness to take part in chapter business. His statement that he often shared Edmund's table and waited on him suggests the relationship between poor scholar and patron. Edmund was well known as a patron of needy scholars.

The final attestation of the letter is of peculiar interest. Three witnesses are listed, namely Sir Robert Asthall, and Andrew and Walter, his servants. Asthall was a demesne manor of the honour of St. Valery which was held by Earl Richard of Cornwall,[1] and Robert of Asthall was the earl's clerk. He held two livings in the earl's patronage,[2] and by 1240 he had evidently risen high in his master's trust, for he was one of those appointed to exercise the earl's ecclesiastical patronage while he was on Crusade.[3] The fact that Robert of Asthall was witness and bearer of Dunstable's letter is the clearest possible indication

[1] *Book of Fees*, ed. Maxwell Lyte (1920), i. 613; ii. 822, 1376.
[2] North Luffenham and North Stoke: *Rotuli Roberti Grosseteste*, ed. F. N. Davis (CYS 1913), pp. 162, 453, 456.
[3] *CPR 1232–47*, pp. 248, 262. He was also the earl's attorney at the Exchequer in 1243: *CLR 1240–5*, p. 198. See the note on him in N. Denholm-Young, *Richard of Cornwall* (Oxford, 1947), p. 41 and note.

that Richard of Cornwall was actively pressing for the canonization of St. Edmund. This is in accord with the earl's subsequent devotion to St. Edmund, and gives added probability to the statement of Matthew Paris that Earl Richard was bitterly disappointed because he could not be present at the translation.[1] It should also make us hesitate before accepting the suggestion of Albert of Armagh that the English court was wholly opposed to the canonization.

It is an obvious presumption that Richard of Dunstable's letter was written in order to postulate canonization proceedings, and that its inclusion with the depositions was an arbitrary proceeding on the part of the compiler of the *Quadrilogus*, who also trimmed it to make it look like a deposition. But although it lacks address or date, the letter contains phrases which strongly suggest that it was addressed to the canonization commission, and that it was intended to be written testimony for their use. A letter of postulation was not usually in the form of an affidavit, but Richard takes an oath on the Gospels and assigns to the bearers of the letter the power to swear *in animam* on his behalf. In explanation of this procedure he writes, 'scio quod in foro isto non sunt admittendi testes non iurati . . . .' The *forum* to which only sworn witnesses were admitted can only be a canonization tribunal. It is precisely the word which we would expect a mid-thirteenth-century writer to use, for the Process was assuming a litigious form. Moreover, identity of matter and verbal parallels clearly link Dunstable's letter with the other three depositions of the *Quadrilogus* and therefore with the Process. As evidence of St. Edmund's sanctity of life, the letter must belong, like the depositions, to the inquiry of July 1244.[2] On the other hand, the admission of

[1] *Chron. Maiora*, iv. 632. In the speech which Matthew attributes to the earl he expresses his own regret and also that of the king, his brother. Richard made a visit to Pontigny later in 1247, ibid. iv. 646–7. Some of the evidence of Richard's devotion to St. Edmund is cited by F. M. Powicke, *Henry the Third and the Lord Edward* (1947), p. 197 n.

[2] When attesting, Richard mentions the absence of his superiors—*licet absentibus prelatis meis*. This may be explained by the fact that in 1244 the

such written testimony by the commission and its incorporation in the procès-verbal is a surprising exception to the rules followed in the Process at this period. It does not conform to the demand for oral testimony, nor could the witness have been cross-examined.

The second and third depositions open with the regular formula used by witnesses before a canonization commission. Stephen the subdeacon and Robert the Cistercian both state their identity, mention that they are giving testimony on oath, and state the duration of their acquaintance with St. Edmund. Each asserts that he had been *clericus et cubicularius ac secretarius* to the archbishop. Both these depositions are in the terse, episodic style of the authentic procès-verbal. They cover much the same ground as Dunstable's letter. There is a good deal of verbal parallelism between the three accounts, but of a kind which suggests verbal reminiscence rather than direct copying. Stephen's deposition is factual, pedestrian in manner, and avoids any reference to the miraculous. He had been clerk and chamberlain to Edmund for just over six years, that is for the duration of his pontificate. Robert, on the other hand, shows a taste for rhetorical ornament, and he describes a modest miracle of which he had been the subject which, he says, 'has given me an unshakable belief in all the others'. Robert was clearly a man of mighty faith.

A comparison between these depositions and the *acta* of other Processes of the mid-thirteenth century reveals some striking points of contrast. In the first place, the depositions of the *Quadrilogus* are written in direct speech, in the first person singular, whereas every other known Process from 1232 onwards employs *oratio obliqua*. Secondly, there is a marked absence of any sign that either witness was interrogated by the commission. As indicated already, papal commissioners were expressly ordered to interrogate witnesses concerning their

General Chapter met at Bologna. It opened at Pentecost, which in that year fell on 22 May. See G. R. Galbraith, *The Constitution of the Dominican Order* (1925), App. iii.

statements, and evidence that they did so abounds in other Processes of the period. The French inquiry which dealt with the miracles of St. Edmund certainly observed these rules, for the fragment of the procès-verbal at Sens is in the normal form. It is written in *oratio obliqua* and there are frequent notes of interrogation. The third point of contrast is the admission of hearsay. Stephen, for instance, states that St. Edmund had never lost his baptismal innocence, and Robert makes the same assertion.

These points of contrast are more strongly marked in the fourth deposition, made by St. Edmund's chaplain, Eustace. Like the others, the deposition of Eustace is in direct speech and bears no trace of interrogation. Most curious of all, Eustace for the most part makes no claim to be giving first-hand testimony at all. He presents a summary account of St. Edmund's life from birth, made on the authority of others: 'quod secundum puritatem multorum et signata veritatis verba testantur . . . .' In fact, up to the time of the archbishop's troubles, his account is composed of extracts drawn from the letters of postulation. As I have endeavoured to show elsewhere (pp. 42–45), Eustace compiled his deposition from his own draft Life of St. Edmund, which is preserved in manuscript R.5.40 of Trinity College, Cambridge. The draft Life was pieced together from the letters of postulation and also borrowed passages freely from John of Salisbury's Life of Becket. The deposition retains this literary character. The whole piece is rhetorical in style. It is much more like a conventional work of hagiography than evidence given by a sworn witness to a canonization tribunal. For instance, it incorporates verbatim a number of the passages drawn from the Life of Becket.

Is it conceivable that, in the stage of development which the papal Process had reached by 1244, a document such as the *Quadrilogus* would have been submitted to Rome as it stands? By comparison, the *acta* of the Process of St. Dominic (1232)[1] or of John Buoni of Mantua (1251)[2] are models of formal

[1] *MOFPH* xvi. 91 ff.   [2] *AA.SS.* Oct. ix. 768 ff.

correctness. Witnesses are listed and presented by the promoter. Testimony to the saints' lives is written in *oratio obliqua*. Depositions are terse and unrhetorical, and any witness showing the least tendency to stray outside the boundaries of personal knowledge is promptly arrested by the question *quomodo scit?* However, both these inquiries were conducted in Italy and by Italians, and it may be assumed that they represent the highest pitch of legal refinement attained by that period.

From Germany, records survive of two Processes held under Gregory IX, a decade or so before that of St. Edmund. The first of these, the abortive Process of St. Hildegarde (1233),[1] is less useful. Since Hildegarde had been dead fifty-four years before the opening of her Process, the testimony concerning her life was necessarily based on literary report and could not be reduced to the form of a procès-verbal. The Process of St. Elizabeth of Hungary and Thuringia (1233) offers a more instructive comparison. In fact an exact parallel to the *Quadrilogus* can be found in the *Libellus Quatuor Ancillarum*,[2] a collection of the depositions made at the Process by four members of St. Elizabeth's household. Moreover, the anonymous compiler of the *Libellus* has some interesting advice to give to other churches faced with a similar case. 'As for the really essential part of this business', he says, 'at the Curia they look for evidence of blameless life and excellence of conduct, rather than miracles, which are, as often as not, feigned by human craft or diabolical deceit.'[3] This observation on papal policy is borne out by the wording of papal mandates and by the increasing care with which evidence of virtue was being sifted. The compiler goes on to introduce the four depositions, explaining that testimony should be simple and plain, and free from borrowed

---

[1] *BHL* 3932. *AA.SS.* Sept. v. 679 ff.

[2] *BHL* 2493. J. B. Mencke, *Scriptorum Rerum Germanicarum* (Leipzig, 1728), ii, col. 2007.

[3] 'quod, quantum ad huius negotii esse ac substantiam, in curia plus vitae laudabilitas et conversationis pulcritudo attenditur quam miraculorum, quae quandoque humana sophisticat versucia quandoque daemonica illusio . . .'; ibid., col. 2011.

improvements (*nihil habens adjectionis extrinsecae*). 'For this is not the place for fine style, whether cursus, metre, or prose, but for bare testimony and strict investigation.' These remarks provide a commentary on the form which depositions were expected to take in the time of Gregory IX. The four depositions of the *Libellus* are all in *oratio obliqua*. The statements are succinct and itemized in a way which suggests question and answer, and there are notes of interrogation by the commissioners. In short, this fragment of the procès-verbal on the life of St. Elizabeth takes the same form as the *acta canonizationis* of St. Dominic and John Buoni.

A comparison of these nearly contemporary procès-verbaux with the *Quadrilogus* throws the singularity of our document into relief. It embodies the very defects which the papal Process was seeking to avoid. It contains hearsay evidence. One witness submits a letter instead of oral testimony. Another adopts a literary and exhortatory style. It contains no evidence of the interrogation of witnesses. All the depositions are presented in direct speech. From this it seems that the English Church was lagging behind the continent in the application of papal requirements to the Process. It is unfortunate that there are no other records of English canonization inquiries of the same period to provide a basis for comparison. The fragmentary procès-verbal on St. Hugh of Lincoln (1219) shows that the scrutiny of miracles had attained strict legal form while the scrutiny of the saint's life was still in a rudimentary stage of development.[1] But the Process underwent important developments during the pontificates of Gregory IX and Innocent IV. The Process of St. Hugh is therefore no guide to what would have been done in 1244. Nevertheless, the Process was still in a formative stage, and it is too early to look for uniformity. The peculiar features of the *Quadrilogus* illustrate the painful progress of the papal inquiry towards uniformity and more rigorous standards of criticism.

[1] A short *cursus vitae* is placed at the head of the roll of miracles: BM Cotton Roll xiii. 27, m. 1.

28   The Quadrilogus *and the Canonization Process*

It is unlikely that the *Quadrilogus* contains all, or even the greater part, of the evidence concerning St. Edmund's life, which was submitted to the pope. The compiler no doubt selected his material. Evidence of this can be found in the *Veriloquium* of the Dominican master Robert Bacon, which Matthew Paris inserted in his Life of St. Edmund.[1] Bacon's so-called *Veriloquium* is a deposition made on oath, of the same type as those included in the *Quadrilogus*. He makes the same points as the other witnesses and there are several points of verbal parallelism. On the other hand, Bacon's deposition contains more historical information than the others, and Matthew Paris displayed sound historical sense in selecting it for insertion in his biography. Bacon's testimony may have been attached to the other four in a copy which has now been lost, for the writer whose work underlies the Anonymous A and the Pontigny Life drew on Bacon as well as on the other four witnesses.

Bacon's deposition seems to have started a false trail among the Tudor bibliographers. Leland listed a Life of St. Edmund among the works of Robert Bacon,[2] and Bale did likewise.[3] Bale gives as his source for this a manuscript seen at Ramsey. Now there is reason to think that what Bale is here referring to was a copy of Bacon's deposition. His notice of Bacon is oddly worded, as follows: 'Robertus Bakon, dominicanus, *Oxonii regens in theologia*, divi Eadmundi Abindonensis *auditor et socius iuratus*, plura de illo scripsit, ut quod studuerit Parisius', &c. The description is a curious one: what exactly is meant by a *socius iuratus*? The explanation is, however, clear if the passage is placed beside the opening of Bacon's deposition as it is reproduced by Matthew Paris: 'Frater Robertus cognomento Bacun de Ordine Predicatorum, *regens Oxonie de theologia*,

---

[1] Below, p. 248.
[2] *Commentarii de Scriptoribus Britannicis*, ed. Hall (1709), ii. 258. From his biographical note it is evident that Leland identified Robert with Roger Bacon.
[3] *Scriptorum Illustrium Maioris Britanniae Catalogus* (Basel, 1557), pp. 294–5; *Index Britanniae Scriptorum*, ed. R. L. Poole and M. Bateson (1902), p. 366.

qui beato Edmundo . . . *auditor et socius, iuratus* dicit: Cum beatus Edmundus in liberalibus artibus studeret Parisius', &c. It can be seen from this that Bale had before him a copy of Bacon's deposition. Mispunctuating, or possibly misunderstanding his text, he produced the meaningless expression *socius iuratus*. It seems then that Bale was referring not to a 'Life' of St. Edmund, but to the *Veriloquium*, a copy of which may have been in the possession of Ramsey abbey. Possibly it was the *Vita* bound up with the Rule of St. Benedict, which the Ramsey cataloguer noted among the books of John the Precentor,[1] and Bale was put off the scent by the shortcomings of the medieval monk librarian. Bale's rather misleading reference was spread abroad by the Swiss edition of his catalogue. Thus Pitseus ascribed a Life of St. Edmund to Bacon, on the authority of Bale,[2] and the Dominican bibliographers made the same assertion on the authority of Pitseus.[3] Perhaps with this, we may lay the question of Bacon's authorship to rest.

The text provides ample evidence that the scribe of the *Quadrilogus* was neither a careful nor a very intelligent copyist. He did not worry himself whether or not his transcript made sense. The text of the depositions as given in the *Quadrilogus* can to some extent be checked by reference to the extracts reproduced in the Anonymous A Life. It can thus be seen that the copyist of the *Quadrilogus* made at least one considerable omission from the deposition of Eustace. Eustace is speaking of St. Edmund's manner of life as a regent Master of Arts and of his conversion to theology, and he follows the text of the Oxford letter of postulation. But the vision of St. Edmund's mother, which played the part of the *dea ex machina* in this story, is omitted in the *Quadrilogus*. Now the Anonymous A reproduces Eustace's deposition verbatim at this point, including

[1] *Chronicon Abbatiae Rameseiensis*, ed. W. D. Macray (RS 1886), pp. 362.
[2] *De Illustribus Britanniae Scriptoribus* (Paris, 1619), p. 318.
[3] J. Quétif and J. Echard, *Scriptores Ordinis Fratrum Praedicatorum* (Paris, 1719–21) i. 118. For an analysis of the sources from which they derived their knowledge of English writings, see R. Creytens, 'L'Œuvre bibliographique d'Echard', *Archivum Fratrum Praedicatorum*, xiv (1944), pp. 43–71.

its minor variations from the letters of postulation.[1] But the Anonymous A has the vision of the saint's mother. There is nothing else to indicate that he had an independent text of the Oxford letter, or that he dodged from the deposition to the letter and back again in order to produce a superior text. It must therefore be concluded that the vision of St. Edmund's mother was in the copy of the deposition which the Anonymous A used, and that the scribe of the *Quadrilogus* has omitted it. The text as it stands suggests that the omission was deliberate: the expression 'ad studium theologie quasi per revelacionem se transtulit' is unintelligible without reference to the story of the dream which he has omitted.

II

THE LIFE BY EUSTACE OF FAVERSHAM

THE records of the canonization process provided the hagiographers with their materials. The Life printed here as the work of Eustace of Faversham is the earliest biography of St. Edmund. As will appear, it was compiled before the Process had ended, possibly even before it had begun, a fact which explains the writer's apologetic tone. It represents as it were the second stratum of the hagiographical tradition, for it is based directly on the letters of postulation. It is to be found in the following six manuscripts, all of which are of English origin:

1. B.M. Royal MS. 2 D vi,[2] (A) a codex of 246 folios, measuring 8 by 6 inches with irregular gatherings. It contains a commentary on the Psalms and various other items written in different hands of the thirteenth century. The volume has a modern binding. An ex-libris on the first folio shows that it belonged to Rochester cathedral

---

[1] Lambeth Palace MS. 135, fo. 122–122ᵛ.
[2] See G. F. Warner and J. P. Gilson, *Catalogue of Western MSS. in the Old Royal and King's Collections* (London, 1921), i. 55–56.

priory. The Life of St. Edmund (fos. 151–65ᵛ) is written in single column in a round well-formed thirteenth-century book hand, with illuminated capitals and a rubricated title of much interest.

2. B.M. Cotton MS. Julius D vi. (B₁).[1] The manuscript is discussed in connexion with the Life by Matthew Paris, of which it contains the sole copy. The Life by Eustace (fos. 161ᵛ–78ᵛ) is written in a fourteenth-century hand, with illuminated capitals.

3. B.M. Royal MS. 8 F xiv (B₂).[2] A volume of 204 folios, measuring 11 by 7¾ inches, containing the Dialogues of St. Gregory (fo. 7), the Philobiblon of Richard of Bury (fo. 76), the Didascalion of Hugh of St. Victor (fo. 90), and other items written in different hands of the thirteenth and fourteenth centuries. The gatherings are irregular. A late fourteenth-century list of contents (fo. 6ᵛ) includes the Life of St. Edmund. The book came from Bury,[3] and the flyleaf bears the ex-libris of the abbey and the press mark (G 15). A note indicates that it was given to the abbey by brother Henry of Kirkestede. It subsequently formed part of Lord Lumley's collection. The Life of St. Edmund (fos. 198–201ᵛ) is written, on a separate quire, in a rather clumsy book hand of the thirteenth century. It is followed by the Pontigny letter and the Office of St. Edmund.

4. B.M. Harleian MS. 2 (C₁).[4] A volume of 289 folios, measuring 11½ by 8 inches. A collection of *Passiones* and *Vitae Sanctorum* written in different hands of the thirteenth and fourteenth centuries. It includes also William of Malmesbury's *Gesta Pontificum* (fo. 98), and St. Bernard's sermons on the Canticle (fo. 234). An ex-libris on fo. 1 shows that the book belonged to the Augustinian abbey of St. Mary, Thornton-on-Humber. The Life of St. Edmund (fos. 88–97) is written in double column in a large and inelegant hand of the thirteenth century.

5. Bibliothèque municipale de Douai, MS. 843 (C₂).[5] A volume of 111 folios, measuring 6¼ by 4½ inches, containing a collection of

[1] *Catalogue of the MSS. in the Cottonian Library* (1802), p. 15.
[2] Warner and Gilson, i. 270–2.
[3] See M. R. James, *The Abbey of St. Edmund at Bury* (Cambridge Antiquarian Society publications, No. xxviii, 1895), p. 58.
[4] *Catalogue of the Harleian MSS. in the British Museum* (London, 1808) i. 1. There is a sixteenth-century transcript of this text, made by John Fox, in the Inner Temple library, Petyt MS. 538, vol. 46.
[5] *Catalogue général des MSS. des bibliothèques publiques des départements*, vi (Paris, 1878), p. 589. See the notice in *Anal. Boll.* xx (1901), pp. 400–1.

Passiones and *Vitae Sanctorum*, including Folcard's Life of St. John of Beverley (fo. 57ᵛ). A calendar on fo. 4 shows that the book is of English provenance. It is written throughout in a fine fifteenth-century book hand, in double column, with illuminated capitals. The Life of St. Edmund (fos. 42–52ᵛ), like the other Lives of the manuscript, had a miniature attached to the title which has been cut out.

6. B.M. Cotton MS. Cleopatra B i (D). A volume of 187 folios, measuring 7¼ by 5¾ inches, made up of diverse fragments which include the Book of St. Gilbert of Sempringham (fos. 33–68).[1] The Life of St. Edmund (fos. 24–28ᵛ) is written in a crabbed, poorly spaced bookhand of the thirteenth century. Together with a treatise on the vision of St. Paul and St. Anselm's letter on the Immaculate Conception, it forms a separate gathering. There is nothing to show the provenance of this part of the book.

A complete collation of these manuscripts has shown that A stands apart from the rest as being nearest to the archetype. At nearly every point it reproduces with greater accuracy the original documents which underlie the Life and is most faithful to the original draft of the Life, which also survives. It therefore provided the obvious basis for the text which follows. The remaining five manuscripts are all associated in descent from a common exemplar. This exemplar is referred to in the diagram as *gloriose* on account of its distinctive variant in the first sentence where it appears to have read *gloriose nutritus* instead of *religiose nutritus*. It also omitted the lengthy and interesting *incipit* of the A version, and apparently contained seventeen variants from the text of A which are reproduced in all the other five manuscripts.

The five manuscripts derived from *gloriose* divide into two groups, (B) and (C), leaving D in a class on its own. Generally D is an inaccurate and perverse copy, but in a number of instances where (B) and (C) have common variants from the

---

[1] This was used by Dugdale as the source for the Life of St. Gilbert which he published in the *Monasticon*, and by Mlle Foreville for her edition of the Process of St. Gilbert: *Le Livre de Saint Gilbert de Sempringham* (Paris, 1943), p. xiv.

The Life by Eustace of Faversham

exemplar, D has reproduced the correct text. As regards (B) and (C), B_1 and B_2 have a considerable number of omissions and variants in common which show that they copied from a common source, (B), and a sufficient number of individual peculiarities to exclude the possibility that either could have copied from the other. The same relationship exists between C_1 and C_2. The text of C_1 is very inaccurate and has a number of omissions which increase in length and frequency towards the end. The relationship between the six texts can be best shown diagrammatically as in Fig. 3.

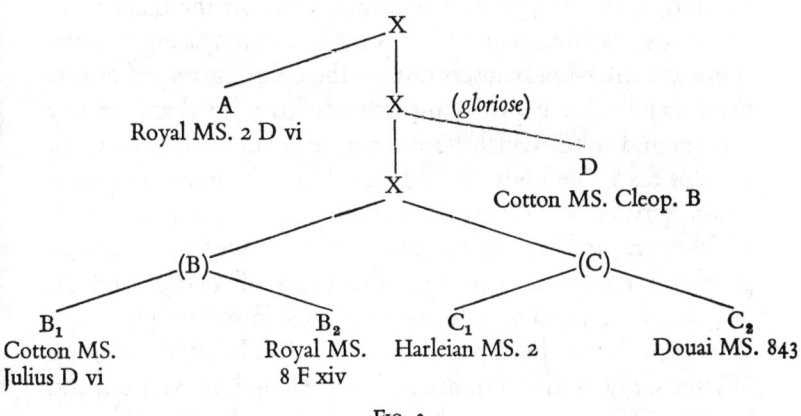

```
                    X
                   / |
                  /  |
                 /   X ___ (gloriose)
                A    |       \
         Royal MS. 2 D vi    \
                 |            D
                 X        Cotton MS. Cleop. B
                / \
              (B)  (C)
              / \   / \
            B₁   B₂ C₁    C₂
        Cotton MS. Royal MS. Harleian MS. 2   Douai MS. 843
        Julius D vi  8 F xiv
```

Fig. 3

The text of these six manuscripts reproduces the Life in its finished form. But an unusual accident has preserved it also in draft form, in MS. R.5.40 of Trinity College, Cambridge. This is a codex of 85 folios, measuring $10\frac{3}{8}$ by $7\frac{7}{8}$ inches, in a modern binding.[1] It contains William of Malmesbury's *Gesta Pontificum* (fo. 5), and other items, written in different hands of the thirteenth and fourteenth centuries. A late fourteenth-century table of contents (fo. 3ᵛ) shows that the book had already assumed its present form at that period and that the Life of St. Edmund formed part of it. The provenance of the book is

[1] See M. R. James, *The Western MSS in the Library of Trinity College, Cambridge* (Cambridge, 1901) ii. 206–8.

uncertain, beyond the fact that it came to the college by the gift of Thomas Nevile, dean of Canterbury. The Life of St. Edmund (fos. 58–60^v) is written in a small neat charter hand of the mid-thirteenth century, with much abbreviation. It forms a separate gathering, the margins of which have been drastically cut to fit into the volume, so that some of the marginal notes have been lost. The arrangement of the text is of special interest because it exhibits a thirteenth-century biography as it were in the process of compilation. The compiler has arranged his work in three columns. The centre column, which is 4⅝ inches in width, contains the main body of the text, written on ruled lines with double spacing to leave room for inter-linear insertions. In the columns on either side the compiler has copied long extracts from his documentary sources and notes which he intends, at a later stage, to work into his text. The body of the text follows the letters of postulation written by Oxford University and Bishop Ralph of Chichester, and amplifies them with conventional hagiographical matter drawn from the Lives of Becket and St. Martin of Tours. The side columns contain transcripts of the letters sent by the bishop and chapter of Salisbury, Archbishop Walter Gray, and the monasteries of Abingdon, Merton, and Reading. The source of each letter is indicated by a heading in rustic capitals. Besides the letters, the margins contain memoranda concerning topics and persons to be consulted for further information, and these provide some interesting pointers to the compiler's identity.

From a biographical point of view, the Life is disappointing. It is a rhetorical and thoroughly conventional work of hagiography. Much of it is unoriginal in the most literal sense, for more than half consists of extracts from the letters of postulation, juxtaposed so as to form a more or less continuous narrative. Its interest lies in the fact that it forms an important link in the hagiographical tradition. Hardy summarily dismissed it as an abridgement of the Life by Matthew Paris,[1] and the

[1] *Descriptive Catalogue of Materials*, iii, nos. 164 and 167.

Bollandists ignored it. Its significance has thus been missed. It is not an abridgement of Matthew's work, but his basic literary source.[1]

The compiler had direct access to the letters of postulation. He did not, however, transcribe them one by one *in toto*, but excerpted a passage here and a passage there first from one letter, then from another, thus constructing a mosaic of quotation. A comparison with the relevant letters printed in the appendix will reveal the dexterity with which the workman wielded his scissors. The mechanics of this typical medieval feat become plain when the draft of the Trinity College manuscript is examined. Having his sources all before him, arranged in three columns, it was a relatively easy task for the compiler to conflate them in this patchwork fashion. The letters, however, only carried him up to a certain point. They contained nothing about St. Edmund's difficulties as archbishop or his departure to Pontigny and death. For this part of the account the writer had to draw on other sources or on his own knowledge. From the point at which the letters fail him up to the archbishop's departure, he borrows frequently from the Life of Becket. When he comes to St. Edmund's death and the funeral procession back to Pontigny, he gives an eyewitness account, occasionally reminding the reader of his presence by slipping into the first person. At one point, he declares himself to have been present as a witness. This part of the narrative, unlike the rest, contains a wealth of circumstantial detail. The Life breaks off unfinished in the midst of this description, and is followed by a transcript of the letter of postulation written by the Pontigny monks. The Harleian copyist has endeavoured to remedy this by the addition of two sentences describing the reception and burial of the body at Pontigny.

The compiler was, of course, familiar with the traditional literature of hagiography. He knew the second book of St. Gregory's *Dialogues*, and he was closely familiar with the Life of St. Martin of Tours by Sulpicius Severus and with John of

---

[1] See below, pp. 79–82.

Salisbury's Life of St. Thomas Becket. At one point he draws a rather forced comparison between St. Edmund and St. Martin (p. 212), claiming, rather rashly, that St. Edmund had, like St. Martin, resurrected three people from the dead. There is, however, a studied ambiguity in the phrasing so that the passage could be taken in an allegorical sense.

The use which the writer makes of John of Salisbury's Life of Becket is interesting. In five places he draws long passages from it verbatim, and a sixth passage shows strong verbal reminiscence. These borrowings are more than rhetorical ornaments. They contain statements of fact. For example, in describing St. Edmund's generosity to the poor, he says that no one was turned empty-handed from the archbishop's door, and that his servants were sent to visit the homes of the sick to inquire about their material wants. The whole of this passage is lifted verbatim from the Life of Becket. The writer draws more extensively on this source when he comes to speak of the archbishop's difficulties with the king. Possibly he felt the need to be guarded at this point. The matters in dispute are not stated. The writer is content to reproduce a purple passage from the Life of Becket. There can be no mistaking the cumulative effect which the writer is aiming at: he is trying to show that Becket's mantle had fallen on St. Edmund. The archbishop's departure is represented as analogous to the flight of Becket and inspired by his example. The residence at Pontigny provided an obvious parallel. Carried on, as he was, by the logic of his analogy, the compiler evidently felt the lack of the dramatic act which ended Becket's career. So he argues that Edmund too, in another way, had earned a title to the crown of a martyr, 'for martyrdom is not accomplished solely by the shedding of blood. To afflict the flesh, to triumph over the world, to conquer the Devil and the flesh, is a martyrdom' p. 216). As has been suggested elsewhere, this effort of the compiler to depict St. Edmund as an *alter* Becket had a permanent influence on the hagiographical tradition.[1]

[1] See below, p. 179.

The Life by Eustace of Faversham

It is useful at this point to discuss the identity of the compiler, but first, it is necessary to clear up a misunderstanding. It has frequently been stated that a Life of St. Edmund was written by his brother, Master Robert of Abingdon. There is no contemporary evidence for this, nor any evidence earlier than Leland, who noted a copy of a Life written by Robert of Abingdon, among the books of St. Mary's priory, Thetford.[1] I think Leland's statement was a mistake caused by misreading the title of the present Life as it stands in the A text. This title, written in rubric, reads as follows:

> Incipit vita gloriosi confessoris Eadmundi archiepiscopi Cantuariensis ecclesie, apud Pontiniacum edita et magistro R(oberto) de Abendonia transmissa ut eius exercicio recipiant obscura lucem, modum superflua, hiancia iuncturam, minus habencia supplementum.

In other words, this Life was produced at Pontigny and sent to Robert of Abingdon for him to inspect and amend. The contents of the Life, and especially of the draft Life, are quite compatible with this description, which is written in the same hand as the rest of the text. The title is omitted in the other manuscripts, but in the margin of D Sir Robert Cotton has written 'Robertus Richius vita Edmundi archiepiscopi cuius frater fuit.'[2] It seems then that in the sixteenth century Robert of Abingdon was thought to be the author of the Life. It is easy to see how a hasty reading of the title in A could lead to this mistake. At any rate, Leland appears to be the starting-point of Robert's literary reputation. Although Leland's notes were not published until the eighteenth century, they were freely used by Bale. Thus the attribution to Robert of Abingdon appeared in the Swiss edition of Bale's catalogue.[3] It was evidently from Bale that Surius took the information,[4] and Pitseus

---

[1] *Collectanea*, ed. Hearne (London, 1774), iv. 26.
[2] Cotton MS. Cleop. B i, fo. 24, top and bottom margins.
[3] *Scriptorum Illustrium Maioris Britanniae Catalogus* (Basel, 1557), p. 281.
[4] *De Probatis Sanctorum* (Cologne, 1575), vi. 366. Oudin increased the confusion by misunderstanding Surius and assuming that the Life published by him was Robert's work: *Commentarius de Scriptoribus Ecclesiae* (1722), iii. 218.

got it from the same source, despite his untruthful claim to have it *ex Lelando*.[1] Thus the statement found its way into the Cistercian menology[2] and into Tanner's catalogue,[3] and troubled St. Edmund's modern biographers. In short, there is no contemporary evidence that Master Robert wrote a Life of his brother, and the assumption that he did so rests solely on a doubtful statement of Leland.

Who then was the compiler of this short Life? The title of the A text states that the Life was produced at Pontigny. This is not surprising in view of the use which the compiler had made of the letters of postulation, for Pontigny was the chief promoter in the movement for the canonization and the place where the Process opened, as well as being the place where the records of the Process were deposited. Moreover, the writer had obviously been at Pontigny since he was able to present an eye-witness account, written in the nominative case, of the funeral procession from Soisy. We may add that he was not a man of superior education or of great intelligence. He was content to conflate the work of others, and where his sources failed him, he drew on the conventional literature of piety. He displays no interest in, or understanding of, public events. His ideal archbishop was evidently Thomas Becket and he was eager to suggest analogies between Becket and St. Edmund. There can be little doubt that the writer with whom we are dealing was a monk.

Besides these indications, the marginalia of the Trinity manuscript provide a number of clues to the compiler's identity. In the first place, three marginal notes indicate that he was someone in close touch with the archbishop's circle. Thus, against the account in the text of St. Edmund's conversion from the Arts to theology (fo. 58), a marginal entry reads: 'De difficultate quam fecit gradiendi in theologiam, Iohannes capellanus exponet, et vos, bone magister R., scitis.' Another marginal

---

[1] *De Illustribus Britanniae Scriptoribus* (Paris, 1619), p. 318.
[2] *Menologium Cisterciense*, ed. Henriquez (Antwerp, 1630), p. 383.
[3] *Bibliotheca Britannico-Hibernica* (1748), p. 630.

note (fo. 58) reads: 'Quomodo vidit diabolum in specie draconis. Unde Iohannes capellanus.' And a third note, referring to damage which the archbishopric had suffered at the king's hands (fo. 60), reads: 'Memorandum de feudo J. militis quod est iuxta Li . . .,[1] de quo vos melius scitis.' It would be unrewarding to speculate on the identity of the persons here referred to,[2] though we may hazard a guess that the 'Magister R.' who knew the details of St. Edmund's early career, was Master Robert of Abingdon, his brother, to whom, as the title tells us, the Life was dispatched. These notes show that the writer was in the position of being able to draw on the personal knowledge of the archbishop's familiars. Another marginal note, laconic but expressive, seems to bring us closer to a solution. Where the text mentions the rebellion of the monks of Christ Church (fo. 60), the compiler has written in the margin: 'Quod ad memoriam anxie revocamus.' Why should the conduct of the monks be a cause of 'anguish' to the writer? It seems permissible to infer from this that he felt himself to be in some way personally involved in the struggle between the chapter and the archbishop. He may therefore have been a Black Monk himself, possibly even a member of the Christ Church community.

Finally, where the text speaks of the archbishop's illness at Pontigny and the unabated vigour of his mind (fo. 60), the compiler has noted: 'Unde dominus Iohannes.' This might be a reference to Abbot John of Pontigny, who could supply personal testimony.

The compiler, then, was someone in close touch with the archbishop's household, and, in all probability, a member of it himself. He felt himself to be personally involved in the rebellion of Christ Church which suggests that he was a Benedictine and possibly a Canterbury monk. This last possibility is strengthened by his preoccupation with the history of St.

[1] The rest of the word has been cut away by the binder.
[2] Master John of Offington might answer to the description of *Iohannes capellanus*: he has been claimed for Oxford.

Thomas Becket which appears in his work. Moreover, he had access to the letters of postulation and he was able to write an eye-witness account of the funeral cortège which brought the archbishop's body back from Soisy to Pontigny.

The evidence so far adduced is admittedly circumstantial, but so far as it goes, it points to Eustace, the archbishop's chaplain. He was a member of the *familia*, and the only one who satisfies all the conditions. Eustace was a monk of Christ Church. He was appointed chaplain to the archbishop sometime before December 1237,[1] and he was the only monk who was a member of the *familia*. The continuator of Gervase of Canterbury makes it clear that Eustace was personally involved in the dispute between the archbishop and the monks. The chronicler remarks ungraciously that Eustace had gone with his master to Rome in 1237 without having sought the permission of the convent.[2] In January 1239 the chapter sent messengers to summon him from the archbishop's house at Teynham to return to the monastery for the election of a new prior. On this occasion the archbishop answered for him. His loyalty to his master was evidently a cause of increasing ill feeling in the monastery. He went with the archbishop on his last journey to the continent, and three days before St. Edmund's death, he received at Soisy a letter, an *inspeximus* of which remains in the archives of Sens cathedral.[3] It is a death-bed testimonial granted to Eustace by the archbishop with the purpose of protecting him against possible reprisals by the monks. Eustace then was present at Soisy and must have taken part in the procession back to Pontigny. Moreover, he was active in promoting the subsequent canonization process. His advice was sought and respected at the papal court[4] and Simon Langton referred to him as 'having laboured in this business more than anyone'.[5] He would clearly have had access to the

---

[1] Gervase, ii. 131. He attests one act on 23 July 1240: App. B, No. 60.
[2] Gervase, ii. 131.   [3] App. B, No. 64.
[4] Sens cath. mun. no. 27; *MD Thes.* iii, col. 1914.
[5] Sens cath. mun. no. 29; *MD Thes.* iii, col. 1914.

letters of postulation. His deposition is one of the four gathered together in the *Quadrilogus*.

In the letters and in Gervase, Eustace appears as *camerarius* of Christ Church and chaplain to the archbishop. His identification as Eustace of Faversham rests on a letter of Archbishop Edmund's, dated 1240, which exists in the Canterbury archives,[1] and on a list of the priors of Dover. The letter nominates Eustace, monk of Christ Church and *capellanum nostrum*, to the priorate of St. Martin's, Dover. The list, which dates from the early fourteenth century, gives the names of two priors of Dover who held office in the time of St. Edmund, namely, Robert of Olecumbe and Eustace of Faversham.[2] This serves to identify Eustace the chaplain as Eustace of Faversham. The only difficulty arises from the fact that no prior by the name of Eustace appears to have held office at Dover. Moreover, the priorate was not vacant in 1240. According to the Dover annals, Robert of Olecumbe was prior from 1235 until his death in 1248.[3] There is no record of any Prior Eustace either in the Dover Cartulary[4] or in the Obituary of Christ Church.[5] The probability is that Prior Robert was ill in March 1240, and that the archbishop's nomination was made, and the letters prepared, in expectation of his death.[6] Whatever the explanation of the fact, it does nothing to invalidate the identification of Eustace. It is clear that he never held the office of prior. After 1240 he appears in the documents as plain *frater Eustachius*, the secretarius and chaplain of the Blessed Edmund.

The facts known about the career of Eustace of Faversham fit the inferences drawn from the marginalia of the draft Life

[1] Canterbury D. and C. mun. Chartae Antiquae D. 76; see App. E.
[2] *Literae Cantuarienses*, ed. J. B. Sheppard (RS 1889), iii. 376.
[3] BM Cotton MS. Julius D v, fo. 30ᵛ; the entries for this period are brief, but the succession of priors is noted.
[4] Lambeth MS. 241.
[5] BM Arundel MS. 68, fos. 10 ff. This obituary was written up to *c.* 1405. Eleven priors of Dover are named.
[6] The suggestion of C. R. Haines, *Dover Priory* (1930), p. 214, that the archbishop's letter intended to designate Eustace sub-prior, is unconvincing, especially since the letter is addressed to the sub-prior.

and from the character of the work itself. He was a member of St. Edmund's household, who held a position of confidence and must have been on familiar terms with the archbishop's intimates. He was a monk of Christ Church and was clearly placed in a most uncomfortable predicament by the conduct of the chapter. He was with the archbishop at Soisy and Pontigny, and he certainly had access to the letters of postulation: he probably sought and collected them. We might add that an analogy between St. Edmund and St. Thomas Becket is one which would appeal to a Canterbury monk. So much for the circumstantial evidence. Of itself it could hardly be conclusive, but it is clinched by the deposition of Eustace in the *Quadrilogus*.

It is obvious at once that the Life and the deposition are not independent productions. Now the writer of a *Vita* who used the deposition of a witness made in the canonization process, would be following a natural and recognized procedure.[1] But here the reverse has happened. Eustace's deposition draws verbatim from the Life. Moreover, the deposition is based not on the completed Life, but on the draft Life of the Trinity College manuscript. The following extract taken from the first paragraph of the draft Life, will illustrate this:

(Text)	(Margin)
	(Abingdon)
extitit a puericia tam religiose nutritus ut, docente eum Christianissima matre sua quam florem postea fuisse viduarum et vita sua clamat et fama, ieiunare inciperet et orare cum adhuc esset puerulus. (fo. 58)	Cuius mater tam sancte vivebat ut loricam ferream sue carni innexam finetenus portaret. Hec dulci puero cum lactis dulcedine lacte dulcius Christi (nomen) induit, amorem inmisit, timorem incussit, crescentem et proficientem suo exemplo informavit.

---

[1] Cf. the use made of documents of the Process by John of Orta in his Life of St. Louis of Toulouse: M. R. Toynbee, *S. Louis of Toulouse and the Process of Canonization*, pp. 13 ff.

The Life by Eustace of Faversham

Deposition	Completed Life
extiterat a puericia tam religiose nutritus ut, docente eum Christianissima matre sua quam florem fuisse postea viduarum et vita sua clamat et fama, ieiunare inciperet et orare cum adhuc esset puerulus. Cuius mater tam sancte vivebat ut loricam ferream sue carni innexam finetenus portavit. Hec dulci puero in ipso inicio viarum suarum Christi nomen indidit, amorem inmisit, timorem incussit, crescentem et perficientem suo exemplo informavit.	extitit a puericia tam religiose nutritus ut, docente eum Christianissima matre sua quam florem postea fuisse viduarum et vita sua clamat et fama, ieiunare inciperet et orare cum adhuc puerulus esset. Hec itaque dulci puero cum lactis dulcedine lacte dulcius Christi nomen indidit, timorem incussit, crescentem et proficientem suo exemplo informavit. Cuius mater tam sancte vivebat ut loricam ferream sue carni innexam finetenus portaret.

In this extract, the text of the draft Life follows the wording of the Oxford letter. The margin contains a transcript of the Abingdon letter. In the completed Life and the deposition, the marginal letter has been incorporated into the text. It will be noticed, however, that the completed Life reverses the order of the two sentences of the Abingdon letter, whilst the deposition reproduces them in their correct order. Again, the completed Life reverses the order of verb and subject in the phrase *cum adhuc esset puerulus*, whereas the deposition reproduces the phrase in the original order.

The deposition of Eustace then, follows the draft and not the completed Life. The completed Life gives a fuller and more developed text of the draft than the deposition does. The deposition sometimes incorporates the marginal notes of the draft and sometimes neglects them. Thus, for example, the letters of Merton and Archbishop Walter Gray, which are copied in the margin of the draft, are totally omitted from the deposition, but are incorporated into the completed Life. Occasionally, however, the deposition develops a marginal memorandum in the draft which is neglected by the completed Life. The following passage offers an example of this. It will be noticed that the draft contains a note to mention the legate. In the deposition this has been developed into a brief mention of the legate's support, but in the completed Life, the note is passed over.

Draft Life

(fo. 60) Unde gravi questione super memoratis inter ipsum et regem Anglorum orta, reformande paci constituti sunt dies plurimi, set, instigante dissensionis auctore, discordes (ab) invicem discesserunt. Convenientibus suffraganeis et proceribus ex mandato regis et archiepiscopi ad excipiendas ecclesie necessitatibus, orta contencio inter regem et ecclesiam que, instigante diabolo, magis ac magis augebatur in dies.

Notabilia de legato ad memoriam revocentur

Deposition	*Completed Life*
Et orta inter regem et ipsum contencione gravi super iure et libertatibus ecclesie . . . reformande paci et ad excipiendas ecclesie necessitates constituti (sunt) dies plurimi, set, instigante discensionis autore, contencio inter ipsos (magis) ac magis augebatur in dies. Vocatis igitur ex parte ipsius regis proceribus, et ex parte archiepiscopi suffraganeis, constituti (sunt) dies multi in corde et ex corde malignancium ad negocium prorogandum, cum presens esset tunc legatus in quo confidebat.	Convenientibus suffraganeis ex mandato archiepiscopi et proceribus ex mandato regis ad excipiendas ecclesie necessitates, orta est contencio inter regem et ecclesiam que, instigante diabolo, magis ac magis augebatur in dies. Reformande paci constituti sunt dies plurimi, sed instigante dissensionis auctore, post prorogacionem dilacionum frustratoriarum discordes ab invicem discesserunt.

Again, in this passage, which is based on a passage in the Life of Becket, the deposition has reproduced the original order of the sentences in the draft Life, whereas the completed Life has reversed the order. Finally, the deposition breaks off at the same point as the draft Life, with St. Edmund's death, and the concluding sentences are identical. In the completed Life, however, the narrative is continued with an account of the funeral procession, and the concluding sentences of the draft are omitted.

The fact that Eustace drew exclusively on the draft Life in order to compile personal testimony for the canonization process can only be explained by the fact that the draft comprised his own notes. This conclusion confirms the inferences about the author's identity drawn from the marginalia of the draft Life and from the whole character of the compilation. Diagrammatically the relationship between the three productions can be expressed as in Fig. 4.

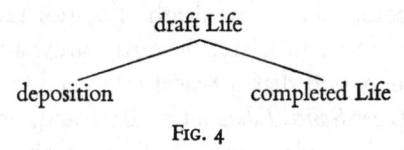

```
              draft Life
           ___/     \___
          /             \
    deposition      completed Life
              FIG. 4
```

It is not easy to say whether the deposition or the completed Life was finished first. The composition of the draft can be dated fairly closely. The original Merton letter, of which it contains a transcript, is dated 27 February 1242.[1] It cannot then be earlier than that. On the other hand, since the draft was used by Eustace to compile his deposition, it was clearly written before the canonization process had ended, or even before the proceedings had begun. Moreover, it is reasonably certain that the depositions reproduced in the *Quadrilogus* belong to the first inquiry held in 1244.[2] The draft Life must therefore have been compiled between 1242 and 1244. The completed Life cannot be much later. The unfinished ending and the addition of the Pontigny letter indicate that it was written up before the canonization had taken place. More conclusive evidence still can be found in the title of the A text which refers to Master Robert of Abingdon as still extant. This makes 1244 the

---

[1] App. A, below, p. 297. The letter is printed in *MD. Thes.* iii. cols. 1899–1900, where, however, it is wrongly dated 1241.
[2] See above, p. 21.

terminus ad quem for the completion of the Life, for Master Robert died in 1243 or 1244.[1]

Eustace then compiled his short Life of St. Edmund either in the early stages of the canonization proceedings, or before they had opened. Eustace was one of the most strenuous promoters of the Process and he most probably compiled the Life with this end in view, a fact which explains its apologetic tone and lack of originality. That it was used in this way may be suspected from three references in the *Historia Canonizationis* of Albert of Armagh. In his prologue Albert mentions the work of an unnamed writer who had composed a biography of Edmund from personal knowledge, Edmund's 'faithful friend both before and after death' ('comes individuus ante mortem et post mortem').[2] The Maurists drew attention to this passage and suggested that it was a reference to the Life contained in the *Liber Sancti Edmundi* by Bertrand, or, as we prefer it, by the Pontigny Anonymous. Such is the psychological compulsion of an editio princeps that this suggestion has been accepted without further question by modern writers. Actually, however, Albert refers back to this *comes individuus* towards the end of his narrative. When the Process was in its last stage, the English cardinal, John of Toledo, sent to France and England to obtain more witnesses. He says that the bearer of this commission was 'that faithful Achates, on whom the whole burden of the affair rested, the *secretarius* of the blessed father Edmund, whom we mentioned at the beginning.'[3] Now the letters containing this commission are preserved in the Sens cathedral archives, and they state that the bearer was Eustace, *dicti sancti servus et alumpnus*.[4] It would appear, therefore, that Albert's reference in the prologue was to the Life by Eustace, and it is interesting to observe that it had been brought to the notice of the president of the papal commission. We are

---

[1] See below, p. 145.   [2] *MD. Thes.* iii, col. 1831.
[3] Ibid. iii, cols. 1849–50.
[4] Sens cath. mun. nos. 27, 28, 29; *MD. Thes.* iii, cols. 1912, 1914. See above, p. 18.

tempted to go a step further and suggest that it had been circulated at the papal court itself. Albert refers to a cardinal who confessed to him in private conversation that he had difficulty in swallowing the story that St. Martin of Tours had resurrected three people.[1] Now the Life by Eustace contains a reference to these three miracles of St. Martin and tries to draw an allegorical comparison with St. Edmund. The passage is found only in this Life and in that by Matthew Paris which incorporated Eustace's work. The *obiter dictum* of the cardinal looks suspiciously like a pointed reference to Eustace's work. In fact, unless it were a reference to Eustace, the remark would be curiously irrelevant, since no such sweeping claims were made for St. Edmund outside this work.

III

THE PONTIGNY LIFE AND THE ANONYMOUS A

THE Pontigny Life, which was published by Martène and Durand, seems to have enjoyed the widest circulation on the continent, and it remains perhaps the best known Life of St. Edmund. It is extant in two recensions of which (*a*) is the complete version and (*b*) is an abridgement of (*a*) made by omitting a number of hagiographical episodes. It has been found in the following eight manuscripts, all of which belonged to Cistercian houses on the continent:

(*a*) 1. Auxerre, Bibl. et Musée, MS. 123 (ancien 110), fos. 1–56ᵛ; written in the mid-thirteenth century; provenance: Pontigny (the *Liber Sancti Edmundi*; printed in *MD. Thes.* iii, cols. 1775–1826).

2. BM. Add. MS. 15264, fos. 87ᵛ–116ᵛ; written in the thirteenth century; provenance: Royaumont.

[1] *MD. Thes.* iii, cols. 1848–8.

3. Leipzig, Universitätsbibliothek, MS. 590, fos. 177–90^v; written in the thirteenth century; provenance: Altzelle, Saxony.

4. Leipzig, Universitätsbibliothek, MS. 633, fos. 68^v–83; written in the thirteenth century; provenance: Altzelle, Saxony.

5. Lille, Bibl. municipale, MS. 761 (ancien 93), fos. 50–76; written in the fourteenth century; provenance: Loos.

6. Munich, Bayerische Staatsbibliothek, MS. lat. 2689, fos. 128–42; written in the thirteenth century; provenance: Aldersbach, Bavaria.

(b) 1. Dijon, Bibl. municipale, MS. 646, fos. 252–72; written in the thirteenth century; provenance: Cîteaux.

2. Namur, Bibl. du Musée archéologique, MS. 73, fos. 125^v–130^v; written in the fifteenth century; provenance: Le Jardinet, Namur.

This Life appears to have achieved something of the status of an official biography in the Cistercian Order and probably supplied the lessons for the Office of the saint prescribed by the General Chapter of 1247 for houses of the Pontigny filiation.[1] Within a few years the eclectic Vincent of Beauvais had incorporated it into his *Speculum Historiale*,[2] and in the next century John of Tynemouth used it as the basis for the Life which he included in his legendary of English saints called the *Sanctilogium*.[3] The identity of the writer remains obscure. In their edition of the Life the Maurists ascribed it to Bertrand, prior of Pontigny, on the authority of the Cistercian bibliographer,

---

[1] Canivez, *Statuta*, ii. 355: 'Historia vero nuper composita tam in domo Pontiniacensi . . . quam per abbatias de generatione sua cantetur.' In the Auxerre manuscript the text has been marked off into twelve lectiones.

[2] *Vincentii Bellovacensis Speculum Maius* (Venice edn. 1591), IV. xxxi, c. 67–88.

[3] Published by C. Horstmann from the Cotton MS. Tib. E 1: *Nova Legenda Anglie* (1901), i. 316–24. Under this title Capgrave compiled a rearranged and compressed version of John's work, which was published by Wynkyn de Worde in 1516.

Charles de Visch.[1] De Visch states that Bertrand wrote the Life in 1247 at his abbot's command, and that the manuscript of his work is to be found at Châlis (diocese of Beauvais).[2] It has been impossible to find any earlier authority for this, and the source from which de Visch obtained his information remains obscure. The eighteenth-century catalogues of Pontigny list the Life as an anonymous work,[3] and, pending a reconstruction of the abbey's library, it seems preferable to refer to the author as the Pontigny Anonymous.

The Pontigny Life has enjoyed a reputation rather out of proportion to its value, for in content it is not an original work. The writer, whose style is florid and highly rhetorical, drew his matter from another Life which is no longer extant. This can be seen by a comparison with the work of the Anonymous A, to which the Pontigny Life is related in the first degree. It is necessary to turn to this work before discussing the matter further.

The Life referred to as the work of the Anonymous A, exists in the following six manuscripts, all apparently of English origin:

1. Lambeth Palace MS. 135, fos. 118–37^v (L). The volume also contains the Life and miracles of St. Thomas Becket. This and the Life of St. Edmund are written in the same thirteenth-century hand. Fo. 138–138^v contains the beginning of the Anonymous C Life, written in the same hand as the others. The book was one of Lord Lumley's, but its provenance is unknown.

---

[1] MD. Thes. iii, col. 1754. They went on to identify Bertrand with the chamberlain of St. Edmund whom Archbishop Albert of Armagh mentions, but on this see above, p. 46.

[2] *Bibliotheca Scriptorum Sacri Ordinis Cisterciensis* (Douai, 1649), p. 52. De Visch says that from this work are taken the lessons of the office used in houses of the Pontigny filiation. In his time, however, the twelve lessons recited in the Cistercian breviary were drawn not from the Pontigny Life, but from the Life published by Surius; see John Çaço, *Lectionarium Sanctorum ex gravissimis praestantissimorum Patrum Historiis et Tractatibus concinnatum* (Palaçuelos, 1603), pp. 394–8. It is probably this Life which he is fathering on Bertrand.

[3] C. H. Talbot, 'Notes on the Library of Pontigny', ASOC x (1954), pp. 106–68; see pp. 142, 153.

2. Worcester cathedral, dean & chapter library MS. Q 27, fos. 243–58[b] (W); written in the fourteenth century, part of a volume of miscellaneous contents including the testament of St. Francis and the treatise *de Duodecim Abusivis*. The book was in the possession of the chapter in the fifteenth century.[1]

3. Dublin, Trinity College MS. C.3.19, fos. 171[v]–3[v] (T).[2] A collection of saints' Lives written in several hands of the late thirteenth century. Fos. 1–205 originally formed a separate volume which bore on fo. 205[r] the following *ex libris*: 'Liber ffratris A(? mauri) de Bredon, capellani parochialis de Stonton'' (possibly the chapel of Stoneton attached to the parish of Priors Hardwick, Warwick).[3]

4. BM. Cotton MS. Vitellius C xii, fos. 280[v]–90 (V). The Life of St. Edmund, together with the Lives of SS. Edward and Thomas Becket, originally formed a distinct volume, all written in a single thirteenth-century book-hand. Fos. 114–57 came from St. Augustine's, Canterbury, but the provenance of the rest is uncertain.

5. Cambridge, University Library MS. MM.4.6, fos. 37–53 (C). A quarto volume containing also the Lives of SS. Francis, Dominic, and Margaret, all written in a single book-hand of the thirteenth century. The book was formerly the property of John Moore, bishop of Norwich.

6. Oxford, Balliol College MS. 226, fos. 48–63[v] (B). A collection of saints' Lives, written in two hands of the thirteenth century. The book came to the college from the humanist William Gray, bishop of Ely.

A collation of these manuscripts with one another and with the depositions of the *Quadrilogus* shows that L reproduces most accurately the text of the exemplar which is no longer extant. At several points W has readings which agree with the deposi-

[1] *Catalogus Librorum Manuscriptorum Bibliothecae Wigorniensis*, ed. I. Atkins and N. Ker (Cambridge, 1944), p. 59.

[2] See P. Grosjean 'Catalogus codicum hagiographicorum latinorum bibliothecarum Dubliniensium', *Anal. Boll.* xlvi (1928), p. 93. Père Grosjean identified the Life of St. Edmund with BHL 2410*b*, i.e. the Anonymous B Life, but in this he was mistaken.

[3] The ex-libris was kindly transmitted to me by Dr. Parke and Mr. O'Sullivan of Trinity College, who were good enough to examine the manuscript for me.

tions against L, but in most other respects it is an eccentric text with odd variants, and its copyist has slightly altered the order of the hagiographical episodes. Manuscripts C, T, and V are apparently derived from the Lambeth text through a common exemplar which is not extant. T is a drastically abridged text of the Life. It omits the titles and items 12–22, 26–60, 62–end.[1] In other words, it is only a fragment of the Anonymous A, containing items 1–11, 23–25, and 61^a–61^b. Manuscript B is copied from C. Tentatively, the relationship of the manuscripts can be represented as in Fig. 5.

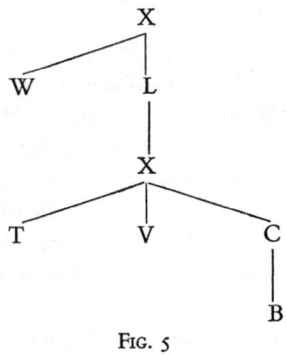

FIG. 5

As will be evident from this, the original text of the Anonymous A must be reconstructed from a collation of L and W.

Because of its obvious affinities with the Pontigny Life, the Anonymous A was thought to be a derivative version of that work. But textual analysis shows that this is not the case. Both writers incorporate the same passages from the depositions of Robert Bacon and the four *familiares*, but A is less rhetorical than the Pontigny writer and reproduces his sources with much greater accuracy. The way in which the two writers handle the following passage, drawn in the first place from the deposition of Eustace, is typical:

Eustace

Cum adholesceret, liberalibus traditus disciplinis inbuendus, via qua prius ducebatur, incedebat spontaneus. Nam ex tunc voluntarie

[1] The references are to the synoptic table on pp. 100–05.

Deo sacrificare cepit, ecclesie limina sponte frequentans, vana et frivola, quibus adholescentior habundat etas, devitans, erudicioni sue diligenter intendens, carnis delicias (non) solum fugiens, sed et crucis mortificationem iugiter in corpore suo portans, toto mentis studio (vite) requisivit auctorem. Videbatur iam illud quod nondum legerat intellexisse proverbium, 'Adholescens iuxta viam suam eciam cum senuerit, non recedet ab ea.' Quod in eo vere invenitur completum esse. Nam ieiunare et vigilare, et cetera penitencie gravia ex tunc tam duxit in consuetudinem facere quod postmodum, ut ipsemet perhibebat, non tam facilia quam delectabilia ei fuerant in provectiori etate.

Anonymous A

Cum puer *adolesceret, liberalibus traditus* studiis *inbuendus, via qua prius ducebatur, incedebat spontaneus. Ex tunc* enim *voluntarie Deo sacrificare cepit, ecclesie limina frequentans, vana et frivola, quibus adholescentior habundat etas, devitans, erudicioni sue diligenter intendens, carnis delicias* non *solum fugiens, sed et crucis mortificationem iugiter in suo corpore portans, toto mentis studio vite requisivit auctorem. Videbatur* enim *iam illud quod nondum legerat intellexisse proverbium,* 'Adolescens iuxta viam suam *ambulans, eciam cum senuerit, non recedet ab ea.' Quod in eo vere invenitur esse completum. Nam ieiunare, vigilare, et cetera penitencie gravia ex tunc tam duxit in consuetudinem facere, quod postmodum, ut ipsemet perhibebat, non tam facilia quam* eciam *delectabilia ei fuerant in provectiori etate.*

Pontigny writer

*Cum*que iam grandiusculus esset effectus et annos attigisset *adolescentie, via qua prius* puer *ducebatur, incedebat* tam *spontanee* quam devote. *Ex tunc enim voluntarie Deo sacrificare* studuit *et ecclesie frequentans limina, vana et frivola, quibus* etas *habundat adolescentior, devitavit. Erudicioni sue* vacans assidue *carnis delicias non* tantum *fugit sed* eciam exhorruit et Christi stigmata *in corpore suo* circumferens, ipsum *toto mentis studio requisivit. Videbatur enim quod proverbium* istud *quod nondum legerat, intelligeret,* 'Adolescens iuxta viam suam positus, ab ea eciam cum senuerit, non recedet.' Cuius proverbii sentencia *in eo* veraciter est impleta. *Nam ieiunare,* orare, *et cetera* vite spiritualis exercitia *ita duxit ex tunc in consuetudinem quod tam facilia quam* iocunda sibi *fuerunt* postquam *provectiorem* pervenerat ad *etatem.*

It is clear that the Anonymous A is not dependent on the Pontigny writer for his text at this point since, saving half a dozen words, he has reproduced the deposition verbatim.

The fact is that both writers used a third source which is no longer extant. This was pointed out by the late H. W. C. Davis, who made a detailed comparison of contents.[1] While the content of the two Lives is nearly identical, each has a number of factual details not found in the other. Thus both writers reproduce a rather macabre anecdote in which St. Edmund has a vision of demons, in the shape of crows, carrying off the body of a dead man. But only A names the place, Chalgrove, where the episode occurred. Again, both writers say that St. Edmund confided the reasons for his last journey to certain persons, described by the Pontigny writer as *quidam religiosi*. A, however, names the persons as the prior and sub-prior of Lewes. On the other hand, the Pontigny writer has three episodes which are completely omitted by A. These are a journey made by St. Edmund from Oxford to Northampton, an account of his association with the countess of Salisbury and the conversion of her husband, Earl William Longspée, and an anecdote about one of the archbishop's chamberlains who was called on to adjust his master's hair shirt and thus discovered his secret austerities. Both writers mention St. Edmund's commission to preach the Crusade and give an account of miracles which occurred at various points on his itinerary through the west of England. Both locate identical episodes at Buckland, which they erroneously supposed to be a Cistercian nunnery,[2] at Crutch, Worcester, and All Saints' churchyard at Oxford. A alone, however, mentions an incident at Hereford, while the Pontigny writer alone records incidents at Leominster, Stratford, and Gloucester. The latter also brings in two analogous incidents, one of which he locates in St. John's churchyard,

---

[1] 'An Unpublished Life of Edmund Rich', *EHR* xxii (1907), pp. 84–92.

[2] Probably a confusion between Minchin Buckland (Somerset), a priory of sisters of the Order of St. John of Jerusalem, and the Cistercian abbey of Buckland (Devon).

Oxford, and the other before the king's hall in the same town. Again, while both writers incorporate the narrative of St. Edmund's death and burial which is found in the Life by Eustace, the Pontigny writer adds two minor details which he probably derived from local knowledge. One of these is a miracle performed by Edmund when preaching at Ligny, near Pontigny.[1] The other is an observation that on his way to Soisy the archbishop personally distributed alms to the poor whom he encountered on the road, a statement which helps to explain the popular demonstrations which occurred when his funeral passed the same way a few days later.

The complementary character of these two narratives can only be satisfactorily explained by the fact that both drew on a common source. There can be no doubt that the Anonymous A reproduces the text of this source more closely since he has the wording of the depositions almost unchanged. The Pontigny writer sits more loosely to his authority. He is rhetorical, flowery, and fond of allegorical exegesis. It is clear that, save for the two incidents located in the Pontigny district, his 'additions' are simply A's omissions from the common source, for he had no first-hand information of his own from which to draw. His anecdote about the earl and countess of Salisbury is a case in point. If we compare the content of the two Lives at this point, we find the following episodes:

1. *Quales habuit in scolis auditores*: St. Edmund's dream of seven brands snatched from his burning schools, followed next day by the departure of seven of his pupils to the Cistercian Order (drawn from Bacon's deposition).

2. *Quomodo apparuit ei Spiritus Sanctus*: Falling asleep before a lecture, St. Edmund has a dream in which the Holy Ghost, in the likeness of a dove, brings him communion.

3. *Qualis fuit in predicatione*: An account of St. Edmund's gifts as a preacher which converted many to religion.

4. *De quadam peccatrice conversa*: A prostitute goes to make fun of him, but is converted.

[1] This was the cure of a girl. The writer probably got it from the procès-verbal of the canonization process: Sens cath. mun. no. 26, m. 6.

The Pontigny Life and the Anonymous A

In the Pontigny Life, the story about the conversion of Earl William Longspée comes between episodes (3) and (4). The Anonymous A ends paragraph (3) with the words, 'multi eciam seculo funditus abrenunciaverunt', and then adds, irrelevantly and lamely, 'Quando autem predicare voluit, nemini ante predicationem facile loquebatur' (a sentence taken from another context in Bacon's deposition). The Pontigny writer, however, ends with the same words, but adds, 'Super hiis, cum plura sint veritatis testimonia, quedam subiciemus quia non possumus universa', thus leading naturally into the Salisbury episode. It is obvious here that the episode existed in the common source, but that A decided to omit it and cast about, not too successfully, for another way of concluding the paragraph. It is curious to see that later on, when he comes to another story about the countess of Salisbury in which a gift of hers is refused by St. Edmund, A reproduces the story, but suppresses the name of the countess. The connexion of these two episodes suggests that A's omissions were dictated by policy rather than by oversight.

Some of the obscurities which Davis discovered in the text of A were attributed by him to unintelligent abridgement from a fuller source. It was unfortunate that he used B, an unsatisfactory version, for the basis of his comparison between A and the Pontigny writer. A number of the obscurities which he fathered on to the author were, in fact, the blunders of copyists. Thus, for instance, in telling the story of the corpse snatched up by crows, B and C write 'Quadam die cum iter ageret versus Habendoniam *una cum illo comite vie*' &c., as if St. Edmund's companion had already been mentioned. But no companion had been previously mentioned. However, the correct reading of A in this case is clearly that given in the Worcester manuscript which has *cum comite suo de Lewekenore* (i.e. Lewknor, near Chalgrove, the scene of the incident). The most striking factual discrepancy between A and the Pontigny writer is in the name of St. Edmund's father, which the Pontigny writer gives correctly as Reginald, and A as Edward.

The mistake appears in L, V, C, and B, but W has a variant opening which avoids the father's name altogether. It is therefore impossible to say whether the error was made by the Anonymous A or whether it was an aberration on the part of the Lambeth copyist. At all events, it seems that the common source had the name right since the correct version is given in the Pontigny Life.[1]

One remaining difference between the two Lives needs to be noticed. Apart from the variations mentioned, both writers reproduce the same hagiographical anecdotes and the verbal parallelism is obvious throughout, but the order in which the anecdotes are presented differs considerably. This can be seen from the synopsis at the end of the chapter. Broadly speaking, the Pontigny writer seems to follow a chronological order, placing the anecdotes at the right point in St. Edmund's career, while the Anonymous A seems to follow an analytical order, grouping the anecdotes according to the identity of their subject-matter. In some cases it is possible to supply the rubrics that the writer has in mind. Possibly he was trying to use the anecdotes to illustrate a scheme of virtues and vices. Thus, if the order of A is compared with the order of the Pontigny writer given in the synopsis, it can be seen that A has regrouped anecdotes together in the following way, under headings which we may suggest:

Influence of St. Edmund's mother   5, 6, 7, 10, 9
Chastity . . . . 13, 14, 15, 62, 16^a, 58
? *Corporal works of mercy* . 26, 40, 19; 20, 44
? *Spiritual works of mercy* . 17, 23, 27, 28, 29, 30, 32, 21

and so on. To illustrate Saint Edmund's resistance to sexual temptation, A has brought together four anecdotes, of which the first two relate to his student days, and the second two to his mode of life as archbishop. The Pontigny writer reproduces

[1] With the exception of the Royaumont copy which has 'Eduuardus': BM Add. MS. 15264, fo. 87^v. The scribe evidently miscorrected his text from a copy of the Anonymous A. The other French manuscripts have 'Reinaldus'; Leipzig Univ. Bibl. MS. 633, fo. 68^v renders it as 'Reinhardus'.

the same stories, but in their right chronological place. It is probable that he reproduces more nearly the order of the common source.

What can be concluded about the common source—we may call it X—which underlies the work of both writers? It is evident that it contained all or much of the depositions of Robert Bacon and the four *familiares*, and that its text of these was an accurate one. X was also the reservoir of miraculous anecdotes which supplied not only the Pontigny writer and A, but the Anonymous C writer also. The facility with which the Pontigny writer, A and C, rearranged the anecdotes to their taste suggests that X was less a finished literary narrative than a collection of documents or a quarry of pre-selected materials, probably similar in format to the draft Life of Eustace of Faversham. The *Quadrilogus* contains testimony relating only to Saint Edmund's virtues. It is known that the English commission collected testimony of miracles also, and it is reasonable to assume that most of the miracle stories of X were drawn from statements taken down in the course of the canonization proceedings in England.

Whether the compiler of X had any information of his own to add to the story is a question that we cannot answer with much confidence. The Benedictines of St. Maur fathered the Pontigny Life on to a chamberlain of the archbishop on the strength of two passages in which the writer appears to claim direct knowledge. Thus, describing the way St. Edmund crossed himself at night, he writes, 'ut ipse testimonium perhibet qui vidit et scripsit hec, et scimus quia verum est testimonium eius'. The other passage describes the sealing of St. Edmund's coffin by the abbot of Pontigny at Trainel, 'presente eo qui scripsit hec et aliis quamplurimis'. These two assertions are found also in A at the same point, and were evidently taken from X. It does not follow, however, that X, any more than his two plagiarists, was claiming to be giving direct personal testimony. It would be most unsafe to infer from these passages that he was himself the chamberlain concerned. He is merely vouching for the authenticity of the original testimony on which his account is based. It is probable that he had before him in the one case a deposition taken from one of St. Edmund's chamberlains, and, in the other, the eyewitness account of the funeral procession written by Eustace of Faversham, the archbishop's chaplain.

Because he is primarily a transmitter, rather than an originator, the compiler of X is an elusive personality. A number of converging pointers suggest a Salisbury connexion. Thus, he alone gives a detailed account of the arrival of the Canterbury envoys at Salisbury, their interview with the dean, and their dispatch to Calne in search of their archbishop-elect. The fact that the compiler knew the name and whereabouts of St. Edmund's prebend itself suggests that he had unusually precise information about this stage of St. Edmund's career, and the report of the dean's observations does not sound as though it was drawn from a sworn deposition. Also the writer displays familiarity with St. Edmund's habits as a canon of Salisbury. He knew, for instance, that Edmund stayed for long periods at Stanley abbey as the guest of his old friend and pupil, Stephen of Lexington. Again, he is the source from which the Pontigny writer drew his story about St. Edmund's acquaintance with Ela, the countess of Salisbury, and Earl William Longspée, an association for which there is documentary confirmation.[1] He was aware too that, since retiring from the world, the countess had become abbess of her own foundation at Lacock. He shows noticeable familiarity with the place-names of western England and, unless he is dependent on his documentation, with the topography of Oxford. We may conclude from these facts that the compiler either did his work at Salisbury, or that he drew an important part of his information from those who knew St. Edmund well at this period of his life.

[1] According to the Lacock register, St. Edmund inspired the foundation; he also attests one of the early charters of endowment: *Monasticon*, vi. 500, 502. He also attests a charter of the countess in favour of Bradenstoke: BM Stowe MS. 925, fo. 143ᵛ.

There are a number of clues to the date at which X was compiled. Both A and the Pontigny writer contain an identical reference to Stephen of Lexington as *nunc abbas Clarevallensis*, and he held that office from December 1243 until 1255.[1] Again, both writers speak of prophecies which St. Edmund made to Albert of Cologne, archbishop of Armagh, and to William Ralegh, bishop of Norwich, later of Winchester, in which these prelates were warned of future trouble. The writers go on to point out that these prophecies have been vindicated by subsequent events. Thus A writes, 'Nam dominus Armachanus gloriatur in tribulacionibus in quibus adhuc pro iusticia desudat, et ille Wintoniensis post immensos tribulacionum aggeres iam de omnibus feliciter triumphat.' The Pontigny writer reproduces the same passage word for word, but instead of *dominus Armachanus*, he has *ille quondam Armachanus*. Archbishop Albert relinquished the see of Armagh when he was nominated metropolitan of Prussia in January 1246, an appointment which involved him in much difficulty with the German Military Orders.[2] William Ralegh was translated to Winchester against the king's wishes and, when he came to take up his see, he found the temporalities withheld and the gates of his cathedral city barred against him. He recovered the king's pleasure in September 1244,[3] and he died in 1250. It appears then that A was written some time after Ralegh's reconciliation with the king in 1244, and before the writer had heard the news of Archbishop Albert's translation, which would have reached him before the middle of the year 1246. The compilation of X may be placed between the same dates. This agrees very well with the character of the compilation as it is known to us through A. It cannot antedate the canonization process since it contains the depositions, but it contains no reference to the act of canonization which, evidently, had not yet taken

---

[1] *Gallia Christiana* (1876), iv. 806; *Chron. Maiora*, v. 596, 651.
[2] *Allgemeine Deutsche Biographie* (1875), i. 202–4; Böhmer-Ficker u. Winkelmann, *Regesta Imperii* (1892), v. 1548–9.
[3] *Ann. Mon.* ii. 88–89, 332; *CPR 1232–47*, p. 435.

place. The Pontigny writer, on the other hand, had evidently heard of Archbishop Albert's translation. Moreover, he wrote after the canonization, to which he refers. He must therefore have written his Life some time between the end of 1246 and 1250, for he refers to William Ralegh as still living.

The surviving manuscripts of the Anonymous A show that in the thirteenth century it was the most widely known Life of St. Edmund circulating in England. It reproduces the miraculous anecdotes in their earliest extant form. A fair number of these, at least, must have originated in depositions laid before the canonization commission and we may believe that of these A has given us a reasonably faithful copy. Other anecdotes no doubt had their origin in oral tradition. Like all such stories, they conform to certain clearly recognizable types. The work of A formed the basis of the Middle English metrical Life which was included in the South English Legendary,[1] and, in the middle of the fourteenth century, Ranulf Higden made an abridgement of it for his huge chronicle.[2] But more important as a factor in its dissemination, it was used to supply the twelve lessons for the feast of St. Edmund in the office of the English Black Monks.[3] It must be said that the portrait of St. Edmund which A put into circulation was neither a wholly fair, nor a very attractive one. The writer is largely oblivious of public events and indifferent to Edmund's contribution to the intellectual world of his time. True to the tradition of

[1] Published from Bodleian MS. Laud 108 by C. Horstmann, *The Early South English Legendary* (EETS 1887), pp. 431–49, and from CCCC MS. 145 and BM Harl. MS. 2277 by C. D'Evelyn and A. J. Mill, *The South English Legendary* (EETS 1956), ii. 492–511. The critical examination of the sources underlying this great collection still remains to be done. A number of the hagiographical anecdotes, detached from the Life, were in circulation, see Carleton Brown, *A Register of Middle English Religious and Didactic Verse*, ii (Oxford, 1920), pp. 1678, 2110.

[2] *Polychronicon Ranulphi Higden*, ed. C. Babington and J. R. Lumby (RS 1865–82), viii. 214–34.

[3] *The Monastic Breviary of Hyde Abbey*, ed. J. B. L. Tolhurst, (Henry Bradshaw Society, 1939), iv, fos. 380–381ᵛ. The Anonymous A was also used for the nocturns of the Hereford office: *The Hereford Breviary*, ed. W. H. Frere and L. E. G. Brown (Henry Bradshaw Society, 1911), ii. 404–6.

The Pontigny Life and the Anonymous A

monastic hagiography, he concentrates attention on the private piety and secret macerations which, during his lifetime, Edmund did his best to hide. But in this he reflects the literary taste of his public.

IV

THE ANONYMOUS B[1]

THE short Life, here called the work of the Anonymous writer B, exists in two manuscripts:

1. B.M. Cotton MS. Faustina B i, fos. 180–3. The Life is written in a neat thirteenth-century book-hand. There is nothing to indicate the provenance of this part of the volume.

2 Oxford, Bodleian MS. Fell, fos. 1–44.[2] The volume contains a collection of saints' Lives written at St. Augustine's, Canterbury, in the twelfth century. The Life of St. Edmund, which is written in a thirteenth-century book-hand, is on a gathering which was added to the book at some later stage.

This Life was printed from the first manuscript by Wallace,[3] and was attributed by him to Robert of Abingdon. The reasons which led him to make this ascription provide an example of the sort of 'evidence' on which too much guessing has been based. He argued that the Fell manuscript came from Abingdon and that the monks of Abingdon would have preferred to have the Life written by an Abingdon man, and also that this was the Life which Surius reproduced and that it was attributed by him to Robert. However, all three of these assumptions are baseless. The Life which Surius printed was based not on this, but on the Pontigny Life, and, as a careful reading of his

[1] *BHL* 2401*b*.
[2] See the history of this manuscript in *Summary Catalogue of Western MSS. in the Bodleian Library*, ii, no. 8690.
[3] Op. cit., pp. 614–24.

note shows, he was far from identifying his text with Robert's work.[1] Moreover, Wallace's suggestion that the writer possessed some special insight into St. Edmund's character and early education took no account of the sources from which the Life is obviously derived.

The source on which the Anonymous B chiefly depends is the deposition of Eustace. This forms the main body of the text. He uses his source fairly freely and has no qualms about altering a phrase or reversing the order of a sentence. He is not, however, dependent solely on Eustace. He has drawn a few phrases from the Abingdon letter of postulation. He also has a few notes on the archbishop's dispute with the monks which are found with identical wording in the Anonymous A. Moreover, he has inserted three miraculous episodes which are found in the Anonymous A and the other derivatives of X. These are the story of St. Edmund's combat with the Devil, the healing of a fistula in a student's arm, and St. Edmund's dispersal of the rainclouds when he was preaching the Crusade. Although these anecdotes are clearly the same as those in the derivatives of X, the Anonymous B reproduces them in a much more succinct form, without any of the place-names, and there is a striking absence of verbal similarity. Matthew Paris drew these three episodes from the Anonymous B, whose wording he reproduces at this point.[2]

It seems at first sight that we have in B another derivative of X, as in Fig. 6.

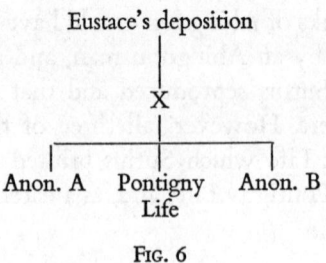

```
        Eustace's deposition
                 |
                 X
                 |
      _____|_____
      |          |          |
   Anon. A    Pontigny    Anon. B
              Life
```

FIG. 6

[1] *De Probatis Sanctorum*, vi (Cologne, 1575), p. 366.
[2] Below, pp. 234–6.

The Anonymous B

But this is impossible for, at a number of points, the wording of the Anonymous B agrees with Eustace against the Anonymous A and the Pontigny writer. Similarly, the possibility that X was derived from the Anonymous B is ruled out by the fact that, elsewhere, the Anonymous A and the Pontigny writer agree with Eustace against B. In fact, the Anonymous B Life can only represent another, and perhaps earlier, recension of the same collection of documents that was used by X, and its relationship to the other Lives is that shown in Fig. 7.

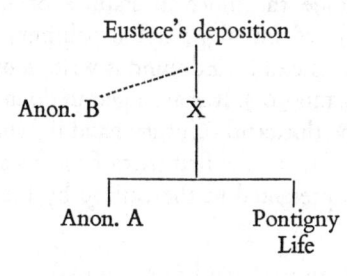

```
              Eustace's deposition
                      |
   Anon. B            X
                      |
              ┌───────┴───────┐
           Anon. A         Pontigny
                             Life
```

FIG. 7

Since the work of the Anonymous B is a pastiche, nothing can be confidently said about its author, except that he was not kindly disposed towards the monks of Christ Church. The apologetic character of the Life and the absence of reference to the canonization suggest that it is an early production, to be dated between 1244 and 1246. It was pointed out by Wallace that it supplied the lessons for the York Breviary.[1] Similarly, it was known to the compiler of the second nocturn for the feast of the translation in the Exeter Breviary.[2]

[1] *Breviarium ad usum insignis Ecclesie Eboracensis*, ed. S. W. Lawley (Surtees Soc. lxxv 1883), pp. 695–99; Wallace, pp. 446–52.
[2] *The Legenda Sanctorum of John de Grandisson*, ed. H. E. Reynolds (1880), fo. 57b.

V

THE ANONYMOUS C

THE Life by the anonymous writer C was published by Wallace[1] from the only known manuscript, namely,

Cambridge, St. John's College MS. 62 (C 12),[2] fos. 129–36ᵛ. The volume, bound in vellum and measuring 9⅜ by 7 inches, is the work of several hands, all of the thirteenth century. Its contents, which are heterogeneous, include the diocesan statutes of Bishop Giles of Bridport (fo. 107ᵛ), which suggests the Salisbury diocese as the place of origin. The Life of St. Edmund is written on a single quire of eight leaves (fos. 129–36ᵛ). It is arranged in double column with rubricated titles. The thirteenth-century hand in which it is written is the same that has written the first part of the bestiary on fos. 12–16ᵛ. The book was presented to the college by the earl of Southampton.

Wallace suggested, though without any real evidence, that this Life was the work of the Dominican theologian, Robert Bacon. He pointed out that the scribe had misplaced an episode on fo. 130ᵛ where he inserted one of St. Edmund's crusading mission miracles in the middle of the narrative describing his interview with his dying mother. The writer discovered his blunder and drew attention to it in a rubric: 'Ista capitula predicta locum habent post "sic thesaurarius".' Wallace concluded from this that the writer was transcribing from another copy or from the exemplar of this Life. However, as will appear, the scribe's blunder can be accounted for in another way.

The C Life stands in close relation to the Pontigny Life and the Anonymous A. As the synopsis shows, the writer has the same stock of hagiographical anecdotes, although he omits much circumstantial detail and omits some of the stories

---

[1] Op. cit., pp. 589–612. *BHL* 2411.
[2] M. R. James, *A Descriptive Catalogue of the MSS. in the Library of St. John's College, Cambridge* (1913), p. 82.

altogether. His order of presentation differs slightly from that of either the Pontigny writer or A, but on the whole he reproduces the order of the Pontigny writer more closely. In two cases he has matter which is to be found in the Pontigny Life but not in A, namely, the etymological explanation of St. Edmund's name, and the story that St. Edmund left his pupils' fees lying in the window. Again, in many points of minor detail C agrees with the Pontigny writer rather than with A. Thus all three writers have the story that, as a student, St. Edmund sold his theological books to help poor scholars. Although they all give an identical book list, their versions of it differ slightly, and it will be seen that C's version more nearly resembles that of the Pontigny Life:

Pontigny: psalterium glosatum et Penthateucum glosatum, cum libro duodecim prophetarum eque glosato, necnon et decretales epistolas,

A: psalterium glosatum, quinque libros Moysi, librum duodecim prophetarum glosatum, decretales et epistolas,

C: glosatum psalterium, pentateucum, epistolas decretales, et librum duodecim prophetarum,

To take another instance, all three writers reproduce the story of the abbot who entered St. Edmund's theological schools and induced seven of his pupils to become Cistercians. Now A alone names the abbot's monastery as Quarr. The Pontigny writer refers to him as *abbas quidam*, and C calls him *abbas ignotus*. It appears then that C is based either on the Pontigny Life or on the source which the Pontigny writer used.

In fact, a textual collation proves conclusively that C is based independently on X, the source underlying both the Pontigny Life and the Anonymous A. This can best be shown by taking a passage where we can compare the text of all three writers with an original document. We may take, for instance, the Vision of St. Edmund's mother, which all three writers reproduce, and which derived from the story in the letter of postulation sent to the pope by Oxford University. The text of the original letter runs as follows:

... *ipso adhuc cursim legente arismeticam quibusdam sociis suis, apparuit ei in sompnis pia mater eius paulo ante defuncta, dicens,* 'Fili, quid legis? Que sunt ille figure quibus tam studiose intendis?' Quo respondente, 'Talia lego', ostensis protractionibus que in illa solent fieri facultate, illa mox dextram manum eius arripuit et in ea tres circulos depinxit in quibus hec tria nomina per ordinem inscripsit: 'Pater · Filius · Spiritus Sanctus.' Et hoc facto, sic ait, 'Fili karissime, talibus figuris et non aliis de cetero intende.'[1]

Now the version of this passage given by the Pontigny writer, A and C respectively, is as follows (in each case, the words reproduced from the original letter are italicized):

Pontigny

Cumque *cursim quibusdam sociis suis lege*ret *adhuc arismeticam, apparentem* sibi *in sompnis* agnovit manifestus *matrem* suam. Que ait, '*Fili, quid legis? Que sunt ille figure quibus tam studiose intendis?' Quo respondente, 'Talia lego'*, ostensis que in ea sunt *facultate protractionibus, mox illa dexteram manum eius arripuit et in ea tres* pinxit *circulos* quos hiis *nominibus, Pater · Filius · Spiritus Sanctus,* per ordinem singulis singulos insignivit. *Et* addidit, '*Fili carissime, talibus figuris* de cetero *intende et non aliis*.'[2]

A

... *ipso adhuc* legente *cursum arismeticam quibusdam sociis suis, apparuit ei in sompnis pia mater eius paulo ante defuncta, dicens,* 'Fili, quid legis? Que sunt ille figure quibus tam studiose intendis?' Quo respondente, 'Talia lego', ostensis protractionibus que in illa fiunt *facultate, illa mox* dexteram *manum eius arripuit et in ea tres circulos depinxit in quibus hec tria nomina per ordinem* scripsit*, Pater · Filius · Spiritus Sanctus.* Quo facto ait, '*Fili carissime, talibus figuris et non aliis de cetero intende.*'[3]

C

... scolaribus magis provectis ad evidenciam probandorum quorundam problematum, geometrie figuras in pulvere protrahebat.

[1] See App. A, pp. 290–3.
[2] *MD. Thes.* iii. col. 1787; Auxerre MS. 123, fo. 14ᵛ.
[3] Lambeth MS. 135, fo. 122–122ᵛ, collated with Worcester MS. Q 27.

Beata vero Mabilia *paulo ante defuncta* tantos labores filii miserans circa mundanam scienciam que vel parum vel nichil edificat ad virtutem, *apparuit illi in sompnis dicens, 'Fili, quid legis? Que sunt ille figure quibus tam diligenter intendis?' Quo respondente, 'Talia lego sociis* meis *ostensis protractionibus que in illa solent fieri facultate'*, illa mox dexteram manum eius arripuit et in ea tres circulos depinxit in quibus hec tria nomina per ordinem scripsit, Pater · Filius · Spiritus Sanctus. Et hoc facto, sic ait, 'Fili carissime, talibus figuris et non aliis de cetero intende.'[1]

It will be seen that C has interpolated some moralization of his own into the narrative, but that in other respects he agrees with the original text sometimes against the Pontigny writer, sometimes against both the Pontigny writer and A. Thus C has the expression *paulo ante defuncta* which is in both the original letter and A, but which is omitted by the Pontigny writer. He also has the expression *que in illa solent fieri facultate*, drawn from the original document, whereas both the Pontigny writer and A have variants of it. This can only be explained by the hypothesis shown in Fig. 8.

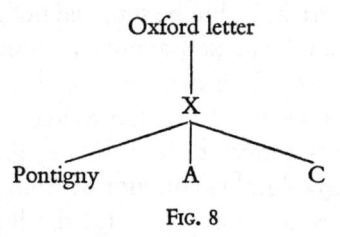

```
           Oxford letter
                |
                X
           ___/ | \___
          /     |     \
      Pontigny  A      C
              FIG. 8
```

This is amply borne out by other passages where C has followed the wording of his source sufficiently closely to make a collation with the other two writers possible. We may take, for instance, the last Latin speech of St. Edmund. He was dying and had just been brought the Viaticum, and he broke into an exclamation which the three writers record as follows:

Pontigny

Tu es domine in quem credidi, quem predicavi, quem veraciter

[1] Wallace, p. 600; St. John's Coll. MS. 62, fo. 133ᵛ.

docui, et tu michi testis es quod aliud quam te, in terra positus, non quesivi. Sicut tu scis quod nichil volo nisi quod tu vis, domine, ita fiat voluntas tua, quia in tua sunt omnia voluntate.[1]

A

Tu es domine in quem semper credidi, quem veraciter docui et predicavi, et tu michi testis es quod, in terra positus, nichil aliud nisi te quesivi.[2]

C

Tu es in quem credidi, quem predicavi, quem docui, et tu testis es mihi quia nichil aliud nisi te, domine, in terra quesivi. Sicut tu scis quod nichil volo nisi quod tu vis, fiat voluntas tua desiderabilis.[3]

Here, in the phrase *nichil aliud nisi te*, C agrees with A against the Pontigny writer. In most respects he agrees with the Pontigny writer against A, who has omitted the second sentence of the passage. On the other hand, the Pontigny writer and A agree together against C in having *veraciter docui* and *terra positus*.

C, then, is a third derivative of X. He omitted several of the anecdotes which were in X, but he supplied nothing of his own in the way of new information about St. Edmund. What he does add to the story is background and moralization. A number of references suggest that the writer knew Abingdon and had some connexion with the Salisbury diocese. Thus he treats us to a topographical encomium of Abingdon, referring to the proximity of the university and the hospitality of its monks, and he remarks on the fact that the cult of Mabel, St. Edmund's mother, is spreading and attracts pilgrims to her tomb as well as local people. In another passage he praises Bishop Richard Le Poore of Salisbury as the great man who translated the city, and elsewhere he refers to the sentiments of the canons of Salisbury who remember the days when St. Edmund was Treasurer.[4] A more striking peculiarity of C is

---

[1] *MD. Thes.* 1815; Auxerre MS. 123, fo. 44ᵛ.
[2] Lambeth MS. 135, fo. 133.   [3] Wallace, p. 611.
[4] Ibid., p. 605.

his fondness for scholastic terminology and his obvious familiarity with the routine of the schools. Thus a sick scholar who tries to detain St. Edmund, when asked the reason for his conduct, 'determines the question proposed' ('determinans igitur sibi propositam questionem respondit').[1] He speaks appreciatively of the disciplines of the Quadrivium ('quadriviali sciencie propter sui decorem et infallibiles necessitates insistens'),[2] and, as will be noted from the passage cited above, when he came to the Vision of St. Edmund's mother, he sensibly altered the wording so that Edmund was caught drawing geometrical diagrams instead of arithmetical ones. Again, when he describes St. Edmund selling his theological books for the benefit of poor scholars, C remarks that this must have been a great handicap to Edmund in the theological schools, for no one could have the Sacred Page entirely by heart.[3] Again, like all the others, C has the story of the seven scholars who quitted St. Edmund's schools for the Cistercian Order, but only he comments on the damage which must have been done to Edmund's school by the departure of seven gentlemen scholars.[4] The seven probably comprised about half of Edmund's school and the financial loss is an aspect that would be most likely to occur to a master who had had schools of his own.

C has made no additions to the *Vita Sancti Edmundi* besides comment and moralization. Apart from dialogue, which he usually reproduces carefully, he makes free with the text of his source. He has stylistic pretensions of his own. He has a liking for scholastic jargon and for extravagant metaphors. We are told, for instance, rather surprisingly, that the king's discontent with the archbishop, 'like a winter torrent plunging downward from the snowy ridge of the Apennine, gathered fury from the obstacle placed in its path'.[5] C's notice of Edmund's career as archbishop is brief. He has little to say about the archbishop's troubles, but it is clear that he feels no sympathy with the monks, whom he regards as the chief

[1] Ibid., p. 598. [2] Ibid., p. 600. [3] Ibid., p. 601.
[4] Ibid., p. 601. [5] Ibid., p. 610.

instigators of opposition and inexcusable rebels. It seems clear, then, that he was a secular clerk, most probably a university master, and possibly a clerk of the Salisbury diocese. There is no positive evidence of the date at which the Life was written, but the absence of any reference to the canonization, either direct or allusive, suggests that it was compiled before the end of 1246.

VI

THE LIFE BY MATTHEW PARIS

THE magnitude of the contribution made by Matthew Paris to our knowledge of the thirteenth century is well known. But the deserved fame of his great chronicles has caused his other writings to be relegated to the background. It is unlikely that he would have approved this order of preference. Hagiography was a recognized province of the medieval historiographer, and the cultus of the saints was a theme which called for his best efforts. Matthew Paris worked as assiduously in this field as in the other. More than a century afterwards, looking back with pride over the literary and artistic achievements of St. Albans, Walsingham wrote of Matthew's contribution to the fame of the abbey: '. . . Rogeri praedicti [i.e. Wendover] Chronicas necessarie ampliavit, et Vitas Sanctorum Albani, Amphibali, Thomae et Edmundi, archiepiscoporum Cantuariae, conscripsit et depinxit elegantissime, et multos libros providit ecclesiae.'[1] Modern research has been able to extend this list of Matthew's hagiographical writings by identifying two more biographies as his work. The list therefore now stands as follows:

1. Life of SS. Alban and Amphibalus.
2. Life of St. Thomas Becket.

[1] *Annales Amundesham*, ed. H. T. Riley (RS), ii. 303.

3. Life of St. Edmund of Abingdon.
4. Life of St. Edward the Confessor.
5. Life of Stephen Langton.

Matthew's Life of SS. Alban and Amphibalus is written in Anglo-Norman verse and is a translation of the Latin prose passion by William of St. Albans. His life of the Confessor, similarly, is an Anglo-Norman metrical translation of the Life by Ailred of Rievaulx. Both of these French Lives have long since been published,[1] but in each case the task of ascribing them to their actual author was left to Montague Rhodes James.[2]

James also identified Matthew's Life of St. Thomas Becket with the fragments of an Anglo-Norman metrical Life which Paul Meyer published from a manuscript at Courtrai.[3] In this case the attribution was based on similarities of diction and on the illustrations: the surviving four folios of the Life have fine miniatures which are unmistakably productions of the St. Albans school. The text appears to be a translation of the Latin *Quadrilogus*, a late twelfth-century compilation made from four existing *Vitae*. Now we have it on Walsingham's authority that Matthew Paris illustrated his Life of St. Thomas (*depinxit elegantissime*), and a note written on the fly-leaf of the manuscript containing the Life of St. Alban, in Matthew's own hand, states that he had translated a book about St. Thomas.[4] There seems no reason therefore to doubt that the Courtrai

[1] *Vie de Seint Auban*, ed. R. Atkinson (London, 1876); *The Lives of Edward the Confessor*, ed. H. R. Luard (RS 1858), pp. 1-157.

[2] In M. R. James, *La Estoire de Seint Aedward le rei* (Roxburgh Club, 1920), and M. R. James, E. F. Jacob, and W. R. L. Lowe, *Illustrations to the Life of St. Alban* (Oxford, 1924). In comparing the French Life of the Confessor with Ailred's Latin work, James noted a number of additions made by Matthew Paris, one of which was the abolition of the Danegeld by the Confessor. This event is, however, in Ailred's *Vita S. Edwardi*, PL cxcv. 753. All that Matthew has done is to change the context. The French metrical Lives by Matthew Paris have recently been discussed from a philological standpoint by Miss Dominica Legge, *Anglo-Norman in the Cloisters* (Edinburgh, 1950), pp. 20-31.

[3] *Fragments d'une vie de Saint Thomas de Cantorbery* (Société des Anciens Textes Français, 1885), with facsimiles.

[4] Cf. p. 76 below, and note.

fragments are Matthew's work. One problem however remains. In the *Historia Anglorum* Matthew refers in five places to a *Vita beati Thomae*.[1] In each case he refers the reader to the text of documents which, he says, are to be found in the Life.[2] The question is, to which Life does Matthew refer? All the documents alluded to are in the text of the *Chronica Maiora*, but three of them at least are not to be found in any known Life of Becket.[3] It is obviously a Latin work that is meant, for Matthew would not have referred the reader to a French poem for the authentic text of diplomatic letters written in Latin.

The existence has been demonstrated of a lost Life of Becket which was known to an earlier St. Albans writer. This precursor of Matthew Paris was the obscure Benedict of St. Albans, who composed an Anglo-Norman verse Life of St. Thomas in *c.* 1183–9.[4] Benedict says that he has 'translaté ceste vie de latin en romanz'. It has been shown that he was in fact translating the same lost Latin source as that which underlies the Icelandic *Thómas Saga*.[5] A good deal can be gleaned about the character of this lost Life from the saga. It evidently contained the text of a number of the diplomatic letters which are also reproduced in the *Chronica Maiora*. The three particular documents mentioned above are not reproduced in the saga, but they may have been in the Latin source. This lost work might therefore be the Life to which Matthew refers in the *Historia Anglorum*. On the other hand, the possibility cannot be

[1] *Hist. Angl.* i. 327, 341, 342 *bis*, 343.
[2] The references 'Respice in Historia ipsius martiris . . . in *Vite beati Thomae . . .*' are written over erasures. In one case where the original is legible, the text read *in cronicis*. It is clearly a separate biography that is referred to.
[3] *Hist. Angl.* i. 327: the bull of Alexander III absolving Becket from his submission to the Constitutions of Clarendon; ibid. i. 342: Gilbert Foliot's letter to the king; ibid. i. 343: the king's letter to Foliot after the Vézelay excommunications.
[4] Ed. F. Michel, *Chronique des ducs de Normandie* (Docs. inédits, 1844), app. ii.
[5] By E. Walberg, *La Tradition hagiographique de saint Thomas Becket avant la fin du xiie siècle* (Paris, 1929), chap. 1, and E. Magnússon, *Thómas Saga Erkibyskups* (RS 1885), introd.

ruled out that Matthew was referring to a Latin Life of St. Thomas written by himself.[1]

The Life of Stephen Langton was written by Matthew Paris in Latin, and survives only in fragments which have been edited by Liebermann.[2] The two fragments, which are in different manuscripts of the Cottonian collection, are in fact two halves of what was originally a single folio, so that, when fitted together, they form a short but continuous narrative covering the period of Langton's life from 1215 to 1220.[3] The piece is written in Matthew's own handwriting,[4] with the marginal headings and additions which are a familiar feature of his manuscripts.

Finally, there is the Life of St. Edmund, which Matthew wrote in Latin and then translated into French verse. Both versions survive and have now been identified. The original version is of particular interest, since it is the only complete Latin hagiographical work by Matthew Paris which we have. Besides the passage of Walsingham's already quoted, there are several references in the writings of St. Albans to the Life of St. Edmund. In three places Matthew mentions it himself. It will suffice to quote the notice inserted in the *Chronica Maiora* under the year 1253, in connexion with the death of Richard Wych. It is as follows:

> Huius (i.e. Richard Wych) igitur assertionibus, necnon et fratris magistri Robert Bacun de Ordine Praedicatorum, certificatus, dominus Mathaius Parisiensis monachus ecclesiae sancti Albani,

---

[1] The suggestion of J. C. Russell in *Dictionary of Writers*, p. 83, that Matthew's Life of St. Thomas is to be found in Cotton MS. Vesp. B XIII, is based on a misunderstanding. The manuscript contains no Life of Becket.

[2] F. Liebermann, *Ungedruckte Anglo-Normannische Geschichtsquellen* (Strasburg, 1879), pp. 318–29.

[3] Thus Cotton MS. Vesp. B XIII, fo. 133, fits on to the bottom of MS. Nero D I, fo. 197.

[4] The vexed question of the Matthew Paris hand has at last received the scientific treatment it deserved from R. Vaughan, 'The Handwriting of Matthew Paris', in *Trans. of the Cambridge Bibliographical Soc.* v. (1953), pp. 376–94. Mr. Vaughan has also identified Matthew's handwriting in the French Life of SS. Alban and Amphibalus.

vitam memorati sancti Edmundi scripsit, et quae indubitanter didicit a fide dignis, diligenter digessit. Quam qui videre desiderat, in ecclesia sancti Albani ipsam poterit reperire.[1]

It will be noticed that the passage mentions the existence of one Life only, that written by Matthew Paris himself. He says that he used the information supplied by Richard Wych and Robert Bacon. There is no suggestion that either of these ever composed a biography of St. Edmund. This Life by Matthew Paris, long unrecognized, was believed to be lost until A. T. Baker published the French metrical version of it which he discovered in the famous Welbeck abbey Legendary.[2] Baker was able to show that the French Life was written by Matthew Paris and that he was translating a Latin work of his own. He correctly identified this Latin Life with that contained in the Cotton MS. Julius D vi. A text of this Life had already been published by Wilfrid Wallace,[3] but Wallace had wrongly, if understandably, ascribed it to Eustace. It survives only in this unique copy.

Cotton MS. Julius D vi is a small volume of 184 folios, measuring 7⅛ by 5¼ inches.[4] Like most of the Cottonian collection, it is a composite book made up of fragments brought together from various places. The first section, comprising Pike's chronicle (fos. 3–66ᵛ), comes from Durham.[5] Another section describing the Invention of the Cross and the founding of Waltham abbey (fos. 73ᵛ–121) was apparently written at Waltham. This part of the manuscript was edited by Stubbs.[6]

---

[1] *Chron. Maiora*, v. 369. The Life is referred to in the same terms in the *Hist. Angl.* iii. 13 and 135. Casimir Oudin took the passage to mean simply that St. Albans library contained a Life of St. Edmund, and added unaccountably 'sed legendo attente locum illum in *Historia*, nullatenus reperio scriptam fuisse ab ipso vitam S. Edmundi': *Commentarius de Scriptoribus Ecclesiae* (1722), iii. 208.

[2] 'La Vie de S. Edmond', in *Romania*, lv (1929), pp. 332–81. The manuscript, which I have been unable to examine, is described by L. Karl in *Zeitschrift f. romanische Philologie*, xxxiv (1910), pp. 297–8.

[3] Op. cit., pp. 543–88.

[4] See *Catalogue of MSS. in the Cottonian Library* (1802), p. 15.

[5] N. Ker, *Mediaeval Libraries of Great Britain* (RHS 1941), p. 41.

[6] *The Foundation of Waltham Abbey* (Oxford, 1861).

The book contains two Lives of St. Edmund, that by Eustace (fos. 161v–78v) and that by Matthew Paris (fos. 123–51v), but there is no resemblance between the hands in which they are written, nor is there anything to show their provenance. Matthew's Life is written in single column, with 28 lines to the page. The hand is a very distinctive one, marked by the broad tapering letter *s*, with an angular hook at the top, and the thick tapering curved stroke used to form the descenders of the letter *p*. It belongs, most probably, to the early fourteenth century. The titles in the text are rubricated and the capitals are illuminated with calligraphic decoration.

Although the Life of the Julius manuscript contains much of what we may call conventional hagiography, it is unique in the amount of historical information which it supplies about St. Edmund's public life and in the animus which the author displays against the legate and the royal court. This enabled Baker to identify it without difficulty as the source of the Anglo-Norman metrical Life. The French is often a close, sometimes a literal, translation of the Latin. In the French version, however, there are indications of the author's identity which are wanting in the Latin. Thus the author of the metrical Life names himself as Matthew:

> La dareine enselée lettre
> Faz ge Maheu en livre mettre.[1]

He dedicates his book to Isabella de Fortibus, countess of Arundel, patroness of Wymondham priory, which was a cell of St. Albans. What is more, in the Envoi, the writer states that he has written the Life in two languages:

> Et ke chescun en seit plus sages
> Escrite l'ay en deux langages[2]

and that he has translated his Latin version into romance especially for the benefit of the countess. It is an interesting fact that the literary interests of the countess and her friendship

[1] *Romania*, lv (1929), 1691.   [2] Ibid. 1975.

with Matthew Paris are attested by another source. A note on the fly-leaf of a St. Albans manuscript now in the library of Trinity College, Dublin, and written in Matthew's own hand, requests her to pass on his Lives of St. Thomas and St. Edward, which she had borrowed.[1]

A collation of the French and Latin Lives shows that the French follows the content of the Latin text closely, omitting only the deposition of Robert Bacon and the testimony of Archbishop Walter Gray and a number of documents at the end. But the exigencies and opportunities of the octosyllabic couplets often prompt the writer to paraphrase rather than to translate exactly. Baker has drawn attention in his footnotes to the stylistic parallels between *la vie de seint Eadmunt* and Matthew's other Anglo-Norman works. The French Life displays the fondness for antithesis and *jeux de mots* which is so characteristic of Matthew's style in both French and Latin. As an example of his method as a translator, we may take the following two versions of St. Edmund's consecration by Bishop Roger Niger:

Consecratus igitur beatus Edmundus in ecclesia Cantuariensi a Rogero Londoniensi episcopo, sanctus a sancto, theologus a theologo, virgo a virgine, ciliciatus a ciliciato, archiepiscopus a suo decano, dominica qua etc. (Below, p. 238)	L'evesque de Lundres, Roger, Del sacrer il fist le mester; Amdeuz (sunt) seint, amdeuz devin, Amdeuz estoré de latin, Des arts et d'autre cleregie, Amdeuz de haute et seinte vie, De logike et devinité; Amdeuz a université Escole grant urent tenu (Op. cit. ll. 845–53)

It will be noticed that the French, recording the same fact, retains the antithesis, but slightly enlarges on the Latin and changes the content. Thus it mentions the fact, unstated in the

[1] *Illustrations to the Life of St. Alban*, op. cit., pp. 15–16. M. R. James translates the note as follows: 'G. send, please, to the lady countess of Arundel, Isabel, that she is to send you the book about St. Thomas the Martyr and St. Edward which I translated and illustrated.'

The Life by Matthew Paris

Latin, that both men had been regent masters in Arts and Theology. It is interesting to observe how Matthew introduces further variations into the same theme in the *Historia Anglorum*. The lower margin of the manuscript contains a pen drawing, showing Bishop Roger blessing St. Edmund, and against this is the caption 'Doctor theologus a doctore, sollempnis predicator a celebri predicatore, sanctus presul a sancto presule feliciter consecratur'.[1]

In a few points of detail the French supplements the Latin text. Thus, for example, the French states that during his period of regency at Oxford, Edmund received a benefice from the archbishop of York, but resigned all and gave his patrimony also to the hospital of Abingdon:

> E tut sun patrimonie done
> a l'hospital de Abinedone.[2]

These pieces of information are peculiar to this version and their authenticity is established by other sources, for the one statement explains an otherwise incomprehensible phrase in Archbishop Gray's letter of postulation,[3] and the other can be verified from the Abingdon cartulary.[4] At one point the French makes an omission which reminds the reader that Matthew is working with the Latin text under his eye. When he comes to the scattering of Edmund's *familia* after his death, he describes the breaking of the archbishop's seal, but he omits the text of Edmund's last letter in favour of Robert of Essex, saying that he has inserted it in the book:

> La dareine enselée lettre
> Faz ge Maheu en livre mettre.[5]

The text of the letter is in fact found at this point in the Latin

---

[1] BM Royal MS. 14 C vii, fo. 122ʳ.
[2] Op. cit., l. 115.
[3] 'quem ... in partem sollicitudinis mee assumpsi': App. A.
[4] Bodleian MS. Lyell 15, fol. 92ᵛ, nos. 37 and 38; see below, p. 109. Edmund granted the house of Reginald of Abingdon to the Hospital of St. John the Baptist, Oxford. It was granted to the hospital of Abingdon by an exchange.
[5] Op. cit., l. 1691.

Life, but it obviously did not lend itself to metrical reproduction.

Matthew, then, was translating into Anglo-Norman verse a Latin Life of St. Edmund composed by himself. What were his sources of information and how far was he indebted to the hagiographical tradition? Or, more specifically, how much of the *Vita* is really Matthew's own work? In the passage of the Great Chronicle quoted above, he says that he got his information from Richard Wych and Robert Bacon, and that he had arranged in order (*digessit*) 'what he had learnt from persons worthy of credit'. Bacon's contribution is given a separate title in the text and thus can be easily distinguished.[1] It consists of a deposition, made in the course of the canonization proceedings, similar to the four statements gathered together in the *Quadrilogus*. Matthew provides the only surviving text of this *disiectum membrum* of the canonization process. The only specific contribution made by Richard Wych is the text of his letter to the abbot of Bayham, reporting the translation of St. Edmund,[2] but he may have supplied other information. He was probably the source for Matthew's account of the breaking of the archbishop's seal and the dispersal of the *familia*.[3]

Matthew's words about the arrangement of his other material presumably refer to his literary sources. Chief among these is the Life by Eustace of Faversham. One of the difficulties hitherto felt in fathering the Julius Life on Matthew Paris is the fact that it contains what purport to be eyewitness accounts of events which Matthew could hardly have seen. Thus, for example, when describing the funeral procession and the sealing of St. Edmund's coffin by the abbot of Pontigny, he writes 'He sealed the bier with his seal, in the presence and sight of him who has written this and of many others'. This difficulty fails, however, to take account of the medieval chronicler's attitude to evidence. The statement of an eyewitness did not, in his view, lose any of its original evidential value in the process of literary transmission, and it would therefore have been

[1] Below, p. 248.   [2] Below, p. 285.   [3] Below, p. 272.

The Life by Matthew Paris

not merely pointless, but wrong, to transpose it into *oratio obliqua*. The passages complained of were in fact not Matthew's own, but statements made by Eustace, whose work he incorporated wholesale into his text. The Life by Eustace has received scant attention because it was thought to be a worthless abridgement of the Life in the Julius manuscript. In fact, it is not an abridgement, but Matthew's basic literary source. To prove this, it is only necessary to demonstrate the originality of the Eustace Life against the work of Matthew Paris, and this can be clearly seen when parallel passages from the two are placed side by side with the original documents of the Process which Eustace pressed into use. The following extract illustrates the point:

The Oxford Letter	The Life by Eustace
Adolescens autem factus cum iam esset literalibus studiis traditus, via qua prius ducebatur, incedebat spontaneus. Nam ex tunc voluntarie Deo sacrificare cepit, ecclesie limina ponte frequentans, vana et frivola, quibus adolescencior habundat etas, devitans, erudicioni sue diligenter intendens, carnis delicias non solum fugiens, sed et crucis Christi mortificacionem iugiter in suo corpore portans, toto mentis studio vite requisivit auctorem.	Adolescens autem factus cum iam esset *liberalibus* studiis traditus, via qua prius ducebatur incedebat spontaneus, *qui iuxta sui nominis interpretacionem mundus vere fuerat atque beatus*. Nam ex tunc voluntarie Deo sacrificare cepit, ecclesie limina sponte frequentans, vana et frivola, quibus adolescencior etas habundat, devitans, erudicioni sue diligenter intendens, carnis delicias non solum fugiens, sed et crucis mortificacionem iugiter in suo corpore portans, toto mentis studio vite requisivit auctorem.

The Life by Matthew Paris

Adolescens autem MATURIOR factus cum ESSET IAM *liberalibus* studiis ARCIUM ADDICTUS, via qua prius ducebatur, incedebat spontaneus, *qui iuxta sui nominis interpretacionem beatus* EXTITIT *atque mundus*. Nam ex tunc PLUS SOLITO voluntarie sacrificare Deo cepit, ecclesie limina SEPIUS ET MATURIUS FREQUENTARE, vana et frivola quibus etas ILLA SOLET IMPLICARE, devitans, erudicioni sue diligenter intendens, carnis delicias non solum fugiens, sed crucis mortificacionem iugiter in suo corpore portans, toto mentis studio vite requisivit auctorem.

(The italics indicate the variations which Eustace has introduced into the text of the Oxford letter, and which Matthew has reproduced. The capitals indicate further variations made by Matthew Paris when copying Eustace.)

This passage not only shows the originality of Eustace as against Matthew Paris, it illustrates the slightly perverse way in which Matthew uses his source. It will be noticed that where Eustace diverges from the text of the Oxford letter, Matthew follows him, whether in alteration, addition, or omission. Thus Matthew, like Eustace, has *liberalibus* for *literalibus*. He has the excursus of ten words on the name of St. Edmund, and like Eustace again, he omits *Christi* from the phrase *crucis Christi mortificacionem*. But Matthew also makes interpolations and trifling alterations of his own. He prefers *cum esset iam* to the original *cum iam esset*. His penchant for the logic of etymology makes him reverse the order of *mundus atque beatus* (Edmundus). Surely only literary hubris makes him reverse the order of *Deo sacrificare* and substitute an infinitive for the participial clause *ecclesie limina sponte frequentans*. The other interpolations can perhaps be said to add slightly to the sense of the original. The psychological implications of these alterations would no doubt make an interesting study. At any rate, it is clear that Eustace follows the text of the original letter much more exactly, and that Matthew followed Eustace. The Life by Eustace is obviously not an abridgement of Matthew Paris, for Eustace has the correct version of the letter, where Matthew has not.

A further illustration will serve to make the matter quite plain. In the following passage, Eustace has put together excerpts from the letters of Reading abbey and Bishop Ralph of Chichester. A collation of Eustace and Matthew with the original letters leaves no room for doubt that Matthew is dependent on Eustace.

READING LETTER	EUSTACE OF FAVERSHAM
. . . multi fratrum nostrorum quorum corda tetigerat Deus, tanta et talia perpendentes in eo sanctitatis indicia, se in comparacione ipsius, in habitu seculari constituti, tepidos arbitrantes et desides, cum haberentur religiosi, iuxta illud vaticinium Ysaie, 'Erubesce Sydon, ait mare', de tepore suo ceperint erubescere et ad talis ac tanti viri imitacionem, vitam ducere solito correctiorem.	viri religiosi non pauci inter quos tempore vacacionis commorari solebat quorum corda tetigerat Deus, tanta et talia perpendentes in eo sanctitatis indicia, se in comparacione ipsius in habitu seculari constituti, tepidos arbitrantes et desides, cum haberentur religiosi, iuxta illud vaticinium Ysaye, 'Erubesce Sydon, ait mare', de *tempore siquidem* suo erubescere *ceperunt* et ad talis ac tanti viri imitacionem, vitam ducere solito correctiorem.
CHICHESTER LETTER	
. . . sicut augebatur et multiplicabatur in eo interius divine lumen sapiencie, sic multipliciter refulsit exterius divinissimorum operum claritate.	Sicut augebatur et multiplicabatur in eo interius divine lumen sapiencie, sic multipliciter refulsit exterius divinissimorum operum claritate.

MATTHEW PARIS

viri religiosi non pauci inter quos tempore vacacionis commorari solebat quorum corda tetigerat Deus, TALIA AC TANTA perpendentes in eo sanctitatis indicia, se in comparacione ipsius in habitu seculari constituti, tepidos arbitrantes et desides, cum haberentur ET ESSENT COMPETENTER religiosi, CONFUSI ERUBUERUNT, iuxta Ysaie vaticinium, 'Erubesce Sy(d)on, ait mare', de *tempore siquidem* suo erubescere *ceperunt*, et EIUS VESTIGIA SEQUI NITEBANTUR.

BEATUS IGITUR EDMUNDUS sicut augebatur DIATIM et multiplicabatur divine lumen sapiencie, sic multipliciter refulsit exterius FRUCTUOSORUM operum claritate.

Here, as in the previous passage, Matthew Paris has followed Eustace in his variations from the original letters, and has added variations of his own. The tendency of the variations in this case is to tone down Eustace where the text implies criticism of the monks of Reading (they were Benedictines). For the slightly derogatory tone of *vitam ducere solito correctiorem*, Matthew substitutes the more laudable *et eius vestigia sequi nitebantur*.

The fact that Matthew used the Life by Eustace as the basis of his own biography of St. Edmund explains a reference which he makes in the French version to a source supplied to him by the monastery or church of Canterbury:

> De cest livret le cumençail
> Deu muster surt de Canterbire.[1]

Whether Matthew is referring to the fact that the writer of the Life was a Canterbury monk, or whether he means that the monks of Christ Church had supplied him with a copy of it, is not clear. From textual comparison, it appears that Matthew used either the A manuscript or its archetype. But the A manuscript is part of a book which belonged to Rochester cathedral priory. It is likely enough that Canterbury possessed the autograph.

Matthew incorporates into his text the whole of the Eustace Life, with the exception of its opening paragraph. As has been seen, he makes fairly free with his authority, altering a word here and inserting a word there to suit his fancy. The performance is reminiscent of the way he treated Wendover's text in the *Chronica Maiora*. At the same time, while strictly preserving the order of Eustace, Matthew makes a number of important interpolations in his source, some of which are of considerable length. A list of these will show their purport. Some of this additional information (marked with an asterisk) is of a purely hagiographical kind and is to be found in other Lives of St. Edmund. But the greater part of it is peculiar to the Matthew Paris Life and comprises real historical matter, and it is this which gives Matthew's Life its unique interest.

---

[1] Op. cit. ll. 73–74.

The Life by Matthew Paris

It is here too that Matthew's characteristic vocabulary and sentiment are to be found. The insertions are as follows:

- * Information about St. Edmund's parents, Reginald and Mabel of Abingdon, his brother, Robert (p. 222).
  A second brother, Nicholas, who entered the Cistercian abbey of Boxley, and a third who became a monk at Eynsham (p. 222).
- * St. Edmund's sisters, Margaret and Alice, whom he placed in the priory of Catesby (p. 222).
- * His mother sends him hair shirts when he is studying at Paris (p. 223).
- * At the age of twelve, when attending the schools, he makes a vow of perpetual chastity to the Blessed Virgin, and places a ring on the finger of her statue (p. 224).
- * When wandering in the meadows, he sees a miraculously flowering shrub, and has a vision of the Child Jesus, who teaches him to cross himself (p. 225).

  He is smitten with compunction for having lingered too long over the liberal arts (p. 230).

  He goes to Oxford from Merton, where he was awaiting the opportunity to lecture (p. 234).

- (a) * He is caught resting by the Devil and throws him in physical combat (p. 234).
- (a) * He heals a student suffering from a fistula in the arm, and the disease is transferred to him (p. 235).
- (a) * He suspends lecturing for a time in order to preach the Crusade. He displays his power over the rain clouds which are prevented from scattering his audience (p. 236).
- * He is appointed Treasurer of Salisbury cathedral (p. 237).

  He is persuaded to accept his election to Canterbury by the suggestion of the monks that the king may otherwise nominate a foreigner (p. 238).

  He is consecrated archbishop on 2 April 1234 by Bishop Roger Niger, in the presence of king and magnates (p. 239).

  Other unsuccessful candidates for the see named: John,

prior of Canterbury; bishop Ralph of Chichester; Master John Blund (p. 239).

Appositeness of his consecration in Lent, since he was also to be canonized in a penitential season (p. 239).

He sets himself to restore peace between the king and magnates. After the death of Richard the Marshal in Ireland, St. Edmund meets the king at Woodstock and intercedes for the rebels. He reconciles Gilbert Marshal, Hubert de Burgh, and others, to the king (p. 240).

He employs his time in correcting books, and determining disputations between the friars (p. 243).

In a conversation with the pope, he expresses a desire for the monastic life (p. 244).

The deposition of Robert Bacon (p. 248).

His chamberlains are ordered to burn his hair shirt, but are unable to do so (p. 254).

The monks of Christ Church burn a privilege on the ground that its authenticity is suspect. The legate Otto intervenes. There is dissension in the community, and some enter the Carthusians for the sake of peace (p. 254).

The archbishop goes to Rome to confirm his agreement with the monks, but finds they have forestalled him (p. 256).

Other troubles with Bishop Roger of London, the chapter of Rochester, Earl Hugh of Arundel, Hubert de Burgh, and Earl Simon de Montfort (p. 257).

The legate sides with the majority to gain favour. He absolves those whom Edmund had excommunicated (p. 258).

After Edmund's death, the monks gain absolution from Rome; papal executors named (p. 258).

The legate Otto given precedence at the baptism of the Lord Edward, though an alien (p. 259).

Edmund is inspired to go into exile. The inscription of his small seal (p. 260).

He is met in France by Blanche of Castile (p. 262).

The Life by Matthew Paris

ꝼ At Pontigny, he preaches to the monks, and is granted confraternity (p. 264).

ꝼ He prophesies his return to Pontigny on the feast of St. Edmund (p. 265).

He writes last letters on behalf of his *familiares*. Text of the letter on behalf of Robert of Essex (p. 267).

Conversation with the prior of Soisy, to whom he promises his heart (p. 270).

He sends his cloak and a silver diptych to his sisters at Catesby (p. 270).

His chancellor assembles the *familiares*, issues testimonial letters, and breaks the archbishop's seal (p. 272).

At the funeral procession, one of the clerks argues that if St. Edmund had been a true saint, he would have chosen burial in one of the Black Monk houses, such as Canterbury or St. Albans (p. 276).

Notice of Canterbury monks present in the procession. Reflections on the hardness of the times (p. 277).

* St. Edmund's burial at Pontigny on 23 November (p. 278).

He is canonized at Lyons after delays caused by the obstruction of certain persons whom it is unsafe to name (p. 279).

* Text of the bull of canonization (p. 280).

Letter of Richard Wych to the abbot of Bayham, reporting the translation of St. Edmund (p. 285).

Text of a sermon delivered by St. Edmund in the chapter house of Pontigny (p. 286).

These additions constitute Matthew's own contribution to the biography of St. Edmund. Broadly, they can be divided into two categories. In the first category are the hagiographical anecdotes. All these were to be found in the common source underlying the Pontigny Life and the Anonymous A. But it is doubtful whether Matthew Paris was directly acquainted with any of these. A group of three miracle stories (marked above (*a*)) were lifted by Matthew from the Anonymous B Life, and inserted in his text *en bloc*. The source from which he drew the rest is not apparent. Although the other incidents are recognizably the same as incidents in the Pontigny Life and the Anonymous A, there is a striking absence of any verbal parallelism between these and the versions given by Matthew Paris. Moreover, in Matthew's account of these incidents there are often considerable variations in detail and context. This perhaps suggests that Matthew's knowledge of these stories was derived from common oral tradition. Some of them indeed are drawn from the *loci communes* of hagiography, and formed part of the biographer's stock-in-trade. The vision of the Child Jesus, for example, is a recurrent theme in thirteenth-century hagiography, and expresses the intimate personal devotion to the Humanity of Christ which is conspicuous in the religious sentiment of the period, and which the Franciscans did much to propagate. Similar episodes are frequent in the contemporary Cistercian hagiography of the Netherlands,[1] and there is a parallel case in the Life of St. Hugh of Lincoln.[2] The obedience of the rain clouds to the saint's commands was an ancient and well-worn theme,[3] and at least one obvious parallel may be found in the thirteenth-century Life of St. Dominic by Jordan of Saxony.[4]

In the second category are the historical details which Matthew has inserted in his text. It will be seen that many of these display an exact and well-documented knowledge of English ecclesiastical affairs. The writer knows the names of the three other candidates for the archbishopric who were rejected. He knows the day of St. Edmund's episcopal consecration and who was present. He appreciates the part which the new archbishop played in ending hostilities in 1234. He clearly knows, though he tries to gloss over, the discreditable conduct of the Canterbury monks which led to the interven-

---

[1] See the examples discussed by S. Roisin, *L'Hagiographie cistercienne dans le diocèse de Liège au xiiie siècle* (Louvain, 1947), pp. 173-4.

[2] *Magna Vita S. Hugonis*, ed. J. F. Dimock (RS), v, chap. 3.

[3] Plummer remarked on its regular occurrence in the Celtic Legendary: *Vitae Sanctorum Hiberniae* (Oxford, 1910), introd.

[4] MOFPH xvi (1935), p. 73.

tion of the papal legate and the deposition of the prior of Christ Church. He can name the executors of the papal absolution obtained by the monks after St. Edmund's death. He gives the text of one of the archbishop's last letters in favour of one of his servants, which is not otherwise known to be extant.

If he is well informed, Matthew also gives full rein here to the prejudices for which he is notorious. Much has been said about the 'constitutional attitude' of the St. Albans school, the pride of an ancient and privileged corporation which caused its writers to align themselves almost instinctively with the critics of royal and papal government.[1] This attitude is apparent here. The rebels, Gilbert Marshal and Hubert de Burgh, are treated sympathetically as victims of official wrongdoing. The king's counsellors are the oppressors of the Church who may be expected to foist an unworthy archbishop on the chapter of Canterbury. Matthew's dislike of aliens is still more pronounced. A friend of St. Edmund's is represented as pleading with him to accept the election of the Canterbury monks 'lest . . . the king's council procure that some foreigner, utterly unworthy of such a great honour, be intruded in the place where God has set up so many saints' (p. 238). The legate, Cardinal Otto, is condemned on both counts, as a foreigner, and as a representative of the bureaucracy of Rome. He is cast for the role of the Achitophel who poses as a peacemaker but who is really an adversary of the saintly archbishop. This is the only Life of St. Edmund which depicts the legate in such an unfriendly light.

On the subject of monasticism, Matthew is particularly sensitive, and his bias is correspondingly strong. The archbishop is made to sigh for the monastic life. The conduct of the Christ Church monks is, as far as possible, extenuated. Matthew places the best interpretation on the destruction by

---

[1] Cf. Hans Plehn, *Der politische Charakter von Matheus Parisiensis* (Staats- und socialwissenschaftliche Forschungen xiv, Hft. 2, Leipzig, 1897), pp. 44–45; and the observations of V. H. Galbraith, *Roger of Wendover and Matthew Paris* (1944), p. 6.

the convent of the charter of St. Thomas, and he glosses over the fact that the monks had forged a replacement. He suggests that some of their number had voluntarily withdrawn to the Carthusian Order owing to contention inside the community. In fact, as he well knew, the prior and others were disciplined and forced to enter a severer Order by the legate.[1] One of Matthew's interpolations towards the end of the Life is especially revealing. Eustace ends his Life with a description of the funeral cortège from Soisy to Pontigny and the acclamation of the crowds along the route. Two clerks of sceptical disposition (*vere Didimi*) express surprise at the universal acclamation and presume to question the merits of the dead archbishop. How could this acclamation of a foreign archbishop by the French peasantry be accounted for? Perhaps the Cistercians had engineered the whole thing. This gives Matthew the opportunity for an interpolation which he cannot resist. A heated colloquy is invented, of a kind which may well have taken place in the locutorium of St. Albans abbey:

> Had he been a real saint, he wouldn't have cared to be buried in a Cistercian house. Nearly all the glorious saints lie in houses of the Black Monks, few or none in Cistercian houses. In confirmation of these words, he instanced the houses of Canterbury, St. Albans, St. Edmunds, Durham, and many others in the kingdoms of both France and England (p. 276).

The archbishop's eccentric wish to be buried at Pontigny had offended Matthew's patriotism and touched his pride in his order.

If the historical interpolations in the Life are compared with the related passages in Matthew's chronicles, the resemblances of matter and language are strikingly obvious. Details of St. Edmund's family and early life are not included in the chronicles, being presumably unsuited to works of that scale, but it is apparent that Matthew had the same stock of information about St. Edmund's public life at his disposal as he had when

---

[1] See the account in Gervase, ii. 133; that Matthew knew the real facts of the case is apparent from his account in the *Chron. Maiora*, iii. 492.

he wrote the Life. There are many instances of verbal parallelism, but these are perhaps less striking than the identity of sentiment and interpretation. These resemblances have failed to make their natural impact because they lie embedded in the conventional rhetoric of Eustace. When decrusted, they stand out sharply, and they provide further and conclusive proof of the author's identity.

Verbally, the Life bears a closer resemblance to the *Historia Anglorum* than to the *Chronica Maiora*, which suggests that it was written at the same period as the *Historia*. A parallel passage from the three works will illustrate this. Take Edmund's consecration as archbishop: the account in the *Chronica Maiora* is as follows:

Eodem anno, in ecclesia Christi Cantuariae, consecratus est Aedmundus, eiusdem ecclesiae electus, a Rogero Londoniensi episcopo in archiepiscopum Cantuariensem, Dominica qua cantatur 'Laetare Jerusalem', quae tunc fuit quarto nonas Aprilis, praesente rege cum tredecim episcopis. Et eodem die missam cum pallio, quod caute ei de curia Romana Simon Legr(ecestria), eius ecclesiae monachus, detulerat, olenniter celebravit.[1]

In the *Historia* Matthew slightly alters and embellishes this account. The purpose of the alteration is to bring out the appositeness of St. Edmund's consecration by Roger Niger, for both were prominent theologians and both had a reputation for sanctity. This point is developed more fully in a caption which Matthew has attached to a pen drawing of the event in the lower margin of the manuscript. Here the parallel with the Life becomes obvious:

Historia Anglorum	*Vita Sancti Edmundi*
Eodem anno in ecclesia Cantuariae consecratus est magister Aedmundus, eiusdem ecclesiae electus, vir quidem Deo amabilis	Consecratus igitur beatus Edmundus in ecclesia Cantuariensi

[1] *Chron. Maiora*, iii. 272. Saving the reference to Simon of Leicester, the account is the work of Matthew's predecessor, Roger of Wendover.

et hominibus, a Rogero, Londoniensi episcopo, sanctus a sancto, in archiepiscopum Cantuariensem, Dominica qua cantatur 'Laetare Jerusalem', quae tunc fuit iiii° nonas Aprilis. . . . Huius consecrationi felicissimae interfuit rex cum xiii episcopis. Et eodem die missam cum pallio, quod ei sponte praemiserat papa, et hoc notabile, sollempniter celebravit.

a Rogero Londoniensi episcopo, sanctus a sancto,

[*in lower margin:*]
Doctor theologus a doctore, sollempnis praedicator a celebri praedicatore, sanctus praesul a sancto praesule, feliciter consecratur.[1]

theologus a theologo, virgo a virgine, ciliciatus a ciliciato, archiepiscopus a suo decano, Dominica qua cantatur 'Letare Ierusalem', quarto nonas scilicet Aprilis, presente rege Henrico cum tredecim episcopis et magnatum copiosa multitudine, sollempniter eo die cum pallio, quod ei gratis transmiserat dominus papa, missam celebravit.[2]

Starting with the simple antithesis of *sanctus a sancto*, Matthew rings different changes on it, in the *Historia* and the Life. Another instance of this stylistic trick, whereby a seminal phrase in the chronicle is developed in the Life, occurs where he speaks of the baptism of the Lord Edward by the legate, cardinal Otto. Matthew observed without pleasure that the legate had, quite correctly, been given precedence over the archbishop at the ceremony. In the account of the *Chronica Maiora*, a parenthesis of four words contains only a hint of reproach: 'legatus eum baptizavit, licet non esset sacerdos;

---

[1] *Hist. Angl.* ii. 367; BM Royal MS. 14 C vii, fo. 122.
[2] Below, p. 238.

The Life by Matthew Paris

archiepiscopus autem Aedmundus ipsum confirmavit.'[1] In the Life, the point is elaborated and Matthew allows his animosity full rein: 'Preelectus fuit ad ipsum baptizandum Otto tunc legatus, qui eciam ad hoc se ingessit, ordine diaconus, natione alienigena, moribus inferior, scientia theologica satis supinus... verumtamen ipsum baptizatum permissus est confirmare.'[2]

When it comes to the archbishop's pacification of 1234, an interesting variation appears between Wendover's treatment of the subject (incorporated by Matthew) in the Great Chronicle, and Matthew's treatment of it in the *Historia* and the Life. The Chronicle is more sympathetic to Richard the Marshal and more critical of the king. Richard goes to Ireland to defend his own property and is killed by a treacherous alliance to which the king is party.[3] Afterwards, Archbishop Edmund produces in council the famous letter sent to Ireland under the royal seal, and reproaches the king with having treacherously contrived the Marshal's death. Henry is stricken with contrition and turns against the counsellors who have betrayed his trust. It has been suggested elsewhere that this account is unsatisfactory at several points and that it lacks a documentary basis. These doubts are strengthened by the fact that the whole incident of the letter is omitted from both the *Historia* and the Life. The episode is one which would have reflected much credit on St. Edmund. Matthew's deliberate omission of it from these later works must shake the credibility of Wendover's narrative.

Here again, the narratives of the *Historia* and the Life are closely allied. According to the interpretation found here, the Earl Marshal was killed in battle as a rebel against the king, and the archbishop came to plead 'that the brother should not expiate the wrong which his brother had done, nor the fault of the guilty recoil upon the innocent'. Matthew's special

---

[1] *Chron. Maiora*, iii. 539.
[2] See below, p. 259. Contrast the more restrained and factual account in *Hist. Angl.* ii. 422.
[3] *Chron. Maiora*, iii. 273.

sympathy is reserved for Gilbert Marshal, whom he seems to have much admired,[1] and for Hubert de Burgh. The interpretation of these events is the same in the *Historia* and the Life, and there is a distinct verbal similarity between the two accounts as may be seen from this passage:

Historia Anglorum	*Vita Sancti Edmundi*
Et in eodem colloquio venit Gilebertus, frater Ricardi, comitis Marescalli iam defuncti. . . . Tunc rex, licet cum magna difficultate—renitebantur enim quidam susurrones ad hoc, ut rex omnia sibi appropriaret, eo quod comes Ricardus in bello contra regem inito captus fuit et rebellio mortuus—reddidit eidem Gileberto hereditatem suam totam.[2]	Unde tunc occiso comite Ricardo Marescallo in Hibernia, rex difficilem se exhibuit in substituendo Gileberto in ipsam hereditatem, ... hac tactus racione, quia comes Ricardus occisus fuit in hostili prelio contra regem abiudicatus. . . . Et accito Gileberto, rex omnem remittens indignacionem, ei suam restituit cum plenitudine dignitatis hereditatem.[3]

This resemblance of language and sentiment between the *Historia* and the Life appears again in Matthew's handling of the dispute between the archbishop and the monks of Christ Church. On this subject Matthew is clearly divided in his feelings. He sympathizes with the anxiety of the monks to protect their privileges, but he cannot very well condone their rebellion against St. Edmund. Canonization was a sentence against which there was no appeal and, besides, St. Edmund was the hero of his story. Thus he says of the monks in the *Historia*: 'habentes quidem zelum bonum, sed non secundum scientiam';[4] and in the *Vita Sancti Edmundi*: 'zelum iusticie habentes, sed non secundum scientiam'.[5]

In one instance Matthew appears to have copied a passage directly from the Great Chronicle into the Life. He is describing the archbishop's death and he records a conversation with

---

[1] *quia vere amabilis erat*: *Vita*, p. 240. *qui bene literatus erat*: *Hist. Angl.* ii. 371.
[2] *Hist. Angl.* ii. 370. [3] Below, p. 240.
[4] *Hist. Angl.* ii. 411. [5] Below, p. 254.

the prior of Soisy in which the saint promises to leave the canons his heart. The passage is written in Matthew's hand in the margin of the chronicle and connected with the text by the familiar frame of red lines:

Chronica Maiora	Vita Sancti Edmundi
... ait prior loci, qui fuit ei specialissimus, 'Domine, ut quid recedis? ut quid nos deseris? vexaberis itinerando; quiesce nobiscum.' Et respondit archiepiscopus,	prior domus archiepiscopo carissimus, qui tunc presens erat, ait, 'Heu. heu. siccine, sic nos penitus deseris et a nobis recedis?' At ille,
Cor meum vobiscum remanebit.'	'Nequaquam. Meum cor et dilectio vobiscum semper est.' Et non intellexerunt verbum, sed post obitum eius facta anathomia de corpore eius, sepulta sunt ibidem cor et viscera eius. Et tunc aperti sunt oculi eorum, et intellexerunt verbum. Hoc autem factum est quia deferendum fuit corpus usque Pontiniacum, quod distat a Soysi, ubi obiit, circiter xx leucis, id est, duabus ad minus dietis.[2]
Et non intellexerunt verbum, sed infirmatus illic obiit, et facta anathomia de corpore suo, ibidem sepulta sunt eius viscera cum corde. Distat locus ille a Pontiniaco viginti leucis, id est, duabus dietis. Et tunc demum aperti sunt oculi eorum, ut verbum intelligerent quod dixerat archiepiscopus.[1]	

This is the only case of complete correspondence between the Great Chronicle and the Life, and in the text of the chronicle the passage evidently represents an afterthought which may have been inserted in the margin of the manuscript at the period when Matthew was working on his Life of St. Edmund. The variations between the two versions illustrate Matthew's attitude to dramatic dialogue, which he clearly regarded as a literary device rather than genuine reportage.

Besides these resemblances of language and content between the chronicles and the Life, there are documents common to

[1] *Chron. Maiora*, iv. 73; in B it is on fo. 139ᵛ, left margin.
[2] Below, p. 270.

the Life and the dossier known as the *Liber Additamentorum*, namely the bull of canonization[1] and the letter of Richard Wych concerning the translation of St. Edmund.[2] The *Additamenta* also contain the description of the archbishop's privy seal which Matthew incorporated verbatim into the Life, and the prayer addressed to St. John the Baptist which follows the Life in the Julius manuscript.[3]

Because of its essentially rhetorical character, hagiography offered more scope for fine writing than the chronicle. Thus in the Life of St. Edmund the stylistic peculiarities of Matthew Paris are thrown into relief. Most of his constructions are exemplified in any representative piece of thirteenth-century Latin, but for some he shows an abnormal fondness. Thus he constantly uses the Ablative Absolute when the subject is the same as that of the main clause, as in 'arrepto brachio suo dextero, illud constrinxit' (p. 234). He almost invariably uses the ablative of the gerund where a more classical Latinist would use a present participle active, as in 'parvulam quietem dormitando pregustaret' (p. 234). But the most distinctive features of Matthew's style are his figures and tricks of speech, some of which are repeated *ad nauseam*. For instance litotes is used in the Life seventeen times. In certain contexts it appears regularly as, for instance, when Matthew is referring to any kind of expenditure. Thus the archbishop conducted his suit at the Roman court 'cum molestia et expensis non minimis' (p. 257) and the monks gained papal absolution, but 'hoc non optinuerunt beneficium sine multa pecunie effusione' (p. 258). The trick of speech is so habitual with Matthew that it sometimes slips out unawares and results in bathos. This is the effect where he builds up to an eloquent climax with the death-bed scene and says that St. Edmund's last words caused in the bystanders no little surprise: 'Non minimam de novitate generarunt admiracionem' (p. 269). Another trick to which he is

---

[1] *Chron. Maiora*, vi. 120–5; it is also reproduced in the text of the Chetham manuscript: *Flores Historiarum*, ed. Luard (RS), ii. 315.
[2] Ibid. vi. 128–9.
[3] Ibid. vi. 127–8.

The Life by Matthew Paris

addicted is oxymoron, and where he is striving for special effect, he will often repeat the contradictory elements in reverse, as in *tristis hilaritas et hilaris tristicia*, and in *delectabili acerbitate vel acerba dilectacione*. Puns and synonyms pour from his pen with extraordinary profusion. Verbs are very frequently combined in pairs, especially participles used adjectively. Occasionally, the second verb adds to, or overlays, the sense of the first, but more often than not the mannerism produces useless verbosity. When Matthew says that St. Edmund was chosen archbishop—*electo et preelecto*, the second participle does suggest a distinct idea: that Edmund had been chosen by God before the monks elected him. On the other hand, it is difficult to see any point in such concatenations as *motus et commotus*, or *censuit et reputavit*.

The Life contains three full-length quotations from Matthew's favourite classical authors, Horace and Ovid. The archbishop's motives for flight are summed up by a line from the *Remedium Amoris*: 'Dum furor in cursu est, currenti cede furori' (p. 260). It seems improbable that Matthew was familiar with the original context of the quotation. It is used also in the *Chronica Maiora*[1] and twice in the *Historia Anglorum*[2] in different but analogous situations. A line from the *Ars Amatoria* is pressed into service with an equally reckless disregard for its original significance. Matthew is more at home with his Biblical quotations. He has a characteristic way of placing them in the mouths of his characters. Thus the legate addresses the monks of Christ Church in the words of 1 Peter v. 6 (p. 255). The archbishop remonstrates with them in the words of Isaiah xlviii. 22 (p. 257). He addresses the pope in the words of 1 Kings xxviii. 22 (p. 244), and, in despair, he quotes Job i. 21 (p. 261). Like all hagiographers, Matthew sometimes uses the dramatic associations of a Scriptural quotation in order to heighten the emotive effect of a situation. At the end, for example, he explains that the prior and canons of Soisy only understood the archbishop's words after his death, evoking

[1] *Chron. Maiora*, iv. 158. [2] *Hist. Angl.* ii. 396, 405.

the sudden revelation of Emmaus with the quotation 'et tunc aperti sunt oculi eorum, et intellexerunt verbum'.

The date at which Matthew composed the Life can be roughly established from internal evidence. He cannot have written it earlier than 1247 because, besides the text of the bull of canonization at the end, it contains a reference to the canonization at a much earlier point in connexion with the archbishop's consecration (p. 240). On the other hand, it was not written later than 1253, for Matthew refers to the French Queen Regent, Blanche of Castile, as still living (p. 262), and she died in that year. The evidence of the St. Albans chronicles may help us towards establishing a closer date. In both the *Chronica Maiora* and the *Historia Anglorum*, Matthew states explicitly that he has written a Life of St. Edmund and that anyone wishing to read it will find it at St. Albans.[1] This statement is introduced, rather arbitrarily, in the annal for 1253, in connexion with the death of St. Richard Wych. It looks as if Matthew seized on the death of Richard Wych as the first opportunity of publicizing his Life of St. Edmund. The natural place to mention it would have been in the passages dealing with St. Edmund's death and canonization. A further opportunity night have been found when Matthew noticed the death of Robert Bacon in 1248.[2] It is impossible to say with confidence when the annals for the years 1240, 1246, and 1248, in the Great Chronicle, were written, though they were evidently completed by 1250.[3] But the absence of any reference to the Life under these obvious headings in the *Historia Anglorum* also, and its arbitrary insertion under the year 1253, suggests that Matthew had not yet written the Life when the *Historia* was undertaken in 1250.

However, Matthew does make another reference to the Life in an amendment to the text of the *Historia*. Speaking of the

[1] *Chron. Maiora*, v. 369; *Hist. Angl.* iii. 135.
[2] *Hist. Angl.* iii. 40.
[3] H. Plehn argues, in *Der politische Charakter v. Matheus Parisiensis*, op. cit., pp. 128-35, that the chronicle for the years 1236 to 1239 was not written until after 1245, but his argument is not very convincing, see below, p. 180 n.

canonization of St. Edmund, he says, 'Cuius canonizationis auctenticum elegantissime in libro *de vita ipsius* poterit, qui curat, reperire'.[1] The words *de vita ipsius* are an amendment written on a slip of vellum which has been pasted over the text. The original reading was 'in libro Additamentorum'. What, if anything, can be inferred from this amendment to the text of the *Historia*? At first sight, it would appear that when Matthew wrote the original passage, the Life of St. Edmund did not yet exist, and so the reader was referred to the *Liber Additamentorum* for the text of the bull of canonization; that subsequently he wrote the Life, and then amended the reference in the *Historia* to read *in vita ipsius*.[2] Such an inference would not, however, be justified. It fails to take account of the question raised by a whole series of amendments which Matthew made in the text of the *Historia*.

It is well known that in his chronicles Matthew Paris frequently refers the reader to the *Liber Additamentorum* for documents and other matter which, for the sake of brevity, he omits from his narrative. This Book of Additions was apparently intended to form a documentary appendix to the chronicles. It has perhaps been too readily assumed that the *Liber Additamentorum* named in each chronicle is to be identified with the volume of miscellanea which we have in Cotton MS. Nero D.i. The contents of this volume were published in part by Luard under the title of *Liber Additamentorum*, as an appendix to his edition of the *Chronica Maiora*.

When writing the *Historia Anglorum*, Matthew originally made twenty-six references to the Book of Additions. In nineteen of these instances, however, the document referred to is not to be found in MS. Nero D i, but is to be found in the text of the *Chronica Maiora*. From this Sir Maurice Powicke inferred (*a*) that the Book of Additions was originally not the same as it is now, and (*b*) that the B text of the *Chronica Maiora*

---
[1] *Hist. Angl.* iii. 135.
[2] I drew this inference in a note in *EHR* lxix (July 1954), pp. 408–17. The difficulties involved in this were pointed out to me by Dr. R. Vaughan.

(CCC MS. xvi) is a 'fair copy', written later than the *Historia*, and that the scribe of B copied the documents in question out of the Book of Additions into the text of the *Chronica* where they are now found. The *Historia* is based not on B, but on an earlier recension of the *Chronica* which did not contain these documents.[1]

Nevertheless, the thesis that B is a fair copy, written up as a whole some time after 1250, remains open to serious objections which have not been met. Not the least of these are the marginal annotations in B which are clearly and expressly intended as directives to the compiler of the *Historia*, and which would have been pointless after the *Historia* had been completed.[2]

If we abandon the theory of the 'fair copy' made all at once some time later than the *Historia*, how can we explain the fact that the text of the *Historia* refers to documents supposed to be in the Book of Additions, which are, in fact, not there, but in the text of the *Chronica*? This is not a very intractable problem. Matthew's avowed purpose[3] in writing the *Historia* was to compose a history, based on the chronicle, which would be more balanced than the longer work and would be mainly concerned with English affairs. In order to achieve this, he abridged the text of B, omitting all save a few incidents which were not directly related to England, and omitting the

---

[1] Sir Maurice Powicke argued from the appearance of B that it was written up continuously all at one period, and he was at first disposed to place the date of writing after 1257 on the strength of a supposed prophecy of Richard of Cornwall's election to the empire: 'The Compilation of the *Chronica Majora* of Matthew Paris', in *Modern Philology*, xxxviii (1941), pp. 304–17. V. H. Galbraith pointed out, however, that the prophecy is not supported by the ordinary meaning of the passage which is, in any case, corrupt: *Roger of Wendover and Matthew Paris* (Glasgow, 1944), p. 27. In the light of this criticism, Professor Powicke revised his article in *Proceedings of the British Academy*, xxx (1944). But he stands by the conclusion that B is a fair copy written up all at once at some date between 1250 and 1260, and that the *Historia Anglorum* was based on an earlier draft of the *Chronica*.

[2] The thesis has been challenged on palaeographical grounds by R. Vaughan, 'The Handwriting of Matthew Paris', in *Transactions of the Cambridge Bibliographical Society*, v (1953), p. 389.

[3] *Hist. Angl.* i. 342.

The Life by Matthew Paris

numerous documents from B. His plan was, it seems, to copy a number of the more interesting documents from B into a separate volume which would form a documentary appendix or *Liber Additamentorum* to the *Historia Anglorum*. What became of this volume it is impossible to say. Either it was never compiled, or it has disappeared.[1] Clearly it cannot be identified with the volume which is now Cotton MS. Nero D i.

If this surmise is correct, Matthew embarked on the *Historia* with the intention of supplementing it with a Book of Additions, and at some stage in the writing he abandoned this plan. That he did in fact do this is borne out by the amendments which he made in the text of the *Historia*. For of the twenty-six references to the Book of Additions, fourteen have been subsequently erased or altered by Matthew, the reader being referred instead to some other place where the document in question may be found. Thus the reader is referred to the 'books of many', the 'books of the Frenchmen', the 'rolls of the clerks of the lord king', &c. In some cases the text has been amended to omit any reference to the document at all.[2] This is clear evidence of a change of plan.

At all events, it is apparent that when Matthew Paris deleted his reference to the bull of St. Edmund's canonization in the Book of Additions, and substituted for it a reference to the Life of St. Edmund, he was only making one of a series of analogous alterations in the text of the *Historia*. It cannot be necessarily assumed that when he wrote the original reference he had not yet composed the Life of St. Edmund.

It remains then that the composition of the Life is to be placed on internal evidence between 1247 and 1253, but that the stylistic similarities between it and the *Historia Anglorum*

---

[1] The copy of the *Chronica* in Cotton MS. Nero D v records under the year 1248 that the *Liber Additamentorum* had been mislaid: *nescio ubi est ille liber*: fo. 371.

[2] Sir Maurice Powicke does not discuss these alterations. But if the original references had been made obsolete when the documents were removed from the Book of Additions and copied into the chronicle, why did not Matthew alter them to refer to the chronicle?

suggest that it was written at the same period as the latter work, namely between 1250 and 1253. This is borne out also by the position at which the Life is referred to in the chronicles. A further piece of evidence may be cited in favour of a relatively late date. Towards the end of the Life Matthew reproduces the text of a letter from Richard Wych to the abbot of Bayham, describing the solemn translation of the relics.[1] The letter states that the opening of the archbishop's tomb took place on the morrow of Trinity last. Matthew kept the copy of this letter in his *Liber Additamentorum*,[2] and when he came to copy it into the Life, he expanded the date—'on the morrow of Trinity last, namely in the year of grace 1247, on the 18th May'. Now in 1247, Trinity Sunday fell on 26 May, so Matthew is nine days out in what appears to have been a chance shot at the date. The error is not a wild one, but it must be remembered that the life of a Benedictine monk was geared to the liturgical year by the changing round of choral office, and in that year Trinity was a pivotal date. It is unlikely therefore that Matthew would have made the error had he been actually writing in 1247 or 1248, but it would be an easy one to make if he were writing a few years later.

VII

A COMPARATIVE SYNOPSIS SHOWING THE ORDER OF CONTENTS IN EACH LIFE

	Pontigny	A	B	C	Eustace	Matthew Paris
The parentage of St. E.	1a	1a	1	3a	1	1
An encomium of Abingdon	—	—	—	2	—	—
How St. E.'s father became a monk at Eynsham	1b	1c	—	3b	—	—
How his brothers became monks at Eynsham and Boxley	—	—	—	—	—	2
Of his mother's austerities	2a	2	2	4	2	4c
Her epitaph quoted	2b	1b	—	9	—	—

[1] p. 285 below, and note. [2] *Chron. Maiora*, vi. 128–9.

A Comparative Synopsis

	Pontigny	A	B	C	Eustace	Matthew Paris
The miraculous cleanness of St. E.'s delivery	3	3	—	1b	—	—
The significance of his name	4	—	—	1a	—	—
How his mother induced him to fast as a child	5	4	—	5	—	—
How St. E. and his brother were sent to Paris to study	6a	5a	—	7a	—	4a
How his mother gave them hair shirts and money	6b	5b	—	7b	—	4b
How St. E. was advised to take the clerical tonsure	7	6	—	—	—	—
The vision of the Christ Child in the meadows	8a	9a	—	6	—	6a
How St. E. crossed himself thereafter at night	8b	9b	—	—	—	6b
How St. E. placed his sisters in religion at Catesby	9	8	—	10	—	3 (30d)
How his mother at death blessed his brothers	10	7	—	8	—	—
The vision of the crows at Chalgrove	11	11	—	—	—	—
The youthful wisdom of St. E.	12	10	3	11	3	7
The espousal of the Blessed Virgin's statue	13	12	—	—	—	5
How St. E. was tempted by his landlord's daughter	14	13	—	14	—	—
How he refused the gifts of a married woman	15	14	—	—	—	—
An exact description of St. E.'s hair shirt	16a	16a	5	20	—	—
A young clerk, called on to adjust it, divulges the secret to the *familia*	16b	—	—	—	—	—
How as a regent master of arts, St. E. heard mass daily and built a chapel for that purpose	17	17	—	—	5	9
How he left his pupils' fees lying in the window	18	—	—	12	—	30b
How he nursed a sick pupil for five weeks	19	32	—	—	—	30k
How he healed a boil in his pupil's arm	20	41	10	13	—	16 (30c)
How he forgot to recite the prayer 'O intemerata' and was cautioned by St. John the Baptist	21	24	—	15	—	30e
His visit to Northampton on a Good Friday	22	—	—	—	—	—
The apparition of St. E.'s mother	23	18	7	16	7	11 (30f)
How as a theological student he attended matins at the church of S. Merri	24	—	—	—	—	—
How he declined the offer of the archbishop of York to procure him a Bible	25	—	—	—	—	30l
He accepts a benefice on his own conditions	—	—	—	—	—	30m
How he sold his theological books to help poor students	26	31a	—	17	—	30j
His inception as a theologian	27	19	8	18	8	12
How he stayed a year at Merton before incepting	—	—	—	—	9	13
His gifts as a preacher and teacher	28	20	—	—	—	—
How seven of his pupils left his schools to become monks (at Quarr), including Stephen of Lexington	29	21	—	19	—	30g

A Comparative Synopsis

	Pontigny	A	B	C	Eustace	Matthew Paris
His vision of the Holy Ghost like a dove	30	22	—	23	—	—
How he converted the earl of Salisbury	31	—	—	—	—	—
How he converted a prostitute	32	23	—	—	—	—
How he threw the Devil in physical combat	34	25	9	30	—	15
His abstinence in food, drink, and clothing	35a	27a	4a	22a	4a (15)	8a
That he never lay in a bed after his inception	35b	27b	4b	22b	4b	8b
How the servants of a certain nobleman jested at his untouched bed	35c	27c	—	22c	—	—
That he never accepted a benefice unless he could reside	36a	28a	13	—	6	10
He becomes Treasurer of Salisbury cathedral	36b	28b	—	24	—	19
An encomium of Bishop Richard of Salisbury	—	—	—	25	—	—
How, on account of poverty, he would stay with his old pupil, the abbot of Stanley	36c	28c	—	—	—	—
His unwillingness to hear pleas or accounts	37	29	—	—	—	—
How he was once angered by the loss of a Bible	38	—	—	—	—	—
How his piety edified certain monks	39	30	6	—	10	14
His generosity to the poor	40	31b	—	—	—	—
How he studied with a statue before him	41	26	—	—	—	—
How he appeared in a vision to a Carthusian	42	—	—	—	—	—
Of relics that he sent to the abbess of Lacock	43a	—	—	—	—	—
How he declined a gift of jewels from the same lady when she was countess of Salisbury	43b	—	—	—	—	—
How a sick scholar tried to detain him	44	42	—	—	—	30i
He is commissioned to preach the Crusade	45	33	11	28	—	17
A miracle worked (at Leominster) when he was preaching the Crusade	46	34	—	29	—	—
The vision of the nun of Buckland	47	35	—	—	—	—
A miracle worked at Stratford	48	—	—	—	—	—
How he dispersed the rain where he preached	49a	38a	12	26a	—	18
in All Saints cemetery, Oxford	49b	38b	—	26b	—	30b
The same in St. John's cemetery	50	—	—	—	—	—
The same before the king's hall	51	—	—	—	—	—
The same at Gloucester	52	—	—	—	—	—
The same at Crutch	53	36	—	—	—	—
The same at Worcester	54	39	—	27	—	—
The same at Hereford	—	37	—	—	—	—
How his candle fell on his Bible but left it unharmed	55	40	—	—	—	—
How a mouse extinguished his lamp and how the lamp was miraculously relit	56	43	—	—	—	—
How he healed a sore in his foot	57	44	—	—	—	—
How his chamberlain was unable to burn his hair shirt	58	16b	—	21	—	31
He is elected archbishop of Canterbury	59a	45a	14	31	10	20

A Comparative Synopsis

	Pontigny	A	B	C	Eustace	Matthew Paris
How the messengers found him at Calne	59b	45b	—	—	—	—
An indiscreet servant is put out of countenance	59c	45c	—	—	—	—
How the bishop of Salisbury urged him to accept	59d	45d	—	—	—	—
His election is confirmed by the pope and he is consecrated	60	46	—	—	—	21a
by Bishop Roger of London on 2 April 1234	—	—	—	—	—	21b
The names of the three other candidates	—	—	—	—	—	22
How St. E. reconciled Earl Gilbert the Marshal, Hubert de Burgh, and others to the king	—	—	—	—	—	23
How he liked to assist at the disputations of the Friars Preachers	—	—	—	—	—	24
His humility and asceticism as archbishop	61	47	15	—	11	27
A comparison between St. E. and St. Martin of Tours	—	—	—	—	13	26
The testimony of archbishop Walter of York concerning St. E.	—	—	—	—	16	28
How he saw a dragon between Wrotham and Otford	—	—	—	—	17	29
The testimony of Robert Bacon concerning St. E.	—	—	—	—	—	30a
How one of his *familia* reproached him with his acquaintance with a certain woman, and his reply	62	15	—	—	—	—
His generosity towards beggars	63a	48a	16	32	14	—
How he used the relief of one of his knights to provide a dowry for the daughters of the same	63b	48b	—	—	—	—
How he would remit the heriot of poor widows	63c	48c	—	—	—	—
His refusal to accept a gift of jewellery	64a	49a	—	—	—	—
or a gift of blankets sent by his brother	64b	49b	—	—	—	—
or a gift of a golden pyx	64c	—	—	—	—	—
How his own chapter troubled him with litigation	65a	50a	18	34	18	32a
How the monks accidentally burned a privilege	—	—	—	—	—	32b
He goes to Rome for advice	65b	50b	19	—	—	25a (35)
How he declined the pope's invitation to drink	65c	50c	—	—	12	25b
He expresses to the pope a desire to be a monk	—	—	—	—	—	25c
How the chapter renewed their opposition	66	51	—	—	—	34
How the legate, Cardinal Otto, intervened and the culprits were removed to the Carthusians	—	—	—	—	—	33
How St. E. was troubled by disputes with Bishop Roger of London, Rochester priory, and others	—	—	—	—	—	36
How he fell into ill repute with the king	67a	52a	17a	33	19	—
and the magnates wronged him	67b	52b	17b	—	20	37

A Comparative Synopsis

	Pontigny	A	B	C	Eustace	Matthew Paris
How meetings were arranged, but were deferred	67c	52c	20a	—	21	38a
How the legate fell in with the majority and quashed the archbishop's acts	—	—	—	—	—	39
How St. E.'s enemies postponed a settlement because of the legate's presence	67d	52d	20b	—	—	—
How St. E. excommunicated those who infringed the liberties of the Church	68	53	21	—	22	38b
Other complaints of St. E., notably Earl Simon's irregular marriage, and the manner in which the baptism of the Lord Edward was performed	—	—	—	—	—	40
How he meditated flight into exile	69	54	—	—	—	—
How he healed sick people with holy water	70	55	—	—	—	—
How he healed a familiar of a quartan fever	71	—	—	—	—	—
How he cured a famous clerk of a knee affection	72	—	—	—	—	—
How he foretold the misfortunes of Albert, archbishop elect of Armagh	73a	57a	—	—	—	—
How he foretold the misfortunes of William Ralegh, then bishop of Norwich	73b	57b	—	—	—	—
His vision of St. Thomas the martyr	74a	—	—	—	—	41
Another vision of the same	74b	56	—	—	—	—
How he explained the reasons for his departure to certain religious (of Lewes)	75	58	—	—	—	—
His flight to Pontigny	76	59	22	35	23	42
His meeting with Blanche, the Queen Regent	—	—	—	—	—	43
How he preached and healed a girl at Ligny	77	—	—	—	—	—
How he was granted fraternity at Pontigny	—	—	—	—	—	44
How he fell sick and was advised to go to Soisy	78	60	23	36	24	45
His generosity to the poor *en route* to Soisy	79	—	—	—	—	—
His exclamation on receiving the Viaticum	80a	61a	24	37	25a	46a
His speech in English afterwards	80b	61b	—	—	25b	46b
How he wrote letters for his *familiares*	—	—	—	—	—	47
The manner of his death	81	62	25	—	26	48
How a certain man had a presage of St. E.'s glory on the night before his death	82	—	—	—	—	—
How he consoled the prior of Soisy	—	—	—	—	—	49a
Bequest of his pallium and diptych to his sisters at Catesby	—	—	—	—	—	50
How his chancellor distributed the letters and broke the seal	—	—	—	—	—	51
How his entrails were buried at Provins	83	63	—	—	—	49b
The funeral procession to Trainel and the intervention of the abbot of Cîteaux	84a	64a	—	—	27a	52a
The procession to Villeneuve l'archevêque	84b	64b	—	—	27b	52b
The procession to Coulours	84c	64c	—	—	27c	52c

A Comparative Synopsis

	Pontigny	A	B	C	Eustace	Matthew Paris
Two of his clerks are sceptical	85	65	—	—	28	53
They discuss his merits and the shrines in the English Benedictine houses	—	—	—	—	—	54
The burial of St. E. at Pontigny	86	66	—	—	—	55
Of miracles worked at Catesby	—	—	—	—	—	56
How Peter the sacrist obtained St. E.'s ring	87	67	—	—	—	—
The vision of brother Hermagnus	88	68	—	—	—	—
How Archbishop Walter of Sens visited the tomb	89	69	—	—	—	—
The first translation of St. E.	90	70	—	—	—	—
The marvellous cures worked at his tomb	91	—	26	—	—	—
Examples of St. E.'s virtues	91	—	—	—	—	—
Answers to critics of the saint and of the conduct of the Roman see	93	—	—	—	—	—
Reasons for his burial at Pontigny	94a	—	—	—	—	—
notably, the prophecy of St. Thomas Becket	94b	—	27	—	—	55b
For this reason, the first man to be cured at St. E.'s tomb was named Thomas	95	—	28	—	—	—
Of St. E.'s canonization by the pope at Lyons	96	—	—	—	—	57
Text of the bull *Novum matris*	—	—	—	—	—	58
A letter of Bishop Richard of Chichester, concerning the translation of St. E.	—	—	—	—	—	59
Text of a sermon preached by St. E. in chapter at Pontigny	—	—	—	—	—	60

Note.—Unfortunately Dr. R. Vaughan's *Matthew Paris* (Cambridge, 1958) appeared too late to be incorporated into this section.

PART TWO

I

THE FAMILY OF ST. EDMUND

EDMUND OF ABINGDON was one of a great company of thirteenth-century prelates who came from humble and obscure families, and for whom the theological schools opened a road to high preferment. The hagiographers have much to say about the piety of his parents, Reginald of Abingdon, called the Rich (*Dives*), and Mabel, but they omit information which might have been more interesting. There is no reference to the date of Edmund's birth or to the social status and occupation of his father. The fact that Edmund was the eldest of a fair-sized family emerges from the confused and conflicting statements in the Lives. Thus the Anonymous A and the Pontigny writer, following their common source, name only one brother, Robert, and two sisters. But elsewhere they reproduce a death-bed colloquy between Edmund and his mother in the course of which he speaks of his absent brothers and she transmits through him her blessing to all of them.[1] Matthew Paris mentions three brothers, namely Robert, who achieved eminence as a secular clerk, Nicholas, who took the Cistercian habit at Boxley, and a third brother, unnamed, who entered the Benedictine abbey of Eynsham. Matthew is clearly well informed on this and the story of the brother who entered Eynsham is particularly interesting. It probably accounts for the statement made by the Anonymous A and the Pontigny writer that Edmund's father had got his wife's consent to retire from the world, and had taken the habit at Eynsham. This spectacular act of fugitive piety is not confirmed by any other independent

---

[1] Lambeth Palace MS. 135, fo. 118ᵛ; *MD. Thes.* iii, col. 1780.

The Family of St. Edmund

source, and if it occurred, it seems unlikely that the Eynsham community would have missed the chance of mentioning it in their letter of postulation. In any case, the Anonymous A is wrong about the father's name, which he gives as Edward. This mistake suggests that the writer has confused the father with the son.

Probably another brother can be added to those mentioned by Matthew Paris. After the mother's death, Edmund placed his two sisters in a convent at Catesby, Northamptonshire, and among the Catesby charters in the Public Record Office there is a deed by William, son of Reginald of Abingdon, assigning the nuns of Catesby a rent from an Abingdon property occupied by Rondulf the mason.[1] In the circumstances, we are justified in assuming that William's interest in Catesby arose from the fact that he had two sisters there.

Having failed to find a husband for either of her daughters, Mabel of Abingdon directed Edmund to place his sisters, Margery and Alice, in a convent. He secured their admission to the small Gilbertine nunnery of Catesby.[2] According to the hagiographers, the reason for Edmund's choice of this obscure and relatively poor convent was a scruple about paying the dowry which was usually demanded from the families of women making the monastic profession.[3] Whether this was so may be doubted, in view of the endowments which Edmund and his brother settled on the house. Possibly the larger women's houses were more exacting or socially exclusive. Catesby, at any rate, was to derive unexpected profit from Edmund's sisters. In 1245, when the Process of St. Edmund was well

---

[1] PRO Anc. Deeds E 326/B 5; see App. C, p. 317.

[2] It is doubtful whether it was a Gilbertine or a Cistercian house, see *Monasticon*, iv. 635 ff. Professor Knowles lists it as a Cistercian nunnery, but notes that Canons Regular and lay brothers were attached to it until the fourteenth century: D. Knowles and R. N. Hadcock, *Medieval Religious Houses of England and Wales* (1953), p. 222.

[3] The provincial statutes of Oxford forbade the exaction of dowry from postulants, thereby reinforcing the decrees of the Third and Fourth Lateran Councils: Wilkins, i. 591.

advanced, Margery of Abingdon was appointed prioress by Grosseteste, who stepped in and quashed a previous election.[1] She died in 1257 with a reputation for sanctity, as was proper in the sister of one whom the Church had raised to its altars.[2] As a result of the presence of St. Edmund's sisters and the personal effects which he had bequeathed to them,[3] Catesby became a centre of his cult and a resort of pilgrims.

To describe the circumstances of Edmund's parents, the hagiographers use the word *mediocris*. If this is taken to be a description of their social status, it means only that they were of free birth, that they occupied a middle position in the social scale between the armigerous class of feudal tenants and the servile class. As an account of their wealth, the word *mediocris* could perhaps be rendered 'average' or 'fair'. Although the Pontigny writer insists that Edmund's father was rich in nothing but pious works, there is evidence to suggest that Reginald of Abingdon was by no means a poor man.[4] He possessed at least two houses and a croft in the borough of Abingdon. One of these properties is described in a deed in the newly recovered Abingdon cartulary.[5] By this deed, which is undated, Master Edmund of Abingdon recorded the conveyance in free alms to the Hospital of St. John the Baptist, Oxford, of 'the house, with all its appurtenancies, which belonged to Reginald the Rich (*Divitis*) in West Street, in the vill of Abingdon, which is situated between the house of Thurbern Manegod on the one side and the house of Gunivilde Ater on the other . . .'.

---

[1] *Rotuli Roberti Grosseteste*, ed. F. N. Davis (CYS 1913), p. 222.

[2] *Chron. Maiora*, v. 621.

[3] Edmund left them his cloak and a silver diptych, see below, p. 270, and *Chron. Maiora*, iv. 102, 324.

[4] Matthew Paris, who was best informed, seems to hint at this: their children were possessions which they had *inter ceteras prosperitates*.

[5] Bodleian Lyell MS. 15, fo. 92ᵛ; see App. C, p. 315. It came to the library with the Lyell bequest in 1949. Part of the deed was known, however, from Twyne's transcripts, see H. E. Salter, 'A Lost Cartulary of Abingdon Abbey', *Berks., Bucks. and Oxfordshire Arch. Journal*, xxiv (1918), pp. 28 ff., and his preface to *The Cartulary of the Hospital of St. John the Baptist, Oxford*, vol. iii (OHS 1916), p. lii.

The following entries in the cartulary show that the brethren of the Hospital assigned the rent of this property to Andrew Halegod of Oxford. Halegod in turn assigned the rent to Abingdon abbey for the support of a hospital in Abingdon.[1] It is apparently this transaction which Matthew Paris has recorded, in syncopated form, in a couplet of his French Life of St. Edmund:

> Et tout son patrimonie donne
> A l'hopital d'Abbendone.[2]

Other properties of the family are described in another undated Catesby deed in the Public Record Office. By this Edmund, who was not yet using the style of a Master, granted to the nuns of Catesby a house with a garden, and a croft situated by the town ditches.[3] Since Edmund had not yet incepted as a Master at the time of this grant, it is unlikely that he had acquired the property himself, and it must have formed part of his inheritance. If to this be added the house occupied by Rondulf the mason out of which William endowed Catesby, Reginald of Abingdon emerges as a man of some means. Under the relatively free tenurial arrangements of the borough he had been able to invest in real estate. There is no reason to doubt that the name 'Rich' signified the reputation which Reginald had obtained among his less prosperous neighbours. The source of his income is nowhere mentioned. The fact that Mabel, his wife, was buried in the church of St. Nicholas suggests a connexion with the abbey.[4] St. Nicholas was not a

---

[1] Bodl. Lyell MS. 15, fos. 92ᵛ and 93. Halegod acquired the rent by an exchange. He owned other property near the east gate of Oxford, where the hospital stood; see H. E. Salter, *Cartulary of the Hospital of St. John the Baptist*, i. 220–1. Salter dates Edmund's grant *c.* 1230, but it is probably a good deal earlier than that. Halegod's deed was executed between 1234 and 1240, since it refers to Edmund as being archbishop.

[2] *Romania*, lv (1929), l. 115. The site of Edmund's birthplace was acquired by Edmund of Cornwall who in 1288 erected a chapel on it; see R. E. G. Kirk, *Accounts of the Obedientiars of Abingdon Abbey*, (CS new ser. li, 1892), pp. xxxix–xl. It stood off West St. Helen Street and is possibly the site in question.   [3] PRO Anc. Deeds E 326/B 4; below, p. 316.

[4] This is stated in the English metrical Life of St. Edmund: *The Early South*

parochial church until a much later date. It lay partly within and partly outside the abbey enclosure and existed to serve the needs of the monastery's lay servants and dependants.[1] It is possible therefore that Reginald was in the employment of the abbey, for unless the monks had some claim over the family, the mortuary of his widow would have been claimed by the vicar of St. Helen's. On the other hand, the hagiographers have much to say about St. Edmund's home background, and their uniform silence on this point is striking. This silence is intelligible on the supposition that Reginald of Abingdon made his wealth from trade. That merchants could hardly be saved was proverbial and the hagiographers, who demanded consistency from the cradle, may have felt that trade was an unsuitable occupation for the father of a saintly archbishop. The fact that Reginald lived in the midst of a trading community and that the family had sufficient means to send two sons to the schools points in the same direction.

II

OXFORD, PARIS, AND SALISBURY

THE difficulty of establishing any certain chronology of Edmund's academic career illustrates the shortcomings of hagiography as historical material. He is far and away the best documented of the early Oxford Masters. In the letters of postulation and the Lives references to his regencies in Arts and Theology abound, but they are not continuous and are mostly unrelated to any context of time or place. Often it is

---

English Legendary, ed. C. Horstmann (EETS 1887), p. 435. After the canonization of St. Edmund, her tomb was transferred to a new chapel inside the abbey precinct; see the extracts of a lost Abingdon chronicle published from Twyne's transcript by H. E. Salter, 'A Chronicle Roll of the abbots of Abingdon', *EHR* xxvi (1911), pp. 727–38.

[1] A. E. Preston, *The Church and Parish of St. Nicholas, Abingdon* (OHS 1935).

not clear whether the hagiographical anecdotes about his student days are supposed to relate to Oxford or to Paris. The absence of any sure chronology is peculiarly exasperating since St. Edmund's academic life fell in a transitional period when the constitution and curriculum of both universities were in a crucial stage of development. The dating of his regency would help to fill an important gap in scholastic history.

The only safe guides to this period of Edmund's life are the depositions of Richard of Dunstable and Robert Bacon, and the letters of postulation written by pupils or colleagues, among which the letter from Oxford University obviously holds first place. From these an outline can be reconstructed. Edmund got his first schooling in grammar at Oxford, where he was sent as a young boy. To this period belong the gracious hagiographical legends of his meeting with the Christ Child in the meadows[1] and his mystical betrothal to the statue of the Blessed Virgin.[2] The Franciscan author of the Lanercost chronicle, who was in Oxford about twenty years after Edmund's death, identifies the statue and speaks of the story as common knowledge in the university.[3] At an early age, Edmund and his brother Robert were sent by Mabel of Abingdon to Paris to take the Arts course. Edmund incepted as a Master in due course and returned to Oxford, where he was regent in the Arts faculty for upwards of six years. At the end of this period he fell a prey to the scruples which afflicted so many of his contemporaries and after a dream in which he was sternly warned to dally no longer with secular learning, he proceeded to theology. For this purpose he returned to Paris. Whether he ever incepted or taught in the theological faculty at Paris is uncertain. He returned to England and eventually, after a year's residence at the Augustinian priory of Merton, he yielded to the pressure

[1] See the version of Matthew Paris below, p. 225.
[2] Below, p. 224.
[3] *Chronicon de Lanercost*, ed. J. Stevenson (1839), p. 36. A. G. Little has shown that the part-author of the chronicle was Richard of Durham who was in Oxford after 1260: 'The Authorship of the Lanercost Chronicle', in *Franciscan Papers, Lists, and Documents* (1943), pp. 42–54.

of his friends and incepted in theology at Oxford. After, or during, his period as a theological Master, he was appointed to a prebend in Salisbury cathedral. These are the bare outlines which can be constructed from the sources.

Interest has lately been focused on Edmund's Oxford regency in Arts on account of a statement made by Roger Bacon in his *Compendium Studii Theologiae*. Illustrating the tardy reception of the New Logic in the West, Bacon says that Edmund was the first Master to lecture on the Elenchi at Oxford, and that a Master Hugh, whom he had seen, was the first to lecture on the Posterior Analytics.[1] If Bacon's statement can be taken at its face value,[2] it would seem that Edmund's regency coincided with the reception of the New Logic at Oxford, and it is therefore of special interest to scholastic history to see whether it can be dated with any degree of certainty.

Through the industry of the translators of Toledo, most of the Aristotelian corpus was accessible in Latin translation by the end of the twelfth century. But the reception of the different books into the schools was a gradual process which was occasionally subject to violent reaction, and which it is difficult to date. The *Heptateuchon* of Theodoric of Chartres shows that the whole Organon, saving the Posterior Analytics, was in use by the Masters of Chartres by 1141.[3] There is evidence that both the Elenchi and the Posterior Analytics were being taught at Paris by 1180.[4] Both are included in the list of prescribed

---

[1] *Rogeri Baconi Compendium Studii Theologiae*, ed. H. Rashdall (Brit. Soc. Franc. Stud. 1911), p. 34. The passage is discussed in an important paper by Fr. D. Callus, 'The Introduction of Aristotelian Learning to Oxford', in *Proc. of the Brit. Academy*, xxix (1943), pp. 229-81.

[2] In view of Bacon's inaccuracy and tendentiousness, one wonders whether too much has been based on an observation written fifty-two years after Edmund's death. The value and the defects of Bacon's contribution to scholastic history are assessed by Grabmann, *Forschungen über die lateinischen Aristoteles-übersetzungen des XIII. Jahrh.* (Beitr. z. Gesch. d. Philosophie d. Mittalalters, xvii. 1916).

[3] M. Grabmann, *Geschichte der scholastichen Methode* (Freiburg, 1909-11), ii. 54-81.

[4] D. Callus, op. cit.

Oxford, Paris, and Salisbury

books compiled by Alexander Nequam shortly after 1191,[1] and 'I', wrote Nequam with engaging modesty, 'have been a small pillar of the Petit Pont', the traditional playground of the dialecticians.[2]

The date at which the new logical books were introduced into the Arts curriculum at Oxford is, as yet, obscure.[3] On the face of it, it is improbable that Oxford would have been far behind Paris in receiving the New Logic. There were already flourishing schools of law and theology at Oxford by 1200, and the strictures of Daniel Morley were directed mainly against Masters who were ignorant of the *libri naturales*.[4] If at Oxford he felt himself to be the only Greek among the Latins, the Masters of Paris seemed to him to be *bestiales*. Morley, with his load of scientific works from Toledo, represented already the second wave of the Aristotelian revolution. If Bacon's assertion is true and Saint Edmund was the first of the Oxford Masters to lecture on the Elenchi, it would be surprising to find that his regency began later than 1200.

An attempt has been made to date Edmund's inception in Arts by reference to two statements in the canonization documents which seem at first sight to be complementary. One of Edmund's personal austerities which received much attention from the hagiographers was his habit of sleeping in a fully clothed state, not in, but beside his bed. In the Oxford letter of postulation, the University state, on the authority of Robert

[1] The book list with incipit *sacerdos ad altare accessurus*, published by C. H. Haskins, *Studies in the History of Mediaeval Science* (1927), pp. 356–76.

[2] *De Laudibus Divinae Sapientiae*, ed. T. Wright (RS 1863), p. 503. On the place of the Petit Pont in the academic topography of Paris at the end of the twelfth century see the encomium of Guy of Bazoches in *Denifle Chartularium*, i. 55–56.

[3] One of the earliest appearances of the Elenchi in an English library catalogue must be the copy, bound up with the Topics, which is listed in the twelfth-century catalogue of Reading Abbey in BM Egerton MS. 3031, fo. 10ᵛ. This is interesting in view of Edmund's connexion with the abbey during the period of his regency in Arts, see the letter of postulation from Reading, below, p. 299.

[4] See R. W. Hunt, 'English Learning in the Late Twelfth Century', in *TRHS*, 4th ser. xix (1936), pp. 19–42.

Bacon and Richard of Dunstable, that Edmund had practised this form of penance from the time of his regency in Arts ('a tempore quo rexerat in artibus'). Now in his Life of St. Edmund, Eustace of Faversham says that Edmund had observed this practice for thirty-six years and more, and his statement is incorporated in the Life by Matthew Paris.[1] If these two statements are taken to be complementary, Edmund's inception in Arts should be placed some thirty-six years before his death, that is about 1204. It must be conceded that at first sight this argument is plausible. On closer inspection, however, it will be seen that the statement of Eustace is based on a passage in the letter of postulation from Bishop Jocelin of Bath, which he has modified or, possibly, mistranscribed. Jocelin's passage runs as follows: 'non iacendo sed sedendo, semper vestitus et cinctus, aliquantulum quiescebat, et hoc per triginta annos creditur observasse'.[2] There is a similar passage in the Eynsham letter which, however, mentions no period of time. Eustace, incorporating this passage, altered *triginta annos* to *triginta et sex annos et amplius*. It is arguable of course that Eustace amended the text in the light of more precise knowledge. But, as indicated elsewhere, Eustace knew little of Edmund's earlier life, and one cannot avoid the suspicion that he wished only to say 'a long time', a suspicion which is strengthened by the addition of the vague covering phrase *et amplius*. At any rate, the original statement of Jocelin deserves at least equal credit. If this is matched with the assertion in the Oxford letter, it would make Edmund's regency begin about 1210. This is certainly too late, and in fact, as will appear shortly, there is reason for rejecting either date. The statements of Jocelin and Eustace on the one hand, and of the Oxford letter on the other, are not really complementary. Had they both been made by the same person, that is had one writer stated that Edmund had not used his bed since his regency, viz. for thirty-six years, the information would have deserved

[1] Below, pp. 205, 208.
[2] Sens cath. mun. no. 16 (an *inspeximus*); *MD. Thes.* iii, col. 1907.

serious consideration. But this is not the case. And the periods of time given are obviously intended to convey no more than approximate knowledge.

A more hopeful approach to dating Edmund's regency may be found in constructing a list of his pupils. It is unfortunate that modern scholarship has concentrated on the theological faculty and left the early Masters of Arts in relative obscurity. Two at least of Edmund's former pupils wrote letters to postulate his canonization, namely Richard, bishop of Bangor, and Walter de Gray, archbishop of York. For this purpose, Richard is disappointing. He was archdeacon of Bangor in 1236, when he was elected to the bishopric.[1] After losing his see by war in 1248, he resided at St. Albans until his death in 1267.[2] Nothing is known of his career before the date of his election, beyond the fact, which he states in his letter, that he had known Saint Edmund from his youth, and had been taught by him.[3] Whether he had been a pupil in Arts or Theology, he does not say. With Walter de Gray the case is rather different. In his letter he mentions that he had heard Edmund's lectures *in artibus*.[4] The son of an influential aristocratic family, and nephew of John de Gray, bishop of Norwich, Walter had a distinguished career in church and state.[5] Walter paid a fine for the chancellorship which he received on 21 October 1205.[6] In 1210 he was bishop elect of Coventry,[7] but this appointment came to nothing owing to John's conflict with the pope. In 1214 he was elected bishop of Worcester, surrendering the Seal, and the same year he was translated to the metropolitan see of York which he ruled until his death in 1255. It is curious that nothing is discoverable about him before he received the

---

[1] *CPR 1232–47*, p. 152. [2] *Chron. Maiora*, v, *passim*.
[3] Sens cath. mun. no. 16 (an *inspeximus*); MD. *Thes*. iii, col. 1906.
[4] 'olim existens eius auditor in artibus'; see App., p. 302.
[5] His family relationship is established by a deed of his mother, Hawysia de Gray, in the Oseney cartulary: H. E. Salter, *The Cartulary of Oseney Abbey* (OHS 1934), iv. 332.
[6] *Rot. Lit. Claus.* (1833), p. 53.
[7] *Pipe Roll 12 John*, ed. C. F. Slade (1951), p. 177.

Great Seal.¹ But it is certain that he cannot have been an untried youth straight from the schools when John chose him to succeed Archbishop Hubert Walter in the highest office of the state. He must have had administrative experience. In fact, all things considered, he can hardly have been much younger than twenty-eight or thirty. On this ground, Edmund's regency in Arts must be placed well before 1200. In fact, we may assign it hypothetically to c. 1195-1201. Although these dates are earlier than any yet suggested, they agree with our presupposition that the New Logic was received into the Arts curriculum at Oxford in the last years of the twelfth century. Courçon's statutes given to Paris in 1215 required that anyone incepting as a Master in Arts should have attained his twenty-first year, and should have attended lectures for six years.² If Edmund fulfilled these requirements, he must have begun the course at Paris before 1190.

The Oxford letter of postulation states that Edmund was regent in Arts at Oxford for six years, and that during that time, though he was unbeneficed, he was accustomed to hear Mass daily, and that out of his fees he constructed a chapel in his parish, dedicated to the Blessed Virgin.³ At the end of this time his mother, now dead, appeared to him in a dream and questioned him reproachfully about the strange geometric figures that he was demonstrating in the schools. His stammered explanations were swept aside. She seized his hand and drew

¹ The absence of any reference to him in records before 1205 is remarked by S. Painter, *The Reign of King John*, p. 64, who concludes, surely wrongly, that 'he seems to have had no experience in the government service'.

² Denifle, *Chartularium*, i. 78-79.

³ Anthony Wood quoted this statement from the deposition of Eustace which he had seen in the Corpus Christi MS., and identified the chapel with the early thirteenth-century Lady Chapel which projects from the north side of St. Peter's-in-the-East: *Survey of the Antiquities of the City of Oxford*, ed. A. Clark (OHS 1890), ii. 100. On this subject I have nothing to add to A. B. Emden, *An Oxford Hall in Medieval Times* (1927), pp. 71-103. Mr. Emden vindicates the dedication of the Hall to St. Edmund, but, as he would be first to admit, the association of St. Edmund with the site or with the parish of St. Peter's remains unproven. He is unable to trace the dedication earlier than the fourteenth century.

on his palm three circles in which she wrote *Pater, Filius, et Spiritus Sanctus*. He was warned thenceforth to make this his sole study. The sermon literature of the period abounds in anecdotes of this type, warning the Master who lingers too long over the *artes* to turn to higher things: 'you still dispute of nouns and syllables. Lucan and Priscian, these be thy gods! Look to it, for death is on the threshold.'[1] Robert Bacon is a good guide here, and from what he says it is clear that Edmund went back to Paris to study theology.[2] At this period the theological schools of Oxford were tributary to Paris, and it was not until much later in the thirteenth century that a strong native tradition was established.

The period of Edmund's two residences at Paris is very obscure. Only one hagiographical anecdote clearly belongs to the days when he was attending the theological schools. This is the Pontigny writer's story that he rose in the night when the bells of St. Merri rang for matins[3] and attended the office there. He evidently lodged in the faubourg St. Merri, which lay on the right bank in the commercial area of the city, not far from the Grève.[4] Whether he ever incepted as a Master in the theological faculty at Paris is uncertain.[5] The dates of his regency at Oxford are equally obscure.

Between 1209 and July 1214 the Oxford schools were in abeyance owing to the quarrel with the town over the hanging of two clerks.[6] It is a fact that none of the sources for St.

[1] Peter of Blois, *Epistolae* 6: *PL* ccvii; cf. the cautionary tale cited by Haskins in *Studies in Medieval Culture* (1929), p. 50: the master who encountered the ghost of his pupil, crushed under the weight of a cope on which were written the vain sophisms of the schools.

[2] 'Paucos libros sacre Scripture quos Parisius habuit, eciam audiens sacram Scripturam, vendidit': below, p. 252.   [3] *MD. Thes.* iii, col. 1788.

[4] L. Halphen, *Paris sous les premiers Capétiens* (Paris, 1909), p. 114.

[5] Glorieux asserts that he was regent at Paris from 1225 to 1229, but cites no evidence: *Répertoire des maîtres en théologie de Paris au xiiie siècle* (Paris, 1933), i. 261. The suggestion that he returned to Oxford at the Great Dispersion of Paris in 1229 takes no account of the fact that he was at that time Treasurer of Salisbury.

[6] See *Rashdall's Medieval Universities*, ed. F. M. Powicke and A. B. Emden (1936), iii. 33–35.

Edmund's academic life mentions the *suspendium clericorum*, and it is legitimate to infer that he incepted in theology after this, since otherwise his regency would have been interrupted.[1] If, then, the year 1214 is taken as a *terminus a quo*, a *terminus ad quem* can be fixed by reference to two of his pupils. Bacon has a vivid anecdote about Edmund when he was lecturing in the theological faculty. The Master is teaching, when the abbot of Quarr enters the schools. The lecture proceeds, but at the end seven of the class, 'fired, it may be thought, as much by the Master's eloquence as by the abbot', approach the abbot and are borne off to take the Cistercian habit. One of these seven was Stephen of Lexington. Stephen of Lexington came of an able and distinguished ministerial family. His father was a royal judge. One of his brothers achieved eminence on the Bench, and another finished up as bishop of Lincoln.[2] He himself after the initial plunge rose rapidly. Abbot of Stanley in 1223,[3] head of Savigny in 1229,[4] and elected to Clairvaux in 1243, he left a permanent mark on his Order by setting up the Chardonnet for Cistercian students at Paris.[5] His association with St. Edmund was not broken when he became a Cistercian. As abbot of Stanley, he gave him hospitality, and years after, when

[1] He can hardly have lectured during the dispersion, for those Masters who had *irreverenter* done so were suspended for three years by the legatine ordinance: H. E. Salter, *The Mediaeval Archives of the University of Oxford* (OHS 1920), p. 4.

[2] See the genealogy of the family in Thoroton's *History of Nottinghamshire*, iii. 110 ff.

[3] In that year he issued new letters of attorney to the proctors of the abbey: *Curia Regis Rolls* xi, 251.

[4] *Gallia Christiana* (Paris, 1876), iv. 806; the Savigny chronicle in *Receuil*, xxiii. 584. His letter book as abbot of Savigny has recently been published from the original at Turin by Fr. Bruno Griesser: *Registrum Epistolarum Stephani de Lexington* in *Analecta Sacri Ordinis Cisterciensis* (Rome, 1952–3).

[5] Matthew Paris has a story that he was deposed in 1255 by the General Chapter on account of his initiative in founding the college: *Chron. Maiora*, v. 596, 651, and this is repeated by the authors of *Gallia Christiana*. *Per contra*, the acts of the General Chapter show that between 1245 and 1255 the chapter supported the project with a series of striking privileges, see Canivez, *Statuta*, ii. 290, 327, 336, 348, 360, 399. Cf. the conclusions of F. E. Kwanten, 'Le Collège saint-Bernard à Paris', *Revue d'histoire ecclésiastique*, xliii (1948), pp. 443–72.

he was immersed in the business of Savigny, he wrote to his friend, the archdeacon of Wiltshire, and asked to be remembered to his old Master, who was then the Treasurer of Salisbury.[1] The date of Stephen's entry into the Cistercian Order therefore provides a clue to the period of Edmund's regency.

The sudden assumption of the Cistercian habit by seven Oxford scholars was a sufficiently striking event to cause comment. The Dunstable annalist, Richard de Morins, noticed it as occurring in May 1221.[2] Richard was a contemporary writer. He was, moreover, a well-informed and judicious observer, a former canon of Merton where Edmund had spent a year of retirement, and a man keenly interested in the theological studies of his time. His report on this point, therefore, deserves credit. Edmund was already regent then in May 1221,[3] and he incepted some time between that date and 1214.

There are in fact good reasons for placing Edmund's inception as a theologian in, or near, 1214. In the first place, there is the evidence of Robert Bacon, the Dominican Master, who describes himself as St. Edmund's *specialissimus scolaris, auditor, et socius*.[4] Bacon was already a Master in 1219. Moreover, in his *Tractatus super Psalterium*, he uses the *reportatio* of a sermon by the French Master, John of Abbeville, which suggests that he was studying theology at Paris about 1210 or earlier.[5] Since Bacon was his pupil, Edmund must obviously have incepted before him. A second reason for placing his inception about 1214, is the evidence of the Merton letter of postulation which states that, before incepting at Oxford, he had stayed for a year or more at the priory.[6] Matthew Paris says that he stayed at Merton 'wishing to lecture' (*lecturiens*), the desiderative form

[1] Griesser, op. cit. ii. 173-4.
[2] *Ann. Mon.* iii. 67.
[3] There is documentary confirmation that he was in Oxford in that year: *Rotuli Hugonis de Welles*, ed. W. P. Phillimore (CYS 1907-9), ii. 5.
[4] Below, p. 248.
[5] Beryl Smalley, 'Robert Bacon and the Early Dominican School at Oxford', *TRHS* 4th ser. xxx (1948), pp. 1-16.
[6] Below, p. 297.

suggesting an enforced interruption of his career.[1] The obvious explanation is that the retirement was forced on him by the suspension of the Oxford schools, and that his stay at Merton fell in the years 1213-14. The Merton letter states that he was called from this retreat to the Master's chair in theology. This would be made possible by the reconciliation between the university and the town in July 1214.

It does not follow from this that Edmund spent the whole period between 1201 and 1213 in the schools. The theology course was long and expensive and it was quite common to take it in stages. The Bachelor could retire to a benefice to restore his shattered finances, and proceed to the Master's degree later. That Edmund did this is suggested by a remark in the deposition of Eustace that he was only willing to accept a benefice on condition that he could reside and that he resigned it whenever he returned to the schools. Now the Oxford letter represents him as being unbeneficed as a Master of Arts, and Eustace must therefore be referring to his attendance at the theological schools.

Not much has been identified of the harvest of Edmund's teaching years. Apart from a stray sermon,[2] there are only his Moralities on the Psalms which survive in a single thirteenth-century manuscript,[3] and the well-known *Speculum Ecclesie*.[4]

[1] Below, p. 234. It is of course possible that he was under the canonical age, but thirty-five was only made the statutory minimum at Paris in 1215. Thereafter it was possible to be a bishop at thirty, but not a theologian.

[2] BM Harleian MS. 325, fos. 162^v-163^v.

[3] Worcester, Dean and Chapter Library, MS. Q 67.

[4] The Latin text in M. de la Bigne, *Bibliotheca Patrum et Veterum Auctorum Ecclesiasticorum*, vol. 5 (Paris, 1610), pp. 981-1004; the French version, together with a preliminary classification of the manuscripts, has been published by H. W. Robbins, *La Merure de Seinte Eglise* (Lewisburg, 1925; limited edition). The Latin manuscripts are very numerous. The Middle English version was printed by C. Horstmann, *Yorkshire Writers: Richard Rolle*, vol. 1 (1895), pp. 219-61.

Quaestiones in BM Royal MS. 9E XIV were identified as Edmund's by G. Lacombe, 'La Summa Abendonensis' in *Mélanges Mandonnet*, ii (Paris, 1930), and P. Glorieux, 'Autour de la Summa Abendonensis', in *Recherches de théologie ancienne et médiévale*, vi (1934). But Lacombe's ascription was shown

The Moralities are a type of gloss which was common in the first two decades of the thirteenth century.[1] They represent the old type of 'spiritual' exegesis with a practical moral bias. St. Edmund's Moralities are a typical class-room product of what has been called 'the Biblical Moral School' created by Stephen Langton and Peter the Chanter[2] but they lack any of the human interest or imagery of the workaday world which enliven the commentaries of Langton and the Chanter.

The *Speculum* belongs to an entirely different genre. Much of it bears a resemblance to the manuals of moral and pastoral theology designed for the parish clergy which drew inspiration from the synodal legislation of the thirteenth century. But the *Speculum* is clearly addressed to religious, and there is that about it that suggests the spacious leisure of the cloister rather than the feverish atmosphere of the schools. It is a treatise on perfect living: the essence of perfect living is to live according to the will of God, and this demands personal sanctification. Sanctification is achieved by knowledge of the self and contemplation of God. St. Edmund analyses four stages of contemplation. In the first, God is contemplated in His creatures. In the second, God is contemplated in Scripture. There follows a catechetical scheme of the necessary doctrines to be found in Scripture—at this point the influence which the *Speculum* exerted on the pastoral manuals becomes most apparent: the seven deadly sins, the seven Evangelical virtues, the seven gifts of the Holy Ghost, the Ten Commandments, the theological virtues, the articles of the creed, the seven sacraments, the cardinal virtues, the seven works of mercy and the seven beatitudes, the seven

---

to be based on a misreading of a marginal note, and the *Quaestiones* have been definitely identified as the work of Alexander of Hales, see F. Pelster, 'Die Quaestionen des Alexander von Hales' in *Gregorianum*, xiv (1933), pp. 401–22, 501–20, and *Alexandri de Hales Summa Theologica*, tome iv, *Prolegomena* (Quaracchi, 1948), pp. lxxix–lxxx, cxxxiv.

[1] Cf., for example, the Moralities on the Psalter by the better known Masters, John of Abbeville, Robert Bacon, and Grosseteste.

[2] See Beryl Smalley, *The Study of the Bible in the Middle Ages*, 2nd edn. (1952), chap. 5.

petitions of the *Our Father*, the joys of heaven and the pains of hell. In the third stage God is contemplated in the Sacred Humanity of Christ. For this purpose St. Edmund outlines a series of meditations on the life and passion of Christ, attaching two themes to each canonical hour of the breviary, an arrangement taken from Hugh of St. Victor. In the fourth stage God is contemplated in His divinity, and this in three progressive ways: by reason, by revelation, and by mystical contemplation. The treatise in fact advances from elementary religious instruction to mystical teaching of an advanced kind. It is difficult to visualize the audience at which such a heterogeneous work was directed. The probability is that the *Speculum* originated as a series of conferences given to a religious community and that it was expanded to include matter which would give it a wider appeal. Its success is attested both by the number of manuscripts extant and by the debt of diocesan legislators and English didactic writers in the later Middle Ages.[1]

If our chronology of Edmund's scholastic life is right, he probably belonged to the group of distinguished men who were learning their theology at Paris in the schoolroom of Langton at the beginning of the century. It was to one of this group, Richard Poore, bishop of Salisbury, that Edmund owed his first important advancement. Some time between January and August 1222 he was appointed Treasurer of Salisbury cathedral.[2] He held this office, with the annexed prebend of Calne, until he was elected archbishop in 1233. It is possible that he continued to teach for a time in the theological faculty at Oxford. During the time of Richard Poore, a roster of residence was drawn up which left members of the chapter free to absent themselves during nine months of the year.[3]

---

[1] See the discussion of the *Speculum* and its influence by W. A. Pantin, *The English Church in the Fourteenth Century* (1955), pp. 222-4.

[2] His predecessor in office, Abraham, attests a chapter act for the last time on 17 Jan.: *Sarum Charters*, ed. W. R. Jones and W. D. Macray (RS 1891), p. 121; Edmund attests for the first time on 18 Aug.: *The Register of St. Osmund*, ed. W. R. Jones (RS 1883-4), i. 339.

[3] *Sarum Charters*, pp. 209-10.

Oxford, Paris, and Salisbury

The Salisbury letter of postulation speaks of Edmund's powers as lecturer and preacher (*legendo et predicando*). Also the Pontigny writer and the Anonymous A have a story that Edmund was often impoverished as Treasurer, and tided over the year as the guest of his old pupil, the abbot of Stanley.[1] When the abbot urged him to cut his prodigal alms-giving, Edmund retorted that it was better to err on the side of generosity, because theological masters (*theologi*) had an unsavoury reputation for avarice.

On the other hand, all these expressions could apply to a theologian teaching at a cathedral school, and this is probably what was meant. Of the chapter acts which Edmund attests, four, in the years 1223,[2] 1227,[3] 1231,[4] and 1233,[5] were executed at dates which fell during the university term. During 1227 he was acting as papal preacher of the Crusade. Moreover the Treasurer's office which, at Salisbury, included the provision of lights and care of the altars and fabric, cannot have been a sinecure in the years when the new cathedral was under construction.[6] It is hardly possible, therefore, that Edmund could have been regent at the schools of Oxford or Paris in these years.[7] On the other hand it is quite probable that he continued to lecture at Salisbury where a fine scholastic tradition existed.

---

[1] The story gains probability from the fact that the inadequate endowment of the Treasurership was the reason for annexing to it the prebend of Calne in the time of St. Edmund: *H.MSS.C. Various Collections*, i (1901), p. 370; *Register of St. Osmund*, ii. 25. Also Edmund was one of the canons notified in 1226 that he was in arrears with his contributions to the fabric fund: ibid. ii. 108.

[2] Ibid. i. 330. 15 May.

[3] *Sarum Charters*, p. 189. 3 Oct.

[4] *Register of St. Osmund*, ii. 24. 3 May.

[5] *Sarum Charters*, p. 229. 19 Oct.

[6] On the Treasurer's responsibilities see the customary in *Register of St. Osmund*, i. 8–12. The new church was founded in 1220 and the use of the choir was solemnly inaugurated by Archbishop Langton at Michaelmas 1225. Edmund was in attendance: ibid., pp. 37–40.

[7] I can find no evidence to support Glorieux's statement that Edmund was regent at Paris from 1225 to 1229: *Répertoire des maîtres en théologie de Paris au xiiie siècle* (Paris, 1933), i. 261.

The English cathedral schools showed a surprising vitality in the face of university competition, and even late in the thirteenth century they were able to command the services of distinguished theologians like Richard Swinfield and Robert Winchelsea.[1]

III

THE CANTERBURY ELECTION AND POLITICS

In the last days of September 1233 monks from Christ Church, Canterbury, rode to Calne to inform Edmund that he had been elected archbishop. The vacancy at Canterbury had been created by the death in Italy of Archbishop Richard le Grand on 3 August 1231. The hagiographers refer in guarded terms to the various political forces of which the election had become a focus. After the see had been much troubled by pope and king, writes Matthew Paris, the convent elected a man 'in whom could be found no reasonable ground of contradiction'. He was in fact the fourth candidate to be elected. The first choice was the Chancellor and bishop of Chichester, Ralph Neville. This was an obvious and safe court nomination. Neville had already been mentioned at Rome as a possible successor to Stephen Langton and had hopes of the primacy.[2] Though educated as a Chancery clerk, he had grown accustomed to office during the Minority and was quite capable of taking an independent line. Wendover states that the scrutiny

[1] See A. G. Little, 'Theological Schools in Medieval England', *EHR* lv (1940), pp. 624–30; K. Edwards, *The English Secular Cathedrals in the Middle Ages* (1949), pp. 200–8.
[2] See the letter from Master Philip of Arden to Neville: Shirley, *Royal Letters*, i. 339; J. Boussard, 'Ralph Neville évêque de Chichester', in *Revue historique*, clxxvi (1935), pp. 217–33.

The Canterbury Election and Politics

of the election was delegated by the pope to Archdeacon Simon Langton, who had been in Rome since the death of Richard le Grand, and that Langton reported him to be a curialist and unlettered.[1] The statement is obviously a travesty. Nevertheless, the election was disallowed. The policy of Rome in this matter remained consistent throughout the thirteenth century. It was to prevent the see of Canterbury from falling into the hands of men whose associations and outlook were predominantly those of the civil service. The ground which had been won by the struggle between Innocent III and King John was not relinquished until the Avignon period.

A new licence to elect was issued on 7 March 1232,[2] and this time the monks chose their prior, John of Sittingbourne.[3] By now there was some anxiety at court lest the election should be called to Rome by the canon law of devolution.[4] Royal assent was therefore granted in haste—John probably promised to be an accommodating archbishop—and the elect set out for Rome on 4 April.[5] Apparently he was persuaded without difficulty to resign into the pope's hands. He was not a strong enough man for the job.

In the meantime, English affairs had reached a crisis. The dismissal and imprisonment of Hubert de Burgh in the same summer signified the accomplishment of a ministerial revolution which was to bring the country to the verge of civil war. For the moment the bishop of Winchester and his kinsman, Peter des Rievaux, held an unchallenged position. It was to be expected that the next nomination to Canterbury would reflect the influence which was now dominant at court. In these circumstances, the chapter elected Master John Blund, canon of Chichester. The political cross-currents which underlay the choice can be discerned in the bitterly partisan accounts of

[1] 'respondit illum curialem esse et illiteratum': *Chron. Maiora*, iii. 207.
[2] *Patent Rolls 1225–32*, p. 465.
[3] Elected 16 Mar.: Gervase, ii. 130.
[4] The monks are warned against sending a *compromissio* to Rome: *Patent Rolls 1225–32*, p. 465.
[5] Gervase, ibid.

the chroniclers. He can hardly be described as a curialist. He was first and foremost a scholar and theologian, a contemporary of Saint Edmund in the schools.[1] According to Matthew Paris, he was among the famous English Masters who left Paris in 1229, at the time of the Great Dispersion.[2] At the time of his election he was regent in theology at Oxford.[3] He had, however, performed services for the king, enough to earn him the style of king's clerk (*dilectus clericus noster*).[4] *Congé d'élire* was given on 12 August 1232, and Blund was elected on the 26th.[5] The king gave formal assent on the 30th, and the archbishop-elect embarked for Rome.[6] But this election too was quashed.

Wendover's explanation is that it had come out at Rome that Blund had received a thousand marks from Peter des Roches after his election, and had been credited with a thousand more to assist him in gaining confirmation. Paris adds that Peter des Roches had sought the emperor's co-operation, and that all this had led the pope to suspect Blund of simony and ambition. Gregory IX, according to Paris, expressed his doubts in a line of Ovid. Also Blund had admitted to holding two benefices *cum cura*, contrary to decrees of the Councils.[7] This is an obviously partisan account. Whatever the canonical definition of simony, it could hardly extend to a gift made by a patron to a successful candidate in order to cover his recognized

---

[1] His place in Aristotelian scholarship is assessed by D. Callus, 'The Introduction of Aristotelian Learning', op. cit. See details of his career collected by J. C. Russell, *A Dictionary of Writers of Thirteenth Century England* (1936), pp. 56–58.

[2] *Chron. Maiora*, iii. 168. But P. Glorieux, *Répertoire des maîtres en théologie de Paris au xiiie siècle* (1936), pp. 302–3, places his Paris regency in 1218–26. This fits the fact that he was in the king's employment in 1228.

[3] *Chron. Maiora*, iii. 223.

[4] He was royal proctor to the Roman court in 1228: *Close Rolls 1227–31*, pp. 80, 118. A Master John Blund received an *ad hoc* commission to sit at the Exchequer of Receipt in 1230: ibid., p. 342. There was, however, another John Blund in the king's service at this time.

[5] *Patent Rolls 1225–32*, p. 497; Gervase, ii. 129.

[6] Gervase, ii. 498.

[7] *Chron. Maiora*, iii. 243–4.

expenses. The various accounts are however unanimous on two points: that Blund's chief opponent was Simon Langton, and that the ostensible reason for his rejection was the fact of his being a pluralist.[1] The French writer William of Andres is a fairly reliable guide to the stories and apologies of the disappointed parties owing to the fact that his monastery in the Pas-de-Calais lay on the highroad between England and the continent. He describes Blund as an upright and learned man and says that he was rejected because he held two benefices and 'on a number of other frivolous counts'.[2]

On the face of it, it is surprising that an otherwise exemplary candidate should have been rejected on the sole ground of pluralism. But Henry of Avranches, who is Blund's apologist, confirms that this was the most important objection raised, and argues that the fault, if it is a fault, is generally prevalent and approved by custom.[3] The issue of pluralism was certainly a live one at the time, as can be seen from a contemporary collection of sermons from Paris University.[4] Thomas of Cantimpré has a story of Bishop William of Auvergne determining a debate at Paris to the effect that no man might hold two benefices and be saved. All the theological Masters determined to the same effect, except two. One of these two was Peter the Chancellor, who would not repent of it even on his death-bed, saying that he intended to find out experimentally whether or not it was a mortal sin to hold more than one benefice. And so he did, according to Thomas. His tortured soul troubled the bishop during his prayers.[5] On the other hand, there are indications that a less rigorous view was taken

---

[1] Thus the Dunstable annalist in *Ann. Mon.* iii. 132.
[2] *Chron. Wilhelmi Andrensis*, ed. Heller, *MGH. SS.* xxiv. 772.
[3] 'Non suus error, | immo communis, si consuetudo probata | et prescripta diu censeri debeat error': J. C. Russell and J. P. Heironimus, *The Shorter Latin Poems of Master Henry of Avranches* (Cambr. Mass. 1935), p. 133.
[4] M. M. Davy, *Les Sermons universitaires parisiens de 1230–31* (Paris, 1931), e.g. John of St. Giles, p. 275, and the anonymous preacher of 1231 who invoked the curse of Habacuc on those who multiplied prebends, p. 412.
[5] *Bonum Universale de Apibus*, ed. Colverinus (1627), i, chap. xix.

at Rome. If it hindered Blund's confirmation, it was to be no impediment to his receiving any other bishopric.[1] This suggests that pluralism was only a pretext, used because the real reason for Blund's rejection could not be voiced: the suspicion that he was too deeply committed to a royal policy. In fact, as Matthew Paris says, the patronage of the bishop of Winchester had done him more harm than good.[2] That he was the especial candidate of Peter des Roches is shown by the metrical broadside of Henry of Avranches, for Henry was a court poet and wrote for his patron. The nomination was at any rate a worthy one, and a credit to Peter des Roches, whose reputation has suffered unduly from the animus of the St. Albans writers.

After quashing the third election, the Pope nominated a candidate of his own to the representatives of the chapter who had accompanied Blund to Rome. As Wendover put it, euphemistically, 'Since, after the quashing of three persons elected to the church of Canterbury, the said church had by now been long widowed of a pastor, he [i.e. the pope] gave the monks, who had come with the unsuccessful candidate, the power to elect Master Edmund, canon of the church of Salisbury.'[3] The monks did not, however, constitute a *compromissio*, and it was necessary for them to return home and place the new choice before the chapter. After papal nomination, the election by the chapter can have been only a formality, and this was completed by 20 September 1233.[4] The royal assent was given on 10 October.[5] It was intimated to Edmund that his personal presence was not required at Rome. Instead a delegation from Canterbury collected the pallium from the tomb of St. Peter on 3 February 1234.[6] This is clear confirmation that he was the approved papal candidate.[7]

It was not the first or last time in the course of the thirteenth century that the pope was to impose his choice on Canterbury

[1] Auvray, i. 777. CPL i. 135.
[2] *Chron. Maiora*, iii. 243.
[3] Ibid., iii. 244.
[4] Gervase, ii. 130.
[5] CPR 1232–47, p. 27.
[6] Auvray, i. 958.
[7] The temporalities were released on 4 Feb., a further indication that papal assent was already known: *Close Rolls 1231–34*, p. 375.

by a direct exercise of his power. Edmund apparently owed his nomination to Simon Langton, who had been Pope Gregory's mentor throughout the affair. He had moved in the Langton circle, and he was already known at the Roman Curia for he had been selected to preach the Crusade in 1227. It is interesting to consider the sort of man whom the papacy, at the height of its hierocratic power, chose as a suitable instrument of its policy. Edmund was a Schoolman, but the thing that impressed his contemporaries was not his originality as a theologian, so much as the moral inspiration of his lecturing and preaching. It is significant that his best known work was a treatise of ascetical theology. He was by instinct an ascetic and a recluse. The premature and over-rigid discipline imposed on him in childhood by his mother left a permanent mark on his character. There was something Manichean in his fear of the senses and in his attitude to sexual delinquency among his servants. Those who knew him both during his time at Salisbury and as archbishop testified that he found administrative business distasteful and that he could hardly be induced to examine the accounts or to attend to chapter business. He was happiest in his study or quietly ministering to the wants of his parishioners on his remote rectory at Calne, or in retreat among his Cistercian friends. The hagiographers speak of his reluctance to accept the Canterbury appointment which was clearly genuine and prolonged. His qualities were seen at their best in a time of crisis. His scrupulous regard for just dealing and his unquestioned moral superiority enabled him to dominate more ambitious or more self-indulgent men like the Earl Marshal or the king. Fastidiousness should not conceal from us the fact that the source of Edmund's power over his contemporaries was his ceaseless self-maceration. He excelled in a form of heroism which thirteenth-century society admired no less than it did physical prowess. It should not be overlooked that the greatest baronial rebel of the century was found, when his body was retrieved from the battlefield, to be wearing a hair shirt.

Edmund was consecrated archbishop in Canterbury cathedral on Laetare Sunday, 2 April, by the bishop of London, Roger Niger, in the presence of the king and court.[1] He had been called to Canterbury at the height of a national crisis. The facts of Richard the Marshal's rebellion have been fully described and are well known. The point at issue was the method of government adopted by the king since the fall of the Justiciar, Hubert de Burgh. The personal element was no doubt important, but the xenophobia of St. Albans gives a false twist to the picture. Baronial animosity was directed not against foreign birth, but against Peter des Roches and Peter des Rievaux and the system of government that they represented. After the long eclipse of the minority, the royal household had suddenly resumed direction of the state. In place of his baronial advisers, the king elevated domestic bureaucrats. As a preliminary to reorganizing the administration of the royal revenue, all the reins of administration were concentrated in the hands of an obscure household clerk who had been brought to power by a palace revolution. While he ruled the household as Keeper of the Wardrobe and Chamber, Rievaux controlled the Exchequer as Treasurer, and held the key to the writing office as keeper of the Privy Seal. As sheriff of twenty-one counties and keeper of escheats and wardships, he touched the baronial class at its most sensitive point.[2] In perspective, these arrangements appear less sinister than they must have seemed to contemporaries. Baronial opposition to the new form of government found a spokesman in Richard the Marshal, who had had the opportunity of observing Rievaux's activities in the escheated lordships of the Welsh Marches.

Hostilities had broken out in the Marches in August, when

[1] *Chron. Maiora*, iii. 272; cf. Matthew's account below, p. 239. There is a contemporary account of the consecration and those present in the St. Paul's cartulary called the *Liber Pilosus*: M. Gibbs, *Early Charters of St. Paul's Cathedral* (CS 3rd ser. lviii 1939), 141.

[2] I follow the account of Rievaux and his offices given by Tout, *Chapters*, i. 216 ff., and F. M. Powicke, *Henry III and the Lord Edward* (1947), i. 84–122.

the royal army had turned aside to besiege the marshal's castle of Usk. By the time of Edmund's election in October, the breach between the king and the Marshal's party seemed irreparable. A strong lead from the Church was necessary if civil war on a wide scale was to be averted. The best opinion was anxious for conciliation and peace. The chief obstacles to understanding had been boldly pointed out by a friar (according to Matthew Paris, the Dominican theologian Robert Bacon, a close associate of Edmund's) who preached before the court in the summer of 1233.[1] He advised the king to reconsider his counsel. The attitude of Edmund is difficult to disengage from the *ex parte* statements of the St. Albans chronicle. He had not the temperament of an ecclesiastical statesman, and had no liking for affairs.[2] He had a scholar's instinctive distrust of the court milieu, which must have been largely incomprehensible to him. A substantial fragment of a sermon of his is preserved in the British Museum Harleian MS. 325, in which he draws out the allegorical sense of a passage from the third Book of Kings, chapter xxii. Achab, the king of Israel, is debating whether he should go up and recover Ramoth-Galaad from the king of Syria. False prophets urge him on with promises of victory, but he is defeated and killed in battle. By the prophets, Edmund understands false counsellors—'false counsellors, grasping persons, flatterers, the hard of heart, and oppressors of the poor. With such people the court of every prince and great man is filled. Whoever, therefore, wishes to lead a good life, let him depart from court.'[3]

[1] *Chron. Maiora*, iii. 244–5. According to Paris, a wag who was present made a daring pun on the name of Peter des Roches—the rock on whom the ship of state was foundering.

[2] This impression, which emerges from the hagiographers, is strongly borne out in Ralph Bocking's Life of Richard of Chichester: *AA.SS.* Apr. i. 282–318. It appears that the chief function of Edmund's chancellor was to ensure his master a quiet life.

[3] 'Hos ergo tales permittit Dominus decipi a spiritu maligno, cum sit spiritus mendax in ore prophetarum eius, suorum scilicet consiliatorum. Procurat enim diabolus ut prelati prava habeant latera, id est falsos consiliarios, raptores, adulatores, immisericordes, pauperum oppressores. Talibus ergo

The sermon cannot of course be related to any particular context, but it illustrates Edmund's atittude to politics and his distrust of the *curialis*. He can have had little sympathy for a man like Peter des Roches.

The archbishop-elect with his suffragans steadily worked to bring the situation under control. He dispatched intermediaries between the king and the Marshal,[1] one of whom was the Franciscan Provincial, Agnellus of Pisa.[2] Wendover has a dramatic account of the interview between Agnellus and the earl, which took place on the night of 22 December in Margam abbey. At the same time efforts were being made to persuade the king to revise the basis of his council. At the beginning of February the bishops, assembled in a council at Westminster, urged on Henry the dangers of retaining Peter des Rievaux in his existing position. They pointed to the disparagement which the king's authority suffered through Rievaux's indiscriminate use of the Privy Seal.[3] On this occasion, Edmund's powers of conciliation were severely tested by a heated altercation which took place between the king and Alexander Stavensby, bishop of Coventry. Preliminary negotiations had now proceeded far enough to make a truce possible, and the archbishop dispatched Stavensby with Henry Sandford, bishop of Rochester, to the Marches. They met Llewelyn and the Marshal's representatives (the earl had already left for Ireland) at the Shropshire village of Brockton, and a truce was concluded on 6 March.[4] The surveillance of the truce was in the hands of the archbishop, and there was to be a meeting at Shrewsbury on 2 May to formulate terms of peace. The clerks of the earl and Llewelyn returned with the bishops to the king to obtain ratification of the truce.[5] This was not granted until 12 April.[6] This was a

repleta est omnis curia principum et magnatum. Exeat ergo aula qui vult esse pius.' BM Harl. MS. 325, fo. 163ᵛ.

[1] *Annales de Theokesberia, Ann. Mon.* i. 92.
[2] *Flores*, iv. 282; Eccleston says that the labour of the journey in mid-winter proved fatal to Agnellus: *De Adventu Minorum*, ed. A. G. Little (1953), p. 76.
[3] *Chron. Maiora*, iii. 270.   [4] *CPR 1232–47*, p. 43.
[5] Ibid., p. 41.   [6] Ibid., p. 43.

The Canterbury Election and Politics 133

long interval. Was the king waiting for news from Ireland or was he simply waiting for the assembly of the council which had been summoned for Passion Sunday (9 April)?[1] At all events, eight days before the truce was ratified, Richard the marshal was fatally wounded in an obscure battle on the boundaries of Meath and Leinster.

Edmund's consecration strengthened his hands, and at the Easter council he exerted himself to secure the dismissal of Peter des Rievaux and the bishop of Winchester. This time he was apparently successful.[2] On 28 April letters were issued revoking Rievaux's authority,[3] and in the course of the following weeks he was stripped of his offices and summoned to render account at the Exchequer.[4] Peter des Roches returned to his diocese.

With the chief stumbling-block to peace removed, the archbishop could address himself to guarding the truce and preparing the ground for peace negotiations. With this in view, he set off for the Marches, and he was continuously employed there during the spring and summer.[5] His task was no doubt facilitated by the Marshal's death, but that event had one interesting repercussion. Late in April the king set out to join the archbishop at Gloucester. From the 6th until the 13th of May he was at Woodstock.[6] According to Wendover, while he was there he received the news of the Marshal's death. The chronicler pictures him unexpectedly prostrated with grief and causing the clerks of his chapel to sing the Office of the Dead for the earl.[7] Proceeding to Gloucester, he published an amnesty to all who should seek his peace by 29 May. The rebels were brought in under the archbishop's conduct, first Gilbert Marshal

---

[1] The king wrote to the citizens of Dublin to say that he was waiting for the council before deciding what action to take in Ireland: *Close Rolls 1231–34*, p. 395.
[2] *Flores*, iv. 298–9; Dunstable Annals, *Ann. Mon.* iii. 136.
[3] *Close Rolls 1231–34*, p. 412. [4] Ibid., p. 419.
[5] He was in the Marches by 8 May: *Close Rolls 1231–34*, p. 421.
[6] See chancery enrolments.
[7] For this and the following account, see *Flores*, iv. 309 ff.

who was pardoned, then Hubert de Burgh, Gilbert Basset, Siward, and the rest. Then, in the presence of bishops and magnates, Archbishop Edmund produced a letter dispatched by the king to Ireland, inciting the Irish magnates to attack the Marshal and promising them a share in his fiefs. The chronicler describes a heated colloquy, the archbishop accusing the king of treacherously contriving the Marshal's death, and King Henry parrying with the curious excuse that he had no cognizance of what the letters contained, and that Peter des Roches and Rievaux had forced him to affix his seal to it. If there is any truth in the story, the seal referred to must have been the small seal of which Rievaux was the keeper, since the letter in question does not appear on the chancery enrolments and the Chancellor was not involved in the scandal. But no such letter is known to survive, and the whole story is such a curious one as to merit further investigation. It rests on the unsupported testimony of a single chronicler.[1] Modern writers on the period have been disposed to accept it, and, albeit with reservations, to charge the king on that account with insincerity and double dealing.[2] The facts as far as they can be ascertained are as follows.

The Marshal had left Wales for Ireland about 2 February,[3] evidently with the purpose of defending his earldom of Leinster. Whether or not at the king's suggestion, the earl's enemies were taking advantage of his struggle with the king to launch an attack on his estates. The lead was taken by Maurice FitzGerald, the Justiciar of Ireland, and the Lacys. The Lacy honour of Meath marched with the north-western boundary of the Marshal lands, and there were grounds of long-standing hostility between the two families. A meeting

---

[1] It is of course also to be found in narratives which are dependent on the St. Alban's chronicle at this point, e.g. the annals of Oseney: *Ann. Mon.* iv. 78.

[2] G. H. Orpen, *Ireland under the Normans* (1920), iii. 66-71. Sir Maurice Powicke takes the view that the king had been tricked by his advisers and that his excuse, though poor, was probably true: *Henry III and the Lord Edward*, i. 137; *The Thirteenth Century* (1953), pp. 57-59.

[3] *Flores*, iv. 300.

The Canterbury Election and Politics

was arranged between Earl Richard and the Anglo-Irish baronage on the Curragh of Kildare on 1 April with a view to discussing a truce. But fighting broke out and the Marshal was carried off mortally wounded. He died on 16 April and was buried in the Franciscan church which his brother had founded at Kilkenny.

Wendover explains these events as the outcome of the 'bloody writing' which the king's counsellors had, with unheard-of treachery, dispatched to Ireland early in January. He quotes the concluding part of the letter and asserts that the Poitevins had compelled the king to affix his seal to it. The Irish lords, however, required confirmation of the king's promises before they would move. When this had been sent under the Great Seal, the Irish barons invaded the Marshal's estates in order to draw him over to Ireland, where he was lured to his death. There are serious improbabilities in this account as well as some demonstrable inaccuracies.[1] In the first place, it is unthinkable that the Keeper of the Wardrobe could have forced the king to seal a letter against his will. In any case, since the seal was in Rievaux's custody, such a stratagem would have been pointless. Secondly, the authenticity of the letter which Wendover cites[2] cannot be sustained. The final protocol with a valediction and no dating clause is very unusual, though not unknown in royal letters of the period. But the letter cannot in any case be a letter under the royal seal for it refers to the king in the third person throughout. It is equally doubtful whether it could have emanated from the council. The king's domestic counsellors would hardly have ventured to refer to themselves as those 'quorum consilio rex et regnum regitur'. These terms suggest the position that the Poitevins held in popular opinion rather than the position that they held in fact.

Archbishop Edmund's accusation of the king as narrated by

---

[1] Some of these were pointed out by Orpen, op. cit. iii. 62–74. Thus Wendover's assertion that Maurice FitzGerald and the Lacys were treacherous vassals of the Marshal is untrue. They held no lands of the Marshal.
[2] *Flores*, iv. 293.

Wendover also fails to carry conviction. It is possible that instructions were sent to the Irish Justiciar. But even if they were as drastic as the chronicler suggests, this was not of itself a reason for accusing the king of treachery. The archbishop could have no reasonable complaint against such a letter which, if it was sent, must have been dispatched in January, when the Marshal was an outlaw engaged in open war against the king. If the archbishop had a genuine grievance it was that during his negotiations in early March he had been placed in a false position. The instructions to the Irish Justiciar should have been revoked or suspended while truce negotiations were in progress in the Welsh Marches. The lack of adequate documentation makes it difficult to allocate the blame for this. We have no record of the negotiations at Brockton until the king ratified the truce on 12 April, and this was already eleven days after the fatal encounter on the Curragh. Probably the substratum of fact underlying Wendover's highly coloured and partisan account is this: the archbishop complained that the king had not taken proper steps to call off the royalists in Ireland while he was engaged in making a truce in the Marches, and the king, in a panic, threw the blame on to his discredited ministers.

These doubts about the authenticity of Wendover's narrative are strengthened by Matthew Paris's Life of St. Edmund. Here we find the archbishop's mediation described in very different terms.[1] The Marshal is killed in battle as an enemy of the king. The archbishop comes to Woodstock to plead for the earl's brother, Gilbert Marshal, and with tears 'pleaded with the king that the brother should not have to expiate and bear the wrong which his brother had done, and that the fault of the guilty should not recoil upon the innocent'. His prayer is heard, and in the same way he obtains pardon for the other rebels, from which, adds Matthew, all sinners may derive encouragement since they have such a strong and merciful intercessor. We catch here an echo of the words that the king is said to have used about Earl Richard five years later: 'a bloody traitor, a

[1] Below, p. 240.

rebel against me and my realm, whom I caught warring on me in Ireland'.[1] The incident of the letter and Edmund's accusation of treachery does not appear in the Life. It is surely remarkable that Matthew should have discarded an incident of such high dramatic effect. It is no less significant that the incident has been dropped from the *Historia Anglorum*. Perhaps the years, bringing with them recognition and royal patronage, had modified Matthew's political views. When he came to rewrite the history of 1234, Wendover's interpretation was no longer acceptable, and the colloquy between the king and the archbishop at Gloucester appeared for what it was, a product of the passions and prejudices of the moment, working on the material supplied by rumour.

Edmund was in the Marches from May to July, occupied in reconciling the rebels and making peace. Henry Sandford and Alexander Stavensby gave constant assistance. While the case was in doubt, Sandford assumed custody of the Braose lands and castles to which the Marshal had laid claim.[2] Gilbert Marshal's castle of Striguil was held by the archbishop until it, with the rest of the Marshal inheritance, was restored to Gilbert on 22 August.[3] The pardon of the rebels and the revocation on 8 June of the sentence of outlawry marked the triumph of Edmund's pacification.[4]

When the barons had been reconciled, there remained the question of making terms with Llewelyn and pacifying the March. The truce of Brockton had envisaged a meeting at the beginning of May to formulate peace terms, but this had been deferred until the reconciliation of the magnates. On 31 May the king issued powers to Edmund, Sandford, and Stavensby, to proceed with the negotiations, and Llewelyn was warned to be at Shrewsbury on 19 June to meet them.[5] The negotiations were actually conducted at Middle, between Shrewsbury and Ellesmere. A truce was made for two years, establishing

[1] *Chron. Maiora*, iii. 523–4.
[2] *CPR 1232–47*, p. 45.
[3] Ibid., pp. 48, 65.
[4] *Close Rolls 1231–4*, p. 564.
[5] Ibid., pp. 564–5.

the territorial status quo which had existed before the war. This was concluded on 21 June, and ratified by the king on 7 July.[1] It was periodically renewed during the following years and efforts were made to arrange a meeting between Llewelyn and the king which would lead to a definitive peace treaty. The truce of Middle completed the archbishop's labours in the Marches, though it did not end his worries. The surveillance of the truce was in his hands, and it was not long before his judgement was invoked.[2]

An archbishop was rarely called on so quickly to assume such a crucial and difficult role in politics as that which had fallen to Edmund. Within a few months of his election he had by his efforts averted civil war and brought about an important reorganization of the government, thereby earning the gratitude and respect of an important section of the magnates. He had of course the assistance of an exceptionally able and loyal corps of suffragans, but it was the archbishop who had dominated the situation. This early demonstration of strength should not be overlooked when the end of his pontificate is under discussion.

IV

THE *FAMILIA* OF ARCHBISHOP EDMUND

THE archbishop's administration was carried on for the most part by members of his household who staffed his chapel, his chancery, and his courts. Although narrative sources often provide valuable help, a reconstruction of Archbishop Edmund's *familia* must rest upon the lists of witnesses found in his surviving *acta*. In many ways this is unsatisfactory material. Only

[1] CPR 1232–47, p. 59.
[2] On 22 Aug. the king complained to Llewelyn of infringement, with a copy of the letter to the archbishop: *Close Rolls 1231–4*, p. 590.

The Familia of Archbishop Edmund

a small proportion of the archbishop's acts are witnessed, and these are sometimes undated and do not contain the curious and compendious lists which give a pleasingly domestic tone to the documents of an earlier age.[1] While in some cases these defects may be the result of apathy on the part of compilers of cartularies, this is by no means invariably the case. Thus, of the thirteen originals listed below,[2] eight are without witnesses, and five are undated. Only one of the originals has both dating clause and witnesses. If for our purpose the surviving acts are defective in form, they are no less defective in quantity. Even a limited search has revealed that the harvest is lean compared with that of earlier pontificates. This is not surprising since Edmund's pontificate was a short one, punctuated by nine months of absence abroad. Moreover, the presence of the papal legate from 1237 onwards must have somewhat reduced the activity of the archbishop's chancery.[3] But the real explanation for the shortage of *acta* lies in the nature of the material. The only acts of an archbishop which are systematically preserved are those which the recipients held to be of lasting value, and this means that the bulk of the survivors consist of deeds of monastic endowment and confirmations of monastic property. But by the time of Archbishop Edmund the heyday of monastic endowment was over, while the increasing efficiency with which the royal courts protected possession was making archiepiscopal confirmation unnecessary.

A single surviving account roll of Archbishop Edmund's time throws some light on that part of the archbishop's staff which was engaged in the management of his estates. This is a fragment of what was apparently a Receiver's roll and contains accounts for six manors probably for the year 1236–7.[4] The

[1] Cf. for instance the list of names given in an act of Gilbert Foliot, bishop of London, printed by C. R. Cheney in *English Bishops' Chanceries 1100–1250* (1950), p. 6.
[2] App. B, Nos. 3, 8, 15, 17, 22, 23, 24, 27, 39, 56, 65, 66, 67.
[3] See the discussion of Cardinal Otto's chancery by Dorothy Williamson, 'Some Aspects of the Legation of Cardinal Otto', *EHR* lxiv (1949), pp. 145–73.
[4] Lambeth Palace, Court Roll collection, 1193. The bailiff of Harrow

forinsec expenses include allowances of provender to many of the archbishop's clerks as they moved about the estates on their master's business and they reveal the constant itinerary from manor to manor of the archbishop's stewards and auditors.

It would be interesting to know to what extent the archbishop's household contained a nucleus of 'permanent civil servants', unaffected by changes at the top, who transmitted their administrative knowledge from one pontificate to the next. The continuity between Edmund's administration and that of his predecessors was probably greater than the existing evidence suggests. Simon Langton, the archdeacon, was the most conspicuous representative of a former régime. He had been appointed by his brother, Archbishop Stephen, in 1227, and held office until his death in 1248,[1] thus performing his duties under four successive archbishops. By reason of his independent and irremovable status, the archdeacon tended to be of the *familia*, but not in it, and Langton's experience particularly set him apart. Only a rash political escapade had barred him from higher office, and in his declining years he had achieved a unique position of influence and power. He had been in Rome since the death of Richard le Grand, and it was apparently on his advice that the pope had disallowed three previous elections, and nominated Edmund. There is no trace of his activity in the diocese until 1237, when he was party to an agreement between the archbishop and St. Augustine's.[2] Towards the end of that year, he accompanied Edmund to Rome where he helped to conduct the archbishop's litigation.[3]

accounts for 4s. 4d. rent *de incremento secundi anni E. archiepiscopi*, which dates the account after Apr. 1236. On the other hand, the bailiff for Lambeth is credited with the expenses of Master Robert of Stafford, who left the archbishop's service in 1237. A reference on the same account to the archdeacon of Bath who died at Lambeth may refer to Hugh of Wells who died in 1234; see Le Neve, i. 163; *Ann. Mon.* i. 94–95.

[1] On his career see the *DNB* xi. 562–3, and K. Major, 'The *familia* of Archbishop Stephen Langton', *EHR* xlviii (1933), pp. 529–53.

[2] No. 22. Until Aug. 1235 he was employed by the king on a diplomatic mission to France: *CPR 1232–47*, pp. 82, 84, 90.

[3] Gervase, ii. 131–2.

To the Christ Church chronicler, he was the *hostis callidus* who suggested to the pope that some of the chapter's title deeds would not stand up to examination. He threw his weight on to the archbishop's side in his struggle with the monks. Even after Edmund's death, Langton pursued the case against the chapter and forced the people of Canterbury to observe the interdict which had been laid on the cathedral church.[1] In the end the monks seem to have bought off their formidable enemy. In August 1241 the prior and chapter conceded to him personally an important part of the *sede vacante* jurisdiction in the diocese.[2]

Another of Stephen Langton's servants who was employed by Archbishop Edmund was Master Thomas of Freckenham. He was rector of Maidstone, had been Langton's Official,[3] and executor to him and to Archbishop Richard le Grand.[4] Although he attests only one of the archbishop's acts,[5] he was probably a senior adviser from the beginning. He was taken by Edmund on his visit to Rome at the end of 1237 and acted as the archbishop's attorney in the papal courts.[6] This was his last service, for he died at Rome.[7]

From the point of view of continuity, Master Elias of Dereham was a most significant member of Edmund's *familia*. He had been steward to Hubert Walter and Langton. Although he was an active canon of Salisbury from 1222 at the latest, a distinguished architect, and a clerk of the king's works, his association with the administration of the archbishopric was unbroken through four pontificates.[8] He was appointed executor by three archbishops. In his old age, he was no less active

[1] Ibid. 180–2.   [2] BM Cotton MS. Julius D ii, fo. 113.
[3] K. Major, *EHR* xlviii (1933).
[4] *Patent Rolls 1225–32*, pp. 472, 474.   [5] *CChR* i. 238–40.
[6] *Annales Roffenses* in *Anglia Sacra*, i. 349.
[7] Gervase, ii. 131.
[8] The details of his career have been traced by J. C. Russell, 'The Many-sided Career of Master Elias of Dereham', *Speculum*, v (1930), pp. 378–87; A. H. Thompson, 'Elias of Dereham and the king's works', *Archaeological Journal*, xcviii (1941), pp. 1–35; and K. Major, op. cit. All of whom, however, believe that Elias's work for the archbishopric ceased after his preferment to the canonry at Salisbury.

in the service of Archbishop Edmund. In 1236-7, as either steward of estates or surveyor, he is to be found touring the archbishop's Surrey and Kentish manors, auditing the accounts.[1] His attestation of acts in 1234 and 1240[2] suggests that he served throughout Edmund's pontificate. One cannot fail to be impressed by the versatile genius and extraordinary industry of Master Elias. It is much to be regretted that no letter-book of his is known to be extant, for no man could have told us more of the ecclesiastical politics of his age. His connexion with Salisbury during Edmund's Treasurership is specially significant in view of the high place which he held in the council of the three previous archbishops and his close association with Simon Langton, the pope's adviser during the vacancy of 1231-3.

Master Aaron, the parson of Wimbledon, who attests five acts of Archbishop Edmund,[3] provided another link with the past. He is to be identified with Aaron of Kent who served as a clerk to both Langton and Hubert Walter.[4] How many more of Edmund's clerks had served a previous archbishop is a matter of conjecture. A Walter of Somercote attests acts in 1237 and 1240,[5] and he is to be found among the witnesses to a Canterbury charter of Langton's in 1227.[6] Another possibility is William, rector of Bekesbourne, who is probably to be identified with the William of St. Edmund whom Langton admitted to Bekesbourne in 1222.[7] The act of admission describes him as the archbishop's clerk. Beyond these surmises we are left with the conviction that the permanent element in

[1] Lambeth Court Roll Collection, 1193.
[2] *CChR* i. 196-7; *Cartulary of the Priory of St. Gregory, Canterbury*, ed. A. M. Woodcock (CS 3rd ser. lxxxviii 1956), p. 157.
[3] *CChR* i. 196-7; *Cartulary of St. Gregory*, p. 139; Canterbury D. & C. mun. Chartae Antiquae L. 7; Oxford, Merton College record no. 957; PRO E 315/45 (Chart. Misc.), no. 139.
[4] *Acta Stephani Langton*, ed. K. Major (CYS 1950), p. xlviii *et passim*. He was presumably dead by 18 July 1241, when Wimbledon church was vacant: *CPR 1232-47*, p. 255. A fine of 100 marks which he owed the Crown was still recorded on L.T.R. mem. roll for 27 Henry III, m. 17.
[5] *CChR* i. 238-40; Lambeth MS. 1212, fo. 135.
[6] *Acta Stephani Langton*, p. 121.   [7] Ibid., p. 68.

the *familia* must have been greater than the archdeacon and the three elder clerks whose antecedents can be definitely established.

With Edmund's own appointments we are on firmer ground. His first Official of whom we have record is a Master R. of Hereford, who attests a single undated act belonging to the early years of the pontificate,[1] but who remains otherwise obscure. Master Nicholas of Burford, who followed him in office, makes his first appearance as one of the trio who bore the archbishop's pallium from Rome in February 1234.[2] It is uncertain when he was appointed as Official, for he does not attest any dated act earlier than 1237.[3] In two documents of which he himself is the originator, he uses a more specific title of *Official of the Canterbury Province*. The first of these,[4] an institution to the church of Seasalter, bears the earliest extant reference to a seal of the Officiality. The second can be dated between January and August 1238,[5] and this and a Dover deed[6] are the last datable appearances of Nicholas as Official. Apparently in the second half of the year 1238 he was replaced by Master Richard of Langdon. Langdon had been employed as a royal proctor at Rome,[7] and doubtless had legal training. He remained in office until the end of the pontificate.[8] He was very active in the affair of the chapter, and we find him executing mandates and issuing citations, convening a chapter to publish a sentence of excommunication, and licensing penitentiaries. Whatever underlay this reshuffle of personnel, Nicholas of Burford did not retire from the archbishop's household. He attests three acts of 1240.[9]

[1] *Cartulary of St. Gregory*, p. 192. The editor's assignment of the inspeximus to 1234–7 is confirmed by the presence of Master Robert of Stafford among the witnesses.   [2] *CPL* i. 138.
[3] *CChR* i. 238–40.   [4] Canterbury D. & C. mun. Reg. A, fo. 320.
[5] PRO Anc. Corresp. xi. 159.
[6] Dated July 1238: Lambeth MS. 241, fo. 176ᵛ.
[7] *CPR 1232–47*, p. 109.
[8] He was in the *familia* by 1237: *CChR* i. 238–40. He first appears as Official on 4 Jan. 1239: Gervase, ii. 144.
[9] *Cartulary of St. Gregory*, p. 156; ibid., p. 157; Lambeth MS. 1212, fo. 135,

The most interesting, if not the most distinguished, figure in Archbishop Edmund's household was his brother, Robert of Abingdon. The unique position which he held among the *familiares* is reflected in the witness lists of the archbishop's *acta*, where he takes precedence over all save mitred heads. Thus an act appropriating the church of Bekesbourne to St. Gregory's priory, Canterbury, bears the following list of witnesses:

magistro Roberto de Abindon' fratre nostro, tunc rectore ecclesie de Wingeham· magistro Elya de Derham· magistro Ricardo de Wichio, tunc cancellario nostro· magistro Nicholao de Bureford. magistro Reginaldo de Lond'. magistro Rogero de Leycestria. magistro Johanne de Wichio. Eustachio monacho· Jordano clerico, et multis aliis.[1]

Robert appears to have held no specific office in the administration. Consanguinity with the archbishop alone gave him precedence over all ranks in the household. When he wrote to the cardinal legate on diocesan business, the only title he used was *germanus domini archiepiscopi*.[2] Because he attracted the attention of the hagiographers, he is better known to us than most of his colleagues. He was only a year or two younger than the archbishop, for, as boys, they were sent off to Paris together to take the Arts course. It nowhere appears that he proceeded to a higher faculty. He was in England in 1214,[3] and he evidently played an active part in the political troubles of 1216–17 which won him the approval of the legate Guala, and for this was rewarded with a licence to hold an additional benefice in plurality.[4] He was rector of Bocking in 1225,[5] but

printed from another copy in *The Register of St. Augustine's Abbey*, ed. G. J. Turner and H. E. Salter (1924), p. 538, which, however, omits the names of Nicholas and one other witness.

[1] *Cartulary of St. Gregory*, p. 218.
[2] PRO Anc. Corresp. xi. 159.
[3] He was involved that year in litigation over land in Isleworth: *Curia Regis Rolls 1213–15*, pp. 236–7.
[4] *CPL* i. 76. On 25 Apr. 1217 he was granted letters of safe conduct anywhere in the king's power: *Patent Rolls 1216–25*, p. 60.
[5] *Acta Stephani Langton*, p. 93.

The Familia of Archbishop Edmund

he had relinquished this benefice by November 1232,[1] probably on being presented to the more important rectory of Wingham.[2] Both these churches were in the archbishop's patronage, Wingham being usually reserved for those holding an important place in the archbishop's administration. A letter from the Franciscan Adam Marsh shows that Robert was also holding the rectory of Risborough at the time of his death.[3] This occurred in 1243 or 1244.[4]

It was no uncommon thing for a thirteenth-century bishop to use his position to help his relatives, and in the case of Canterbury, at least, the use which Stephen Langton made of his brother provided Edmund with an obvious precedent for associating his brother with the government of his diocese. Robert of Abingdon attests four of the archbishop's acts.[5] During Edmund's absence abroad in the first half of the year 1238 he enjoyed the powers of a later vicar-general. He exercised the archbishop's ecclesiastical patronage,[6] and shared with the Official the power of visiting the non-exempt religious houses of the diocese.[7] After his brother's death Robert disappears into obscurity. At the end of 1240 he was the object of royal proceedings in the legate's court,[8] but how he fared it is impossible to say. 'The Lord raised him up', writes Matthew Paris, 'and gave him a rich reward, brilliantly endowed as he

---

[1] *CPR 1232–47*, p. 2.

[2] As rector of Wingham he makes an institution in 1237–8: Canterbury D. & C. mun. Reg. A, fo. 320, and attests three acts in 1240.

[3] *Monumenta Franciscana*, ed. J. S. Brewer (RS 1858), p. 247.

[4] Wingham was vacant by 27 Sept. 1243: *CPR 1232–47*, p. 396. Matthew Paris reports miracles at his tomb in the annal for 1244: *Chron. Maiora*, iv. 378. See the details of his career collected by J. C. Russell, *Dictionary of Writers of Thirteenth Century England* (*BIHR* suppl. 3, 1936), pp. 128–9.

[5] *CChR* i. 238–40; *Cartulary of St. Gregory*, p. 156; ibid., p. 157; *Register of St. Augustine's*, p. 538. He also appears beside the archbishop as witness to a grant made by Earl Humphrey de Bohun: C. E. Woodruff, 'Some Early Documents relating to the Priory of Bilsington', in *Arch. Cant.* xli (1929), p. 21. From Lambeth Court Roll 1193, it appears that his herd of swine were maintained at the archbishop's expense on the manor of Northfleet.

[6] Canterbury D. & C. mun. Reg. A, fo. 320.

[7] PRO Anc. Corresp. xi. 159.   [8] *CPR 1232–47*, p. 241.

was with gifts of sanctity, liberality, urbanity, and profound learning.'[1] When due allowance has been made for the language of the encomiast, it is still evident that Robert was not dependent solely on the family connexion for his advancement in the Church.

The organization of the archbishop's chancery in the thirteenth century is obscure. It has not yet proved possible to construct a continuous list of archiepiscopal chancellors for the first half of the century, and even where the existence of the man is undoubted, the precise nature of his functions remains uncertain.[2] In the later middle ages the legal aspect of his office was more pronounced and his secretarial functions were increasingly allocated to a registrar. In the early thirteenth century, however, differentiation had hardly begun, and the archiepiscopal chancellor seems to have been both head of the secretariat and judge.[3] Edmund's chancellor, Richard de Wich, can be seen acting in both capacities. He was the most distinguished member of the *familia*, the future bishop of Chichester who, like his master, was to find a place in the calendar of the Church. He had been regent in Arts at Oxford and, according to his Dominican biographer, had gone on to the canon law.[4] If there is any substance in the hagiographer's statement that the archbishop and Grosseteste contended for Master Richard's services,[5] he cannot have entered the *familia* until some time after the spring of 1235, and archbishop Edmund had another chancellor. We do not know the name of anyone holding the office between Richard de Wich and the obscure Master Reginald, archdeacon of Middlesex, who attests acts of 1231

[1] *Vita*, below, p. 222.
[2] See the evidence presented by C. R. Cheney, *English Bishops' Chanceries 1100–1250* (1950), pp. 22–43.
[3] Perhaps he was primarily the custodian of the seals, cf. Fleta's definition of the royal chancellor: 'Officium vero Cancellarii est sigillum Regis custodire, simul cum conrotulis suis de proficuo regni': *Commentarius Juris Anglicani* (1647), ii, c. 29.
[4] *AA.SS*. Apr. i. 286–7. See the account of J. C. Russell, *Dictionary of Writers*, whose references, however, require revision.
[5] *AA.SS*. Apr. i. 278. His earliest attestation is in 1237: *CChR* i. 238–40.

as chancellor of Richard le Grand,[1] but there is an unfortunate scarcity of dated *acta* for the first years of the pontificate.

Richard de Wich attests six[2] of the nine acts of St. Edmund which contain witness lists. He appears to have been the member of the council most constantly at the archbishop's side. He accompanied him abroad in 1237, and again in 1240. In an interesting passage of the Life, Matthew Paris describes the breaking of the archbishop's seal after his death and the dispersal of the *familia*. This account suggests that the chancellor personally supervised the imposition of the archbishop's seal and that letters were only issued from the writing office with his authorization:

> On the day after his death, he who discharged the chancellor's office sealed the letters we have mentioned and, on the following morning, handed them to those to whom the saint had granted them, to be delivered to his friends. . . . The seal was then broken, as is the custom, in the presence of all who had been summoned, because of the danger of fraudulent counterfeit . . . .[3]

However, the archbishop may have taken only a skeleton staff abroad, and the occasion was too unusual to form a safe basis for generalization.

The chancellor, Official, and a few senior clerks like Thomas of Freckenham, Elias of Dereham, and Robert of Abingdon, occupied a privileged position in the *familia* by reason of their closeness to the archbishop. It was this group which formed the nucleus of the ill defined body which was increasingly referred to as the archbishop's council.[4] They surrounded their master

[1] PRO Anc. Deeds B 8723; Register of Archbishop Warham, fos. 99ᵛ-100.

[2] *CChR* i. 238-40; Oxford, Merton College record no. 957; *Cartulary of St. Gregory*, p. 156; ibid., p. 157; Lambeth MS. 1212, fo. 135; PRO E 315/45 (Chart. Misc.), no. 139.

[3] Below, p. 272.

[4] In their letter to the legate, Robert of Abingdon and Nicholas of Burford refer to a monk of Christ Church who had confessed to forgery *coram consiliariis domini archiepiscopi*: PRO Anc. Corresp. xi. 159. In Lambeth Palace MS. 1212, fo. 112, there is an interesting account of Archbishop Boniface's deliberation with his council behind locked doors at his manor house of Wingham, when he was appointing a new prior of Christ Church.

with a net of watchfulness which only the greatest of the land could penetrate.[1] To this group belonged also the stewards of the archbishop's estates, Simon of Seinliz and Brother Walter of Ferriby, and his chaplain, Eustace of Faversham. Simon of Seinliz had been steward to Bishop Ralph Nevill of Chichester before he passed into the archbishop's service.[2] He was already Edmund's steward by April 1235.[3] He appears frequently on the Receiver's roll, often in the company of Elias of Dereham, with whom he toured the archiepiscopal manors, auditing accounts.[4] Although Simon of Seinliz and Walter of Ferriby are the only stewards who appear in the records *eo nomine*, it is probable that Edmund had a third estates steward in Reginald the abbot of Bayham, who attests acts relating to the temporalities. It is to be observed that later in the century Pecham employed three stewards of the estates, one of whom also was a Premonstratensian abbot.[5]

Eustace of Faversham, the archbishop's chaplain, appears to be the only member of the monastic chapter who was taken into Edmund's service. He attests an act of the archbishop's only once.[6] The evidence of his constant presence at the archbishop's side comes from his own account of himself in the *Quadrilogus* and from the invidious references of the Canterbury chronicler. He was, it seems, *camerarius* of Christ Church,[7] though he can hardly have carried out the duties of an obedientiary while he followed the archbishop's court. His earliest appearance in the records is in 1237, when the monks observed that he had gone with the archbishop to Rome without having

[1] Ralph Bocking says that the chancellor's chief merit lay in providing a quiet life for Archbishop Edmund: *AA.SS.* Apr. i. 287.
[2] An interesting series of letters addressed by Simon to Bishop Ralph were published by W. H. Blaauw in *Sussex Archaeological Collections*, iii (1850), pp. 35–76. He was in the bishop's service at least as late as 21 June 1232: *Close Rolls 1231–4*, p. 77.
[3] *Close Rolls 1234–7*, p. 84.
[4] Lambeth Court Roll collection, no. 1193.
[5] D. Douie, *Archbishop Pecham* (1952), p. 58.
[6] *Cartulary of St. Gregory*, p. 157.
[7] Gervase, ii. 146.

sought the leave of his monastery.[1] When the chapter summoned him from Teynham to take part in the election of a new prior, the archbishop excused him on the ground that he had no other chaplain.[2] It is obvious that the rebellion of the chapter involved him in a distressing conflict of loyalties, and his abortive nomination to the priorate of Dover in March 1240[3] may represent an attempt on the archbishop's part to extricate him from an intolerable position. Edmund made a final effort to protect him against reprisals with a letter, given at Soisy three days before his death.[4]

The archbishop could delegate his jurisdiction, but not his order. Acts which required bishop's orders, such as ordinations, confirmations, or the consecration of chrism, would demand the services of an auxiliary bishop.[5] It is probable that these duties were performed in Edmund's absence by John, formerly bishop of Ardfert, but since 1224 bishop *in universali ecclesia*. A Benedictine, he had been removed from his see by papal mandate owing to the irregularity of his election.[6] His habitual residence was St. Albans, where, as a venerable and respected figure, he ended his days.[7] He had already acted as suffragan in the Canterbury diocese under Langton.[8] He appears in St. Edmund's service in 1238 and 1240,[9] both years in the course of which the archbishop made journeys abroad.

It is well known that an archbishop's household offered a ladder as well as a schooling to men of talent. The point is well illustrated by the history of three of St. Edmund's clerks who, although they never attained episcopal rank, had subsequent careers of distinction. These three men, Robert of Stafford, Geoffrey of Ferring, and John of Offington, were all

[1] Ibid., p. 131. [2] Ibid., p. 145.
[3] Canterbury D. & C. mun. Chartae Antiquae D. 76.
[4] Sens cathedral charter no. 3.
[5] In the early thirteenth century Irish bishops were frequently used as suffragans in English dioceses, see A. H. Thompson, *The English Clergy in the later Middle Ages* (1947), pp. 48–50.
[6] *CPL* i. 68, 98, 100.   [7] *Chron. Maiora*, iii. 394; iv. 324, 501; v. 2.
[8] *Acta Stephani Langton*, xx, n. 6.
[9] Gervase, ii. 139; *Register of St. Augustine's*, p. 538.

university masters. They were apparently already members of the *familia* in 1234, for the compiler of the *Liber Pilosus* of St. Paul's singled them out for notice among the throng of clergy present at the archbishop's consecration.[1] Master Robert of Stafford attests four acts dating from the earlier years of the pontificate,[2] and he presumably left Edmund's service in 1237 when he was appointed archdeacon of Stafford.[3] Master Geoffrey of Ferring passed from the archbishop's service into that of William Ralegh, bishop of Winchester, whose Official he became.[4] It was, no doubt, the association with Ralegh which brought him into the orbit of the royal court. In 1246 the king entered into a bond to provide him with a benefice to the value of fifty or sixty marks, and empowered the provost of Beverley and the chancellor of St. Paul's to make such provision for him.[5] The record of his benefices, though incomplete, suggests the picture of a pluralist on a fair scale.[6] He finished up as dean of St. Paul's,[7] and apparently died in 1268.[8] Master John of Offington, the third of this group of

[1] *Early Charters of St. Paul's Cathedral*, ed. M. Gibbs (CS 3rd ser. lviii 1939), p. 142.

[2] *CChR* i. 196-7; ibid. i. 238-40; Canterbury D. & C. mun. Chartae Antiquae L. 7; *Cartulary of St. Gregory*, p. 139.

[3] *CPL* i. 167. His early career is obscure apart from his institution to the church of Bradeley in 1221-3 on the presentation of the Lady Milicent de Stafford: *Magnum Registrum of Lichfield Cathedral*, ed. H. E. Savage (WM. Salt Arch. Soc. 1924), p. 15.

[4] *CPL* i. 221; he first appears in that capacity on 16 May 1245: *Cartulary of Winchester Cathedral*, ed. A. W. Goodman (1927), p. 395. As such he attests acts of William Ralegh in 1249 and 1250: ibid., p. 212a; BM Cott. MS. Nero C iii, fo. 218.

[5] *CPR 1232-47*, p. 484.

[6] He was admitted to the rectory of Denham on 3 Sept. 1236: *Rotuli Roberti Grosseteste*, ed. F. N. Davis (CYS 1913), pp. 341, 343. He held a portion of the church of Elham for life: Merton College record no. 957. He was authorized in 1245 to hold three benefices with cure of souls: *CPL* i. 221. In additon to his prebends in Beverley and St. Paul's, he was precentor of Chichester not later than 1256: *Chartulary of the High Church of Chichester*, ed. W. D. Peckham (Sussex Rec. Soc. xlvi 1946), p. 261.   [7] *CPL* i. 392.

[8] C. N. L. Brooke, 'The deans of St. Paul's, *c.* 1090-1499', *BIHR* xxix (1956), p.239.

The Familia of Archbishop Edmund

distinguished *magistri*, was evidently a trained lawyer, since he had been commissary to the chancellor of Oxford before entering the archbishop's service.[1] He attests three of St. Edmund's acts, but does not appear later than 1237–8. He had been canon of Wells since 1236 at latest, and after Edmund's death he passed into the *familia* of Bishop Grosseteste.[2] A papal dispensation from the impediment of illegitimacy, obtained in 1247, indicates that he was marked out for a bishopric,[3] but he died in 1251[4] without having reached the purple.

It is interesting to observe the ease with which the *magistri* passed from the service of one diocese to that of another. Ecclesiastical administration must have been for them a profession as the Home Civil is to modern men, only the prizes might be higher. Besides the three mentioned, Master John de Wich and Master Roger of Burwardiscote both found similar employment elsewhere after the archbishop's death. John de Wich was a lawyer and he acted as the archbishop's proctor at Rome in the case against the chapter.[5] He was one of the archbishop's executors.[6] Later, as canon of South Malling, he appears in the *familia* of Bishop Richard of Chichester.[7] Roger of Burwardiscote who appears in the household in 1240, had by August 1242 joined the service of Grosseteste.

The bishop of a secular cathedral could draw on the learning and administrative experience of his canons to help him in running the diocese, but a bishop with a monastic chapter was less favourably placed. As far as can be ascertained, St. Edmund's chaplain was the only monk in his service.[8] The support of a

---
[1] *The Cartulary of Oseney Abbey*, ed. H. E. Salter, i. 137.
[2] See his career traced by Miss Major in *Robert Grosseteste, Scholar and Bishop*, ed. D. Callus (1955), p. 232.
[3] *CPL* i. 238.   [4] *Chron. Maiora*, v. 230.
[5] Gervase, ii. 183–4; he attests two acts in 1240: *Cartulary of St. Gregory*, pp. 156, 157.   [6] *Close Rolls 1237–42*, p. 280.
[7] *Chartulary of the High Church of Chichester*, pp. 286, 839, 860. It is possible that he was related to Richard de Wich.
[8] The profession of Brother Walter of Ferriby, steward of the estates, remains an enigma. It is quite possible that he was an officer of one of the archbishop's hospitals.

substantial *familia* must obviously have been a serious problem. The Official was normally a stipendiary, but to maintain the rest, the archbishop resorted to the same methods as were used by the king and the pope. He provided them with benefices. The exempt parishes, which were in his patronage, offered one valuable source of remuneration. Thus Robert of Abingdon was collated to Bocking by Stephen Langton, and to Wingham, probably by his brother. Elias of Dereham was rector of Harrow[1] as well as canon of Salisbury. Another of Edmund's clerks, Master Richard, was rector of Hollingbourne.[2] Aaron of Kent was collated by Edmund or his predecessor to Wimbledon, and one of the archbishop's acts shows him providing for Master Geoffrey of Ferring out of the revenue of the church of Elham.[3] It is probable that most of his clerks were maintained in the same way, although the livings which they held cannot be traced. Master Robert of Stafford, for instance, was already holding two benefices with cure of souls when he was appointed archdeacon of Stafford in 1237,[4] and in 1240 Edmund received a papal faculty to license five of his clerks to hold an additional benefice each, with cure of souls.[5] Whatever personal scruples St. Edmund may have had on the subject of plurality and non-residence,[6] they evidently failed to withstand the hard pressure of administrative necessity. It was no doubt this problem of providing for his staff which underlay his attempt to revive the plans of his predecessors for the endowment of a new collegiate church in the diocese.

A bishop had one reservoir of cheap yet highly skilled labour in the friars, provided that he was in a position to tap it. Their superior intellectual and spiritual equipment made the Mendicants valuable auxiliaries in diocesan work, and Grosseteste continually pressed the Dominican provincial chapter to send

[1] *Close Rolls 1237–42*, p. 420.
[2] *CChR* i. 238–40; PRO E 315/45 (Chart. Misc.), no. 139.
[3] Oxford, Merton College record no. 957.
[4] *CPL* i. 167.
[5] Ibid. i. 189.
[6] See the statements of Eustace, below, p. 198.

The Familia of Archbishop Edmund

him friars to help in the diocese.[1] Although no friars appear among the witnesses of St. Edmund's acts, it is clear from other sources that they were frequently to be found in his household. Trivet remarks that the archbishop constantly had friars in his retinue, one of whom the chronicler had met as a young man.[2] Edmund's association with the Dominicans dated from his teaching days at Oxford. It was the Dominican theologian, Robert Bacon, and the prior of Oxford, Richard of Dunstable, who supplied the university with information when they were pressing for the archbishop's canonization.[3] It is uncertain, however, whether either of these men served Edmund as archbishop.[4] Edmund made use of the friars when he was working for peace in 1234. How far he used them for more routine tasks it is impossible to say. Matthew Paris refers in the *Vita* to friars who dined at Edmund's table and remarks that, as archbishop, he liked to determine theological disputations held between them.[5] It is not clear, however, whether these disputations were held in the priory or in the archbishop's household.

It will perhaps be useful to have a list of the archbishop's *familiares*, defective though it necessarily is, with a record of acts attested by them.[6]

Chancellor

Richard de Wich, Master, 24, 35, 39, 58, 59, 62, 65.

Officials

R. de Hereford, Master, 28.

---

[1] *Epistolae*, pp. 61, 304; cited by W. A. Hinnebusch, *The Early English Friars Preachers* (Rome, 1951), pp. 448–51.

[2] *Nicholai Triveti Annales*, ed. T. Hog (1845), p. 228.

[3] Below, p. 292.

[4] Richard of Dunstable states in his deposition that he had been associated with St. Edmund for ten years, but this was *priusquam intrarem in Ordinem*: below, p. 187. There is some evidence that Bacon's association with Edmund continued after he had become archbishop in *CLR 1240–5*, p. 71.

[5] Below, p. 243. Matthew uses the expression *questio collata*, an informal type of debate held amongst students for practice.

[6] The numbers refer to the list in App. B, pp. 303–14. Bracketed numbers refer to attestation without title.

The Familia of Archbishop Edmund

Nicholas de Burford, Master, 24, 27, 31, 39, (58, 59, 62).
Richard de Langdon, Master, (24), 47, 49, 55.

Chaplains

Eustace, the monk, 56, 63.

Clerks

Aaron, parson of Wimbeldon, Master, 6, 27, 28, 39, 65.
Elyas de Dereham, Master, 6, 59.
Geoffrey de Ferring, Master, 58, 65, (named 39).
Geoffrey de Stapelhurst, 28.
Henry de Bech', 65.
Henry de Bissopstone, Master, (named 35).
Henry Luvel.[1]
Henry de Wells, 24, 59.
John de Offinton, Master, 6, 27, 39.
John de Wich, Master, 58, 59.
Jordan, the clerk, 58, 59, (named 54).
Peter de Carsing.[1]
Richard, rector of Hollingbourne, 24, 65.
Robert de Abingdon, Master, 24, 58, 59, 62, (named 47).
Robert de Dorking, 24, 39, 65.
Robert de Stafford, Master, 6, 24, 27, 28.
Roger de Burwardiscote, Master, 58.
Roger de Leicester, Master, 39, 58, 59, 65.
Thomas de Frekenham, Master, 24.
Walter de Somercote, 24, 62.
William, rector of Bekesbourne, 24.
William de Burne.[1]

Stewards

Simon de Seinliz.
Brother Walter de Ferriby.
? Reginald, abbot of Bayham, 6, 39, 62.

Treasurer

Robert de Bath.[2]

Almoner

John.[2]

[1] Lambeth Palace MS. 1212, fo. 86.
[2] Lambeth Palace Court Roll 1193.

The Familia of Archbishop Edmund

Chamberlains
Robert, the priest.[1]
Stephen, the subdeacon.[1]
Gilbert.[2]

Knights
Henry de Wintreselle, 58.[3]
William Talbot, 58.[3]

V

ARCHBISHOP EDMUND

LIKE that of the king, the life of a thirteenth-century archbishop was a perpetual eyre. The coronation of the queen, a legatine council, or more humdrum business of state took him to London. Less frequently, ecclesiastical business took him to his own cathedral city, where he stayed on the sufferance of the most touchy and cantankerous chapter in England. Neither place was his normal habitat. As a rule, he resided on the archiepiscopal manors, passing from one to another of his Kentish and Sussex manor houses. Archbishop Edmund's movements can be accounted for with certainty on only 105 days out of approximately six years which he spent in England. Of these 105 days, 17 were spent at Canterbury, 26 at London,[4] 39

---

[1] See the *Quadrilogus*, pp. 189, 191.
[2] In Lambeth Court Roll 1193 Gilbert *de camera* receives wages on the Wimbledon account. It is possible that he was domiciled on that manor.
[3] Both men witness Humphrey de Bohun's grant of Bilsington: C. E. Woodruff, 'Some Early Documents relating to the Priory of Bilsington', *Arch. Cant.* xli (1929), p. 21.

Record has been found of the following bailiffs of Archbishop Edmund: Peter (South Malling), Peter Bacun (Wingham), Richard de Fairford (Croydon, Harrow, Lambeth and Southwark, Wimbledon), William Bullok (Bexley, Northfleet).

[4] Residence at Lambeth manor is included in this figure.

on the archiepiscopal manors,[1] and 23 elsewhere. The most favoured places of residence appear to have been the Kentish manors of Wingham and Aldington and the Sussex manor of South Malling. When due allowance has been made for the fragmentary and haphazard character of the data, the figures serve to illustrate the general pattern of the archbishop's existence.

The itinerary which can be worked out from St. Edmund's surviving *acta* is too patchy to show whether he exercised the ancient right of metropolitan visitation, or even whether he visited his own diocese. Luckily there is other evidence. In November 1239 Robert Grosseteste wrote a letter to Simon of Arderne, his proctor at Rome.[2] Invoking both Ordinary and Apostolic authority,[3] he had set out to visit his chapter and the prebendal churches of the canons. Resistance had been carefully co-ordinated and successful, and the bishop had had to suspend the dean, precentor, and subdean. The rebels were now offering to treat. There follows a page of anxious heart-searching. Should he force them with excommunication, a dangerous course which might lead to a public outcry, 'for it had not been customary for an English bishop to attempt anything of this sort'? Would it not be better to refer the dispute to an independent judge? An independent judgement could not fail to be in favour of the bishop's visitatorial rights and it would have the excellent result of strengthening the hands of other bishops. Also it would stir up the negligent to undertake visitations. But how was a suitable judge to be found? It would require a brave man to incur the wrath of every cathedral chapter in England. Few bishops, even, would wish to pronounce unreservedly in favour of visitation, for they hate having their own churches visited by the archbishop, and the action over visitation between the archbishop of Canterbury and the bishop of London is still pending.

[1] Viz. Wingham 12, Aldington 10, South Malling 8, Teynham 4, Slindon 2, Lyminge 1, Maidstone 1, Croydon 1.
[2] *Epistolae*, ed. H. R. Luard (RS 1861), pp. 253–60.
[3] Probably the legatine statutes of Cardinal Otto were intended.

Archbishop Edmund

In his dilemma Grosseteste reveals how far the English clergy of his time were from regarding regular and systematic visitation as a normal state of affairs. He seems, however, to hint that metropolitan visitation was an evil with which his fellow bishops were not unfamiliar. Hubert Walter, certainly, had visited his province,[1] but Langton seems to have been negligent in the matter.[2] Presumably therefore it was the visitatorial activity of Archbishop Edmund that Grosseteste had in mind. The dispute which he mentions between the archbishop and Bishop Roger Niger occurred in 1239 over St. Edmund's claim to visit religious houses in the London diocese.[3] But earlier than this there is clear evidence that Edmund attempted a provincial visitation; on 8 May 1237 the pope sent him a rescript[4] empowering him to use ecclesiastical sanctions against certain prelates and religious who had impeded him when he was visiting his province. There is a gap in the history of the archbishop's movements between 11 July 1236, when he was negotiating with Llewelyn at Tewkesbury,[5] and 20 January 1237, when he was in London, but two letters, chance survivors copied on to the fly-leaf of a manuscript now in Clare College, show that he proposed to visit the cathedral priory of Worcester in the middle of July 1236.[6] He evidently took advantage of his engagement in the Marches to visit the western parts of his province during this period.

In an age of ecclesiastical reform and legal definition a conscientious bishop might be hard put to it to reconcile his spiritual obedience with what he owed to the secular power.

---

[1] C. R. Cheney, *From Becket to Langton* (1956), pp. 140–1.

[2] *CPL* i. 86, cited C. R. Cheney, *Episcopal Visitation of Monasteries in the Thirteenth Century* (1931), p. 32, who also summarizes the legislation on the subject.

[3] *Ann. Mon.* iii. 151.

[4] Auvray, 3646.

[5] *CPR 1232–47*, p. 153.

[6] Clare College, Cambridge, MS. Kk.5.6, fo. 1ᵛ. In one letter Bishop William of Blois asks Edmund to cancel his proposed visit on Tuesday, the feast of St. Mary Magdalen, on the ground that the priory had not been visited by the archbishop's two predecessors.

During the crisis of 1234, Archbishop Edmund had shown himself a fearless critic of government in the Langton tradition. He had a receptive pupil in Henry III who could hardly forget that he owed his throne to the clergy. The archbishop doubtless felt that some sacrifices were worth making in order to preserve the fund of confidence and good will created in the early months. But rigid-minded churchmen with high sacerdotal views, like Grosseteste, were scandalized at the lengths to which he was prepared to go. It is clear that he did not feel justified in making a major issue over the employment of heads of religious houses as royal justices.[1] Possibly his friendship with William Ralegh, one of the outstanding judges of his generation, convinced him that the arrangement was not without advantage to both Church and State. But to Grosseteste all such accommodations were treason against divine law.

A direct conflict of legal principles was a more severe test of the archbishop's eirenic powers. Just such a conflict arose over the different treatment of bastardy in the ecclesiastical and secular courts. Since the time of Alexander III, the canon law had held that a child born out of wedlock was legitimized by the subsequent marriage of its parents.[2] The royal courts, however, refused to admit this doctrine: a child born out of wedlock, even though he had been subsequently covered by the marriage mantle, could not claim an inheritance against the children born after marriage. Questions of bastardy belonged to the matrimonial jurisdiction of the Church and were normally referred to the bishop. But in a case of *legitimatio per subsequens* difficulty arose, since the ecclesiastical court was

[1] Grosseteste wrote twice to St. Edmund on this subject. From the second letter it appears that the archbishop had advised procrastination until the bishops met in a forthcoming council which he proposed to hold: *Epistolae*, pp. 105–8, 108–13. In 1239, however, Grosseteste wrote to the legate on the same matter, and said that he had twice sought the archbishop's help, but had achieved nothing: ibid., pp. 262–4.

[2] c. 6, X. iv. 17. *Tanta est vis*, addressed to the bishop of Exeter. See the classical discussion of the question in F. W. Maitland, *Canon Law in the Church of England* (1898), pp. 53–55; F. Makower, *The Constitutional History of the Church of England* (1895), pp. 420–3; Powicke, *Henry III*, pp. 150–2.

Archbishop Edmund

bound to reach a decision inadmissible in common law. Consequently, in the thirteenth century the royal courts began to abandon their practice of sending such pleas to the bishop, and questions as to the fact of a man's birth before or after the marriage of his parents were referred instead to a lay jury.[1] Such an arrangement was doubly objectionable to zealous churchmen. It deprived the ecclesiastical courts of a sector of their jurisdiction, and it produced a result which was in flat contradiction to the law of the Church. It appears that soon after St. Edmund became archbishop, a move was made to recover this class of pleas for the Church. Bracton records that at a council held on 12 October 1234 the king conceded to the archbishop and bishops that when a suitor pleaded exception of bastardy, it should be referred to the bishop, who would inquire whether the person concerned was born before or after the marriage of his parents.[2] But this concession made the situation more difficult for a scrupulous bishop: he was required to provide information for purposes which he considered unlawful. Grosseteste was cited before the royal courts for refusing to

---

[1] In 1200 Archbishop Hubert Walter submitted the facts of such a case to the justices when required: *Curia Regis Rolls*, i. 335. But in 1224 and 1226 such cases were being referred to a jury: ibid. xii. 2000; *Bracton's Notebook*, ed. F. W. Maitland (1887), ii. 184.

[2] *Bracton's Notebook*, iii. 134–6. In the printed edition this entry follows Bracton's account of the discussions at the council of Merton in 1236, and begins with the words 'Postea vero die Jovis proxima post festum S. Dionisii', &c. But it is obvious that the concession was not made after Merton, for at the council the fact that just such inquiries were being addressed to them was a ground of complaint by the bishops. The record of the council of Merton is an insertion in the text, and the note of the king's concession belongs with the other concessions mentioned earlier and dated on the octave of St. Michael, 18 Henry III. The king refers back to this concession when writing to the archbishop of Dublin and the Irish Justiciar in May 1236. He says that the archbishop and bishops discussed the question with him *anno praeterito*, and asked that the inquiry on such matters should be left to the court christian, but that subsequently they objected to the form of the writ, which required them to state whether a person was born before or after the marriage of his parents: *Close Rolls 1234–7*, p. 354. Cf. also the citation of Grosseteste, dated 21 Oct. 1235, which refers to this concession and the form of writ agreed: ibid., pp. 201–2.

answer these questions, and he reproached St. Edmund for having consented to such a formula.[1]

It is clear from the correspondence that, rightly or wrongly, Grosseteste believed that the archbishop had sold the pass, that he had fallen into the last infirmity of the official mind, that of placing administrative order before questions of principle. The formula of 1234 may have represented in Edmund's view a diplomatic success in that it had restored the jurisdiction of the Church over all questions of legitimacy, but it had left the fundamental issue untouched. Under pressure from Grosseteste, the archbishops and bishops raised the matter again in 1236 at the council of Merton and sought to have the common law brought into line with canon law on this point. To this request the magnates gave the famous reply 'quod nolunt leges Angliae mutare quae usitatae sunt et approbatae'.[2] This refusal to interfere with the established law of succession created an impasse. The account of the situation which the king sent to Ireland shows that, while the courts had not yet decided on the best way of dealing with bastardy pleas of this type, they had ceased to refer them to the ecclesiastical judge.[3] Eventually, they resorted to a jury, as they had done before 1234.

Conflict between the competing jurisdictions of ecclesiastical and royal courts was not new in the thirteenth century. Between the acknowledged sphere of each lay an area of disputed ground, 'that debatable land which is neither very spiritual nor very temporal' to which belonged so many actions relating to ecclesiastical benefices. As is well known, actions in which the Crown claimed an interest could be stayed in the ecclesiastical

[1] *Epistolae*, pp. 101–5; *Close Rolls 1234–7*, pp. 201–2. Grosseteste also wrote a long letter to William Ralegh, proving that *legitimatio per subsequens* was postulated by divine and natural law. He appears to have received a somewhat barbed reply: *Epistolae*, pp. 76–97.

[2] *Statutes of the Realm*, i. 4. On the sources of this version, which is a composite text, see F. M. Powicke, 'Note on the Recording of Statutes and the Text of the Statute of Merton', *Henry III and the Lord Edward*, app. D, pp. 769–71.

[3] *Close Rolls 1234–7*, p. 354.

court by a writ of prohibition. But a writ of prohibition was not normally issued unless it was sought by the defendant in the court christian who had some reason, perhaps a disreputable reason, for preferring royal justice.[1] The increasing resort to writs of prohibition, especially by clerical litigants had come to constitute a mounting threat to ecclesiastical jurisdiction, and in the time of St. Edmund gave rise to the first organized protest against the encroachments of the royal courts. Under the year 1237, the Burton annalist records a list of clerical grievances which, he states, the archbishop and clergy asked the cardinal legate to take up with the king.[2] Prominent among these are complaints that benefit of clergy is being disregarded in personal actions, and that writs of prohibition are being used to stop actions in the court christian concerning tithes, advowsons, and the appropriation of chapels to parish churches. One of the items demands the renewal of canonical penalties against clerks who improperly seek writs of prohibition. A similar, if not identical, list of complaints was laid before the king in 1240 in the legate's presence,[3] and again in 1253.[4] It is not clear what part the archbishop had in drawing up this memorandum which embodies the points made by Grosseteste in a long letter written to the archbishop about this time,[5] but it is clear that he gave it his active support.

There are several indications of an explosive situation existing in 1237. The archbishop himself had been forbidden to pursue litigation before papal judges on the ground that the case concerned the temporalities of the archbishopric.[6] In June 1236

---

[1] On this whole subject see G. B. Flahiff, 'The Use of Prohibitions by Clerics against Ecclesiastical Courts in England', *Medieval Studies*, iii (1941), pp. 101–16; 'The Writ of Prohibition to the Court Christian in the Thirteenth Century', ibid. vi (1944), pp. 261–313; vii (1945), pp. 229–90.

[2] *Ann. Mon.* i. 254–7.

[3] *Chron. Maiora*, iv. 3. According to Matthew Paris, the bishops in 1240 presented *capitula circiter triginta*. The list of the Burton annalist comprises 28 articles, but some items contain more than one complaint.

[4] *Ann. Mon.* i. 305; *Chron. Maiora*, v. 373–5.

[5] *Epistolae*, pp. 205–34.

[6] *Close Rolls 1234–7*, pp. 356, 524, 540. The judges were warned to desist

Grosseteste provoked an angry warning from the king by forbidding clerks of his diocese to answer in the royal courts for contempt of writs of prohibition.[1] Indeed the last item in the list of clerical gravamina seems to suggest that there was an officially inspired campaign in London to intimidate any layman who attempted to bring an action in the ecclesiastical court in any case except matrimonial or testamentary. Grosseteste was all for thorough. The fact that there was no explosion is credit in part to the conciliatory conduct of the archbishop, and in part to the tact of the legate.

The use which the archbishop and his suffragans made of the cardinal legate in their negotiations with the king suggests that the relations between the legate and the English bishops deserve fresh examination. Cardinal Otto was despatched to England in the summer of 1237 at the request of the king. He was not a popular figure, as the attack on his *familia* at Oseney demonstrated.[2] But it does not follow from this that he was regarded with hostility by the English episcopate, or that relations between him and the archbishop were bad. Recent research has tended to reveal his work in a more favourable light and to emphasize the tact and restraint with which he wielded his great powers.[3] The examination of thirteenth-century English synodal legislation has shown the wide and lasting influence exerted by the decrees which he promulgated in the Council of London. Against this, the assumption that his presence was a source of annoyance to Archbishop Edmund rests largely on the ex parte statements of Matthew Paris, whose prejudices on this subject are well known.[4]

from citing the archbishop in May 1236, Mar. 1237, and again in July 1237. As so often happened, the impasse was solved by the parties reaching an agreement out of court, viz. Canterbury D. & C. mun. Chartae Antiquae C. 34; see App. B, No. 22.

[1] *Close Rolls 1234–7*, p. 360.
[2] *Ann. Mon.* iv. 84–85. See the ensuing inquiry in *Close Rolls 1234–7*, pp. 47, 53, 72, 133–6.
[3] See Dorothy Williamson, 'Some Aspects of the Legation of Cardinal Otto', *EHR* lxiv (1949), pp. 145–73, and the authorities there cited.
[4] For example, Matthew felt that the precedence given to the legate at the

The fact that the cardinal enjoyed the confidence of the higher clergy is indicated by their readiness to resort to him not only for justice, but also for mediation and advice. Grosseteste more than once confided to him his anxieties on the use of religious as royal justices and on other matters. In the *Quadrilogus* Eustace of Faversham says that the archbishop relied on his support,[1] and this assertion is borne out by the history of Edmund's dealings with his chapter. A striking case is the letter addressed to the cardinal, during Edmund's absence abroad, by Robert of Abingdon and the archbishop's Official.[2] They lay before him the case of Ralph of Orpington, who is being maltreated by the monks of Christ Church, despite the archbishop's protection. They state that in case of difficulty they have been instructed by the archbishop to approach the legate for help, and in the event their confidence seems to have been justified. Ralph of Orpington was one of the monks involved in the forgery of a privilege. Smitten with compunction, he had confessed all to the archbishop who, being *en route* for Rome, had taken Ralph with him to save him from the reprisals of his fellow monks, and had lodged him at the abbey of St. Bertin in Flanders, to await his return. The monks of Christ Church had, however, lured the penitent back with false promises and put him in chains. The archbishop pursued the matter while in Rome, and returned home with a papal mandate ordering the legate to inspect the privileges of the monastery.[3] The two men lost no time in carrying out the visitation. The results of the legate's visit were satisfactory to the archbishop and painful to the monks. The forgery of the charter was exposed and the culprits were summoned to appear before the legate in London.[4] The prior, John of Chetham, was forced to resign and to enter the Carthusian Order.

baptism of the Lord Edward in 1238 was a slight to the English bishops, but it is unlikely that they were conscious of being disparaged.

[1] 'quia presens erat tunc legatus in quo confidebat': below, p. 199.
[2] PRO Anc. Corresp. xi. 159.   [3] *CPL* i. 173-4.
[4] Gervase, ii. 133, presents a tendentious account of these events. The facts are clearly stated in *CPL* i. 194.

The cardinal displayed his readiness to assist the archbishop in other ways. When the chapter appealed against Edmund's plan for a collegiate church in the Canterbury diocese, it fell to the legate to inquire into the matter and report. His findings were favourable to the archbishop, who received from Rome the necessary faculty to proceed.[1] He did his best to bring about a reconciliation between the rebellious chapter and the archbishop, but after the failure of his efforts to persuade the monks to submit, he abandoned further intervention. The picture of Cardinal Otto which emerges from these incidents is not a disagreeable one. He appears to have been a modest man.[2] He was not to be bought, even by the king.[3] He was obviously unwilling to interfere in the domestic quarrels of the English Church, and he only acted if he was directly appealed to, or when expressly bidden by a papal mandate.[4] It is clear that he discharged his difficult mission with tact and firmness. Matthew Paris's portrayal of the legate in the *Vita* as a time-server, ready to betray the archbishop's interests in order to curry favour at court,[5] is a gross distortion.

The cathedral priory was a survival from an age of monastic bishops. In the thirteenth century relations between a secular bishop and a monastic chapter were seldom harmonious for long. Archbishop Edmund was engaged in almost constant litigation with his chapter. In 1235 he had to take them to law to induce them to shoulder their share of the expenses incurred in promoting the election of John Blund.[6] In 1236 they reopened the old question of the archbishop's patronal rights in the liberty of Christ Church. They sued him before papal

[1] *CPL.* i. 173, 180, 182.
[2] Even Matthew Paris concedes so much: *Chron. Maiora*, iii. 403. Grosseteste, who was not given to sycophancy, comments on the grace and humility of the legate's reply to a letter of his: *Epistolae*, p. 185.
[3] A gift of silver plate which the king had caused to be made for him was declined: *Close Rolls 1237-42*, pp. 33-34.
[4] Miss Williamson points out his unwillingness to intervene in disputed elections until instructed by the pope to do so.
[5] Below, p. 258.
[6] Auvray, 2590.

judges for the recovery of the advowsons of churches and the *exennia* which the archbishops claimed on the priory manors, and also for the right to return of the king's writ without the archbishop's intermission. The abbots of Boxley, Bradsole, and Lesnes were appointed judges-delegate to try the case, but before they could get both parties into court, the action was stopped by a royal writ of prohibition.[1] The king claimed cognizance of the case because it affected the temporalities of the archbishopric in which the Crown had a vital interest. Squeezed between papal orders to proceed and repeated royal prohibitions, the judges sought escape from their dilemma by referring the parties to Rome.[2] Meanwhile the archbishop tried to negotiate an agreement out of court. On 18 December 1237 a concord was drawn up[3] which left the archbishop undisturbed possession of the rights in dispute, while reserving to the priory advowsons and their customary share of the *exennia* in certain specified places. This agreement was expressly made subject to papal and royal confirmation. The sequel, which led to the bitter struggle between Edmund and his chapter, has to be disentangled from the vague allegations of Matthew Paris and the partisan account of the Christ Church chronicler. It appears that when the archbishop arrived in Rome in the spring of 1238 and presented the agreement for confirmation, the proctors of the chapter startled everyone by repudiating it. The explanation of this volte-face is to be found not, as Matthew Paris suggests, in the desire of the lawyers to keep the ball in play, but in another issue which touched the cathedral monastery very closely.

The Christ Church chronicler says that when the archbishop reached Rome, he sought against the monks a licence to erect a prebendal church.[4] A papal mandate of May 1238 shows that

[1] *Close Rolls 1234–7*, pp. 356, 524, 540.
[2] A copy of the judges' report is to be found in Canterbury, D. & C. mun. Chartae Antiquae A. 168; printed by Wallace, pp. 488–95.
[3] Canterbury D. & C. mun. Chartae Antiquae C. 34; see App. B, No. 22.
[4] Gervase, ii. 133. He makes no mention of the chapter's repudiation of the agreement which they had made in 1237.

the lawyers of the archbishop and the chapter had in fact joined issue on this point.[1] Both Archbishops Baldwin and Hubert Walter had attempted to found a college of secular canons in the Canterbury diocese and had been defeated by fierce opposition from the monastic chapter.[2] What the archbishops chiefly sought was a means whereby they could provide for the numerous secular clerks whom they employed in diocesan administration. They were at a disadvantage in having a monastery for a chapter.[3] The fears of the monks appear from the guarantee which was offered them by Hubert Walter. The setting up of a great collegiate church in the diocese, endowed out of the possessions of the archbishopric and peopled by the learned clerks who served the archbishop, might prove to be the first step in transferring the chapter's electoral rights, and even the see itself. There is no doubt that it was Edmund's revival of this project which provoked the monks to such bitter resistance. Historically, the old question of the *exennia* and advowsons on the Canterbury manors was connected with the collegiate church. Archbishop Richard of Dover had granted a number of these rights to the cathedral priory, but Archbishop Baldwin had recovered them with the express purpose of using them as an endowment for his new college.[4] The news that Archbishop Edmund was planning to do likewise must have thrown the monks into panic and must have placed the agreement of December 1237 in a new and sinister light. Hence their anxiety to repudiate it.

As a result of the appeal lodged by the chapter, Cardinal Otto was instructed to hold an inquiry and to inspect the site of the proposed foundation.[5] The place chosen was Maidstone, an exempt parish in the archbishop's patronage. Plans were

[1] *CPL* i. 173.
[2] The dossier of this dispute was published from Lambeth Palace MS. 415 by Stubbs, *Epistolae Cantuarienses* (RS 1865).
[3] As Hubert Walter unkindly explained to the monks, secular canons were 'prudentiores et faciliores ad propugnandum ecclesiam quam monachi, qui nil aliud saperent quam claustrum': ibid., p. 537.
[4] Ibid., pp. 8–10.   [5] *CPL* i. 173.

drawn up by Elyas of Dereham for conventual buildings and a great church to contain fifty prebends.[1] In May 1239 the archbishop was notified that the appeal of the chapter had failed,[2] and building on the site began. The monks, who now despaired of help from Rome, appealed to the Crown, representing that the new foundation would impoverish the temporalities. The king now intervened. In November 1239 a writ was dispatched to the sheriff of Kent ordering him to halt the building operations, if necessary by force.[3] This put an end to a project which was only to be realized, on a modified scale, in the time of Archbishop Pecham. By this time Edmund was at open war with the chapter.

It was a purely personal squabble that led to the open breach between the archbishop and the monks, but the petty incident which provoked it was magnified by the underlying conflict of interests. As the astute archdeacon realized, by foolishly tampering with their documents the monks had offered their adversary a handle. An examination of their archives led to the deposition of the prior. In November 1238, at the convent's request, Archbishop Edmund entered the chapter to supervise the election of a new superior.[4] When he announced, however, that he had deposed the sub-prior, there was an angry scene which ended in the monks walking out of the chapter house. For this insult the archbishop suspended the community from sacred functions. But the monks defied this sentence, taking their stand on the appeal which they had lodged, and, in January 1239, they further aggravated the situation by electing themselves a new prior, without the archbishop's consent. This brought down a sentence of excommunication, first on the group which had elected Roger de la Lee, and finally on the entire community. The monks refused, however, to bow before

[1] Gervase, ii. 174; *Ann. Mon.* iii. 150–1.
[2] *CPL* i. 180, 182.
[3] *Close Rolls 1237–42*, p. 234.
[4] The history of the wrangle is to be found in Gervase, ii. 131 ff., and is described in detail in Wallace, pp. 279–301. For the documents see App. B below.

the storm, and they lodged a fresh appeal. It was evidently felt in some quarters that the archbishop's treatment of the chapter had been rather high-handed, for when he raised the subject at the legatine synod in March 1239 he was unable to carry all his suffragans with him. The attitude of the Crown remained equivocal.[1] An effort made by the legate to bring about a reconciliation came to nothing, and a complete impasse was reached. The futile and wearisome dispute was only terminated by the archbishop's death. Underlying the contest there was a real and deep conflict of interests, but, as so often happens, the parties came to blows on a personal issue of trivial importance. The manner in which the dispute was conducted reflects small credit on either the chapter or the archbishop.

The last days of Archbishop Edmund are wrapped in an obscurity on which the hagiographers cast only a feeble and uncertain light.[2] It is well known that he left England in the autumn of 1240 and made his way to Pontigny where he was taken ill, and that he was subsequently buried there. The story that he had withdrawn from the country into voluntary exile appeared early in the hagiographical tradition and has been so long accepted that some of the difficulties inherent in it have escaped notice. The hagiographers represent the archbishop's death in exile as a kind of martyrdom. His chosen place of residence suggested a parallel with Becket and Langton which they were glad to exploit. It seemed fitting that Pontigny, which had offered a refuge to fugitive English prelates, should at last be handsomely rewarded with the bones of an English saint.

On examination, however, the parallel between Archbishop Edmund and his distinguished predecessors is less convincing than at first sight appears. Becket, after all, fled because he could not stay without surrendering fundamental principles.

---

[1] The archbishop's right to return of writ on the Christ Church manors was suspended after the excommunication: *Gervase*, ii. pp. 166–7.

[2] The outline of what follows has been worked out in an article in *Journal of Ecclesiastical History*, vii (1956), pp. 160–73.

Archbishop Edmund

Langton remained abroad because King John would not have him. But it is difficult to discover any important issue which could have induced Edmund to withdraw from England in 1240. It seems natural to turn to the *Vitae* for help in solving this problem. The Life by Eustace, however, is hardly more than a literary pastiche at this point. In order to describe the archbishop's difficulties leading to his decision to leave the country, he is content to reproduce a rhetorical passage from the Life of Becket by John of Salisbury.[1] The Anonymous 'A' and the Pontigny writer have more to say, although they deal in generalities. They refer to the dispute with the chapter, to unspecified difficulties with the king, and to infringement of the rights and liberties of the church of Canterbury. Matthew incorporated the passage from Eustace in his work, but, writing ten years or so after the event, he endeavoured to infuse some historical facts into these studied platitudes. He describes in detail, though not always accurately, the development of the conflict between the archbishop and his chapter. He points to his failure in litigation with the chapter of Rochester, and his failure to prevent the irregular marriage of Earl Simon de Montfort with the king's sister. He speaks of the overbearing conduct of Cardinal Otto, who quashed the archbishop's acts and procured the absolution of the Canterbury monks, and he refers guardedly to trouble made by 'the mightier of the kingdom whom, out of respect for pope and king, I do not consider it proper or safe to accuse by name'.[2]

It does not appear that any of these allegations, when closely examined, offers a satisfactory explanation of the archbishop's retirement. There is, for instance, the matter of the legate. It has already been suggested that Matthew's account of hostility between the cardinal and the archbishop is not supported by the known facts. When he attempts to connect the archbishop's flight with the conduct of the legate, Matthew's sense of chronology seems to desert him, as well as his sense of proportion. Thus, he suggests that in the end the archbishop was persuaded

[1] Below, p. 216.   [2] Below, p. 261.

to retire because he had been made to look small when the legate was asked to baptize the Lord Edward, but, apart from the incongruity of the explanation, the baptism took place in June 1239, at least fifteen months before the archbishop went. Similarly, he says that the legate procured the absolution of the chapter, but this is beside the point, for it was not done until after the archbishop's death, and then only for the purpose of electing a new archbishop.[1] In fact Matthew's case against the cardinal hardly stands up to examination. It would be odd, anyway, if the archbishop, after enduring the legate's presence for three years, should have beaten a retreat at the very time when the legate's own departure was known to be imminent.

The other explanations of Matthew Paris are no more satisfactory. He points out that the archbishop had a setback in losing his case against Rochester cathedral priory. Edmund had refused to consecrate Richard of Wendene, whom the monks had elected bishop in 1235, on the ground that the patronage of the see belonged to the archbishops.[2] Also he had failed to prevent the irregular marriage of Eleanor, the king's sister, who had taken an oath of chastity after the death of her first husband. How far Matthew's treatment of this question was coloured by the widespread disapproval of the marriage, it is impossible to say. It seems unlikely at any rate that failure in litigation would have been enough to make the archbishop throw up his responsibilities. In any case, both these judgements were given against him in 1238, while he was in Rome. If he wished to register a protest in this curious and novel form, why did he return to England in the summer of that year and remain at his post for the next two years? The obvious procedure, surely, would have been to remain abroad.

On the subject of the archbishop's difficulties with the king, Matthew Paris seems to have nothing to add to the vague

---

[1] The mandate was issued on 6 Mar. 1241: *CPL* i. 194.
[2] The account of the dispute is in the Rochester annals: *Anglia Sacra*, i. 348–9; the judgement is printed in Auvray, 4197.

Archbishop Edmund

allusions of Eustace, and these are in fact borrowed from the Life of Becket. The Anonymous 'A' and the Pontigny writer draw on Eustace's deposition. The only specific incident in the quarrel which Eustace records is the archbishop's excommunication of 'those who had unjustly invaded the rights and liberty of the church of Canterbury'. There is no doubt that relations between the king and the bishops were strained in 1240, for Henry's manipulation of episcopal elections was causing much anxiety. Grosseteste complained to Edmund of the use of bribery and intimidation at Hereford to induce the canons to elect the royal candidate.[1] The vacancy at Winchester, caused by the death of Peter des Roches in 1238, had led to a prolonged struggle. In his efforts to get the queen's uncle elected, the king had resorted to the unprecedented step of packing the chapter.[2] These high-handed proceedings formed the subject of a protest which the archbishop made to the king at a meeting held on 13 January 1240.[3] He seems to have acted on Grosseteste's advice and reminded the king of his obligations to the Church under the Great Charter.

The archbishop had also personal grievances against the Crown. The court was claiming the prerogative wardship of the entire estate of Ralph fitzBernard, one of the archbishop's tenants, and the archbishop was apparently not prepared to give up his claims to Ralph's three Kentish fees without a struggle.[4] Edmund also reacted sharply to the king's suspension of his right to return of writ on the liberty of Christ Church. In March 1240 he ordered his Official to publish the excommunication of any persons who entered the fees of Christ Church in order to execute the royal writ in contravention of the archbishop's franchise.[5] It is apparently to these incidents

---

[1] *Epistolae*, pp. 264–6.
[2] Henry appointed the prior and a number of obedientiaries: *Ann. Mon.* i. 243; *Close Rolls 1237–42*, p. 158. See the account in F. M. Powicke, *Henry III and the Lord Edward*, pp. 270–3.
[3] *Chron. Maiora*, iv. 3.
[4] See the fees of the archbishopric in *The Red Book of the Exchequer*, ed. H. Hall (RS), ii. 472, 725, 727.   [5] Gervase, ii. 177.

that the hagiographers refer when they speak of an attack on the liberty of the church of Canterbury. Such incidents could engender bad feeling, but they were after all commonplace in the life of a thirteenth-century bishop. It is hard to see in them any reason likely to compel the archbishop to abandon his duties and retire from the country. He was certainly not conducting himself like a defeated man. He seems if anything to have been over-aggressive. His readiness to employ spiritual sanctions in defence of the archbishop's temporal rights is striking, and exemplifies one of the less agreeable developments of the period.[1]

Perhaps the least plausible of all the explanations which the hagiographers offer us is that his nerve was broken by the rebellion of the chapter. It may be thought that he was guilty of roughness in the handling of the monks, but not of pusillanimity. Time was on his side. His interdict lay heavily on Canterbury. The cessation of pilgrim traffic had serious economic repercussions, and neither monks nor townspeople could afford to put up with the situation indefinitely. Constitutional conflicts between bishop and chapter are all too common in the thirteenth century, but we shall look in vain for a chapter which drove its bishop into exile.

If we lack any really satisfactory explanation of the archbishop's withdrawal, we are met, more curiously, by a seeming conspiracy of silence on the part of the contemporary chroniclers. The one exception is the chronicle of St. Albans, and to this we may return later. The self-imposed exile of the archbishop of Canterbury was surely a matter for comment, yet, Matthew Paris apart, the contemporary chroniclers do not even notice it. Thus the Rochester annalist makes no mention of the archbishop's departure, despite the fact that Rochester cathedral priory was at that time engaged in litigation with him.[2] Richard of Morins, the Dunstable annalist, who was a papal

---

[1] Another instance is the archbishop's excommunication of Hugh of Albeney, earl of Arundel, for impounding a number of the archbishop's hounds: *Red Book of the Exchequer*, ii. 758.   [2] *Anglia Sacra*, i. 349.

judge-delegate in various cases concerning the archbishop and one of the best-informed commentators of the time, also ignores the archbishop's departure. He records, however, his death in Burgundy and burial at Pontigny, remarking only that before leaving Edmund had excommunicated his chapter. This annal was evidently written some time after March 1241, since Richard goes on to say that he was one of those deputed by the pope to relax the archbishop's sentence.[1] The continuator of Gervase of Canterbury notices the archbishop's departure and says that on his disembarkation at Gravelines, he was seriously ill, and that he pursued his journey to Pontigny, where he died.[2] He says nothing, however, about the archbishop's reasons for leaving the country. The Oseney annalist says that the archbishop crossed the seas about the Feast of All Saints, that he was taken ill at Pontigny, and that continuing on his way to Soisy, he died at that place.[3] The annalist excusably thought that the village of Soisy-en-Brie was south, not north, of Pontigny. The slip is interesting as the writer evidently believed that Pontigny was only a stage in the archbishop's journey to some other destination, and not his ultimate goal. None of these writers, who were writing up their annals year by year, saw anything in the archbishop's departure which called for special comment.

However, two writers referred in passing to the purpose of the archbishop's travels, a purpose so natural and commonplace that the other chroniclers did not trouble to mention it. The first, the writer of the unpublished annals of Hailes, writes in the annal for 1240, 'Magister Edmundus Cantuariensis archiepiscopus transfretavit versus curiam Romanam, qui itinerando apud Pontiniacum obiit, ubi Deus pro eodem multa operatur miracula.'[4] The other writer, the Tewkesbury annalist, has 'Dominus Eadmundus Cantuariae archiepiscopus

[1] *Ann. Mon.* iii. 156.
[2] Gervase, ii. 179–80.
[3] *Ann. Mon.* iv. 87–88; reproduced by Wykes, ibid. iv. 88.
[4] Cott. MS. Cleop. D iii, fo. 43ʳ. I am much indebted to Mr. Eric John for drawing my attention to this reference.

transfretavit in Augusto', and later, 'Obiit Sanctus Eadmundus archiepiscopus Cantuariae circa festum Sancti Eadmundi, itinerando versus Romam.'[1] These statements offer a perfectly natural explanation of the archbishop's journey and death in France and, if they are correct, account for the silence of the other contemporary annalists on the subject of the 'exile'. They obviously merit serious consideration.

In the first place, the two notices represent the statement not of two independent authorities, but of one. Textual collation shows that the annals of Hailes and Tewkesbury are based on a common source which is no longer extant. Moreover, this lost source is the same as that which underlies the annals of Worcester, at any rate up to the year 1229, and a short chronicle in Cott. MS. Faustina B i, fos. 12–29ᵛ, which extends to the year 1231.[2] We have in fact to do with a whole group of West Country annals, all of which are dependent at some point on a single unknown source. From the common Tewkesbury matter shared by this group it is evident that this source was a Tewkesbury chronicle.

The version of St. Edmund's departure given by the Hailes annalist has every appearance of being the earlier form of words, derived from the lost Tewkesbury source.[3] The writer

[1] *Ann. Mon.* i. 116.
[2] The existence of a common source underlying the Tewkesbury and Worcester annals was pointed out by Luard, *Ann. Mon.* i, p. xvii, and the investigation of the Worcester sources was carried a stage further by Felix Liebermann, *Ungedruckte anglo-normannische Geschichtsquellen*, pp. 173–202. Worcester's dependence on 'Tewkesbury perditus' apparently ceases in 1229. Thereafter he is independent until 1261, when he falls back once more upon Cott. MS. Vesp. E iv, a Waverley recension of the Winchester annals; see N. Denholm Young, 'The Winchester-Hyde Chronicle', *EHR* xlix (1934), pp. 85–93. Local references and Augustinian matters show that the annals of Cott. Faust. B i were compiled at Cirencester. On the Hailes annals see Hardy, *Catalogue of Materials*, iii. 352.
[3] The date at which the existing recension of the Tewkesbury annals was compiled is hard to establish. It would be unsafe to infer from the writer's use of the word *sanctus* in regard to St. Edmund that he wrote after 1246. In the thirteenth century this term was not confined to those officially canonized; cf. Matthew Paris's references to Roger Niger in *Chron. Maiora*, v. 13, 195, and to Richard Wych, ibid. v. 419.

had heard reports of miracles at Pontigny, for the archbishop's *familiares* were already propagating his reputation for sanctity in the spring of 1241.[1] But canonization proceedings were not yet in the wind, for the annalist was content to describe the archbishop as 'Magister Edmundus' without any qualification. We conclude then, that the unknown Tewkesbury chronicler wrote the annal for 1240 either in the second half of 1241 or in 1242, and that at that date he had, in common with other well-informed writers, heard nothing about the archbishop's 'exile', and believed the archbishop to be *en route* for Rome at the time of his death.

Apart from its inherent probability, the statement of the Tewkesbury writer explains the absence of any reference to an exile in the letters written to postulate the archbishop's canonization. The point would presumably have been one worth making when petitioning for canonization. The Pontigny letter, it is true, makes ambiguous references to the archbishop's enemies who had avoided his presence when he was alive and who were now confounded by his miracles. This letter was written rather later than the others, some time after June 1243,[2] and it may be that here already we have the theory of the exile germinating. But this may be to read too much into words which can bear a simpler and more straightforward interpretation.

Reasons for the archbishop's visit to Rome are not far to seek. The profession of obedience which he made on receiving the pallium laid on him the obligation of making a triennial visit *ad limina*.[3] His litigation with the church of Rochester and the monks of his own chapter, whose proctors were busy in Rome, may have persuaded him to go in person to the papal court, while the king's proceedings at Winchester provided a compelling reason for seeking an audience with the pope.

---

[1] Gervase, ii. 182.
[2] It is addressed to Innocent IV: *MD. Thes.* iii, col. 1902.
[3] See the profession made by Archbishop Edmund in *Le Liber Censuum de l'Église romaine*, ed. P. Fabre and L. Duchesne (Paris, 1910), i. 286^b, 449^a.

A summons to a general council had gone out on 9 August 1240.[1] The council was to meet the following Easter, and an archbishop, with fish of his own to fry, might wish to arrive early to get his business dealt with before the fathers of the council began to assemble.

It would be interesting to know how long the archbishop stayed at Pontigny, but unfortunately it is impossible to fix the precise date at which he left England. The Patent Rolls for the years 23 and 24 Henry III were already missing in the fourteenth century, so that there is no record of a safe-conduct.[2] The two annalists who date the archbishop's crossing differ by as much as three months. Thus the Tewkesbury annalist places his departure in August,[3] and the Oseney annalist places it around the feast of All Saints.[4] No act of his given on English soil has come to light later than one dated at Wingham on 23 July 1240,[5] but this does not mean that none exists. The last episcopal consecration which was certainly performed by him was that of Hugh Pateshull, which took place at Newark on 1 July 1240.[6] Wykes says that this was some time (*diu*) before the archbishop crossed the seas. A copy of the *Flores Historiarum* made at St. Paul's notes that Edmund was present on 1 October, when Roger Niger consecrated St. Paul's cathedral.[7] Although this is a later copy, its provenance gives it some title to consideration on this point. On this evidence there is something to be said for placing the archbishop's departure in October.

The route taken by the archbishop was the one which he might be expected to take if he was on his way to Rome. He

[1] Potthast, 10927.
[2] The Canterbury chronicler states that Edmund went without seeking the king's permission: Gervase, ii. 179.   [3] *Ann. Mon.* i. 116.
[4] Ibid. iv. 72. Wallace rejected this on the ground that it would allow the archbishop too short a residence at Pontigny. But Matthew Paris writes that he stayed at Pontigny for only a few days (*per aliquot dies*): *Chron. Maiora*, iv. 72.
[5] App. B, No. 60.
[6] There is serious doubt about the consecration of Howell ap Ednevet to St. Asaph's. The *cautio* cited by Wallace, p. 517, is probably that for Bishop Hugh.
[7] *Flores Historiarum*, ed. H. R. Luard (RS), ii. 237 and note.

embarked at, or near, Sandwich, and landed at Gravelines, thus crossing eastward of the *via rectissima* which was from Dover to Wissant. He probably chose this crossing because Gravelines was a better port for the abbey of St. Bertin.[1] From there he made his way to Senlis, where he encountered the French court.[2] How he proceeded from there to Pontigny is uncertain. The manuscript of the *Historia Anglorum* of Matthew Paris contains a thirteenth-century itinerary to Italy which passes through Provins (*la bone faire*), Nogent, Troyes, Bar-sur-Seine, Beaune, Châlons-sur-Saône, Mâcon, and Lyons, up the Rhone valley and over the Mt. Cenis.[3] This was the route to Rome taken by St. Anselm a hundred and forty years earlier.[4] An alternative highway passed up the Yonne valley as far as Auxerre where it linked up with the Grand Chemin Tonnerrois leading east to Tonnerre and Langres.[5] Pontigny lay midway between Auxerre and Tonnerre, a few miles north of the main route. In view of its associations with Canterbury, as well as its size and eminence, it was a natural resting place for the archbishop. It is highly probable that Edmund had stayed there already on his way back from Rome in 1238, for the Pontigny archives contained an *inspeximus* and grant which he made to the monastery in that year. In the autumn of 1240 he had cogent reasons for interrupting his journey: the Alpine passes were in the grip of the imperial forces and the emperor had refused a safe conduct to any prelates attempting to reach the pope. The archbishop may have thought it prudent to wait until the situation in north Italy was clarified. If his last sickness had not been upon

---

[1] Becket took this route for the same reason in 1164: Gervase, i. 189–90. St. Edmund had rested there on his way to Rome at the end of 1237: PRO Anc. Corresp. xi. 159. Cf. above, p. 163.

[2] Matthew Paris, below, p. 262.

[3] BM Royal MS. 14C vii, fos. 2ᵛ–3.

[4] *Eadmeri Historia Novorum et Opuscula*, ed. M. Rule (RS), pp. 89, 90, 385–9.

[5] See the reconstruction of roads in J. Richard, *Les Ducs de Bourgogne et la formation du duché du xie au xive siècle* (Dijon, 1954), xi; and *Le Guide des chemins de France de 1553 par Charles Estienne*, ed. J. Bonnerot (Paris, 1936).

him, he would presumably have attempted the sea route and would have shared the fate of the other prelates who defied the emperor's threats in 1241. As it was, after a period of rest he was obliged to turn back. His itinerary northwards to Soisy suggests that he was making for Provins, and probably home. But on reaching Soisy he was too weak to go any farther, and there, under the roof of a small Augustinian priory, a cell of St. Jacques de Provins, he died on 16 November 1240.[1]

This account seems to be the most reasonable interpretation that can be placed upon the facts of St. Edmund's departure and death. But how then did the story of the exile originate? The contemporary chroniclers, with one exception, ignored it, and so too did the people who wrote to ask for the archbishop's canonization. In fact, the earliest references to it are to be found, wrapped up in rhetorical and ambiguous language, in the deposition of Eustace of Faversham and in the *Vita* which he wrote. It will be useful to see the two versions side by side:

The Deposition	The Vita
Et cum debitum pastoris officium, quamquam ad ecclesie liberacionem manus eius fuisset extenta, premissis obstantibus, mimime potuit adimplere, mari transito, venit Pontiniacum, quo, ut fieret fortior, infirmabatur.	Qui, cum cure pastoralis officium libere non poterat exercere, licet manus eius ad ecclesie liberacionem fuisset extenta, cedendum tamen censuit malicie, gloriosum martirem Thomam in hoc facto volens imitari. . . . In orientali igitur parte Anglie que dicitur Sandwicus, navigio clam preparato, prospero vento optatum portum advenit. . . . Qui, cum ad Pontiniacum devenisset, quadam infirmitate corripitur.

[1] The hagiographers suggest that he was advised on account of the heat at Pontigny to retire to Soisy for his health. But the heat at Pontigny can hardly have been very intense in early November and it is hard to see what improvement in the climate could be expected such a short distance away. It is also unlikely that a small Augustinian priory would have been able to accommodate the *familia* of an archbishop for an indefinite period.

Archbishop Edmund

The only existing text of the *Quadrilogus* is defective and there are signs of copyist's omissions at this point. It appears, for instance, from the text in the Anonymous 'A' Life that the deposition contained the phrase *cedendum tamen censuit malicie*, which Eustace reproduces in the *Vita*. Nevertheless, it is clear that the deposition is more guarded, as well as briefer, on the subject of the archbishop's departure. This is not surprising since the deposition was prepared for the critical scrutiny of a papal commission. It contains no reference to the example of Becket or the secret preparations for flight. The *Vita* shows unmistakable traces of 'development'. Although the word 'exile' is not used and the possibility of a journey to Rome is not completely excluded, the narrative clearly suggests that the archbishop had decided to throw up the unequal struggle and go into retirement.

What Eustace had stated by implication was gladly seized and elaborated by the hagiographers who followed him. The writer used by the Anonymous 'A' and the Pontigny monk made use of the *Quadrilogus*, and in his hands the implication half hidden in the original words of Eustace was brought into the open and developed as follows:

The Anonymous 'A'

Cedendum censuit maliciis, et quoniam *debitum pastoris officium, quamquam ad ecclesie liberacionem manus eius esset extenta*, non *potuit adimplere*, vehementi dolore introrsum affectus quasi in se penam intorsit et pro aliorum reatibus penas luiturus, extra regnum Anglie extorris et exul esse elegit . . . et *mari transito* ad *Pontiniacum*, ubi est asilum omnium prelatorum extra regnum Anglie pro iusticia exulancium, Domino ducente, provenit.

Thus the story of the archbishop's self-sought exile was fairly launched. By the time that Matthew Paris came to write his Life of St. Edmund, using the work of Eustace as a basis, the story already had a literary history and was well established. Matthew's literary dependence on Eustace explains the presence of the exile story in the *Historia Anglorum* and in the *Chronica*

Maiora. The close connexion in content and date of composition between the *Historia* and the Life has been indicated elsewhere. The presence of the story in the great chronicle can be explained by the fact that the annal for the year 1240 was not written up in its existing form until some years after Eustace had put his story into circulation.[1]

The question remains, how did Eustace of Faversham perpetuate what at first sight appears to be a literary fraud? But this is to mis-state the question. If the *Vita* is read continuously, it is possible to see how he wrote up Archbishop Edmund's last journey in terms of an exile without any preconceived plan of distorting the truth. As can be seen from the text, he made frequent and extensive use of John of Salisbury's Life of Becket. As he approaches the end of St. Edmund's career, he draws more and more heavily on this source. He seems to feel the lack of a dramatic finale like that which ended Becket's career, and at one point he argues that St. Edmund too had, in his own way, merited the martyr's crown. The cumulative effect of these passages is unmistakable: the writer is trying to show that Becket's mantle had fallen on St. Edmund. He seems to be increasingly absorbed by this analogy, and he presses it to the end, or at any rate as far as it will go. The archbishop's stay at Pontigny, with its memories of Becket, no doubt provided welcome fuel to the imagination of a Canterbury monk who had fed and pondered for years on the biographies of

[1] It is doubtful exactly when the annal for 1240 was written. The question is connected with the wider problem of dating the B text of the chronicle. H. Plehn, *Der politische Charakter von Matheus Parisiensis* (*Staats- u. socialwissenschaftliche Forschungen* xiv, hft. 2, Leipzig, 1897), pp. 128–35, argues that the chronicle for the years 1236 to 1239 was not written up in its existing form until 1245 at the earliest. But the evidence which he cites for this is not altogether convincing. Thus he refers to Ralph Neville's refusal to surrender the Great Seal on the ground that it had been conferred on him by the great council, *Chron. Maiora*, iii. 364, 491, and argues that these passages must have been written subsequently in the light of the paper constitution of 1244. But this seems most doubtful. Again, he argues that a reference to the ill luck of Gilbert Marshal and his brother, under the year 1239, ibid. iii. 524, was written with knowledge of their premature deaths in 1241 and 1245, but it is by no means certain that the words will bear this meaning.

St. Thomas Becket. It would be unwise to accuse Eustace of deliberate deception. He was attempting to depict St. Edmund as a *pedisequus* of Becket. He apparently believed that the spiritual likeness between Becket and his master was a real one, and that was what he wished to convey. But the service that he rendered his master's memory was a dubious one.

Later judgements on Archbishop Edmund have all been coloured by the story of his supposed withdrawal into exile. He has been depicted as a saintly, gentle, but ineffectual reformer, driven by disillusionment and despair to desert his office. I have tried to show that he was a stronger and greater man than the hagiographical tradition would have us believe. If he lacked the wide-ranging intellectual curiosity and speculative power of Grosseteste or the humanity of Langton, he was nevertheless a teacher of distinction who had to school many of the most outstanding churchmen of the next generation. Primarily, he was an ascetic and a master of the spiritual life. He was a man of great moral force to whom all parties instinctively turned for leadership in a time of crisis. Nor were they disappointed. The events of 1234-6 provide the most impressive example in the century of the English Church united in political action. Edmund's pacification was long remembered with gratitude. It is indeed significant that while royal children were baptized in his name, his memory was invoked by the desperate company of rebels who held out in the Fens after Evesham and Kenilworth.

Insufficient records remain to enable us to follow the archbishop in his daily work of administering his diocese and province, but there is enough to show that in visitation, in his care for the maintenance of the pastoral office in parish churches, and in his anxiety for the unhindered working of the ecclesiastical courts, he maintained the work set on foot by the great reforming councils of 1179 and 1215. Even the querulousness of Grosseteste was silenced in the end. Moreover, two visits to Rome, undertaken in the course of six years, show that the view which Edmund took of his task as primate of the English Church was no insular one. But it was not as a statesman or even as a zealous pastor that he became the object of a widespread cultus after his death. He appealed to the popular imagination because he satisfied the profound conviction of simple people that those who ruled the Church should be learned, humble, and holy men.

AN ITINERARY OF ARCHBISHOP EDMUND

The numbers cited as evidence refer to the list of *acta* in Appendix B.

Year	Date	Place	Evidence
1234	Jan.	South Malling	No. 1.
	2 Feb.	Westminster	Attended council: *Chron. Maiora*, iii. 268–70.
	2 Apr.	Canterbury	The day of his consecration: *Early Charters of St. Paul's Cathedral*, ed. M. Gibbs (CS 3rd ser.), lviii (1939), p. 141; *Chron. Maiora*, iii. 272.
	9 Apr.	Westminster	Attended council: *Chron. Maiora*, iii. 272.
	10 Apr.	Westminster	*Charters and Docs. relating to Selbourne Priory*, ed. W. D. Macray (Hants. Rec. Soc.), iv (1891), p. 13.
	13 May	Leominster	No. 2.
	15 May	Hereford	No. 3.
	18 May	Gloucester	*CPR 1232–47*, p. 45.
	25 May	Gloucester	Ibid., p. 75.
	8 June	Gloucester	*Close Rolls 1231–4*, pp. 566–7.
	19 June	Shrewsbury	Ibid., p. 564.
	21 June	Middle	Engaged in peace negotiations with Llewelyn: *CPR 1232–47*, p. 59.
	26 June	Leominster	No. 4.
	14 July	Westminster	*Chron. Maiora*, iii. 294–5.
	25 July	Rochester	*CChR* iii. 361.
	26 Sept.	Marlborough	*CPR 1232–47*, p. 70.
	30 Sept.	London	No. 6.
	14 Oct.	Westminster	*HMC Report*, Wells, i. 495.
	9 Dec.	Reading	*CPR 1232–47*, pp. 45, 46, 48.
1235	20 Jan.	Westminster	Attended council: *Close Rolls 1234–7*, pp. 160–1.
	17 June	Reading	Consecrated Robert Grosseteste: *Registrum Sacrum*, p. 57.
	23 June	Farnham	No. 9.
	17 Aug.	Westminster	Cott. MS. Claudius A vi, fo. 217.
	21 Oct.	Westminster	*Close Rolls 1234–7*, p. 202.
	3 Nov.	Woodstock	Ibid., p. 203.
	24 Nov.	Aldington	No. 10.
	10 Dec.	Aldington	No. 11.
1236	14 Jan.	Canterbury	*Chron. Maiora*, iii. 336.
	20 Jan.	Westminster	Ibid. iii. 337.
	30 Jan.	Merton	Attended council: *Close Rolls 1234–7*, pp. 337–9.
	21 Feb.	South Malling	No. 13.
	5 Mar.	South Malling	No. 14.
	4 Apr.	Croydon	No. 15.
	19 May	Slindon	No. 16.
	1 June	Slindon	No. 17.
	11 July	Tewkesbury	*CPR 1232–47*, p. 153.

An Itinerary of Archbishop Edmund

Year	Date	Place	Evidence
1237	20 Jan.	Westminster	*Close Rolls 1234–7*, p. 543.
	28 Jan.	Westminster	*Magnum Registrum Album of Lichfield*, ed. H. E. Savage (1924), p. 100.
	22 Apr.	Wingham	No. 19.
	4 May	Maidstone	No. 20.
	9 June	Canterbury	Lambeth Palace MS. 1212, fos. 85–86.
	c. 17 July	Dover	To meet the legate: *Chron. Maiora*, iii. 395–6; this was in late July; see *Close Rolls 1234–7*, p. 541.
	13 Oct.	Worcester	At the enthronement of Walter de Cantilupe: *Ann. Mon.* iv. 428.
	18–21 Nov.	London	Legatine Council at St. Paul's: *Chron. Maiora*, iii. 415; *Ann. Mon.* i. 105.
	18 Dec.	Canterbury	Nos. 21, 22.
	19 Dec.	Canterbury	No. 23.
	19–24 Dec.	Crossed the seas for Rome, passing by St. Bertin, Flanders.	*Chron. Maiora*, iii. 470. PRO Anc. Corresp. xi. 159 mentions that he dismissed a follower at St. Bertin.
1238	*c.* 15 Aug.	Returned from Rome	*Ann. Mon.* i. 110.
	17 Nov.	Canterbury	Gervase, ii. 134.
	21 Nov.	Canterbury	Consecrated Richard of Wendene: *Ann. Roff.* in *Anglia Sacra*, p. 349.
	c. 3–9 Dec.	Aldington	Gervase, ii. 138–9.
	11 Dec.	Canterbury	No. 35.
	13–15 Dec.	Canterbury	Nos. 36, 37, 38.
	23 Dec.	Canterbury	Gervase, ii. 141.
	23–*c.* 27 Dec.	Wingham	*Ibid.*, p. 141.
1239	2–5 Jan.	Canterbury	*Ibid.*, pp. 142–5.
	5–6 Jan.	Teynham	*Ibid.*, pp. 145–6; Nos. 41, 42.
	10 Jan.	Hadlow	No. 43.
	14–15 Jan.	Hadlow	*Ibid.*, pp. 150–1; No. 44.
	20 Jan.	Lambeth	No. 45.
	7 Feb.	Tunbridge	*Ibid.*, p. 155.
	4–6 Mar.	London	Meeting of bishops summoned by the legate: Gervase, ii. 159; *Chron. Maiora*, iii. 524.
	18 Mar.	South Malling	Gervase, ii. 160.
	12 Apr.	South Malling	No. 48.
	17 Apr.	London	Meeting with the legate: Gervase, ii. 166.
	24 Apr.	Teynham	*Ibid.*, p. 166.
	24 Apr.	Shalmsford	*Ibid.*, p. 166.
	24–27 Apr.	Wingham	*Ibid.*, pp. 166–8; Nos. 49, 50, 51.
	1 May	Canterbury	Preached at St. Sepulchre's: *ibid.*, p. 168.
	20 June	London	At baptism of the Lord Edward: *Chron. Maiora*, iii. 539; *Vita*, below, p. 259.

An Itinerary of Archbishop Edmund

Year	Date	Place	Evidence
	31 July	London	At meeting with the legate: *Chron. Maiora*, iii. 567.
	25 Sept.	London	Consecrated William Ralegh: *Ann. Mon.* iv. 86; *Chron. Maiora*, iii. 617.
	5 Oct.	Wingham	No. 52.
	3 Nov.	London	Grosseteste, *Epist.*, pp. 253–60.
	16 Nov.	Teynham	No. 53.
1240	2 Jan.	Lyminge	No. 54.
	13 Jan.	London	Attended council: *Chron. Maiora*, iv. 3.
	4 Mar.	South Malling	No. 56.
	7 Mar.	South Malling	No. 57.
	15 Mar.	South Malling	No. 58.
	1 July	Newark	Consecrated Hugh Pateshull: *Ann. Mon.* iv. 86–87.
	9 July	Aldington	No. 59.
	23 July	Wingham	Nos. 60, 61.
	Oct.	Crossed the seas for Rome; disembarked at Gravelines; travelled via Senlis to Pontigny	*Ann. Mon.* i. 116; iii. 88; cf. pp. 175–6 above.
	c. 5–10 Nov.	Pontigny	The *Vitae*.
	13 Nov.	Soisy	No. 64.
	14 Nov.	Soisy	No. 65.
	16 Nov.	Soisy	*Dies obitus.*

PART THREE

TEXT OF THE *QUADRILOGUS*[1]

GLORIOSISSIMI confessoris Eadmundi felicis memorie, nuper Cantuariensis archiepiscopi, vitam et mores volens describere, si paupertas mei ingenii sufficeret, set secundum quod ego[2] Ricardus de Dunstapel'[3] de Ordine Fratrum Predicatorum vidi et audivi per decem fere annos quibus sum conversatus circa eum, priusquam intrarem in Ordinem predictam, de hiis testimonium perhibeo. Confiteor in primis et do gloriam omnipotenti Deo quod, cum pluries assisterem ei in prandio set et plerumque ei servirem, numquam memini me vidisse eum comedere meo iudicio usque ad communem hominum satietatem. Sparissime[4] bibebat. Sextis feriis totum per annum in pane et aqua ieiunabat. Nec recolo quod hoc ieiunium solidabat[5] nisi propter notabilem infirmitatem vel magnam festivitatem, vel raro propter magnum hospitem grossis cibariis vescebatur. Delicata aut non omnino contingebat aut raro aut parum inde sumebat. Illud autem quasi pro statuto penes se firmiter tenebat quod quanto cibus vel potus esset preciosior et delicatior tanto minus inde sumebat. Ieiunia Quadragesimalia solebat absque piscibus observare et solo pane et pulmento contentus esset. Ceteris autem temporibus frequenter per quindecim dies vel amplius abstinere solet a carnalibus et maxime postquam ad gradum sacerdotii fuerat provectus. Ex tunc enim duxit in consuetudinem tam pridie quam celebraret quam ipsa die simpliciter a carnalibus abstinere, unde mensis transibat in quo carnes | omnino non gustabat. Rarissime autem et hoc propter socialitatem cenare consueverat. Vestimenta grisei coloris ut sepius habebat, que nec preciosa nimium nec plurimum abiecta set mediocria fuerant, prout honestatem clericalem decebat. Cilicio utebatur ad carnem quod tam vestiendo quam deponendo studiose ab omnibus occultare curabat. Vestitus et

---
[1] *titulum supplevi*   [2] *add* sum *cod*   [3] Drinstapel' *cod*
[4] Sparississime *cod*   [5] solidet *cod*

cinctus dormiebat, nec omnino lectum introibat set super bancum ante lectum vel ad ipsum lectum se inclinando requiescere solebat. Coopertorium[1] seu lintheamina non habebat, set tantum cappa sua vel pallio suo se cooperire permittebat. Post primum sompnum surgere consueverat et deinceps in oracione et meditacione seu lectione pro tempore tam post matutinas suas quam ante pervigil usque ad diem perseverabat, raro namque tam in hyeme quam in estate post matutinas sompnum capiebat. Quod si forte aliquam (diu)[2] sopor in eum irruerat, non ad lectum recurrebat, set in loco oracionis vel in sede sua reclinato capite paululum dormitabat. Raro visus est in ecclesia in orando sedere, set semper stando vel genuflectando (orare)[3] consuevit, unde et deprehensus est ex magna frequencia genuflectandi scalosa genua habere. Primum et principium opus ei fuerat in die studio vacare, sacre lectioni intendere. Cui ut liberius vacaret, solet se a mane usque ad horam prandii in cella sua includere, ne quis ad eum impediendo[4] facile posset accedere. In hoc autem studio tanquam in | Rachelis amplexu tantum delectabatur quod cetera omnia eciam huic vite necessaria quasi non reputare videbatur. Tria autem tempora dixit se perdita reputare, videlicet tempus comestionis, dormitionis, et equitacionis, ob hoc solum quod in hiis non poterat prefato studio insistere. Placitis et causis non interfuit, set nec tractatibus capituli sui nisi invitus et quodam modo compulsus interesse voluit. Tantus erat contemptor temporalium ut pecuniam tangere vel videre cellaria sua, vel alias officinas intrare, set computaciones suas audire, dedignaretur. Plus expendit quam habuit, unde et debitis semper obligatus fuit. Hospitalitatis graciam nulli denegavit. Pauperibus et egenis elemosinas largiter erogavit. Munera ab indigentibus se scienter non accepit, set iuxta evangelicum preceptum, omni petenti se gratis tribuit.[a] Cetera virtutum eius insignia quis ad plenum referat? Nam si de zelo animarum quem habuerat, si de gracia et fervore,

---

[1] Coopertorio *cod*   [2] -diu *supplevi*   [3] orare *supplevi*
[4] impedimentum *cod. Sed fortasse legendum* ad eius impedimentum

[a] omni petenti &c. Cf. *Luc.* vi. 30.

necnon et fructu predicacionis quem Dominus ei contulerat, si de eius humilitate, paciencia, mansuetudine, ceterisque virtutibus vel breviter aliquid tangerem, timeo ne prolixitate sermonis aures sanctitatis vestre pluribus occupatas gravarem. Hec ergo ad presens de vita et moribus eius breviter tacta sufficiant, in quibus si diligenter inspicere volueritis, qualis in victu, qualis | in habitu, qualis eciam in actu fuerit, ex parte cognoscetis. Quod si, teste beato Gregorio, *vite vera estimacio est in virtute operum, non in ostentacione signorum*,[a] ex premissis perpendite quid de eo vestre discretioni sit arbitrandum. Set enim unica virtus pluris sit estimanda multis miraculis, unde idem Gregorius, *ego*, inquid, *virtutem paciencie signis et miraculis maiorem credo*.[b] Quante sanctitatis ac meriti iure censendus erit qui tot virtutibus claruit, tot et tanta nobis exempla virtutum reliquit. Verum quia premissa virtutum ipsius opera simplici vobis relacione texui, et scio quod in foro isto non sunt admittendi testes non iurati, ideo, ut testimonia mea vobis credibilia fiant nimis,[c] ecce iuro vobis in Domino tactis sacrosanctis quod omnia premissa et multo plurima relacione digna vidi et audivi de ipso tempore supra memorato. Large dico intelligendo singula hec pro sentencia pro qua fuerit, non pro sensu quem stricte intellecta faciunt. Ad huius vero testificacionem iuramenti quod licet absentibus prelatis meis me tamen qualicunque vice[1] eorum in omnibus interim constituto, de plenaria eorum potestate coram fratre Iohanne de Monte Mirabili et aliis quibusdam fratribus feci, licencia conventu nostro Parisiensi petita et obtenta, sigillum eciam commune coram fratribus presentibus appendi. Hiis testibus: domino Roberto Asthall', presencium latore, Andrea et Waltero servientibus suis. Quibus eciam, si opus | fuerit, potestatem committo iurandi in animam super premissis secundum formam quam iuravi coram ipsis.

Ego Stephanus subdiaconus, requisitus de vita venerabili et conversacione insigni beati Edmundi quondam Cantuariensis

[1] vita *cod*

[a] *Dialogi*, i, c. 12. *PL* lxxvii. 213.   [b] Ibid. i, c. 2. *PL* lxxvii. 161.
[c] testimonia &c. Cf. *Ps.* xcii. 5.

archiepiscopi, cuius ego per annos sex et amplius clericus et cubicularius ac secretarius fui, iuratus, et confidenter protestor et dico quod de eo et in eo et circa eum vidi et cognovi et quod quasi manus mee contrectaverunt de viro vite admirabilis. Erat namque singularis abstinencie, nec enim recolo quod unquam viderim eum usque ad communem hominum satietatem in meo iudicio comedere. Comedebat parce; bibebat parcius. Ferias sextas per annum in pane et aqua ieiunabat: pro maiori parte dico. Aliquando solvit hoc ieiunium vel propter festivitatem precipuam vel infirmitatem notabilem vel hospitis specialis et venerabilis susceptionem. Raro tamen cibis grossioribus vescebatur, et quanto cibus vel potus preciosior et delicatior[1] extitit, eo ipse in sumendo parcior fuit, ut verum fatear, preciosa et delicata magis degustans quam sumens. Omni feria secunda a carnalibus abstinebat. Omni eciam die quo missam celebravit, rarissime cenabat. Vestimenta grisea ut sepius habebat, nec nimium preciosa nec nimium abiecta. Cilicio ad carnem utebatur asperrimo, non contexto, set ex cordulis in se invicem ad modum retis densissimi connodatis connexo. Que connectura nodos innumerabiles spisso ordine | continebat. Cilicium ex parte anteriori fuit apertum et laqueolis hinc inde appositis arcius colligatum, quod ut carni coniunctus adhereret fune grossiori et triplici illud desuper a scapulis usque ad renes constrinxerat. Manuum quoque et colli nuda de nocte cilicio contegebat. Vestitus et cinctus dormiebat, non in lecto set ante lectum vel lecto innitens.

Coopertorium non habebat culcituram vel lintheamina, sed cappa sua vel pallio cum tapeto tegebatur. Circa mediam noctem surgere solitus, deinceps in oracione et contemplacione persistebat. Ad maioris ecclesie Sarrisbiriensis[2] matutinas sine intermissione perrexit, et post matutinas in ecclesia pervigil usque ad primam missam permansit. In oracione genua creberrime flexit et ad terram allisit, et toto corpore vel capite frequentissime adoravit. Unde propter genuflexionum frequenciam genua habuit scallosa. In lectionibus assiduus erat, omne tempus

[1] delicior *cod*   [2] Sarribiriensis *cod*

perditum reputans quod non in divinis expendisset obsequiis. Placitis et causis non interfuit nisi in hiis in quibus periculum parochianorum suorum versabatur, ut causis matrimonialibus et huius(modi)[1] et hec in parochiis suis. Tractatibus capituli sui raro interfuit et quodam modo invitus. Adeo temporalia contempnebat quod computaciones rerum suarum audire, cellaria vel alias officinas suas intrare, despexit. Hospitalitatem nulli negavit. Pauperibus et infirmis compacientissimus et largissimus fuit, unde et debitis semper obligabatur. Munera libenter non accepit. Corporis aut capitis lavacrum omnino non admisit. Iactanciam vel laudem humanam summo studio vitavit et aliis vitandam demonstravit. Inimicos suos gratis dilexit, adeo ut eorum iniurias amicorum obsequiis preferre videretur. Erat confessionum auditor sedulus et confessor discretus, in maioribus pius, humilis, benignus, dulcis et mitis, misericors et affabilis omnibus, maxime pauperibus, in caritate fervidus, in predicacione assiduus et devotus, cum gracia lacrimarum quibus uberrime orando et predicando rigabatur. Et ut breviloquio utar, *sobrie et iuste et pie vixit in hoc seculo*.[a] Innocenciam quam recepit in baptismate nullo postea peccato mortali maculavit, ut certissime credo, quod ipsi constanter asserunt qui cum eo ab annis primis usque ad diem mortis successive noverunt.[2]

(fo. 378b)

Ego frater Robertus, sacerdos, olim canonicus regularis Ordinis Sancti Augustini, nunc ob arcioris vite frugem in probacione Ordinis Cisterciensis constitutus, de beati Edmundi quondam Cantuariensis archiepiscopi vita venerabili et conversacione insigni requisitus, cuius ego per annos multos clericus extiti necnon et cubicularius ac secretarius, iuratus, dico quod oculata fide didici et protestor quod de eo propriis quasi manibus contrectavi. Erat igitur pater iste precipuus castitate precellentissimus, fide firmissimus, longanimis in spe, diffusus in caritate, potens in opere et sermone, abstinencia singularis, in

---

[1] -modi *supplevi*
[2] noverunt: dixerunt *cod, sed iuxta epistolam Abindoniensem correxi*

[a] Cf. *Tit.* ii. 12.

vigiliis et oracionibus assiduus, in genuflexionibus[1] creberrimus, Scripture sacre doctor insignis, predicator fervens, mirabiliter et devotus, confessionum | auditor assiduus, confessor piissimus et discretus, uti in me ipso expertus sum, paupertatis amator et amicus pauperum et elator animarum, osor inhonestatis et viciorum que semper et ubique curavit evellere, infirmorum baculus, debilium et destitutorum refugium, et pauperum scolarium libentissimus educator, sobrius in prosperis, fortissimus in adversis, omnibus affabilis, eloquio dulcis, cum gravitate debita letus et hilaris et gaudens in Spiritu Sancto, humilis in oculis suis, compaciens afflictis, elemosinarum multigenarum affluentissimus erogator, consolator merencium, auxilium miserorum, qui cum beato Iob dicere poterat, *ab infancia mea crevit mecum miseracio, et de utero matris mee egressa est mecum.*[a] Carnem quoque suam inmensa penitencie asperitate perdomuit. Ferias sextas per annum in pane et aqua frequentissime transigebat. Aliquociens vero solius panis contentus edullio, nullius liquoris poculum per totum diem pergustavit. Feria secunda et diebus quibus missas celebrabat, ab esu carnium abstinere solebat, reliquis quoque diebus carnes potius pregustare quam sumere, pane et pulmento se reficiens. Raro plusquam semel in die refecit. Dies Adventus et Septuagesime sine esu carnis et sanguinis peregit. Corporis et capitis lavacrum non admisit.[2] Species et diversi generis electuaria respuebat. Cilicio ad carnem indutus, vestitus et cinctus ante lectum quiescebat, pluma, culcitra, coopertorio, et lintheaminibus a lecto semper sublatis, quia huius(modi)[3] stramenta omnino non habuit. Circa mediam noctem, ubicunque | esset, locum quietis deserens, reliquum noctis spacium lectionibus, meditacionibus, et oracionibus deputavit, quas enim pro fluvio lacrimarum, suspiriis, et gemitibus, et devocione sincerissima coram Deo effundebat. Cum autem moram faceret aput Sarum, ubi officium thesaurarii gerebat, noctibus ad ecclesiam hora matutinarum sine intermissione perrexit, et post matutinas solus in ecclesia pernoctavit

---

[1] genuflexionum *cod*   [2] amisit *cod*   [3] -modi *supplevi*
[a] *Iob* xxxi. 18.

usque ad lucem, oracioni et contemplacioni intentus. A potu ante prandium mirum in modum abstinuit. In estate vero, cum nimius estus et sitis aridior eum urgeret, aquam coctam, que 'cisona' dicitur, in poculum sumpsit. Unde contigit quod aliquando propter humorum paucitatem, pilis barbe et capitis fluentibus, depilis[1] videbatur ad tempus. Et quia singulos et singulares vite sue artissime modos nec memoria revolvere nec lingua sufficit explicare, hoc tamen brevitatis causa dico, quod carnem suam parcitate victualium, modicitate sompni, asperitate cilicii, assiduitate studendi et meditandi, aliisque laboribus quamplurimis adeo mortificavit quod mirabile fuit in oculis suorum quomodo vires eius ad tot et tantos labores sufficere poterant, cum vires humanas excedere viderentur.

De operibus misericordie que[2] superius omisi, hic adicio videlicet quod hostium eius viatori patuit, quod ab eius ianuis nemo publice mendicans vacuis manibus recessit nisi per famulorum negligenciam accidisset, quod, quando accidit, molestissime tulit, cum id in eius noticiam forte pervenisset, et ob hoc necgligentes durius increpavit. Tempore | famis modo (fo. 380ᵃ) panem, modo pulmentum vel bladum, omnibus undecunque a servientibus[3] fecit plena manu compassionis erogari, et preterea de omnibus sibi ad prandium appositis in disco magno coram se posito partem uberiorem posuit, quam infirmis mitti mandavit. Quandoque vero pauperibus peregrinis ea ipse manu sua distribuit, potu competenti adhibito. Minutas decimas, oblaciones, et admerciamenta piis usibus deputavit. Multos eciam victu et vestitu cotidiano procuravit. Sicut animam ab avaricia ita quoque manus a munere excuciebat. Visitandis infirmis solicitus intendebat, et seminans super omnes aquas Verbum vite, omnibus publice et privatim predicavit et quociens occasionem lucrandis animabus invenire poterat, non mediocriter exultans. Caritas quippe que veritati congaudet[a] in omnibus eius actibus et verbis evidentissime relucebat. Unde

---

[1] depilatis *cod* [2] quod *cod* [3] servientibus: ferventibus *cod*

[a] Cf. *1 Cor.* xiii. 6.

inimicos suos propter Deum perpensius dilectioni (habuit),[1] et eorum promocioni, non minus quam si amici essent, intendit. Ex eiusdem caritatis quoque plenitudine processit quod proles numero sibi prorsus ignotos in scolis exhibuit. Qui fere omnes eius exemplo admoniti, seculum[2] salubriter relinquentes, ad religionem confugerunt. Nec modo eius alumpni, verum et eius in scolis discipuli, eius sunt quasi stimulis excitati, eandem viam sunt aggressi. Et cum hiis et aliis innumeris virtutibus et bonis operibus choruscaret, appetitum inanis glorie cum occasionibus[3] suis adeo fugiebat et prodetestabatur, ut aliquid aliquando quod simplicitati[4] possit ab aliis ascribi, mallet publice demonstrare, quam ad inanem ostentacionem aliquid pretendere virtuosum. Quam pestem, viris virtutum importunam (fo. 380ᵇ) multipliciter saluti, | quadam mirabili et tanta simplicitate semper studebat elidere et ab aliis verbo et exemplo repellere. Et ut breviter omnia concludam, semper sobrie, pie, et iuste vixisse,[a] semper ab omni peccato mortali liber et immunis certissime creditur, et firmiter confirmatur ab eunte etate usque ad supremum diem vite per successiones temporum pugnam[5] traxisse[6] longiorem. Plurima quoque et pulcherrima miracula tamen in vita sua a viris fidelissimis didici, ea eciam que prelati Anglie, pusilli cum maioribus, sub literarum suarum testimonio perhibent de ipso. Alia[7] frequenter audivi que omnia una cum miraculis predictis in vita sua perpetratis inrefragabili veritate teste consciencia credo esse subnixa. Miracula vero innumera que post eius sacram deposicionem pluribus in locis ad eius nominis invocacionem Dominus operatus est, mihi *credibilia facta sunt nimis,*[b] nichilque minus de eorum veritate certus sum quam si omnia propriis oculis aspexissem. Nam unum in meipso exhibitum indubitatam mihi fidem omnium facit aliorum. Erat mihi aliquando[8] per duos dies cum tumore magno sinistre faucis dencium dolor intolerabilis. Cumque tanto

---

[1] habuit *supplevi* [2] admoniti, seculum: admonuit secundum *cod*
[3] occationibus *cod* [4] simpliciter *cod* [5] pugnam: moram *cod*
[6] traxisse: traxere *cod* [7] Alias *cod* [8] aliquam *cod*

[a] Cf. *Tit.* ii. 12. [b] *Ps.* xcii. 5.

Text of the Quadrilogus

constrictus incommodo, me in lectulo nocte alia collocassem, dolor et angustia plus solito circumdederunt me et acrius urgere ceperunt. Quid facerem miser ignorabam. Dolor non quievit et, nisi dolore quiescente, quiescere ipse non poteram. Tandem memorabilem patrem meum, beatum scilicet Edmundum, ad memoriam reducens, eius auxilium precibus et lacrimis, quas non minus dolor quam devocio deducebat, cepi flagitare. Paulo post | in soporem resolutus, quievi et quietissime, donec signum pro fratribus convocandis ad matutinum pulsaretur, (fo. 381ª) dormivi. Quo excitus, me sanissimum reperi et tam a dencium dolore quam a faucis tumore penitus liberatum. Multa quidem et alia in eo vidi et de eo audivi et ab eo in me expertus sum, que[1] brevitatis causa sponte pretereo, hoc in talone[2] sermonis adnectens et constanter affirmans quod vir ille venerabilis vas erat virtutum, via morum, spectaculum sanctitatis, religionis exemplar, sciencie armarium, sanctorum thesaurus. Erat denique verus Dei cultor, abstinens se ab omni opere malo, et in innocencia, quam in baptismo receperat, semper usque ad finem vite quantum humane fragilitati perseverans.

Ego frater Eustachius, monachus, iuratus, et requisitus super vita et moribus recolende recordacionis Edmundi, Cantuariensis archipresulis, cuius lateri per plures annos adhesi, et capellanus ac cubicularius eiusdem extiti, fide consciencia constanter assero quod secundum puritatem[3] [a] multorum et signata veritatis verba testantur, *extiterat a puericia tam religiose nutritus, ut docente eum Christianissima matre sua, quam florem fuisse postea viduarum et vita sua clamat et fama, ieiunare inciperet et orare cum adhuc esset puerulus.*[b] *Cuius mater tam sancte vivebat ut loricam ferream sue carni innexam finetenus[4] portavit. Hec dulci puero in ipso inicio viarum suarum Christi nomen indidit, amorem inmisit, timorem incussit, crescentem | et perficientem suo exemplo informavit.*[c] Cum adholesceret, *liberalibus traditus disciplinis inbuendus*, (fo. 381ᵇ)

---

[1] quo *cod* [2] talose *cod* [3] purita *cod* [4] fune tenus *cod*

[a] i.e. iuramentum; on this use see *Du Cange*, vi. 575.
[b] extiterat . . . puerulus: *Oxford letter.*
[c] Cuius . . . informavit: *Abingdon letter.*

via qua prius ducebatur, incedebat spontaneus. Nam ex tunc voluntarie Deo sacrificare cepit, ecclesie limina sponte frequentans, vana et frivola quibus adholescencior habundat etas devitans, erudicioni sue diligenter intendens, carnis delicias (non)[1] solum fugiens, sed et crucis mortificacionem iugiter in corpore suo portans,[a] toto mentis studio (vite)[2] requisivit auctorem. Videbatur iam illud quod nondum[3] legerat intellexisse proverbium, 'Adholescens iuxta viam suam ambulans, eciam cum senuerit, non recedet ab ea'.[b] Quod in eo vere invenitur completum esse. Nam ieiunare et vigilare, et cetera penitencie gravia, ex tunc tam duxit in consuetudinem facere quod postmodum, ut ipsemet perhibebat, non tam facilia quam delectabilia ei fuerant in proveciori etate.[c] *Beati itaque Iohannis Evangeliste imitator existens,* carnem suam nulla unquam immundicie macula maculavit, quod et *firmiter asserunt qui ipsius confessiones audierunt et qui ipsum ex familiari cum ipso conversacione ab annis puerilibus noverunt.*[d] Et sic in carne uixisse creditur preter carnem. *Crescente vero etate, crevit et in virtute.* Nam *sic, gracia sibi divina favente, proficit quod*[e] *dum in annis iuvenilibus intenderet disciplinis, non sacre pagine auditor effectus, honesta, matura, et sancta conversacione doctor videbatur* sacre *Scripture, non solum (prius)*[4] *incipiens facere quam docere*[f] *sed et prius incipiens facere quam audire. Factus itaque magister arcium, nondum ad sacros ordines promotus, nec adhuc racione alicuius beneficii ecclesiastici compulsus, sed solo Dei instinctu et studio pietatis ductus, supra morem tunc legencium singulis diebus priusquam legeret, missam suam audire consuevit. Quod ut devocius faceret, (capellam)*[5] *de beata Virgine, quam speciali quodam privilegio amoris semper dilexit, in parochia in qua tunc habitabat, construxit, ubi adhuc solempnes misse non desinunt celebrari ad laudem et gloriam ipsius. Porro transactis fere sex annis quibus in artibus rexerat, cum iam placuisset ei qui eum segregavit*

---

[1] non *supplevi*
[2] vite *supplevi iuxta epistolam Oxon*
[3] -dum *supplevi*
[4] prius *supplevi*
[5] capellam *supplevi*

[a] crucis mortificacionem &c. Cf. *2 Cor.* iv. 10.
[b] Adholescens &c. *Prov.* xxii. 6.
[c] *Oxford letter.*
[d] Beati . . . noverunt: *Abingdon letter.*
[e] Crescente . . . quod: *Eynsham letter.*
[f] *Chichester letter.*

Text of the Quadrilogus

ex utero matris sue, ut in eo et per eum revelaret Filium suum,[a] *fieretque vas electionis,*[b] *ad studium theologie quasi per revelacionem se transtulit. In quo tam mirabiliter in brevi profecit quod cito post paucos annos, suadentibus multis* cum instancia, *cathedram magistralem* quasi invitus, quamquam doctus amore iusticie et veritatis, *ascendit.*[c] *Et sicut augebatur et multiplicabatur in eo interius divine lumen sapiencie sic multipliciter refulsit exterius divinissimorum operum claritate. Erat enim predicator eximius, doctor egregius, ignitus in predicacione, et doctrina habens eloquium, mentes auditorum ad veritatis cognicionem illuminans et affectus ad bonitatem accendens,*[1] *ut ex effectu verbi in auditoribus luce clarius pateret quod in eo et per eum loquebatur de quo scriptum est, 'Deus noster ignis consumens est.'*[d] *Pauper et dives, subiectus et prelatus, ut esset vere beatus, manus suas excussit ab omni munere. Habens victum et vestitum, novit hiis contentus esse. Indefessus operator operum misericordie et ad imitacionem* | *precursoris Domini, vir mire et velud singularis abstinencie, carnem edomans* nova et inaudita cilicii asperitate, sompni modicitate, *ante lectum recubans, vestitus et cinctus sompnum brevissimum capiebat. Residuum noctis in lectione seu oracione cum gemitibus et lacrimis et in divinis obsequiis peragebat. Omnia ipsius tam verba quam opera quasi cuiusdam latentis energie voce in mentibus hominum clamabant quod operator eorum non que sua sed que Iesu Christi (sunt)*[2] *per ipsa veraciter querebat.*[e] In eius ore iugiter pax, castitas, veritas, pietas, caritas,[f] que superhabundanter preeminebat in eo pre ceteris virtutibus, quod satis lingua exprimi non possit, nisi quatenus opere iam Deus manifestat. Inimicos vero sibi inimicantes dilexit in tantum ut gratis obsequiis quorumlibet[3] amicorum graves iniurias visus

(fo. 382ᵇ)

---

[1] ascendens *cod*
[2] sunt *supplevi*
[3] quorumlibet: et *cod*

---

[a] cum iam placuisset &c. Cf. *Gal.* i. 15.
[b] *Act.* ix. 15. At this point the deposition contained the vision of St. Edmund's mother, which the copyist has omitted.
[c] Factus . . . ascendit: *Oxford letter.*
[d] Deus noster &c. *Hebr.* xii. 29.
[e] Et sicut . . . querebat: *Chichester letter.*
[f] In eius ore &c. Cf. Sulpicii, *Vita S. Martini,* PL xx. 176.

est pretulisse.[1] Beneficium ecclesiasticum et unicum tantum, quamquam plura fuissent sibi pluries oblata, nunquam nisi cum residencia voluit accipere. Qui quociens lectionibus vacabat, illud et semper resignabat. Quando alios docebat, seipsum pascebat, et cum residenciam faceret, *in exercenda hospitalitate et aliis liberalibus operibus* dapsilis dispensator *sic pollebat, ut quicquid*[2] *erat in facultatibus suis commune bonorum omnium credi posset.*[a] Innumeris *igitur virtutum floribus in beato viro gratissima venustate vernantibus, cepit honestatis (odor)*[3] *necnon et sanctitatis eius circumquaque diffundi*[b] et sicut[4] placuit Altissimo 'talis sanctus, innocens, inpollutus, segregatus a peccatoribus,'[c] sede Cantuariensi | vacante,[d] in pastorem canonice electus est. Et ut illa autoritas quasi tunc primo inter eos in quos fines seculi devenerunt, scilicet 'indignus est sacerdotio nisi fuerit ordinatus invitus', impleretur, contradixit, et sepe et multum reluctatus est. Evocatus recessit, fugiebat invitatus. Set electio divina tam prevaluit ut, suadentibus et inducentibus multis et magnis viris et prout creditur sibi fuisse inspiratum consilium amicorum, adquiesceret et electioni consentiret. *Pastor autem et dux inclitus in populo Dei factus, priorem humilitatem non deposuit,*[e] dignitatis oneri succumbens, non honori. Manum misit ad fortia, quia manus Domini erat cum eo confortans in ministeriis suis sibi commissis, actus suos ordinate dispensans.[5] Non sicut prius set magis ac magis in omnibus virtutibus theologicis, scilicet fide, spe, caritate, et cardinalibus, fortitudine, iusticia, prudencia, temperancia, pollebat. O quam mirabilis modus huius confessoris, qui sub *veste preciosa spiritu pauper* (erat),[6] *in facie leta contritus corde, in mensa lauta penuriam*[7] *eligens,*[8] *nonnunquam*

---

[1] pertulisse *cod* [2] quicunque *cod* [3] odor *supplevi*
[4] sic *cod* [5] dispensantem *cod*
[6] erat *supplevi, sicut hic requirit sensus*
[7] penuria *cod* [8] erigens *cod*

---

[a] *in exercenda &c. Vita S. Thomae auct. Joanne Saresberiensi,* Materials, ii. 307.
[b] igitur ... diffundi: *Oxford letter.*
[c] talis sanctus &c. Cf. *Hebr.* vii. 26.
[d] *Oxford letter.* [e] Ibid.

Text of the Quadrilogus 199

ventre magis vacuus quam refectus,[1] *sepius magis refocillatus quam plenus!*[a] Et sic membrorum vigor animi vigore mutatur, vigor corporis in virtutem spiritus migrat. Pallescit ieiunio speciosa facies, ita quod repente totus ex alio alius ostenditur. In altaris ministerio totus *effundebatur lacrimis, et sic in altaris versabatur officio ac si*[b] fieret actu quod[2] ministerio figurabatur. Qui plane in omnibus exhibuit semetipsum tanquam | Dei ministrum, proba- (fo. 383[b]) *bilem*[3] *operarium in moribus, inconfusibilem*[4] *in actibus et recte tractantem verbum Dei in sermonibus. Erat enim quasi sol refulgens in doctrina et quasi thus redolens in operacione, implens illud Apostoli*[c] '*Sic loquimini, sic et facite*'.

Demum athleta Christi, dum in cura animarum sibi commissa solicitus extitisset, ut animas Deo lucrifaceret, et *antiquus hostis*[e] doleret ab eo esse superatum, *tanti viri profectum vidit et invidit et, ne pace diu frueretur, multos et magnos* excitavit contra eum *incentores*[5] *discordie, per quos* regi Anglorum et curialibus innocens factus est odiosus. Et *orta inte regem et ipsum contencione gravi super iure* et libertatibus ecclesie Cantuariensis, fratribus sibi lites alias voluntate magis inferentibus, magnatibus terre sibi undique iniuriantibus, reformande[6] paci et ad excipiendas ecclesie necessitates constituti (sunt)[7] dies plurimi. Sed *instigante* discensionis autore, contencio inter ipsos (*magis*)[8] *ac magis augebatur in* dies. Vocatis igitur ex parte ipsius regis proceribus, et ex parte archiepiscopi suffraganeis, constituti (sunt)[7] dies multi in corde et ex corde malignancium ad negocium prorogandum, cum presens esset tunc legatus in quo confidebat. Verum tamen archiepiscopus cum quibusdam suffraganeis tanquam subiectus rogavit regem humiliter, velud fidelis consuluit[9]

[1] refetrus *cod* [2] quo *cod* [3] probabile *cod*
[4] inconfusible *cod* [5] innocentores *cod* [6] remando *cod*
[7] sunt *supplevi* [8] magis *supplevi* [9] consul' *cod*

[a] *Vita S. Thomae, Materials,* ii. 308.
[b] Ibid., p. 306.
[c] *Iac.* ii. 2.
[d] in omnibus . . . facite: *Oxford letter.*
[e] The following passage is based on the *Vita S. Thomae, Materials,* ii. 309–10.

fideliter, et ad instar prelati cum omni mansuetudine caritatis monuit frequenter, ut iura ecclesie Cantuariensis, contra sanctorum patrum privilegia et sua suorumque patrum propria iniuste occupata, sibi restitueret. Sed quanto, Deo autore, archiepiscopus humilior extitit in sui[1] iuris prosecucione, tanto, instigante adversario, emuli eius perstiterunt | opere et consilio. Protervitate contumacium exigente, post intolerabiles iniurias, sentencia excommunicacionis occupatores iniuste iuris et libertatis ecclesie Cantuariensis in genere et quosdam, de quibus legitime constabat, specialiter innodavit. Et cum debitum pastoris officium, quamquam ad ecclesie liberacionem manus eius fuisset extenta, premissis obstantibus, minime potuit adimplere, mari transito venit Pontiniacum quo, ut fieret forcior, infirmabatur. Et cum apud Soysi[a] ad tempus se cedere voluisset, dolentibus et flentibus monachis Pontiniaci de suo, licet ad horam, recessu, compassione motus, promisit se in sequenti festo beati Eadmundi martiris reversurum. Quod utique sine prophetico spiritu factum minime fuisse probat non tam veritas sanctitatis ipsius, quam rei promisse consequens eventus. Eodem quippe die, quod non est ei concessum a Domino ut adimpleret vivus, datum (est)[2] ei celitus ut in delacione sui corporis suppleret vel defunctus. Eo vero die apud Soysi translato, corpus gravabatur, sed mente sanior perseverabat. Cum igitur, ingravescente morbo, diem sibi novissimum videret imminere, iussit Viaticum afferri, paratus interim lampadem suam ut, veniente Domino, non imprudenter ei possit obviam exire. Porro quam preclaram lampadem, quam preciosum oleum penes se recondita haberet, testantur ista verba que oblato sibi Viatico, tanquam ad se venienti Domino, protulit, dicens,

'Tu es, Domine, in quem credidi, quem docui, quem predicavi, et tu michi testis es quod in terra positus, nichil aliud

[1] suis *cod*   [2] est *supplevi*

[a] Soisy-en-Brie (Seine-et-Marne). Saint Edmund died there at the Augustinian priory, which was a dependency of Saint-Jacques de Provins: Cottineau, *Répertoire Topo-bibliographique*, ii. 2369.

quam te quesivi. In tua protectione commendo spiritum meum.'

Audientes qui aderant os illud | congruens vite, in quo erat conscia purificati pectoris sermonis luculencia, stupidi admirantur, putantes illum in mentis excessu translatum, eo quod sic loqueretur. Siquidem ad premissa verba, sicut testati sunt qui tunc affuerunt, quasi subito circumfulsit eum lux de celo, ita subito perfudit eum quedam luculenta rubedo, et facies, quam prius cinereus pallor obtexerat, mox erumpente caritatis eius fervore, velut rosei coloris decorem induebat. Stupebant omnes et mirabantur tam subitam mutacionem factam. Contra eum accedunt propius, et contemplantur virum iam quasi transfiguratum, et in amicicia Dei decoratum, sed et quodam modo corpori claritatis sue configuratum. Sumpsit ergo Dei electus eum a quo sumebatur, comprehendit in quo comprehensus fuit. Et inter sumendo, volens, sed non valens, gaudium suum depromere, tandem in vulgari suo proverbiale quoddam protulit, per quod mentis sue leticiam utcumque designavit, dicens (fo. 384ᵇ)

'Men seith, game god en wombe; ac ich segge, game gos en herte,' quod interpretatum, Latinus sermo exprimit sic, verbo ad verbum: 'ludus vadit in ventrem,' quod profecto dicitur cum cibus aliquis ludendo sumitur, de quo venter iocundatur, et subdens, 'set ego dico quod ludus vadit in mentem', de illa nimirum spirituali refectione loquens, de qua mens eius ineffabili iocunditate letabatur. Quam, quo ad cor ineffabilem, quo ad faciem vix inexplicabilem, si quis niteretur[1] exprimere, forsan a veritatis tramite videretur deviare. Completo itaque reverenter sacramento | extreme unctionis, petit sibi tradi signum Dominice crucis. Quam sibi oblatam miro devocionis affectu intuens, et amplectens, loca clavorum frequenter et morose suxit, ac si quiddam latentis inibi dulcedinis conaretur elicere. Osculis frequentibus et affectuosis eam allambens, signum vero lateris lanceati (deosculans),[2] ex mera mentis devocione lacrimis pluentibus, ait (fo. 385ᵃ)

[1] i'teretur *cod*   [2] osculis *cod*

'*Haurietis nunc aquas de fontibus*'[a] etcetera. et adiecit,

'Domine, ego volo quod tu vis, et te invoco testem quod nichil aliud[1] volo. Tua fiat voluntas.' Iam sine fletu quis referat quantam ex hiis fontibus copiam hauriebat? —sine fletu dixerim, ausus[2] risu. Sed certe melius utrumque dicemus quia *musicam in luctu*[b] fecit ei Dominus, et ideo dignum est ut nos lugendo ei congaudeamus.[3] *Inundacionem maris, quasi lac suggebat,*[c] et vinum quod ei Dominus miscuerat cum lacte suo bibebat.[d] Denique laudabilis vita laudabilem exitum est sortita. Nam ut *contempnet vivos impios iustus mortuus,*[e] et ut gloriosus appareat in sanctis suis sanctorum auctor et remunerator Deus, quem[4] prius instituerat meritis, informaret exemplis, iam miraculis confirmat evidentibus et probatis, quorum numerus est innumerabilis et inestimabilis magnitudo, quia multiplicata sunt nimirum, et humanum transcendunt sua magnitudine modum, per que aperte[5] patet qualis spiritus in eius sanctissimi gleba (corporis)[6] habitaverat. Si igitur diabolum vincere, mundo triumphare, carnem domare, proximorum[7] adversa propria reputare, martirium est, martirum corona, confessorum gloria beatissimo rite debetur Eadmundo.

[1] alio *cod* [2] ausum *cod* [3] condeamus *cod*
[4] quoque *cod* [5] apte *cod*
[6] corporis *supplevi ex Trin. Coll. MS. R. 5.40. fo. 60*ᵛ
[7] pro Christianorum *cod, sed correxi iuxta Vitam Anon. B*

[a] *Is.* xii. 3. [b] *Eccli.* xxii. 6. [c] *Deut.* xxxiii. 19.
[d] et vinum &c. Cf. *Cant.* v. 1. [e] *Sap.* iv. 16.

TEXT OF THE
VITA SANCTI EDMUNDI AUCTORE EUSTACHIO DE FAVERSHAM

INCIPIT vita gloriosi confessoris Eadmundi archiepiscopi Cantuariensis ecclesie apud Pontiniacum edita et magistro R(oberto) de Abendonia transmissa, ut eius exercicio recipiant obscura lucem, modum superflua, hiancia iuncturam, minus habencia supplementum.[1] (fo. 151)

Beatus Eadmundus Cantuariensis archiepiscopus *ex piis parentibus* Abendonie *genitus*, extitit *a puericia tam religiose nutritus ut, docente eum Christianissima matre sua quam florem postea fuisse viduarum et vita sua clamat et fama, ieiunare inciperet et orare cum adhuc puerulus esset.*[a] Hec itaque dulci puero cum lactis dulcedine lacte dulcius Christi nomen indidit, amorem immisit, timorem incussit, crescentem et proficientem suo exemplo informavit. Cuius mater tam sancte vivebat ut loricam ferream sue carni innexam finetenus portaret.[b] Infancie siquidem primordia vir iste beatus decora honestans indole *ab ipso puericie tempore cor gessit senile.*[c] Ex utero enim matris sue electus est a domino et meditabatur a pusillo opere placere deo, *semper nitens in carne preter carnem vivere, hostiam vivam, sanctam, deo placentem*[d] *seipsum offerre,* (fo. 151ᵛ) *optinere per graciam quod non habuit per naturam,* | *scilicet quam modo invenit celestem vitam.*[e]

Adolescens autem factus, cum iam esset liberalibus studiis traditus, via qua prius ducebatur incedebat spontaneus,[f] qui iuxta sui nominis interpretacionem mundus vere fuerat atque beatus. Nam ex tunc voluntarie deo sacrificare cepit, ecclesie limina sponte frequentans, vana et frivola quibus adolescentior habundat etas devitans, erudicioni

---

[1] Incipit *om* BCD

[a] ex ... esset: *Oxford letter.*   [b] Hec ... portaret: *Abingdon letter.*
[c] S. Gregorii dialogi, ii, PL lxvi. 125.
[d] hostiam vivam &c. Cf. *Rom.* xii. 1.
[e] semper ... vitam: *Abingdon letter.*
[f] Adolescens ... spontaneus: *Oxford letter.*

sue diligenter intendens, carnis delicias non solum fugiens sed et crucis mortificationem iugiter in suo corpore portans,[a] toto mentis studio vite requisivit auctorem. Videbatur enim[b] iam illud quod nondum legerat intellexisse proverbium: 'Adolescens iuxta viam suam, eciam cum senuerit non recedet ab ea.'[c] Quod in eo vere completum esse invenitur. Nam ieiunare et vigilare sed et cetera penitencie gravia ex tunc tam duxit in consuetudinem facere quod postmodum, ut ipsemet perhibebat, non tam facilia quam eciam delectabilia ei fuerant in provectiori etate.[d] Insolenciam namque carnis restringens baltheo castitatis, asperitate cilicina dura et nodosa carnem studuit edomare, ita quod, excogitato novo cilicii usu, in nocte et manuum et colli nuda tegebat. Et ut afflictus magis affligeretur | corpus ciliciatum funiculo triplici de grossa seta circumcingendo constrinxit, videlicet constringendo circumduxit.

Beati itaque Iohannis Evangeliste imitator existens, carnem suam nulla unquam immundicie macula maculavit, quod et firmiter asserunt qui ipsius confessiones audierunt et qui ipsum ex familiari cum ipso conversatione ab annis puerilibus noverunt.[e] Et sic in carne vixisse creditur preter carnem. Crescente vero etate crevit eciam in virtute. Nam sic gracia sibi divina favente profecit quod[f] dum in annis iuvenilibus liberalibus intenderet disciplinis nondum sacre pagine auditor effectus, honesta, matura, et sancta conversatione doctor videbatur sacre scripture, non solum prius incipiens facere quam docere,[g] sed prius incipiens facere quam audire. Abstinenciam verbi, cibi, potus, et sompni, et rerum omnium mundanarum ab infancia illibatam servavit. Ubi vero occurrunt spectacula numquam tamen spectaculis se immiscuit nec sedit cum concilio vanitatis[h] sive ludencium. Oracioni instabat sedulus, noctes cum brevissima sompni degustacione deducens, non in lecto

---

[a] crucis mortificationem &c. Cf. 2 Cor. iv. 10.

[b] The following sentences, taken from the Oxford letter, are drawn from the Legenda S. Dominici auctore Petro Ferrandi, MOFPH xvi. 212.

[c] Adolescens &c.: Prov. xxii. 6.

[d] Nam . . . etate: Oxford letter.

[e] Beati . . . noverunt: Abingdon letter.

[f] Crescente . . . quod: Eynsham letter.

[g] dum . . . docere: Chichester letter.   [h] Ps. xxv. 4.

sed ante lectum iacens vel sedens semper vestitus et cinctus aliquantulum quiescebat,ᵃ *et hoc per triginta et sex annos et amplius creditur observasse*.ᵇ Semper sibi rigidus et durus, aliis semper affabilis et benignus, vir extitit sanctissime conversacionis, castitate precipuus, abstinencia singularis, in vigiliis, oracionibus, et disciplinis assiduus, scripture sacre doctor egregius, predicator fervens et devotus, confessionum auditor sedulus, pauperum scolarium nutritor piissimus, paupertatis amator, animarum zelator, viciorum extirpator, omnium bonorum exemplum prebuit semetipsum. *Omnia ipsius tam verba quam opera quasi cuiusdam latentis energie voce in mentibus omnium clamabant quod operator eorum non que sua sed que Iesu Christi sunt perquirebat ipsa veraciter*.ᶜ

Tanta quoque penitencie asperitate carnem suam mortificavit pane et aqua frequencius abstinendo aliisque modis quamplurimis, ut vix inveniretur qui vires humanas ad tot et tantes labores sufficere posse estimaret. Sed et ad occultandum hominibus asperitatem quam gerebat interius, semper letum, semper hilarem gratissima et matura iocunditate se exhibuit. Hoc eciam speciale virtutis exemplar | ex aliis duximus exprimendum, quod, licet tantis pollere videretur virtutibus, in hoc se imitatorem mirabilem exhibebat, quod appetitum inanis glorie, que virtuosis viris se multipliciter ingerit importunam, sub quadam simplicitatis cautela et modo mirabili elidebat ab aliis non minus (exemplo)¹ eciam quam verbo doctrine hoc pestiferum et generale vicium repellendo. Mirum eciam in modum² quantum amplius in virtutum adquisicione profecit, tanto magis studuit humilitatem servare, in tantum ut aliquid quod simplicitati possit ab huius mundi sapientibus imputari mallet in

---

¹ exemplo *supplevi iuxta* Trinity Coll. MS. R. 5.40. fo. 58ᵛ
² modum: *add* quod *cod*

ᵃ Oracioni . . . quiescebat: *Eynsham letter.*
ᵇ et hoc . . . observasse: Letter from Bishop Jocelin of Bath: MD. Thes. iii, 1907. Cf. the *Oxford letter*: a tempore quo rexerat in artibus numquam vel raro lectum intraverat, sed vestitus et cinctus, iacens ante lectum &c.
ᶜ Omnia . . . veraciter: *Chichester letter.*

opere publico demonstrare quam ad ostensionem inanem aliquid facere virtuosum. Oppressorum erat refugium, miserorum solacium, afflictorum benignissimus consolator, manus suas ab omni munere immunes conservabat[a] et a suis familiaribus sordes avaricie et immundicie eliminabat pro posse.

Factus itaque magister arcium, nondum ad sacros ordines promotus, nec adhuc racione alicuius adepti beneficii ecclesiastici compulsus, sed solo dei instinctu et studio pietatis ductus, supra morem tunc legencium (fo. 153ᵛ) *singulis diebus priusquam legeret missam | audire consuevit. Quod ut devocius faceret, capellam de Beata Virgine, quam speciali quodam privilegio amoris semper diligebat, in parochia in qua tunc habitabat, construxit, ubi adhuc solempnes misse non desinunt celebrari ad laudem et gloriam ipsius.*[b] Cumque hiis atque aliis plurimis virtutibus excellenter premineret, addidit dominus suo servo illam graciam meritorum ut vivens eciam miraculis choruscaret prout illi qui oculata fide viderunt et interfuerunt fida assercione protestantur. Sic enim nutrix gracia magnificum fidei zelatorem prosequebatur, sicut a multis viris fide dignis qui eum ab infancia plenius noverunt creditur, quod ab omni peccato mortali fuit immunis, *ut cum beato Iob dicere possit 'ab inicio coaluit michi miseracio et pietas de utero matris egressa est mecum'*.[c] Illud autem spectabile fuit in eo quod beneficium ecclesiasticum non retinuit nisi faceret residenciam, ita quod, quando transtulit se ad studium, resignavit, si quod habuit, quod antea apud nostrates fuerat inauditum.

Porro transactis fere sex annis quibus in artibus rexerat, cum iam placuisset ei qui eum segregavit ex utero matris sue ut in eo et per | (fo. 154) *eum revelaret Filium Suum,*[d] *fieretque vas eleccionis,*[e] *ipso adhuc cursim legente*[f] *arismeticam quibusdam sociis suis, apparuit ei in sompniis pia mater eius paulo ante defuncta dicens,*

---

[a] manus suas &c.: Cf. *Vita S. Thomae auct. Ioanne Saresberiensi* in *Materials*, ii. 307.   [b] Factus . . . ipsius: *Oxford letter*.

[c] ut . . . mecum: *Vita S. Thomae auct. Ioanne Saresberiensi*, p. 303. An adaptation of *Iob* xxxi. 18.

[d] cum iam placuisset &c. Cf. *Galat*. i. 15.   [e] fieretque &c.: *Act*. ix. 15.

[f] i.e. 'cursorary' as opposed to 'ordinary' lectures. On these terms see Strickland Gibson, *Statuta Antiqua Universitatis Oxoniensis* (1933), p. lxxxi.

Vita S. Edmundi auctore Eustachio

'*Fili, quid legis? Que sunt ille figure quibus tam studiose intendis?*'

Quo respondente,

'*Talia lego*', *ostensis protractionibus que in illa solent fieri facultate, illa mox dexteram manum eius arripuit et in ea tres circulos*[1] *depinxit. In quibus hec tria nomina per ordinem inscripsit: Pater · Filius · Spiritus Sanctus. Et hoc facto sic ait,*

'*Fili karissime, talibus figuris et non aliis de cetero intende.*'

Quo sompnio quasi per revelacionem edoctus, statim ad studium theologie se transtulit, in quo tam mirabiliter in brevi profecit ut cito post paucos annos suadentibus multis cathedram magistralem ascendit.[a] Idem quoque pater antequam theologie publicus rector existeret, per annum et amplius in domo et cenobio Meretonie iugiter morabatur, et postea per longum tempus quasi unus ex eiusdem ecclesie filiis sepius intravit et exivit quia quidam fratrum in ipsius sancti valde delectabantur colloquiis et fovebantur consiliis conversacionem ipsius ineffabiliter admirantes. Nam in mundo | conversans mundum conculcaverat, et etate iuvenis quosque senes fide, doctrina, sciencia, consilio, (fo. 154v) excedebat et quod mirabile (est)[2] dictu inter scolares[3] gradiens non solum religiosus sed eciam forma tocius religionis inter eos videbatur. Erat enim in lectionibus et meditacionibus assiduus, in oracione devotissimus, semper in ieiuniis et vigiliis continuus, horam nullam matutinarum dormiendo preteriens, sed ad omnes horas una cum fratribus quasi deditus esset, accedens. Nec solum gestus exteriores religionis sed eciam secretissimos quos in Spiritu Sancto didicerat, pretendebat, clavem scilicet tocius religionis habens. Quia fedus in tantum cum oculis pepigerat ut quemdam fratrem per annum in mensa ei ministrantem minime cognosceret. Equidem qualiter de virtute in virtutem celitus creverit ut deum deorum in Syon videret,[b] non solum illis sed et omnibus innotuit.[c]

---

[1] ortulos *cod*
[2] est *supplevi*
[3] scholares: *fortasse legendum* seculares *ut in* Trinity Coll. MS. R. 5.40. fo. 58

[a] Porro . . . ascendit: *Oxford letter.*
[b] de virtute &c. Cf. Ps. lxxxiii. 8.
[c] Idem quoque pater . . . innotuit: *Merton letter.*

Tanta denique diligencia, tantaque discendi aviditate sacris literis prius inheserat quod pene noctes ducebat insompnes et videbantur ei dies pauci pre amoris magnitudine qua ad speciose Rachelis castos hanelabat amplexus. Nec est fraudatus a desiderio suo.[a] Nam iuxta estimacionem suam modicum in opere eius laboravit | et cito de generacionibus percepit.[b] *Etenim divini verbi semina intenta[1] cordis aure suscipiens, tamquam terra celesti rore perfusa, non solum sanctarum meditacionum et affectionum segetes sed eciam bonorum operum fructus uberrimos ex se producebat. Verum eciam legendo et disputando eiusdem verbi strenuus et egregius seminator ad aliorum edificacionem tamquam imbres eloquia divine sapiencie mittebat.*[c] Unde factum est ut ob tantam edificacionem tam in maturitate sermonum quam in exhibicione salubrium exemplorum, viri religiosi non pauci inter quos tempore vacacionis commorari solebat quorum corda tetigerat deus, *tanta et talia perpendentes in eo sanctitatis indicia, se in comparacione ipsius in habitu seculari constituti[2] tepidos arbitrantes et desides cum haberentur religiosi, iuxta illud vaticinium Ysaye 'Erubesce Sydon ait mare',*[d] *de tempore siquidem suo erubescere ceperunt et ad talis ac tanti viri imitacionem vitam ducere solito correctiorem.*[e]

Sicut augebatur et multiplicabatur in eo interius divine lumen sapiencie, sic multipliciter refulsit exterius divinissimorum operum claritate.[f] Quod vero nocturno sompno sine gravi dispendio corporis deducere poterat, lacrimis | et oracionibus indulgebat et meditacionibus sanctis, castimoniam sectans in corpore, servans in corde pudiciciam, modestiam in sermone, in opere iusticiam, ut quos erudiurus erat verbo sanctitatis sue moneret exemplo. Erat enim predicator eximius, doctor egregius, ignitum in predicacione et doctrina habens eloquium, mentes auditorum ad

[1] intenta D in tanta A B₁ B₂ C₁   [2] add se A B₁ B₂ C₁

[a] Nec est fraudatus: Cf. *Ps.* lxxvii. 30.
[b] Cf. *Eccli.* vi. 20.
[c] Tanta ... mittebat: *Oxford letter.* Much of the passage was drawn by the authors of the letter from the *Legenda prior* of St. Dominic.
[d] *Is.* xxiii. 4.
[e] Unde ... correctiorem: *Reading letter.*
[f] Sicut ... claritate: *Chichester letter.*

Vita S. Edmundi auctore Eustachio

veritatis cognicionem illuminans et affectus ad bonitatem accendens, ut effectu verbi in auditoribus luce clarius pateret quod Ipse in eo et per eum loquebatur de quo scriptum est:[a] '*Ignis consumens est.*'[b] *Unde et effectus est clericis gratus, laicis acceptus, ipsis eciam principibus reverendus. Cumque sederet inter primos erat tamen merencium consolator. Ab infancia quippe cum eo creverat miseracio,*[c] *que aliorum sibi coacervans miserias, nullius afflictionis aspecte permittebat eum non esse participem.*[d] Cuius mens ad pietatem mollior, cuius esset cibus durior? Cuius sermo blandior, cuius amictus asperior? Quis loqui rarius, quis orare crebrius possit! Quem minus ab adolescencia detineret lectulus, quem magis lectio? Quem minus moveret iniuria, quem magis misericordia? Quis daret promptius quod sibi detraxisset? Cui honore rarior mundus, cui frequencius Christus? Quis in illa | sublimitate (fo. 156) virtutum positus, sibimet ipsi minor videretur, et quo magis merito ascenderet, hoc magis conpunctione decresceret?

Superhabundantem graciam caritatis, qua preminens in sublimitate charismatum multorum corda ad se convertit, sicut multi noverunt qui hoc per experimentum didicere, non possumus satis habundanter exprimere, quia quoslibet inimicos sibique inimicantes dilexit in tantum, ut gratis obsequiis quorumlibet amicorum graves eciam iniurias visus fuit pretulisse. Quod quibusdam displicebat austeris. *In exercenda vero hospitalitate et aliis liberalibus operibus sic pollebat, ut quicquid erat in facultatibus suis commune bonorum omnium credi potuisset.*[e] Vicium detractionis, quod in locutionis cursu surripere consuevit viris eciam sibi studiose caventibus, summa intentione vitabat, ita quod cum occasio detractionis incideret, aut verba detractoria incidebat mutando materiam, aut, si verba persisterent detrahentis, penitus abscedebat, nolens pollui audiendo qui vix aut nunquam ipsum polluere consueverat in loquendo. In altari existens *totus effundebatur lacrimis et sic in altaris versabatur*

---

[a] *Hebr.* xii. 29.   [b] Erat ... est: *Chichester letter.*
[c] Ab infancia &c. *Iob* xxxi. 18.
[d] Unde ... participem: *Oxford letter.*
[e] *Vita S. Thomae auct. Joanne Saresberiensi,* p. 309.

(fo. 156ᵛ) *officio ac si presencialiter | in carne geri dominicam cerneret passionem. Reverentissime quidem divina sacramenta tractabat ita ut intuencium fidem et mores ipsa contractacio informaret.*[a] Si quis autem velit inspicere in quanta mansuetudine ubique subditos pertractavit et quot ubique virtutum propagavit exempla, nimia prolixitate onerabit auditores. Erat quippe in divinorum munerum gracia ubique precipuus, in corpore castus, mente devotus, affabilis colloquio, amabilis aspectu, prudencia preditus, temperancia clarus, interna fortitudine firmus, censura iusticie stabilis, longanimitate assiduus, paciencia robustus, humilitate mansuetus, caritate sollicitus, et ita in eo omnium virtutum decorem sapiencia adornabat ut, secundum Apostolum,[b] semper illius sermo in gracia sale esset conditus.

Nunquam in ore eius nisi pax, nisi castitas, nisi pietas, nisi caritas, nunquam in corde eius nisi omnium horum fons Christus[c] habitavit, qui ei et per eum plurimos caritatis, gaudii, pacis, longanimitatis, fidei, modestie, continencie, fructus ministravit exuberantes. *Talibus virtutum floribus in beato viro gratissima venustate vernantibus, cepit odor honestatis necnon et san-* (fo. 157) *ctitatis | eius circumquaque diffundi.*[d] Nam *doctrina ipsius ita erat catholica et lucida ut de eo per totam regionem anglicanam passim ab omnibus diceretur, 'Lingua eius calamus scribe velociter scribentis.'*[e] *Scivit eciam iuxta humanam capacitatem quodam modo excellentissimo de thesauro sacre scripture proferre nova et vetera, ita quod cum legeret vel predicaret, visum esset auditoribus suis quod digitus dei scribebat in corde suo verba vite que procedebant de ore eius.*[f] *Et quia talis decebat ut esset pontifex sanctus, innocens, impollutus, et segregatus a peccatoribus,*[g] *vacante postmodum sede Cantuariensi, divina inspirante gracia in archipresulem sollempniter est electus.*[h] Verum electioni de se concorditer, communiter, et canonice facte per

---

[a] totus ... informaret: *Vita S. Thomae, Materials*, ii. 307.
[b] Cf. *Col.* iv. 6.
[c] Nunquam ... Christus. Cf. *Sulpicii Vita S. Martini*, PL xx. 176.
[d] Talibus ... diffundi: *Oxford letter*.   [e] *Ps.* xliv. 2.
[f] doctrina ... eius: *Salisbury letter*.   [g] Cf. *Heb.* vii. 26.
[h] Et quia ... electus: *Oxford letter*; the writers of the letter are here drawing on the Legend of St. Dominic, see p. 292.

Vita S. Edmundi auctore Eustachio 211

duos dies noluit consentire. Qui tandem multorum persuasionibus invitus, et vi tractus, consensit. Unde sicut de beato Gregorio legitur[a] ita et de eo: capitur, trahitur, et in nomine sancte Trinitatis metropolitanus tocius Anglie cum summa devocione et leticia cunctorum consecratur.

Pastor autem et dux inclitus in populo Dei factus, priorem humilitatem non deposuit sed in abstinencia iugi, in vestis asperitate, in vigiliis multis, carnem spiritui et sensualitatem racioni servire coegit, dignitatis | oneri succumbens non honori. Pristina retinetur (fo. 157ᵛ) humilitas conservata in tantum ut pontificalis fastigium dignitatis mentem eius nulla elacionis ostensione corrumpere videretur. De animarum sibi commissa cura sollicitus, aut recipiendis confessionibus eorum quos in multa lenitate spiritus confovebat ut lucrifaceret Christo, aut predicacioni,[1] per se vel per alios sedulus intendebat. Et vere (puto)[2] neminem diffiteri sibi ad martirium tempus, non animum, defuisse. Cui non fuit aliud vivere nisi Christum cum dilectione timere et cum timore diligere. Abstinencie consuetudo prioris, licet archiepiscopales delicias inveniret, usum sobrietatis antique retinuit illibatum. Oracionum instancia consueto cursu olim noctes cum sompni brevissima degustacione deducens, non amittitur in mutacione officii, sed mutatur. Negociorum enim occupacio quam officii necessitas ingerebat, horam consuetam orandi prepediens, consuetudinem orandi, non studium alternavit. Quia datum sibi tempus in ocio non consumpsit, sancte meditacioni quam predicacioni consultius reservababat vel oracioni vacando quam pro se ac pro commisso sibi populo fundere necesse habebat. De silencio vero suo in ecclesia et nocturnis horis et post Completorium, fuit inestimabile.[c] Nam dum | fuit Rome, (fo. 158)

[1] predicacione *cod*
[2] puto *supplevi iuxta Trinity College, MS. R. 5. 40. fo. 59ᵛ*

[a] *Vita S. Gregorii auct. Ioanne Diacono, PL* lxxv. 81.
[b] Pastor . . . coegit: *Oxford letter.*
[c] This and the following sentence represent Eustace's efforts to develop the following note in the left margin of the Trinity MS. fo. 59ʳ: 'De summo silencio post Completorium, ita quod, quando fuit in curia Romana, ad vocacionem pape post Completorium vix voluit ad eum ire.'

quodam sero ad vocacionem domini Pape pulsatus post Completorium, invitus et a suis increpatus, accessit ad eum et hoc ideo quia noluit infringere silencium post Completorium. Morose siquidem et tarde ivit ad aulam et citissime ad ecclesiam.

Erat autem sicut de beato Martino legitur,[a] hic *pauper et modicus, sed celo dives et magnificus, subiectus et prelatus, ut esset vere beatus, manus suas excuciens ab omni munere, habens victum et vestitum, novit hiis esse contentus, indefessus operator omnium operum misericordie.*[b] Misericordia exuberans quam erga pauperes et afflictos semper habuerat, in assumpto pontificali officio non defecit, sed perquisitarum simul cum officio habundancia facultatum usu largiori mentem simul et intencionem secuta est largitoris. Sed ne quis forte moveatur quod Eadmundum Martino equiparaverim, qui hoc dicis, si recte percenseas, pene similia ab utroque potes videre completa. Martinus[c] adhuc cathecuminus Algentem pauperem divisa clamide vestivit; Eadmundus fide robustus tot milia veterem hominem exuta fidei veste[1] contexit. Martinus primo solitariam delegit vitam ut Christi dulcedine singulariter frueretur; Eadmundus exteras regionis partes expetiit ut multorum animas lucraretur. | Martinus in virtute Trinitatis deifice trium mortuorum est magnificus suscitator; Eadmundus totidem et plures ad vitam revocans mortuos, tociens mortis extitit victor. Martini corpus hii, qui ductu eius mundum vicerant, prosequuntur. Eadmundi exequiis hii, qui eo duce celestia iam tenebant, famulantur. Quid plura? Uni regi militarunt, uni domino servierunt, uno spiritu sanctificati sunt, supra petram unius fidei sunt. Restat ergo ut par sit eis honor et gloria quos virtutis actio pares in Christi constituit disciplina.

Ostiatim mendicancium nullus ab eius ianuis vacuus recessit. Lares egrorum et debilium per suos diligencius scrutabatur et beneficiis

---

[1] tot milia &c.: multus viciorum frigore torpentes caritatis veste predicando C₁

[a] *Sulpicii Severi Epistolae*, iii, PL xx. 184.
[b] pauper . . . misericordie: *Chichester letter*.
[c] The following comparison is based on Sulpicius, *Dialogi*, ii, PL xx. 201–12.

Vita S. Edmundi auctore Eustachio

visitabat quamplurimis, cotidiano victu vestituque sustentans.[a] *In oracione continuus erat, in lacrimarum effusione profluus, in animarum zelo fervidus, ad prospera non remissus, ad adversa securus. Quid plura?*[b] Informatur pontificalis auctoritas in delinquentes sic zelo rectitudinis ne[1] mansuetudinis[2] deserat lenitatem, sicque iudiciorum studeat equitati ne dissolucionem redoleat indulgencia vel vindicta seviciam. Convenitur predicatorum vita non indoctis humane sapiencie verbis Evangelium ponere, sed in ostensione spiritus et virtute, ne gloriam querens ab hominibus, gloriam que a solo Deo est non optineat, et foris effusa mercedis interne munere vacuetur. Componitur | popularium status non (fo. 159) recedere a fidei fundamento, persistere in lege testamenti, principalibus edictis esse subiectus, nec publicis execucionibus adversari. Sic fructificatis omnibus unius exemplo,[3] in omni opere[4] eius pietatis cultus et semita veritatis elucet. Laudemus Deum qui fecit illum, qui sicut in sanctis suis semper est et ubique mirabilis, sic est in beati virtute miranda laudabilis. Ipse in illo nomini suo dat gloriam qui magnificavit eum in laude,[c] qui fecit eum excelsum in verbo glorie,[d] et in verbis monstra placavit.[e] Quid plura? *In omnibus exhibuit semetipsum tamquam Dei ministrum, probabilem in moribus, operarium inconfusibilem in actibus, et recte tractantem verbum Dei in sermonibus.*[f] *Erat enim quasi sol refulgens*[g] *in doctrina et quasi thus redolens*[h] *in operacione, implens illud Apostoli, 'sic loquimini et sic facite'.*[i] *Et quasi alter Iohannes Baptista in deserto angelus factus generalis predicator, turbis et publicanis et militibus, magnis et parvis utriusque sexus, religiosis et clericis verba sancte predicacionis et exhortacionis cum affectu et effectu, lucide, salubriter, et incessanter proposuit.*[j]

[1] origine AB₁B₂C₂D ne C₁   [2] *add* ne A
[3] *add* eo A   [4] tempore B₁B₂C₁C₂D

[a] Ostiatim &c.: *Vita S. Thomae, Materials*, ii. 307.
[b] In oracione ... plura: *Oxford letter*.
[c] magnificavit &c. Cf. *Ps.* lxviii. 31.
[d] Cf. *Eccli.* xlvii. 9.   [e] Cf. *Eccli.* xlv. 2.
[f] operarium &c. Cf. *2 Tim.* ii. 15.
[g] Cf. *Eccli.* l. 7.   [h] Cf. *Eccli.* l. 8.   [i] *Iac.* ii. 2.
[j] Et quasi ... proposuit: *Salisbury letter*.

Sane quid est aliud Deo dignius (quam)¹ vita pontificis (que prestat)² bene vivendi lumen eximium, speculum sanctitatis, iusticie zelus, magisterium | pietatis, formam³ doctrine, discipline sanctionem,⁴ religionis exemplum. Habent omnis in eo sexus, etas, condicio, gradus, ordo, statusve, quid eligat, et in omnes habundanter emanat luminis huius sancta serenitas. Invenit in eo puericia quid imitetur, adoptat robur virile quid appetat, quid imitetur, quid sequatur vigilancia senectutis. Instruitur in eo nobilitas plus anime quam carnis affectare delicias, et ornare natalium dignitatem decore virtutum, humiliari et obedire. Status ordinis edocetur ne, perversi turbinis aura supra se raptus, inaniter animus elacionis superbiam gestans intumescat, et ad eius sortem pertinere videatur qui est rex super omnes filios superbie. Potestas enim a Deo est.ᵃ Non (oportet)⁵ altum sapere, sed timere et in terrene sublimitatis eminencia celestibus imperiis humiliter subici nec divinam refellere voluntatem. Et quidem *in veste preciosa* vir iste beatus *spiritu pauper, in facie leta, contritus corde, in mensa lauta penuriam eligens, nonnumquam ventre magis vacuus quam refectus, sepius magis refocillatus quam plenus.*ᵇ Membrorum vigor animi vigore mutatur, virtus corporis in virtutem spiritus migrat, pallescit ieiunio speciosa facies ita quod repente totus ex alio alius ostenditur. Aliquando a potu | sic abstinebat quod pili capitis sui et barbe ceciderunt, quia humorem nutritivum non habebant. Cuius depilacionis deformitas socios suos in arte medicinali tunc regentes minime latuit. Quibus inter se sciscitantibus et disputantibus que huius rei esset causa, argumenti scrutinio inventum est hoc ex defectu humorum accidisse.

Archiepiscopus Eboracensis inter multa de beato Eadmundo scribens, ita loquitur:ᶜ *Fuit itaque* vir iste gloriosus, *ut firmiter*

---

¹ quam *supplevi*
² que prestat: quam ABCD, *sed correxi sicut requirit sensus*
³ forma *cod*   ⁴ sanctio *cod*   ⁵ oportet *supplevi*

ᵃ *Rom.* xiii. 1.
ᵇ in veste &c. *Vita S. Thomae, Materials,* ii. 308.
ᶜ What follows is from the letter of Archbishop Walter Gray.

credo, *a lapsu carnis omnino immunis, fide firmus, spe robustus, caritate ferventissimus, lingua facundus, abstinencie plurimum deditus, in oracionibus sedulus, in vigiliis creber, strenuus in disciplinis, doctor egregius, predicator eximius, confessor discretus, cilicio ad carnem indutus, in lecto vix aut numquam quietis gracia recubans, in adversis fortissimus, in prosperis mansuetus, affabilis omnibus, verbo pius, cum debita maturitate semper gaudens et hilaris, compaciens miseris, elemosinarum largitor largissimus, merencium consolator usque adeo quod tanquam alter Iob dicere potuit,* 'Pes fui claudo, oculus ceco, pater pauperum, solacium miserorum.'[a] *Et, ut breviter dicam, ita se universis exemplar bonitatis exhibuit ut eius merita vix humana lingua sufficeret enarrare.*

Cuius cum recolo inexpugnabilem in operibus fidem, precipuum in victu rigorem, diuturnam cum mundo et diabolo colluctacionem, incunctanter affirmo hunc, non impleta passione, implesse martirium. Non enim martirium sola sanguinis effusione[1] consummatur, nec sola dat fidei palmam exustio illata flammarum aut contagio funesta carnificum. Contemptu quoque corporis nec occasu solo ad coronam venitur. Absque iniuria sanctorum qui in persecucionibus sunt defuncti, dicere liceat, carnem afflixisse, de mundo triumphasse, diabolum et carnem vicisse, martirium est. Nam, ut ipsa rerum comparacione altrinsecus conferamus, martir vicit subitum tortoris ignem; beatissimus Eadmundus vicit cotidianam corporis flammam. Martir habet brevem cum persecutore conflictum; hic habuit adversus carnis vicia certamen. Ille in gentili colluctacione, hic servavit in diabolica infestacione, pacienciam. Martir pro Christo patitur quia pati desiderat; et hic pati voluit. Ille abnegans idola, Deum confitetur; hic, quo clarius Christum confitetur, seipsum negavit sibi. Post martiris certamen mors consummat, dum ingeritur; huius certamen actum est, dum mors negatur. Apostolus enim dicit,[b] 'Michi vivere Christus est et mori lucrum.' Quia vero *celestis docebat unctio sive* cum

---

[1] effusione B₂C₁C₂D infusione AB₁

[a] Iob xxix. 15.   [b] Phil. i. 21.

illitteratis sive cum *litteratis colloquebatur, mirum in modum eius collacio tam pondere sentenciarum quam puritate verborum placens erat et efficax. Post epulas autem et sompnum, ubi necessitas poscebat, exactum, aut scripturis aut honestis colloquiis insistebat, ocium summopere fugiens, ne viderent eum hostes et deriderent sabbata eius.*[a] Raro cenavit et rarissime post prandium potavit. Post matutinas clericis et eciam capellanis suis euntibus dormitum, ipse tam tempore hiemali quam estivali remansit in oratorio solus, reliquum noctis in meditacionibus, lacrimis, et oracionibus expendebat. Cum diabolo conflictum sepius habebat. Vidit eciam aliquando diabolum inter Wroteham et Ottefordiam in specie draconis ex ore suo ignem fulminantis, cuius caput nunc in celum, caudam vero nunc in terram, vice versa habebat.

Videns[b] *hostis antiquus tantum virum ecclesie Dei plurimum profuturum, invidit et, ne pace* principis *diucius frueretur, multos et magnos elegit incentores discordie per quos in corde regis et curialium odii seminarium sparsit. Orta siquidem hiis procurantibus questione* (fo. 161ᵛ) *super iuribus et dignitatibus* | ecclesie, *filios perdicionis in perniciem sancti viri excitavit, qui subvertere ecclesie libertatem moliebantur. Sed cum* alie (ecclesie)[1] cathedrales *opprimerentur, ecclesia Cantuariensis ipsum angebat. Cuius potestati, honori, et utilitati plurimum derogabatur, insurgentibus in eum primum quibusdam viris religiosis, deinde proceribus multis, et ipso rege dampna et iniurias graves inferente. Convenientibus* suffraganeis ex mandato archiepiscopi *et proceribus ex mandato regis ad excipiendas ecclesie necessitates, orta est contencio inter regem et ecclesiam, que, instigante diabolo, magis ac magis augebatur in dies. Reformande paci constituti sunt dies plurimi, sed, instigante dissensionis auctore, post prorogacionem dilacionum frustratoriarum discordes ab invicem discesserunt. Tunc archiepiscopus securus ascendens ex adverso opponensque se murum pro domo*

---

[1] ecclesie *supplevi*

[a] ne viderent &c. Cf. *Lam.* i. 7. Quia ... eius: *Vita S. Thomae, Materials*, ii. 308.

[b] The following account of the archbishop's difficulties is taken from John of Salisbury's *Vita S. Thomae, Materials*, ii. 309.

Israel, post innumeras vexaciones et iniurias, de consilio suffraganeorum suorum, in pacis ecclesie perturbatores sentenciam tulit excommunicacionis. *Vir siquidem Dei fundatus in petra et solidatus, nec blanditiis emolliri potuit nec minis terreri ut a cultu iusticie deviaret. Hanc itaque mutacionem dextere Excelsi*[a] *maligna interpretacione conati sunt impii obfuscare.* | *Supersticioni ascribentes quod vitam duceret altiorem, zelum iusticie crudelitatem mentiebantur. Quod ecclesie procurabat utilitates, avaricie attribuebant. Contemptum mundani favoris veneracionem vane glorie esse dicebant. Curialis magnificencia fingebatur elacio. Quod divinitus edoctam voluntatem sequebatur in plurimis nota supercilii dicebatur. Quod antecessorum metas utendo iure sepe videbatur excedere, temeritatis arbitrabantur indicium. Quid plura? Nichil iam ab eo vel dici vel fieri poterat quod non malicia hominum depravaretur.*[b]

Tantis itaque dissimulacionibus, quas enumerare perlongum est,[2c] dabantur cornua peccatoribus, et contra sanctum rex appellavit et precipui ecclesie filii precipui ecclesie fiunt inimici. Qui cum cure pastoralis officium libere non poterat exercere, licet manus eius ad ecclesie liberacionem fuisset extenta, cedendum tamen censuit malicie, gloriosum martirem Thomam in hoc facto volens imitari. Sed quia ecclesia sua ere alieno nimis extiterat onerata, cum paucis transfretare disposuit. In orientali igitur parte Anglie que dicitur Sandwicus,[1] navigio clam preparato, prospero vento optatum portum advenit, se et suos et ecclesie sue causam Deo et gloriose Virgini | et beato martiri (fo. 162ᵛ) commendans. Qui, cum ad Pontiniacum devenisset, quadam infirmitate corripitur que, licet dolorem ingereret infirmanti, minus tamen sensum eius vel racionis vigorem pristinum immutavit. Sed, cum de Pontiniaco recessisset et ad Soysy

---

[1] Tanathos B₁B₂ Thanathos C₁C₂ Thanatos D   [2] est *add* quibus ABCD

[a] Hanc mutacionem &c. Cf. *Ps.* lxxvi. 11.
[b] The preceding account is wholly derived from the *Vita S. Thomae, Materials,* ii. 309–10.
[c] This disjointed sentence is a clumsy expansion of a note in the margin of the Trinity College MS. fo. 60ʳ. Matthew Paris, when copying Eustace, wisely decided to drop it altogether.

pervenisset, eius infirmitas in dies ingravescebat. Quadam autem die Eucharistiam cum debita veneracione fecit deferri. Ante cuius perceptionem proposuit omnes articulos fidei, et ex fervore fidei ita loquebatur et ita se habebat, suis et aliis astantibus et videntibus, *ac si presencialiter in carne geri dominicam cerneret passionem.*[a] Cuius fidei fervor et devocionis affectus multo maior fuit quam sermo sufficiat animi meditacione describere. Inter cetera que proposuit, hec et hiis similia dixit,

'Tu es domine, in quem credidi, quem dilexi, quem amavi, quem predicavi, quem docui, et tu michi testis es quod non quesivi in terra nisi te.'

Que verba nonnulli sapientes stupidi admirantur. Post perceptionem dixit Anglice,

'Me seid, game gath on wombe, ac ich segge game goth on horte,'[1] quod est dictu, 'Dicitur, ludus vadit in ventrem, at ego dico nunc ludus intrat cor,' id est, nimis letificat cor pre nimio gaudio. Et re vera tantam pretendebat hilaritatem et iocunditatem quod circumstantes non modicum admirarentur. Cuius hilaritatem qui veraciter vellet depromere, veritatis metas forsitan videretur excedere, videlicet de vultu hilari et leta facie. Vidimus illas pietatis lacrimas, illam iugem ac perpetuam mentis serenitatem, cuius testimonium vultus immutabilis erat. Audivimus quoque os illud congruens vite in quo erat consciencia purificati pectoris, sermonis luculencia.

Sacramento extreme unctionis reverenter accepto, accepit crucem non sine gemitibus et lacrimis eam amplectens, et mira devocione loca clavorum morose et frequenter deosculans, vulnus vero lateris lanceati oculis illacrimantibus respiciens, et diu suggens locum vulneris, dixit,

'Haurietis nunc aquas de fonte Salvatoris' etcetera.[b]

Cuius devocio et devocionis modus sensibus astancium ultra

---

[1] Men seid game goth on wombe ac ic segge game got on herte B_1B_2 Men seith gamen gamen goth in wombe, ac ich saie gamen gamen goth in hert C_1 It is saeid game game goth in wambe, ac ich segge game goth in herte C_2 Man seid gamen god an uombe, and ich sigge game god on herte D

[a] *Vita S. Thomae, Materials,* ii. 307.   [b] *Is.* xii. 3.

modum erant admirandi eo quod in eo mixtam tanta hilaritate viderunt disciplinam. Deficiente denique membrorum ministerio, nova semper mentis gracia pullulabat. Sompno deinde ultimo exceptus, in mortis quietem sub quiete dormientis transiit sine ullo, ut se habent, supremo[1] luctamine. Nullas difficilis obitus moras sensit. | Angelicis choris anima illa sancta, generosa, (fo. 163ᵛ) sincera, et ab omni contactu mundi incontaminata, suscipitur. In transitu vero ipsius sexto decimo kalendas (Decembris)[2] terminus est assignatus, et undecimo kalendas eiusdem mensis corpus eius in ecclesia beate Marie Pontiniacensis humane condicionis lege sepultum est. Quo in loco vere se in Christo vivere demonstrat frequentissima consolacione vivencium. Ut condempnet vivos impios iustus mortuus[a] et ut gloriosus appareat in sanctis suis sanctorum auctor et remunerator Deus, quos prius instituerat meritis, informarat exemplis, iam miraculis confirmat evidentibus et probatis que, glorioso confessore Eadmundo in Pontiniacensi ecclesia sepulto, statim choruscare ceperunt. Etenim preter opera sanctitatis et signa virtutis quibus in carne positus claruit, multorum et diversorum iam curatis languoribus et pristine sanitati restitutis, aperte patet qualis spiritus in eius sanctissimi gleba corporis habitaverit. Vivens eciam in carne prophecie spiritu pollebat vir iste gloriosus sicut per sequencia patebit. In recessu namque suo a Pontiniaco doluerunt monachi et fleverunt quidam. Quibus sanctus dixit,

'Nolite fratres et amici de recessu meo tristes fieri, quia in festo | sancti Eadmundi regis et martiris per Dei graciam ad (fo. 164) vos revertar.' Quod ita factum est. Eadem siquidem die beati confessoris corpus Pontiniacum constat esse delatum.

Cum igitur prima die post dormicionem eius sanctissimum illud corpus de Soysoy apud Triangulum Pagum[b] fuisset delatum, magna fidei ambicione et populi devocione vestitum est. Distentis agminibus incredibili reverencia corpus

[1] suprema A
[2] Novembris ABCD; *sic quoque in Trinity College MS. fo. 60ᵛ, sed correxi*

[a] Cf. *Sap.* iv. 16.
[b] Trainel (Aube), about 18 kilometres from Soisy.

suscipiunt. Omnes pariter delectantur aspectu, sancta iudicantes que corpus tetigissent et se sanctificari tactu eorum vel usu credentes. Neque enim ullus non magno sibi dampno affici visus est, si conspectu corporis sacri caruit, si non ut quemque res aut reverencia aut amor suaserit osculum ori ipsius aut quibuscumque membris ipsius impressit aut feretro, et tetigisse eum singulis salutare videbatur. Cumque abbas Pontiniacensis vidisset populi concursum et cleri et populi admirabilem devocionem et reverenciam corpori exhibitam, et quod veneracio excederet modum, ammotis prius extraneis, in hunc modum locutus est, dicens,

'Bone pater, in eo quod es frater ecclesie Pontiniacensis, teneris michi obedire. Unde rogo quatinus nullum facias signum antequam pervenias ad locum requiescionis tue Pontiniacum.' Abbas vero timens | ne corpus ei auferretur, signavit feretrum sigillo suo, presente illo et vidente qui scripsit hec et aliis quamplurimis.

(fo. 164ᵛ)

Cum vero secunda die cum sancto corpore transitum faceremus per Villam Novam archiepiscopi,[a] occurrit ei multitudo virorum ac mulierum letabundis acclamacionibus sancto applaudencium et feretrum mira devocione deosculancium intra agminum spissamenta detentum. Et licet hoc moleste acciperemus, nulla tamen potuimus pronos et devotos racione compescere, nulla interdictione repellere quin vi et virium suarum violencia corpus ad ecclesiam deportarent, illud maiori altari imponentes. Irruunt alii in ecclesiam, alii propter magnum populi concursum, donec corpus exeat, pre foribus prestolantur. Tandem maiores de villa post diutinam expectacionem ad instanciam quarumdam personarum sibi notarum cum fustibus populum abscedere compulerunt. Accepimus igitur corpus et precedentibus et subsequentibus turbis delatum est eadem die usque ad domum Templariorum de Colors,[b] per quam, cum

[a] Villeneuve-l'Archevêque (Yonne).
[b] Coulours (Aube). I have been unable to find any other reference to a house of the Templars at this place. The order had a commandery at Provins, see V. Carrière, *Histoire et cartulaire des Templiers de Provins* (Paris, 1919).

in recessu suo a Pontiniaco transitum fecisset vir sanctus et domum illam vidisset, quesivit cuius esset illa domus. Cui quidam respondit,

'Templariorum.' At ille,

'In domo | illa iacebo in reditu meo.' Et ita factum est. In (fo. 165) domo namque superius memorata cum corpore sancto eadem nocte pernoctavimus.

Tercia vero die, cum inde progrederemur, occurrerunt nobis nonnulli utriusque sexus clamantes et ingeminantes,

'Ubi est sanctum corpus? Ubi est sanctum corpus?' Hinc psalmicines clericorum phalanges, illinc religiosorum pre parsimonia turme pallentes. Hinc ruricole ex agris et vicis, illinc nonnulli ex vicinis castellis.[a] Tunc duo ex nostratibus admirantes populi concursum et in populo fidei fervorem, dixerunt ad invicem,

'Quid est hoc quod homines in tanta reverencia corpori exeunt obviam illi veluti sancto applaudentes, cum de sanctitate sua nichil audierint nec aliquod sanctitatis signum de ipso viderint?' Et adiecerunt quod monachi Pontiniacenses quosdam de suis premiserant ad predicandum talia de sancto. Tunc illi socios suos precedentes pre nimia admiracione et adhuc vere Didimi eo quod ullum signum nondum viderant, ex condicto equis desiliunt inquirentes quid quererent homines illi et qua de causa sic currerent. At quidam ex eis Spiritu Sancto edocti, dixerunt,

'Procedimus obviam sancto.' Alii autem a nostratibus inquirentes | quando veniret sanctus, non perstiterunt in quo (fo. 165ᵛ) cepto constiterunt. . . .[b]

[a] Possibly here 'towns'; cf. this usage in *Matt.* x. 11. This would give the antithesis: 'On this side the countryfolk from fields and by-ways, on that the people from the neighbouring towns.'

[b] The account is evidently incomplete. The Anonymous A, who reproduces the same account, has the following sentence: 'Alii autem quando veniet sanctus inquirentes, effrenate progrediebantur, responsum minime prestolantes.'

TEXT OF THE
VITA SANCTI EDMUNDI AUCTORE MATTHAEO PARISIENSI

(fo. 123ʳ)   Vita beati Edmundi Cantuariensis archiepiscopi

I

BEATUS Eadmundus Cantuariensis archiepiscopus ex piissimis parentibus fortune mediocris in pago Abendonie extitit oriundus, patre editus Reginaldo, cognomento Divite, matre vero Mabilia, matrimoniali federe copulatis. Quibus tale cognomen congrue immo, nec sine divino nutu, competebat. Ipsos namque inter ceteras prosperitates utriusque sexus maxime fecunda ac sancta soboles divites fecit et beatos. Suscepit enim dictus Reginaldus ex gremio uxoris sue Edmundum de quo michi ad presens sermo est, quem Deus postea ad dignitatem, ut (infra)[1] dicetur, vocavit archipresulatus. Habuit et Robertum quem sicut et Edmundum, meritis suis preclaris exigentibus, (ad)[2] uberrimorum redituum[3] opulenciam Dominus ditando sublimavit, qui sanctitatis eximie, dapsilitatis facete, et profunde sciencie dotibus choruscavit. Habuit et Nicholaum qui mundum despiciens cum flore sterili[a] habitum religionis in domo de Boxele[b] Ordinis Cisterciensis devotus suscepit. Habuit et duas filias Margaretam et Aliciam que ab ineunte etate, ut virginali puritate custodite et literis informate, apud Katebiam[c] sanctimoniales Edmundo procurante sine symonie scrupulo[4] facte, velum perpetui celibatus susceperunt. Habuit, et memoratus Edmundus fratrem quemdam qui apud Eynesham,[d] vir

---

[1] supra *cod*   [2] ab *cod*
[3] redditur *cod sed fortasse legendum* ab uberrimarum reditu opulenciarum . . . sublimavit   [4] scripulo *cod*

---

[a] Cf. *Vita S. Benedicti*, PL lxvi. 126: despexit iam quasi aridum mundum cum flore.
[b] Boxley, Kent.   [c] Catesby, Northants.
[d] Eynsham, Oxon.

Vita S. Edmundi auctore Matthaeo Parisiensi

discretus et compositus, habitum suscepit religionis. Hec iccirco scripserim ut tam beate prolis sit memoria in perpetua benediccione.[a] Patre igitur post paucos annos defuncto quem, ut dictum est, in hoc seculo Dominus uxoris honestissime individua societate et sanctissime sobolis fecunditate letificaverat et divitem fecerat ut competenter et vere | dives cognominaretur, (fo. 123ᵛ) mater in viduitate irreprehensibili perseverabat ut, ieiuniis elemosinis et oracionibus intendens, omnium matronarum quas habuit Abendonia gemma diceretur. Ipsa igitur filio suo Edmundo electo et inter ceteros fratres suos preelecto et dilecto transmisit[1] adhuc Parisius studenti pannos lineos materna sedulitate et asperrimum cilicium involutum cum eisdem, deprecans eum ut pro Christo preeligeret uti cilicio, quod et ipse obediendo complevit. Cum autem redisset Oxoniam, mater eius iam universe carnis viam sanctissime ingressa, reliquerat ei loricam qua, dum viveret, utebatur. Que consulens obnixius supplicaverat ut exemplo sui pro Christi amore ipsa lorica Deo militans pro camisia utetur. Filius autem pius pie matris precibus et consilio dulciter obtemperavit. Et sic matris ad Deum sequens vestigia, studuit matrissare. Nec cessavit filium suum adhuc eciam moritura feliciter informare et Deo per omnia complacere. Viva enim *dulci nato cum lactis* primitiva *dulcedine lacte dulcius Christi nomen indidit, amorem immisit, timorem incussit, crescentem et* proficiscentem[b] *suo exemplo* (et)[2] *virtutibus* multipliciter *informavit*, nunc persuadendo, nunc supplicando, nunc increpando, vices matris, vices patris, vices magistrique supplevit.

Liberet igitur tam infancie primordia quam rudimenta adolescencie et iuventutis sue maturitatem, dum adhuc matre superstite scolarum studiis sedulo intenderet, audientibus explicare. Seriem enim tocius vite sue sub ferula districte discipline continuavit, et sub regimine honestissimorum necnon et peritissimorum a primis annis usque ad ultimos totam vitam

---

[1] transivit *cod*

[2] et *supplevi*

[a] Cf. *Eccli.* xlvi. 14.

[b] Eustace has proficientem.

deduxit sciencia et moribus instruendam, utens lorica super nudo vel rudi cilicio. Et sic infancie principia virtutibus subarravit ut, sicut de beato Benedicto legitur,[a] *ab ipso puericie tempore cor gessit senile. Ex utero enim matris sue* | alter Nicholaus[b] *electus est a Deo et meditabatur a pusillo placere Deo, nitens in carne preter carnem vivere, hostiam sanctam, Deo placentem se ipsum offerre, optinere per graciam quod non* poterat *per naturam*, gloriam scilicet sempiternam.

II. Qualiter anulo quodam ymaginem (beate)[1] Virginis subarravit

Beatus vero Edmundus dum adhuc puer etate existeret duodennis sub pedagogo scolas frequentans sepe cuiusdam sancti sacerdotis cui frequenter confitebatur disciplina instructus regebatur. In conspectu igitur sui confessoris cum virginitatem suam illibatam castissime Dei genetrici Marie dare et vovere et omnibus vite sue diebus conservare promisisset et hec dicta ante ymaginem dicte Virginis in ecclesia recitasset,[c] surrexit concito et digito ymaginis quemdam anulum quem ad hoc adquisierat, imposuit et adaptavit dicens,

'Tibi, Virgo virginum, mater domini mei Ihesu Christi purissima, virginitatis mee voveo, spondeo ac libo donativum. Et hoc anulo te subarrans, in dominam ac sponsam eligo et gratanter adopto ut, virgo virgini, gracius de cetero tibi ac conformius merear famulari.

Et genibus flexis ante ipsam ymaginem velut ante ipsam Dei genetricem oravit devotissime lacrimis uberrimis profusis, ita ut exitus aquarum deducerent oculi eius,[d] dicens,

---

[1] beate: de *cod*

[a] S. Gregorii *dialogi*, ii, *PL* lxvi. 125.

[b] Perhaps a reference to the story that St. Nicholas sucked the breast only once on Wednesdays and Fridays, see Surius, vi. 795.

[c] According to the Franciscan author of the Lanercost chronicle, the statue was at Oxford, see *Chronicon de Lanercost*, ed. J. Stevenson (Edinburgh, 1839), p. 36.

[d] exitus aquarum &c. Cf. *Lam*. iii. 48.

'O domina mea serenissima, sponsa iam michi precordialis, Filium tuum dominum meum efficaciter deprecare ut in obsequiis vestris perseverans, beati Iohannis Evangeliste vestigia sequi promerear.'

Et post oracionem cum vellet anulum quem digito ymaginis apposuerat, ne vulgo generaret admiracionem, avellere, non potuit, licet omnibus quot poterat modis cum conamine niteretur. Unde gaudens spem concepit quod beata Virgo votum suum favorabiliter acceptavit, ut sicut ipse puer purissimus se castissime Dei genetrici ac semper virgini sponsum | sic et ipsa Beata Virgo feliciter beato Edmundo sponte copulandam se promisit.

III. Qualiter apparuit ei Dominus quando vidit rubum florentem

In adolescencia vero iam pubescens cum provectioribus scolaribus associaretur et quadam die medie estatis tempore cum eis iret in prata spaciatum et ipse ne singularis haberetur, sequeretur, noluit se ludis eorum immiscere set solus seorsum semotus, in lege Dei meditabatur.[a] Et ecce rubum repperit quemdam preter morem et contra temporis exigenciam floribus mirifice pulcherrimis redimitum et incomparabilis odoris fragranciam longe lateque circumquaque dispergentem. Quod cum in spiritu certissime perpenderat hoc aliquid celitus significare, genibus flexis devotus oravit dicens,

'Deus qui in monte Sinay sancto Moysi figuraliter in rubo ardente et non combusto apparuisti, revela michi quod istud miraculosum portendat.'

Et cum flens et orans solo procubuisset, en claritas de celo copiosa circumfulsit eum in qua Christus infans lucidissimus apparuit, ipsumque vehementer stupefactum consolans ait,

'Ego sum Ihesus Christus, Beate Marie Virginis sponse tue Filius, quem anulo subarrasti et in dominam adoptasti. Ego tuorum conscius secretorum tibi soli vago fui socius indivisus.

---

[a] Cf. *Ps.* i. 2.

Amodo me et matrem meam sponsam tuam polliceor[1] tui adiutores et consolatores.'

Hecque dicens impressit signans fronti adolescentis benediccionem hoc modo: 'Ihesus Nazarenus Rex Iudeorum'. Et addidit,

'Frequenter te signans, sic hec replica in mei commemoracionem.'

Et cum prolixius ibidem procumbens adhuc orasset, postulans sibi a Spiritu Sancto donum sciencie salutaris cum ceteris virtutibus suis concedi, surrexit et ecce socii eius festinanter (fo. 125ʳ) advenientes[2] interrogabant | quenam esset ipsa claritas maxima quam iuxta rubum viderant choruschare. At ipse caute dissimulans noluit alicui misterium illud temere[3] revelare. Beatus igitur adolescens extunc in omni virtute et sciencia felix suscepit incrementum. Et hoc memoriter retinens, sepissime diebus ac noctibus omni vite sue tempore se signans in fronte et oculis devotissime recitavit. Fidelisque sponsor et sponsus usque ad mortem in illa beata virginitate indubitanter perseveravit. Cui in presencia[4] tu Christe, etsi homo dubitet, certum in crebris miraculis presertim in sui corporis integritate perhibes testimonium. Et *testimonia tua credibilia facta sunt nimis*.[a]

IV. Qualiter extunc de virtute in virtutem diatim ascendit beatus Edmundus

Adolescens autem maturior *factus, cum esset iam liberalibus studiis* arcium addictus, *via qua prius ducebatur incedebat spontaneus qui iuxta sui nominis interpretationem, beatus* extitit *atque mundus*. Nam extunc plus solito *voluntarie sacrificare Deo*[b] cepit, ecclesie limina sepius et maturius frequentare,[5] *vana et frivola quibus* etas illa solet implicare[c] *devitans, erudicioni sue diligenter intendens*, carnis

---

[1] pollicio *cod*   [2] advenientibus *cod*   [3] tenere *cod*
[4] presenciarum *cod*   [5] frequentans *Eustace*

[a] *Ps.* xcii. 5.   [b] *Voluntarie* &c. Cf. *Ps.* liii. 8.
[c] Matthew's alteration seems to have been suggested by reminiscence of St. Bernard's *Vita S. Malachiae, PL* clxxxii. 1075.

delicias non solum fugiens set crucis mortificacionem iugiter in suo corpore portans,[a] toto mentis studio vite requisivit auctorem. Videbatur enim iam illud quod nondum legerat intellexisse proverbium, 'Adolescens iuxta viam suam primam; cum eciam senuerit, non recedet ab ea.'[b] Quod in eo vere completum est. Nam vigilare et ieiunare sed et cetera penitencie gravia extunc tam duxit in consuetudinem facere quod postmodum, ut ipsemet testimonium perhibebat,[1] non tam facilia quam eciam delectabilia ei fuerant in etate provectiori. Insolenciam namque carnis restringens balteo castitatis, asperitate cilicina | dura dira et nodosa ipsam studuit edomare ita (fo. 125ᵛ) quod excogitato novo cilicii usu, in nocte et manuum et colli nuda tegebat. Et ut afflictus magis affligeretur, corpus ciliciatum funiculo triplici de seta grossa circumcingendo constrinxit et[2] constringendo circumduxit. Beati itaque Iohannis Evangeliste imitator existens, carnem suam nulla umquam immundicie macula coinquinavit, quod et firmiter asserunt[3] qui ipsius confessiones audierunt et qui ipsum ex familiari cum ipso conversacione ab annis puerilibus noverunt. Et sic in carne vixisse creditur preter carnem.

V. De vite sue mira severitate

Crescente vero etate crevit eciam in virtute. Nam sic gracia sibi divina favente profecit quod dum in annis iuvenilibus liberalibus intenderet disciplinis, nondum sacre pagine auditor effectus, honesta, matura, et sancta conversacione doctor videbatur sacre scripture, non solum prius incipiens facere quam docere set prius incipiens facere quam audire. Abstinenciam verbi, cibi, potus, et sompni, rerumque omnium mundanarum ab infancia illibatam servavit. Ubi vero occurrunt spectacula numquam tamen spectaculis se immiscuit, nec sedit cum consilio vanitatis[c] sive ludencium. Oracioni insistebat[4] sedulus, noctes cum brevissima sompni degustacione deducens, non in lecto

---

[1] perhibeat cod [2] videlicet Eustace [3] asseruerint cod
[4] instabat Eustace

[a] mortificacionem &c. Cf. 2 Cor. iv. 10. [b] Prov. xxii. 6.
[c] nec sedit &c. Cf. Ps. xxv. 4.

set ante lectum nuda terra *iacens vel sedens, semper vestitus et cinctus, aliquantulum quiescebat. Hoc* autem *per triginta annos et sex ampliusque creditur* inviolabiliter observasse nisi gravissima infirmitate impediretur. *Semper sibi rigidus et durus, aliis semper affabilis et benignus, vir* utique *extitit sancte*[1] *conversacionis, castitate precipuus, abstinencia singularis, in vigiliis, oracionibus, et disciplinis assiduus, scripture sacre doctor egregius, predicator fervens et devotus, confessionum auditor, pauperum scolarium nutritor piissimus, paupertatis amator,* | *animarum zelator, viciorum exstirpator, omnium bonorum exemplum prebuit semetipsum. Omnia ipsius tam verba quam opera quasi cuiusdam latentis energie voce in mentibus omnium clamabant quod operator eorum non que sua set que Ihesu Christi sunt perquirebat. Tanta quoque penitencie asperitate carnem suam mortificavit in pane et aqua frequenter*[2] *ieiunando aliisque modis quamplurimis, ut vix inveniretur qui vires humanas ad tot et tantos labores sufficere posse estimaret. Set ad occultandam hominibus asperitatem quam gerebat interius semper letum semper hilarem gratissima et matura iocunditate se exhibuit. Hoc eciam specie virtutis exemplar ex aliis duximus exprimendum, quod, licet tantis pollere videretur virtutibus, in hoc se imitatorem mirabilem exhibebat quod appetitum inanis glorie que virtuosis viris se multipliciter ingerit importunam sub quadam simplicitatis cautela et modo mirabili elidebat* actu et *verbo hoc pestiferum vicium et* doctrina viriliter *repellendo. Mirum eciam in modum quanto* amplius *in virtutum adquisicione profecit, tanto magis studuit humilitatem servare, in tantum ut aliquid quod simplicitati possit* (ab)[4] *huius mundi sapientibus imputari, mallet in opere publico demonstrare quam ad ostensionem inanem aliquid facere virtuosum.* Oppressorum quippe *refugium* extitit, *miserorum solacium, afflictorum benignissimus consolator, manusque suas ab omni munere immunes conservabat et a suis familiaribus sordes avaricie et inmundicie eliminabat pro posse*

[1] sanctissime *Eustace*
[3] quantum *Eustace*
[2] frequencius *Eustace*
[4] ad *cod*

VI. Quod amator et frequentator fuerit ecclesie incomparabilis

Factus itaque magister arcium nondum ad sacros ordines promotus, nec adhuc racione alicuius accepti[1] *beneficii ecclesiastici compulsus, set solo Dei instinctu et studio pietatis ductus, supra morem tunc legencium singulis diebus priusquam | legeret missam audire con-* (fo. 126ᵛ) *suevit. Quod ut devocius faceret, capellam de Beata Virgine, quam speciali quodam privilegio amoris semper diligebat, in parochia in qua tunc habitabat construxit, ubi adhuc sollempnes misse continue celebrantur ad ipsius gloriam et honorem. Cumque hiis et*[2] *aliis plurimis virtutibus excellenter premineret, addidit Deus suo servo illam graciam meritorum ut vivens eciam miraculis choruscaret prout illi qui oculata fide viderunt et interfuerunt fida assercione protestantur. Sic enim nutrix gracia magnificum fidei zelatorem prosequebatur sicut a multis viris fide dignis qui eum ab infancia noverunt, creditur ab omni peccato mortali fuisse immunis, ut cum beato Iob dicere possit, 'ab inicio coaluit me miseracio et pietas de utero matris egressa est mecum.'*[a] *Illud autem spectabile fuit in eo quod beneficium ecclesiasticum non retinuit nisi faceret residenciam ita quod, quando transtulit se ad studium, resignavit si quod habuit, quod antea apud nostrates fuerat inauditum. Porro transactis fere sex annis quibus in artibus rexerat, cum iam placuisset Ei qui eum segregavit ex utero matris sue ut in eo et per eum revelaret Filium suum,*[b] *fieret(que)*[3] *vas eleccionis,*[c] *ipso adhuc cursim*[4] *legente arismeticam quibusdam sociis suis, apparuit ei in sompnis piissima mater eius paulo ante defuncta dicens,*

'*Fili, quid legis? Que sunt ille figure quibus tam studiose intendis?*'

Quo respondente,

'*Talia lego*', *ostensis protraccionibus que in illa solent fieri facultate,*[5] *illa mox dexteram manum eius arripuit et in ea tres circulos*

---

[1] adepti *Eustace* [2] atque *Eustace* [3] -que *supplevi*
[4] cursum *cod* [5] facultates *cod*

---

[a] *Iob* xxxi. 18.
[b] qui eum segregavit &c. Cf. *Galat.* i. 15.
[c] Cf. *Act.* ix. 15.

depinxit. In ipsis[1] quoque *hec tria nomina per ordinem* scripsit,[2] *'Pater · Filius · Spiritus Sanctus.' Et hoc facto sic ait,*
  'Fili karissime, talibus figuris et non aliis amodo *intende.'*
(fo. 127r) Quo sompnio[3] *quasi per revelacionem edoctus* | *statim ad theologie se transtulit* exercicium. Cepit igitur fastidire iam philosophie sterilitatem et ad theologie fructus profuturos hanelare.[a] Set cum adhuc delectabili acerbitate vel acerba dilectacione liberalium arcium maxime Quadriviali adhuc dentes eius opstipescerent, non sapiebant ei divine pagine rudimenta que animam esurientem plenius reficere consueverunt pocius quam vagum animum ambagibus illudendo demulcere. Reversus igitur ad se, cepit vehementer formidare ne peccatis irretitus adeo et eius speciali sciencia veluti reprobus repelleretur, scriptum illud recolens, *'in malivolam animam non intrabit sapiencia'*.[b] Recurrens igitur ad lavacrum mundacionis que per confessionem requiritur et adquiritur, sese ab omni mentis scrupulo confitendo veraciter emundavit. Ex tunc igitur in ipsa theologie facultate a Deo expedienter in brevi profecit ut omnes eius collaterales aut equiparavit aut precessit. Opponens igitur, respondens et determinans,[c] tenebras ignorancie delucidavit et apparencium contrarietatum repugnancias denodavit. Unde *cito post paucos annos suadentibus multis cathedram magistralem ascendit.*

VII. Qualiter per aliquod tempus Mertone[d] commorabatur

Deinde *quoque pater, antequam theologie publicus rector existeret per annum et amplius in domo et cenobio Mertone iugiter morabatur et*

---

[1] ipsius *cod* [2] inscripsit *Eustace* [3] sompno *cod*

[a] The sterility of dialectic is a favourite theme with moralists in the first half of the thirteenth century, and Matthew expresses the prevailing attitude. Cf. the remarks of Stephen of Tournai in Denifle, *Chartularium*, i. 43, and of Jacques de Vitry: G. Frenken, *Die Exempla des Jacob von Vitry* (Quellen u. untersuch. z. lateinischen Philologie des Mittelalters, Munich, 1914).

[b] *Sap.* i. 4.

[c] See the place of disputations in the theology curriculum of the thirteenth century in Little and Pelster, *Oxford Theology and Theologians* (OHS 1934), introd., pp. 28 seq.   [d] Merton (Augustinian Priory), Surrey.

Vita S. Edmundi auctore Matthaeo Parisiensi 231

postea per longum tempus quasi unus ex eiusdem ecclesie filiis sepius intravit claustrum *et exivit.* Quidam enim *fratrum in ipsius sancti valde delectabantur colloquiis et fovebantur consiliis et conversacionem*[1] *eius ineffabiliter admirantes. Nam in mundo conversans mundum conculcaverat et etate iuvenis quosque senes fide, doctrina, sciencia et consilio excedebat. Et quod mirabile* est *dictu, inter scolares gradiens non solum religiosus* set *eciam forma tocius religionis inter eos videbatur. Erat enim in leccionibus et meditacionibus assiduus, in oracionibus*[2] *devotissimus, semper in ieiuniis et vigiliis continuus, horam | nullam matutinarum dormiendo preteriens,* set *ad omnes una* (fo. 127ᵛ) *cum fratribus, quasi eorum* officio *deditus esset,* accessit. *Nec solum gestus exteriores religionis* set *eciam secretissimos quos in Spiritu Sancto didiscerat pretendebat, clavem scilicet habens tocius religionis. Fedus* insuper *in tantum cum oculis pepigerat*[a] *ut quemdam fratrem per annum in mensa ei* perministrantem ex nomine vix *cognosceret. Equidem qualiter de virtute in virtutem celitus* proficeret *ut Deum deorum in Syon videret,*[b] *non solum illis* set *et in omnibus innotuit. Tanta denique diligencia tantaque discendi aviditate sacris literis inheserat quod pene noctes deducebat insompnes et videbantur ei dies pauci pre amoris magnitudine quo ad speciose Rachelis castos amplexus hanelans*[3] *preveniret. Nec est fraudatus a desiderio suo.*[c] *Nam* complens *in brevi tempora multa, iuxta estimacionem suam modicum in eius opere laboravit et cito de generacionibus* benediccionis fructus percepit. *Etenim divini Verbi semina cordis aure suscipiens tamquam terra celesti rore perfusa, non solum sanctarum meditacionum et affeccionum segetes set eciam bonorum operum fructus uberrimos ex se producebat. Verum eciam legendo et disputando eiusdem Verbi strenuus et egregius seminator ad aliorum edificacionem tamquam ymbres eloquii et sapiencie divine mittebat.*[d] *Unde factum est ut ob tantam edificacionem tam in maturitate sermonum quam in exhibicione salubrium exemplorum viri religiosi non pauci inter quos tempore vacacionis commorari solebat,*[e] *quorum corda tetigerat Deus,*

---

[1] conversacione *cod*   [2] oracione *Eustace*   [3] hanelabat *Eustace*

[a] *Fedus* &c. *Iob* xxxi. 1.   [b] Cf. *Ps.* lxxxiii. 8.
[c] *Ps.* lxxvii. 30.   [d] *tamquam imbres* &c. Cf. *Eccli.* xxxix. 9.
[e] i.e. the monks of Reading Abbey; see Eustace.

talia ac tanta perpendentes in eo sanctitatis indicia,[1] *se, in comparacione ipsius in habitu seculari constituti, tepidos arbitrantes et desides, cum haberentur et essent competenter religiosi,* confusi erubuerunt, *iuxta Ysaie vaticinium,* 'Erubesce Syon ait mare'.[a] *De tempore siquidem suo* salubriter *erubescere ceperunt* et eius vestigia sequi nitebantur.

VIII. Item de moribus illius multiplicibus

Beatus igitur Edmundus *sicut augebatur* diatim *et multiplicabatur* | (fo. 128r) *divine lumen*[2] *sapiencie, sic multipliciter refulsit exterius* fructuosorum *operum claritate.* Illam namque noctis particulam quam *sine corporis dispendio* insompnem *deducere* non valebat *lacrimis et oracionibus et* sacris *meditacionibus* expendebat.[3] *Castitatem* quippe servabat *in corpore, pudiciciam in corde, modestiam in sermone, in opere iusticiam, ut quos eruditurus erat verbo, sanctitatis sue moneret exemplo. Erat enim predicator eximius, doctor egregius, ignitus in predicacione et doctrina habens eloquium, mentes auditorum ad veritatis cognicionem illuminans et affectus ad bonitatem accendens,*[4] *ut effectu*[5] *verbi in auditoribus luce clarius pateret quod Ipse in eo et per eum loquebatur de quo scriptum est,* 'Non vos estis qui loquimini, set Spiritus Patris vestri',[b] et 'Ignis consumens est'.[c] *Unde et effectus est clericis gratus, laicis acceptus, ipsis eciam principibus reverendus. Cumque sederet inter primos erat tamen merencium consolator. Ab infancia quippe cum eo creverat miseracio,*[d] *que aliorum sibi coacervans*[6] *miserias nullius afflictionis aspecte permittebat eum non esse participem. Cuius* umquam *mens ad pietatem mollior? Cuius cibus durior? Cuius sermo blandior? Cuius amictus asperior? Quis loqui rarius, quis orare* prolixius *potuit? Quem minus ab adolescencia*[7] *detineret lectus, quem magis leccio? Quem minus moveret iniuria, quem magis misericordia? Quis daret prompcius quod*

[1] indicta *cod*   [2] lumine *cod*   [3] exponebat *cod*
[4] accedens *cod*   [5] effectum *cod*   [6] coadcervans *cod*
[7] holescencia *cod*

[a] Is. xxiii. 4.   [b] Matt. x. 20.   [c] Heb. xii. 29.
[d] *Ab infancia* &c. Cf. Iob xxxi. 18.

sibi detraxisset? Cui rarior mundus, cui frequencior Christus? Quis in illa sublimitate virtutum positus sibimet minor videretur? Et quis sic *quo magis merito ascenderet, magis compunccione decresceret? Superhabundantem* igitur *graciam caritatis*[1] *qua, preminens in sublimitate karismatum, multorum corda ad se convertit sicut multi noverunt qui hoc experimento*[2] *didicere,*[3] *non possumus satis habundanter demonstrare. Quoslibet* | enim eciam sibi hostiliter adver- (fo. 128ᵛ) santes *dilexit in tantum ut gratis obsequiis quorumlibet amicorum graves iniurias visus fuit pretulisse, quod quibusdam austeris displicebat.*

IX. De liberalitate ipsius et quam reverenter se habuerit circa altare et in ecclesia

In exercenda hospitalitate et aliis liberalibus operibus sic pollebat ut quicquid erat in facultatibus suis commune bonorum omnium credi potuisset. Vicium detraccionis quod in locucionis cursu surripere consuevit viris eciam sibi studiose caventibus summa intencione vitabat ita quod cum occasio detraccionis incideret aut verba detractoria incidebat mutando materiam aut, si verba persisterent detrahentis, penitus abscedebat, nolens pollui audiendo qui vix aut numquam ipsum polluere consueverat in loquendo. In altari autem *existens totus effundebatur lacrimis et sic in altaris officio versabatur ac si* visibiliter ac personaliter *in carne geri dominicam cerneret passionem. Reverentissime quidem divina sacramenta tractabat ita ut intuencium fidem et mores ipsa* tractacio[4] *divinitus* informabat.[5][a] *Si quis velit inspicere in quanta mansuetudine ubique subditos pertractavit et quot ubique virtutum propagavit exempla, nimia prolixitate onerabit auditores.* Erat nempe *in divinorum munerum gracia ubique precipuus, corpore castus, mente devotus, affabilis colloquio, amabilis aspectu, prudencia preditus, temperancia clarus, interna fortitudine firmus, censura iusticie stabilis, longanimitate assiduus, paciencia*

---

[1] caritatis: *bis in cod*
[2] per experimentum *Eustace*
[3] didicere: *add* quod *cod ad damnum sensus*
[4] contractacio *Eustace*
[5] informaret *Eustace*

[a] effundebatur &c. Vita S. Thomae *auct.* Johanne Saresberiensi, Materials, ii. 306. Cf. Eustace.

robustus, humilitate mansuetus, caritate diffusus. Et ita in eo omnium virtutum decorem sapiencia divina ordinaverat ut, secundum Apostolum, semper illius sermo in gracia sale esset conditus.[a] *Numquam*[d] *in ore eius nisi pax, nisi castitas, nisi pietas, nisi caritas. Numquam in corde suo nisi horum omnium fons, Christus, habitavit, qui et aliis per eum plurimos caritatis, gaudii, pacis, modestie et continencie* (fo. 129ʳ) *fructus ministravit.* In almariolo igitur | cordis quasi in horreo messis tempore dum lecturiens[c] apud Mertonam multiplicem segetem postquam exaggerasset, Oxoniam lectum vadit vocatus a multis et instanter flagitatus. Ubi aliquot annis laudabiliter legens et predicans, fructum fecit exuberantem, talentum sibi commissum multiplicando.

X. Quomodo diabolum vicerit cogitando de passione Domini in cruce

Contigit[d] *autem quadam die quod habito multorum colloquio* apud ipsum propter diversas causas maxime tamen propter edificaciones spirituales *confluencium, in suis meditacionibus et leccionum* studiosis provisionibus parvulam *quietem* dormitando pregustaret fatigatus. Fecerat enim scolaribus quibusdam ut memorie eorum preaudita firmius[1] imprimeret, annotare.[e]

[1] firmus *cod*

---

[a] *sermo* &c. Cf. *Col.* iv. 6.

[b] For the following passage, incorporated from Eustace, cf. *Vita S. Martini*, PL xx. 176.

[c] Matthew's use of the desiderative form *lecturiens* is interesting, cf. Sidonius, *Ep.* ix. 7. It implies that Edmund desired to lecture, but was prevented. This probably refers to the suspension of the Oxford schools from 1209 to 1214, see above, p. 119. The sense of the passage is that Edmund used the period of enforced inactivity in the cloister to lay up a hoard of spiritual treasure.

[d] The following version of Edmund's combat with the Devil is taken from the Anonymous B: Wallace, p. 618.

[e] The construction here is doubtful: either 'he had caused notes to be made for certain scholars' or 'he had caused certain scholars to make notes'. In either case, *annotare* seems to be used intransitively. It seems to be some kind of private and informal note taking that is meant, rather than a *reportatio*. On the subject of note taking in the thirteenth-century universities, see J. Destrez, *La 'Pecia' dans les mss. universitaires du xiiiᵉ et du xivᵉ siècle* (Paris, 1936).

Vita S. Edmundi auctore Matthaeo Parisiensi

Cui hostis humani generis apparuit, set ipsum vir sanctus *crucis signaculo* affugare *nitebatur*. *Diabolus* autem *arrepto brachio suo dextero, illud* constrinxit violenter, ut sic pro tutela sancti facienda ne fieret *signum* impediret. Magister igitur *erecta manu sinistra*, ut dextere officium in signo faciendo adimpleret se preparavit. At hostis eadem qua prius temeritate et illam manum *forcius* constringendo adhuc munimen tale ne fieret, *impedivit*. Sanctus autem in hoc certamine in Dei adiutorium *confidens*, *Christi passionem cum preciosi sanguinis sui effusione ad memoriam reducens*, *collisum cum* ingenti *sonitu in terra diabolum fortiter arripuit*, *adiurans*[1] *per sanguinem Christi per quam rem* magis *confundi* et repelli solet, ut recederet irrediturus. *Et sic* victus recessit et confusus.

XI. Qualiter curatus est quidam scolaris a gravissima infirmitate per ipsum

Quadam[a] vero dierum *contigit quod quidam suus scolaris in uno brachiorum* suorum graviter *infirmabatur* infistulatus, ita *quod de* vita sua *desperaret*. *Cui valde compaciens*, magister *dixit* illi miserabiliter ingemiscenti,

'*Confide, fili.* | *Rogabo Deum ut tuam in me transferat infirmitatem.*' (fo. 129ᵛ)

Et oracione cum lacrimis et suspiriis *facta* prolixa, *quod petiit optinuit, translata in ipsum* quam alter habuerat mirabiliter *egritudine. Brachium* autem *dicti scolaris* morbo *quo circiter quindecim diebus* intolerabiliter torquebatur, *ex integro* statim *sanitati restitutum est, nulla remanente*, quod admirabile et insolitum est, *cicatrica*. Illam enim infirmitatem phisici solent antracem vocare, quia antrum facit in recessu. Magister autem postea in brevi leviter et leniter, caritate medicinam conferente salutarem,[2] sanabatur.

---

[1] admirans *cod*   [2] scelerem *cod*

[a] This version of the anecdote is taken from the Anonymous B: Wallace, p. 619.

XII. Nubes ei obediunt[1]

Cum[a] *per multos annos legem* theologus lector egregius *docuisset, in qua tota sua voluntas nocte dieque versabatur, et videretur ei disputacionum subtilitates non sine quadam vana gloria posse exerceri, cessavit ob hoc et ad horam cathedram suspendit magistralem. Verbum* autem pro *Crucis* negocio de *mandato Summi Pontificis* non sine fructu multiplici seminavit. *Cuius imperio per invocacionem nominis Christi nubes sepe et pluvie obedierunt,*[2] *ne a sermone plebs fidelis recederet* congregata.

XIII. De bono odore fame sue

Talibus igitur *floribus in beato viro* cum *gratissima venustate vernantibus, cepit odor honestatis necnon et sanctitatis eius* per tocius regionis Anglicane *circumquaque diffundi* latitudinem. *Nam doctrina eius ita erat catholica et lucida ut de eo per totam provinciam passim ab omnibus diceretur 'Lingua eius calamus scribe velociter scribentis'.*[b] Quippe erat ei promptum et sponte fluens eloquium et sub succincta brevitate tam retoricum quam sentenciosum (fo. 130ʳ) stilo Gregoriano subornatum,[c] iuxta illud | poeticum,
    Omne tulit punctum qui miscuit utile dulci.[d]
Scivit eciam supra *humanam capacitatem quodam modo excellentissimo de thesauro sacre scripture nova et vetera* indubitanter *proferre, ita ut, cum legeret vel predicaret, visum esset auditoribus suis quod digitus Dei scribebat in corde suo verba vite que de ore suo ut* profluvium paradisi *procedebant.*

[1] obediant *cod*

[a] This version of the anecdote is drawn from the Anonymous B: Wallace, p. 619.

[b] Cf. *Ps.* xliv. 2.

[c] The masters of *Dictamen* expounded four styles, the Gregorian, Tullian, Hilarian, and Isidorean, according to the arrangement of the stressed syllables in the *clausula*; see the exposition in John of Garland's *Poetria de arte prosaica*, in Rockinger, 'Briefsteller und Formelbücher des elften bis vierzehnten Jahrhunderts', *Quellen u. Erörterungen z. bayerischen u. deutschen Geschichte*, ix (Munich, 1863), p. 501.

[d] Horace, *Ars Poet.* 343.

XIV. Quomodo factus est thesaurarius Saresbiriensis et quomodo[1] dignus censetur pontificari[2]

Collata est igitur quedam prebenda ei ecclesie Saresbiriensis[a] ut thesauri custos diceretur et esset. Quia igitur *decebat*[3] et expediebat *ut talis esset pontifex, sanctus, innocens, impollutus et segregatus a peccatoribus*,[b] *vacante sede Cantuariensi*, videlicet anno divine Incarnacionis millesimo ducentesimo tricesimo quarto, *divina inspiracione* post relatu indignas papales et regales vexaciones dicte sedi irrogatas quamplurimas, in archipresulem solempniter est electus. Dicebat enim Cantuariensis conventus, ad quem ab antiquo dinoscitur ius eleccionis pertinere,[c]

'Eligatur talis in quo non inveniatur alicuius scrupulus iuste contradiccionis et in quo merito elidantur omnium morsus detractorum.'

Invocata igitur Sancti Spiritus gracia et facta oracione devota, post multorum ponderacionem[4] quorum virtutes prout humanum est ipsi electores racionis statera diligenter trutinabant, tandem Deo procul dubio sic volente, omnium resedit sentencia et quievit in magistrum Edmundum de Abendonia, lectorem theologum. Decantato igitur angelorum ympno, scilicet 'Te Deum laudamus', ipsum adeuntes ipsi electores eundem Edmundum, quem legentem inveniunt, alloquuntur, assensum benignum suppliciter postulantes. *Verum de se concorditer, communiter, canoniceque eleccioni facte per duos | dies* nullatenus (fo. 130ᵛ) voluit electus *consentire*. Porro multorum pulsus precibus et persuasionibus et usque ad spiritus amaritudinem impulsus, cepit hesitare. Quidam eciam amicorum secrecius ei dicebant,

[1] quo *cod*
[2] pontificem *cod. Huius capituli titulus per errorem est inferius in codice scriptus*
[3] dicebat *cod*
[4] ponderat *cod*

---

[a] The prebend of Calne (Wilts.). St. Edmund first appears as Treasurer in a chapter act dated 18 Aug. 1222; see *The Register of St. Osmund*, ed. W. H. R. Jones (RS 1883-4), i. 339.

[b] *pontifex* &c. Cf. *Heb.* vii. 26.

[c] Cf. with this passage the identical wording used by Matthew to describe the Winchester election of 1238 in *Hist. Angl.* ii. 410.

'Nisi tu consentiens ibidem sine mora instituaris, procurabit regis consilium ut ibi aliquis alienigena, tali prorsus ac tanto indignus honore, ubi tot Deus sanctos ordinavit, intrusus subrogetur.[1] Et cum nolle iustis postulacionibus adquiescere genus sit ariolandi, noli esse piis inexorabilis. Cave eciam ne tua pusillanimitas[2] et rebellio tante sit causa confusionis in nobilissima ecclesia Cantuarie.'

Instabant eciam monachi flexis genibus, iunctis manibus et profusis lacrimis postulando ut benigne consentiret, dicentes,

'Domine, qui tam pius diceris et es, ne nos ter vel quater repulsos iterum confundi permittas.'

XV. Consentit sanctus[3] vix in eleccione de se facta

Hiis igitur precibus ac racionibus motus et commotus, beatus Edmundus tandem set vix consensit. *Unde sicut de beato Gregorio legitur,*[a] *ita et de eo* dici potest, *capitur, trahitur, et in nomine sancte Trinitatis metropolitanus tocius Anglie cum summa devocione* constituitur feliciter. *Pastor autem et dux in populo Dei factus*, pristinam *humilitatem non deposuit, set iugi abstinencia, in vestium asperitate, in vigiliis multis,* in oracionum devocione, *carnem spiritui, sensualitatem racioni,* Evam scilicet Ade, *coegit* de*servire, dignitatis oneri succumbens non honori.* Anterior affabilitas *pristina*que benignitas nullatenus immutatur. *Pontificalis fastigium dignitatis mentem eius* penitus aliqua *elacionis ostentacione* (non)[4] *corrumpit*.

XVI. De primis factis eius post consecracionem

(fo. 131ʳ) Consecratus igitur beatus Edmundus in ecclesia Cantuarie | a Rogero Londoniensi episcopo,[b] sanctus a sancto, theologus a

[1] subrogabitur *cod* [2] pusillamitas *cod* [3] se *cod* [4] non *supplevi*

[a] *Vita S. Gregorii auctore Joanne Diacono*, PL lxxv. 81.

[b] Roger Niger, bishop of London 1229–41. The following passage is almost exactly paralleled by Matthew's account of the same event in *Hist. Angl.* ii. 367 and note. In the lower margin of the *Historia* Matthew has drawn a pen sketch of St. Edmund kneeling before Roger Niger.

Vita S. Edmundi auctore Matthaeo Parisiensi

theologo, virgo a virgine, ciliciatus a ciliciato, archiepiscopus[1] a suo decano[a] dominica qua cantatur 'Letare Ierusalem', quarto nonas scilicet Aprilis, presente rege Henrico cum tredecim episcopis et magnatum copiosa multitudine, solempniter eo die cum pallio quod ei gratis transmiserat dominus papa,[c] missam celebravit.

XVII. Nota quod divinitus fuit illa dignitas beato Edmundo reservata[2]

Nec pretereundum censeo eventum de ipso mirabilem a Deo preordinatum. Quod scilicet cassatis ante eius promocionem tribus electis, videlicet priore Cantuariensi Iohanne, Cicestrensi episcopo Radulpho, magistro quoque Iohanne cognomento Blundo, dignitas illa preclara ipsi sancto Edmundo, veluti de multis preelecto, divinitus reservabatur. Qui quidem in hoc assimulabatur Tobie iuniori, cui amplexus Sare filie Raguelis, prefocatis multis maritis, specialiter assistante angelo debebantur et dabantur Gabriele.[d]

XVIII. Nota de fortunatis eventibus in ipsius (honore)[3]

Notandum quoque est non hoc accidisse sine Dei providencia quod in Quadragesima, tempore scilicet penitenciali ac parsimoniali et spirituali, consecratus est beatus Edmundus in archipresulem Cantuariensem. Et in Adventu Domini, tempore similiter penitenciali, parsimoniali, et spirituali, consecratus[4] est. Eodemque tempore postea, sicut sequens sermo declarabit, a

---

[1] archidiaconus *cod*   [2] reservatus *cod*   [3] ho *cod*
[4] consecratus: *sic in codice, sed aliquid deesse videtur. Fortasse voluit dicere auctor* in presbyterum consecratus, *vel forte legendum* canonizatus

---

[a] The bishop of London was dean of the Canterbury province.
[b] The Introit of the mass for the fourth Sunday in Lent.
[c] Gregory IX confirmed the election on 22 Dec. 1233, and dispatched the pallium on 3 Feb. 1234: Auvray, i. 907 and 958.
[d] *Tob.* vii. The angel was, however, Raphael not Gabriel.

domino papa Innocencio Lugduni canonizatus est, post se omnibus dedisset[1] formam et exemplum vere penitencie et parsimonie. Bene igitur divina ordinacione evenit quod in die consecracionis eius canitur in ecclesia 'Letare Ierusalem', et in die canonizacionis sue, 'Gaudete in Domino'.[a] Utrobique leticia, utrobique resultat exultacio. Quicumque autem eius sequuntur vestigia | post penitenciam et abstinenciam, leticiam et honorem sempiternum, que in eius consecracione et canonizacione designantur, consequantur.

XIX. De augmentacione sanctitatis eius

Ex tunc autem solito diligencius operibus caritatis, precipue que regnum et magnates contingebant, conatus est efficaciter insistere et discordantes ad pacis tranquillitatem amicabiliter revocare, satis caute considerans quod a magnatum odio et discordia dependent pericula subditorum. Unde tunc occiso comite Ricardo Marescallo in Hybernia, rex difficilem se exhibuit in substituendo Gilberto in ipsam hereditatem ipsum tamquam fratrem proximum contingentem, hac tactus racione quia comes Ricardus occisus fuit in hostili prelio contra regem abiudicatus.[b] Archiepiscopus igitur diligens Gilbertum quia vere amabilis[2] erat, condoluit afflicto, utpote qui super afflictos pia semper gestabat viscera, regem festinus adiit tunc apud regale manerium suum Wudestoke existentem. Quem cum rex satis reverenter ac civiliter in osculo assurgens suscepisset, dixit ei,

'Bene veneris, pater. Et que causa adventus et laboris tui?'

At ipse,

'Magna, domine mi, videlicet salus anime vestre et regni prosperitas et salvacio.' Et pro fundamento locucionis sue ponens et exponens eleganter et rethorice virtutem caritatis, iunctis manibus et obortis lacrimis regem pro memorato Gilberto devotissime deprecabatur, ut frater fratris noxam

[1] datus est *cod*   [2] amabilia *cod*

[a] The Introit of the third Sunday in Advent.
[b] Cf. the account of the same incident in *Hist. Angl.* ii. 370.

nullatenus lueret ac portaret, nec innocentem culpa nocentis aliquatenus redundaret. Et cum theologicas, quibus habundavit, induceret ad hoc cum racionibus auctoritates, efficaciter orans et persuadens ut non tantum omnem animi rancorem remitteret, immo eidem ad cumulum amplioris beneficii, | totam (fo. 132ʳ) cum officii dignitate concederet hereditatem suppliciter deprecabatur. Cui respondit rex pietate motus, vultu inquiens serenissimo,

'O bone archiepiscope, multum ponderis et nescio quid supra quod humanum est gracie et efficacie habent preces tue que me, in concepta ira fixum, ad clemenciam et favorem inopinabiliter revocarunt.'

Et ut vulgariter loquens ea, que benignus rex pronunciavit, recitem, planius ait modeste ridens,

'O quam pulcre scis precari. Precare eodem modo pro me Deum et non dubito, cum sit me Deus benignior, quin te clementer exaudiat. Porro ego te iam exaudivi. Fiat ut petisti.'

Et accito Gilberto, rex omnem remittens indignacionem ei, suam restituit cum plenitudine dignitatis hereditatem.

XX. Quomodo reconciliavit Hubertum de Burgo et alios nobiles regni[a]

Comitem quoque Cancie, Hubertum de Burgo, cuius erumpne et iniuriose persecuciones speciales tractatus exigerent,[b] ipse piissimus beatus antistes Edmundus, tactus super eo dolore cordis intrinsecus, simili precum instancia, regi misericorditer reconciliavit. Quid de Gilberto Basset et Stephano de Segrave et aliis preclaris ac viris potentibus quos in regno regi reddidit tantum non pacificatos set amicissimos, auditores

---

[a] The wording of this chapter is paralleled by Matthew's account of the same events in *Hist. Angl.* ii. 370–1.

[b] *speciales tractatus exigerent*: this is one of Matthew's favourite expressions, cf. its use in connexion with St. Edmund in *Hist. Angl.* ii. 442; iii. 27. Its use here suggests that Matthew may have contemplated a biography of Hubert de Burgh; cf. the sympathetic notices in *Chron. Maiora*, iv. 243, and *Hist. Angl.* ii. 477.

onerando percuncter?¹ Quorum perturbaciones dampnificas² non sine magna sollicitudine et labore tam prudenter quam clementer sedare procuravit. O peccatores qualescumque, ad sinum misericordie talis ac tanti intercessoris confugite confidenter,—ut hoc enim persuaderem hec predicta retexui. Misericordiam proculdubio consequimini nunc, cum sit causa favorabilior | animarum quam corporum et Deus omni rege terreno deprecabilior et pronior ad salvandum si modo quo decet et expedit preces, expiatis viciis, porrigatis salutares.

(fo. 132ᵛ)

Sic igitur omni misertus cunctosque miseratus, dum in hac vita Deo militaret, beatus archipresul Edmundus universorum pressuras pro posse propicius relevavit, singulorum honores et commoda procuravit. *De cura animarum* vero *sibi commissa* et spiritualium tutela *sollicitus, recipiendisque confessionibus eorum quos in multa spiritus lenitate confovebat ut* multos Deo *lucrifaceret, aut per se* aut per alios sedulus intendebat. Elemosinarum quoque irriguum³ que peccata dicuntur extinguere tam affectuose quam largiter pauperibus diffudit, ut quicunque de adventus sui presencia per tocius provincie latitudinem certificaretur ad patulas eius portas confugiens famelicus adveniret, tam potus quam cibi sustentacione diurna recreabatur. Et quamvis numerose pauperum multitudini in corporalibus cooperimentis subveniret, verecundatis tamen, quos aliquando honeratos⁴ paupertas precipitaverat, esu lauciori vestibusque honestioribus lineiis et laneis ac calciamentis secreto et civiliter respiciebat, ita videlicet ut impensum beneficium docta et faceta industria duplicaret. *Abstinencie* quoque *consuetudo prioris* diatim suscepit augmentum, et cum nobilium hospitum in mensa crebro suscepisset frequenciam, *consuete sobrietatis usum retinuit illibatum.* Verum tamen archanum ieiunium sub serena facie mirabili prudencia novit sub sancta dissimulacione palliare. Et cum ipsi pransuro tam deliciose quam speciose dapes et fercula carencia apponerentur commedenda, minima buccella cibos ipsos pregustatos vel commensalibus circumsedentibus vel alicui advene |

¹ percunter *cod* ² dampnas *cod* ³ irruguum *cod*
⁴ oneratos *cod*

hospiti iussit distribui vel pauperibus qui Fratres appellantur (fo. 133ʳ) in presencia sua prandentibus,[a] errogari.

XXI. Qualiter numquam tempus consumpsit ocium

Desidiam autem et ocia detestans beatus Edmundus semper vel orans vel meditans vel librorum correccionibus vel confessionibus vel inter Fratres collatarum questionum sollucionibus[b] vel exortarum licium decisionibus occupatus detinebatur ne umquam inveniret eum humani generis inimicus vacantem a bonis operibus et ociosum. Quem si aliquis de immoderato labore corriperet, respondit, illud repetens sapientis,

> 'Nunc lege, nunc ora,
> Sacra vel in arte labora.
> Sic erit hora brevis
> Et labor ipse levis.'

Maxime tamen *oracionum* prolixitati crebrius intendens, *noctes* eciam hyemales in *brevissima sompni degustacione* pervigil in genuflexionibus, fletibus, et meditacionibus usque ad ultimum gallicinium expendebat. Et tunc diurnas et cotidianas preces, quas consuetudinarias appellavit, ac si tunc diesceret vel mane foret, inchoavit. Nos autem torpentes et sompnolenti vix potuimus ad eius horas finales pervenire cum iam tempus erat matutinas inchoare. *Negociorum enim* diurnorum *occupacio, quam*

---

[a] On the presence of Dominican friars in St. Edmund's household, see Trivet, *Annales*, p. 228, and W. H. Hinnebusch, *The Early English Friars Preachers* (Rome, 1951), pp. 446–7.

[b] The *questio collata* was an informal type of disputation, held among students for practice. The Dominican General Chapter of 1259 decreed 'quod fiant repetitiones de questionibus et collationes de questionibus semel in septimana, ubi hoc potest commode observari'; see Little and Pelster, *Oxford Theology and Theologians*, pp. 53–56. It is not clear whether the *collationes* mentioned here by Matthew took place between the friars in the archbishop's household or perhaps in the priory of Canterbury of which Edmund was a patron.

[c] The *oratio recta* is clearly drawn from the deposition of one of the archbishop's *familiares*, which is omitted in the extant copies of Eustace's Life.

officii pontificialis *necessitas ingerebat, consuetam horam orandi prepediens, consuetudinem orandi non studium alternavit. Datum* enim *sibi tempus in ociis* numquam *consumpsit.*

De silencio vero suo in ecclesia et nocturnis horis et post completorium,[a] silencii pacem (numquam)[1] infregit, illud sepe recitans autenticum 'Silencium cultus iusticie'[b] et 'Sedebit silens solitarius; levabitque se supra se'.[c] De qua consuetudine inviolabili quiddam relatu dignum huic libello duximus inserendum.

(fo. 133ᵛ) *Dum Rome fuit quodam* | *sero,* cum prolixius orasset, solus *ad vocacionem domini pape pulsatus post completorium, invitus et a suis increpatus* de mora et hesitacione, *accessit ad eundem.* Et inter loquendum recitans illud Samuelis a mortuis vocati atque provocati, ait domino pape,

'O domine sancte pater, tali hora quare inquietasti me?'[d] Et cum causam huius dicti querentibus plenius exposuisset, ait papa iocose vultuque sereno,

'Bene scires monachus esse.'

At ipse,

'Utinam hiis exutus[2] sollicitudinibus bonus monachus essem. O quam (bona)[3] est monachorum pax et condicio.'

XXII. De quadam comparacione eius ad beatum Martinum et eius similitudinem

Erat autem de beato Edmundo sicut de beato Martino legitur,[e] hic *pauper et modicus, set celo dives et magnificus, subiectus et prelatus,* magnus Deo, modicus sibi, officii dignitate severus, vultus hylaritate et eloquii melliflui affabilitate socialis. Semper insuper *ab omni munere palpancium excuciens manus,* sua *novit*

---

[1] numquam *supplevi*   [2] executus *cod*   [3] bona *supplevi*

[a] This clause represents a note which Eustace neglected to write up into a grammatical sentence. Matthew Paris has altered the rest of the sentence, but the anacoluthon remains.
[b] *Is.* xxxii. 17.
[c] Cf. *Lam.* iii. 28.
[d] Cf. *1 Reg.* xxviii. 15.
[e] Sulpicius Severus, *Epist.* iii, *PL* xx. 184; see Eustace.

gratanter *esse contentus*, cum usu rei familiaris sibi competente, condicione. *Indefessusque operator omnium operum misericordie, pietate exuberans, quam erga pauperes et afflictos semper habuerat, in assumpto pontificali* numquam *defecit*. Perquisitarum quoque simul cum officio habundancia facultatum vel reddituum vix ad exhibicionem eorum,[1] manu auxiliatrice semper extenta ad Christi pauperes, suffecit. Non enim sustinebat ut aliquis mendicus *vacuus* aut desolatus a portis eius aliquando *recessisset*. Set[2] ne quis moveatur si, salva tanti sancti reverencia, *beatum Edmundum* sancto *Martino equiparaverim* vel sane assimulaverim, cum in utroque | similium virtutum insignia fallibiliter consideraverim. *Martinus* enim *adhuc cathecuminus algentem pauperem*, immo in ipso paupere Christum, *divisa clamide vestivit.*[a] *Edmundus* numerosam pauperum multitudinem quolibet anno eciam antequam beneficiaretur pro posse vestiens, multo plures *fidei et doctrine vestibus* adornavit. Martinus sancte Trinitatis gloriam in partibus occiduis gentibus manifestavit. Edmundus in partibus Anglicanis doctor celeberrimus theologie doctrinam elegantissime dilucidavit, et predicando longe lateque non in cassum seminavit et scriptura posteris profutura reliquit. Pro Martini corporis desiderata possessione orta est sacra contencio. Pro sancto corpore Edmundi, prout sequens sermo declarabit,[b] possidendo, pia exorta est controversia. Martinus flos Francorum, Edmundus gemma Angligenarum choruscabat. Martinus Turonencium archipresul, Edmundus Cantuariensis archiepiscopus refulgebat. *Martinus in virtute Trinitatis trium* vivens *mortuorum suscitator erat magnificus.* Edmundus adhuc vivus tres a mortuis, quod tamen in tota vita sua iussit supprimi, revocavit. Quid pluribus immorer? Uni ambo regi militantes,

(fo. 134ʳ)

[1] earum *cod*   [2] se *cod*

[a] Cf. Sulpicius Severus, *Dialogi*, ii, *PL* xx. 201-12.
[b] Apparently a reference to the argument between the *familiares* of the dead archbishop which Matthew reports below, p. 276. The letter of Richard Wych, in Sens cath. mun. no. 2, attesting the archbishop's wish to be buried at Pontigny, suggests that the claim of Pontigny to St. Edmund's body did not pass uncontested.

uno spiritu sunt sanctificati. Uni Domino fideliter famulantes supra multa constitui[a] feliciter promeruerunt.

XXIII. De quarumdam ipsius virtutum titulis

Laudemus igitur *Deum qui* sanctum suum sic glorificavit. Gratuletur Anglia qui talem ac tantum celicolam generavit et in gremio suo tam felicem alumpnum educavit. Letetur Francia, qui corpus tanti patroni retinere meruit intumulatum. Exultent angeli et omnes celestis curie milites de tanti commilitonis (fo. 134ᵛ) associacione. *Erat* namque *quasi sol* in terra | *refulgens*[b] *doctrina et quasi thus redolens*[c] *fama et operacione, implens illud Apostoli, 'Sic loquimini et sic facite'*.[d] *Et quasi alter Iohannes Baptista in deserto angelus factus generalis predicator, turbis* publicis, *militibus* et urbanis, *religiosis et clericis, utriusque sexus* fidelibus, *verba sancte predicacionis et exortacionis cum affectu et effectu lucide, salubriter, et incessanter* propinavit. *Sane* cunctis[1] extitit *bene ac digne vivendi lumen, eximium speculum sanctitatis, iusticie zelus, magisterium pietatis, forma doctrine, discipline sanccio, religionis exemplum. Habet in eo omnis sexus, etas, condicio, gradus, ordo, statusve quid eligat, et in omnes habundanter emanat luminis huius sancta serenitas. Invenit in eo puericia quid imitetur. Speculatur robur virile quid appetat et miretur. Instruitur clerus et informatur ad quid debeat anelare. Membra corporis ipsius debilitantur. Robur anime suscepit incrementum. Pallescit ieiunio speciosa facies* adeo *quod repente totus* immutatur. *Aliquando* eciam *a potu sic abstinebat quod pili capitis sui et barba ceciderunt quia humorem nutritivum non habebant. Cuius depilacionis deformitas socios suos in arte medicinali tunc regentes* et valde peritos non latebat. *Quibus intersciscitantibus*[2] *et disputantibus que huius rei esset causa argumenti scrutinio inventum est hoc ex defectu humorum* nutritivorum *accidisse*. Corpus quoque ipsius ossibus desiccatis et medullis

---

[1] cuntis *cod*
[2] inter se sciscitantibus *Eustace*

[a] Cf. Matt. xxv. 23.   [b] Cf. Eccli. 1. 7.   [c] Cf. Eccli. 1. 8.
[d] Iac. ii. 2.

evacuatis, tysis[a] que est substancialis humiditatis consumptiva fere demersit et adnichilavit.

XXIV. Testimonium archiepiscopi Eboracensis[b] de virtutibus beati Edmundi

Inter multos qui veritati testimonium de eius incomparabili sanctitate perhibebant, *archiepiscopus Eboracensis scribens ita loquitur, Fuit itaque vir* Edmundus archiepiscopus Cantuariensis gloriosus, ut | *firmiter credo* et ut humanum est scio, *a lapsu carnis* (fo. 135r) prorsus *immunis*, pre omnibus prout cognovi *fide firmus, spe robustus, caritate ferventissimus, lingua facundus,* sentencia copiosus, *abstinencie plurimum deditus, in oracionibus sedulus, creber in vigiliis, strenuus in disciplinis, doctor egregius, predicator eximius, confessor discretus,* semper ciliciatus, *in lecto vix aut numquam quietis gracia recumbans,* dormiens vestitus et cinctus assidue, discalciatus raro. Virgarum flagellaciones quas disciplinas appellamus qualibet nocte, nisi precipuum festum ipsas suspenderet, usque ad livorem et aliquando sanguinis effusionem suscepit, teporem disciplinantis cum parceret increpando. Hic *in adversis fortissimus, in prosperis mansuetus, affabilis omnibus, verbo pius, cum debita maturitate semper gaudens et hilaris, compaciens miseris, elemosinarum largitor* benevolus,[1] *merencium consolator* usque adeo quod tamquam alter Iob vere *dicere potuit, 'pes fui*[2] *claudo, oculus ceco, pater pauperum, solacium miserorum'.*[c] Cuius cum recolo inexpugnabilem *in operibus fidem,* precipuum in victu rigorem, diuturnam cum mundo et diabolo colluctacionem, *incunctanter* et indubitanter *affirmo hunc,* quamvis *non completa* in gladio *passione,* longum et quasi intolerabile traxisse (*martirium*)[3] (et)[4] martirii palmam suscepisse, ut dixisse posset cum Apostolo, *'michi vivere Christus et mori lucrum est.'*[d] Et *quia* ipsum *celestis docebat unctio* et Ipse qui in linguis igneis apparens, apostolos instruxit, verbis

[1] benivolus *cod* [2] sui *cod* [3] supplevi
[4] supplevi

[a] i.e. phthisis. [b] Walter de Gray, archbishop of York, 1215–55.
[c] Cf. *Iob* xxix. 15. [d] *Phil.* i. 21.

ut essent proflui et caritate fervidi, *mirum in modum eius collacio*[a] *tam pondere sentenciarum quam puritate verborum* elegantissime placens erat ut *efficax* et nescio quem celestis gracie effectum in se confortans. *Post epulas autem et sompnum* de consuetudine quem sedendo gustavit, *aut scripturis* sacris *aut honestis* et (fo. 135ᵛ) edificativis *colloquiis* intendebat, *ocium* | *summo opere* devitans, *ne* videntes hoc *hostes deriderent sabbata* illius.[b] *Raro cenavit et rarissime* post prandium potavit, illud adimplens Sapientis, 'Sobrietas est sanitas anime et corporis'.[c] *Post matutinas* vero *clericis et capellanis* recedentibus et *dormitum euntibus*, ipse archiepiscopus, licet distincte et articulatim omnia rite complevisset, *tam tempore hyemali quam estivali remansit in oratorio solus* et *reliquum noctis in meditacionibus, lacrimis, et oracionibus expendebat*. Horis itaque illis *conflictum cum diabolo sepius* visibilem *habebat*. Unde quasi obiurgans audiebatur. Videbat quoque *aliquando diabolum inter Wrotham et Ottofordiam in specie draconis igni*vomi *nunc* ad *celum* erectum, *nunc in terram* proiectum et demersum.

XXV. Veriloquium ac breviloquium fratris Roberti cognomento Bacun de sanctitate beati (Edmundi)[1] Cantuariensis archiepiscopi[d]

Frater Robertus cognomento Bacun de Ordine Predicatorum, regens Oxonie de theologia, qui beato Edmundo specialissimus fuit scolaris, auditor, et socius, iuratus dicit: Cum beatus Edmundus in liberalibus artibus studeret Parisius, mater eius cum lineis pannis, quos ei misit, solebat cilicium mittere, deprecans eum ut eo uteretur. Cuius peticionem ipse gratanter adimplevit. Cum autem Oxoniam devenisset, mortua matre

---

[1] Edmundi *supplevi*

[a] Here *collacio* has its commoner meaning of a sermon and, by metonymy, preaching.

[b] *hostes* &c. Cf. *Lam.* i. 7.

[c] Cf. *Eccli.* xxxi. 37.

[d] This is the only extant text of this deposition by the distinguished theologian, which was the source of many of the hagiological anecdotes about St. Edmund. See above, pp. 28–29.

Vita S. Edmundi auctore Matthaeo Parisiensi

sua, ipse uti lorica, quam ad hoc reliquerat ei mater sua, (incepit),[1] que in vita sua eadem utebatur. Uti eciam solitus fuit in Adventu Domini et in Quadragesima quodam indumento plumbeo. Constringere eciam solebat carnem suam funiculis in locis plurimis corporis sui. Numquam lectum maxime linthiaminibus stratum intravit, set ante lectum, vestitus et cinctus, iacuit. Clausis et talaribus utebatur vestimentis, quia ea conferre solebat veris viduis vel honestis puellis. Cirotecis | et mitra non utebatur. Rarissime quasi numquam lavabatur (fo. 136ʳ) capud eius. Quasi nichil de carnibus vel piscibus vescebatur. In Adventu Domini et Quadragesima solo pulmento utebatur. Species et electuaria et medicinalia non curabat, immo pro frivolis habebat. Numquam voluit ut sibi propter se diceretur quid manducaturus esset. Immo frequenter cibum, cum coram ipso laudaretur, non illum gustavit, dicens quod laus sibi satis illi cibus erat. Aliquando vero tantum abstinuit quod pili barbe et corone sue defluxerunt. Die quo celebravit carnes non gustavit, sic nec secunda feria nec in Septuagesima. In ieiuniis, vigiliis, et oracionibus ardenter instabat. In ecclesia vero non sedebat, stabat vel genua aspere flectebat. Iocundus (erat) et[2] dulcissimus aliis, set sibi durissimus, dicens quod oliva retinet sibi radicis sue amaritudinem, set aliis infundit olei sui suavitatem[3] et lumen cum refeccione. Bursam vel loculum non portabat, set cum denarios a scolaribus recepit, solebat eos in fenestra sua quasi omnibus exposita ponere et pocius iactare, et accipiens pulverem ait,

'Pulverem pulveri, cineremque cineri'.

Unde sepe et quasi furto asportabantur. Regens in artibus singulis diebus audivit missam antequam scolas intraret, et sic assuefecit scolares suos ut similiter secum missam suam audirent. Contigit autem quod quidam de scolaribus suis in brachio suo infirmaretur, qui accessit ad magistrum suum Edmundum et ostendit ei morbum suum. Qui dicit huiusmodi verbum, 'sanet te Deus.' Ille autem in crastino[4] reversus, dixit se sanum

---

[1] incepit *supplevi* [2] erit *cod* [3] suavitate *cod*
[4] crastinum *cod*

esse. Et sicut michi retulit magister Edmundus, ipse morbum scolaris sui per aliquantum temporis in brachio suo portavit.

(fo. 136ᵛ) Mater | sua in morte sua commisit ei duas sorores suas cum quadam summa pecunie ut eas traderet religioni. Ipse autem super hoc sollicitus, conatus est hoc adimplere nec potuit, nisi exprimeret quid cum eis dare vellet, quod et ipse renuit. Et tandem pervenit ad Kateby, et antequam colloquium haberet cum priorissa, ipsa eum ignotum proprio nomine nominavit et negocium pro quo venerat ei expressit. Et dixit ei ut eas sibi mitteret et eas faceret moniales. Et sic factum est. Hoc michi ipse retulit. Item quadam die, regens in artibus, occupatus esset studio, oblitus dicere quamdam oracionem beate[1] Virgini et beato Iohanni Evangeliste quam qualibet die dicere consueverat. Nocte autem sequenti apparuit ei beatus Iohannes ferulam baiulans et dixit ei,

'Extende manum tuam.' Qua extensa, beatus Iohannes ferula, quam manu tenebat, comminatus est ei, set vultu non torvo, ipsum percutere. Quod si fecisset, videbatur ei pre magnitudine comminacionis qua potens erat si vellet, quod[2] mortuus fuisset. Dixit autem ei quod ex inde illam oracionem nulla die omitteret. Hoc eciam michi retulit magister Iohannes de Wiz,[a] cui magister Edmundus hoc narraverat. Cui et illam oracionem scripsit. Incipit autem illa oracio sic: 'O intemerata' et cetera alia.[b] Cum autem leccionem quamdam festinam suis auditoribus de sciencia disciplinali legeret et frequenter figuras in pulvere protraheret, quadam nocte in sompnis apparuit ei mater sua et dixit ei,

'Fili mi, extende manum tuam.' Et ipsa in manum quam extendit tres circulos descripsit, dicens,

---

[1] beati *cod* [2] *add* si vellet *cod*

[a] Master John de Wych was a member of the archbishop's *familia* and one of his executors, see above, p. 151.

[b] For the earlier history of this prayer, which enjoyed great popularity in the twelfth century, see A. Wilmart, *Auteurs spirituels et textes dévots du moyen âge latin* (Paris, 1932), pp. 474–504.

'Hii tres circuli sunt tres troni trium personarum. Has figuras, non alias, amodo addisce.'

Et sic postquam sex annis in artibus rexerat et mirabiliter profecerat, ad sacram scripturam audiendam se transtulit. In qua predicando, legendo, et disputando[a] multum fructum attulit. Multi enim divites barones | in medio tempore ipsum (fo. 137r) audientes, Cruce signati, omnia pro Christo reliquerunt et sese peregrinacionis periculis subdiderunt, alii claustra subierunt, alii vero bonis moribus informati, theologie paginis intenderunt. Quadam autem nocte in sompnis ei visum fuit quod magnus ignis in scolis suis accensus erat et quod septem ticiones vel torres de igne extraherentur. Ipso autem die, scilicet crastino, eodem in cathedra sedente et docente, intravit abbas de Lapidicina,[b] Cisterciensis Ordinis, et completis magistri leccionibus, septem de scolaribus suis a monitu[1] tam magistri quam abbatis ut credi potuit, igne caritatis accensos, secum adduxit habitum suum assumpturos. Quorum unus fuit magister Stephanus de Leixentuna, postea abbas Clarevallensis.[c] Contigit insuper quod cum versus partes Wallie die quadam predicaret, nubes quedam aquosa nimis et imbre manifeste repleta super congregatos ad audiendum suspensa esset imbres effusura. Ipso autem et ipsis orantibus hinc inde in pluviam resoluta est ipsis ab (ea)[2] minime complutis. Et sic prospere in predicacionem processit. Quadam eciam die visitavit quemdam scolarem infirmum nobilem virum. Quem cum vellet ab eodem recedere infirmus detinuit. Cuius rei causam ego ab infirmo postea quesivi. Qui michi respondit et dixit,

'Dum magister mecum erat, videbatur michi quod tota domus plena esset aromatibus.'

---

[1] a monitu: ammonitu *cod* [2] ea *supplevi*

[a] The threefold obligation of the Master of the Sacred Page, cf. Peter the Chanter, 'In tribus igitur consistit exercitium sacre scripture: circa lectionem, disputationem et praedicationem': *Verbum Abbreviatum*, PL ccv. 25.

[b] Quarr, Isle of Wight, of the filiation of Savigny.

[c] Stephen of Lexington, abbot of Clairvaux 1243–57. The Dunstable annalist places Stephen's departure from the Oxford schools for Quarr in 1221; see *Ann. Mon.* iii. 67.

Cum predicaret, vix[1] cum aliquo maxime infirmo loqui voluit donec predicasset.

Cum servientibus suis semper pactum iniit, ut, si quandoque in lapsu carnis deprehensi essent, accepta mercede pro rato, ab eo recederent. Officium regendi in sacra scriptura et omnes (fo. 137ᵛ) sacros ordines invitus et coactus suscepit. | Orare solebat ut nunquam vacaret ecclesia ad eius spectans donacionem. Antequam Bibliam suam aperiret, de more osculabatur eam. Paucos libros sacre scripture quos Parisius habuit, eciam audiens sacram scripturam, vendidit et precium pauperibus scolaribus errogavit. Ipso adhuc regente in artibus contigit unum de pauperibus scolaribus infirmari, quem ipse portari fecit in domum suam. Et ipse per quinque fere ebdomadas qualibet pene nocte iacuit coram eo et ministravit ei in urinali[2] suo et in aliis nature necessariis quasi vulgare mancipium, et nichilominus in crastino[3] legebat et disputabat. Frequenter autem cadebat de manu infirmi pre vanitate capitis nec tamen, licet vas fragile super aspera caderet, frangebatur.

Archiepiscopus Eboracensis Walterus ipsi magistro Edmundo carissimus, optulit ei, quia erat[4] specialis et amantissimus[5] ei, quod faceret ei scribi totam Bibliam glosatam quod et ipse renuit, respondens ei quod formidabat ne forte oneraret abbatias et prioratus, scriptoribus ad hoc deputatis, et maluit libris carere quam religiosis sic inde gravari. Aliquando autem a demone vexatus, adiuravit eum ut sibi diceret in quo maxime ei nocuit. Qui ait,

'In recordacione effusionis sanguinis Christi'.

Ipse qualibet die solebat membra sua a capite usque ad pedes signo Crucis consignare et in consignacione cuiuscumque membri dicere 'Adoramus te Christe et benedicimus te quia per sanctam Crucem tuam redemisti[6] mundum.'

Celeberrimi igitur viri et preelecti regionis Anglicane prelati, Cantuariensis videlicet Stephanus et Eboracensis Walterus

---

[1] vix: add enim cod, sed textus vitiatus esse videtur
[2] veniali cod
[3] crastinum cod
[4] erit cod
[5] amantissimus: add optulit cod
[6] rede cod

archiepiscopi simul et alii viri magni talia de viro sancto fama referente cognoscentes, ipsum amplioribus honoribus et redditibus uberioribus certatim ditare festinarunt. De quorum recepcione causa | et modo vobis duximus referendum, et sit unum (fo. 138ʳ) exemplum plurimorum. Cum igitur ad ipsum nuncios suos dominus archiepiscopus destinasset offerens ei regimen cuiusdam ecclesie que circiter ducentarum marcarum summam annuarum eius rectori persolvere consuevit, respondit magister Edmundus post modicum deliberacionis tempus et dixit nuncio qui advenerat,

'Amice, nosti qualiter ecclesia illa, quam collaturus est michi sui gracia dominus tuus, cancello, vestimentis, libris, et aliis que ad rectoris pertinent exhibicionem communitur?'

Responsum est,

'Domine, certe, pauperrime.'

At ipse super hoc certificatus,[1] nuncio respondit,

'Gracias referas domino tuo. Oblatum enim redditum accipio et accepto ne forte in ipsum Romani vel alii ipsis consimiles qui nichil de ovibus Christi preter lac et lanam querunt, avidas manus iniciant.'

Apposito igitur eidem ecclesie ad cancellum ampliandum, cooperiendum, et decorandum, et ad ornamenta et que fuerant necessaria emenda fideli ac diligenti procuratore, omnes ecclesie proventus in hoc exposuit, nichil inde sibi penitus reservando. Et hoc per plures annos continuavit officium donec omnes illius ecclesie defectus plenius supplerentur. Postea vero ne de animarum reddendis racionibus obligaretur vel curie curis ipsum implicari oporteret quominus scolarum studiis interesset, omnia resignavit.

XXVI. Nota quoddam miraculum

Cum autem haberet beatus Edmundus pontifex ciliciorum mutatoria, contingit quod uno per usum contrito et inveterato aliud sibi sumpsit eiusdem vel maioris asperitatis novum ad

---

[1] certificatur *cod*

utendum, precepitque cubiculariis duobus quos ad secretiora sua habuit fideles ac familiares ut continuo cilicium vetus quod turpe et scissum fuit et ad nullius rei usum valens, clam comburerent. | Qui obedientes in loco competenti accenso igni copioso illud ad comburendum apposuerunt. Set flamma vorax nec unum valuit pilum consumere. Mirabantur famuli nec ausi fuerant, ne adulatores viderentur, talia domino suo nunciare. Impositis igitur lapidibus ponderosis cilicio quot poterat continere, illud in profundo quodam gurgite, ut putrefaccione consumeretur, submerserunt.

XXVII. Oritur contra beatum Edmundum multiformis tribulacio

Videns autem humani generis publicus inimicus *tantum virum ecclesie Dei* quam *plurimum profuturum, invidit et ne pace principis* gratularetur ut consuevit, *multos et magnos elegit incentores discordie per quos in corde regis et curialium odii* detestabile *sparsit seminarium.*[a] Monachi autem Cantuarie quibus specialius ceteris prefuit, videlicet de gremio ecclesie sue zelum iusticie habentes, set non secundum scienciam,[b] quasdam suas libertates ipsum, ut dicebant, conventum specialiter contingentes, quas archiepiscopales occuparant, constanter reposcebant. Quas eciam cum archiepiscopus,[1] eo quod caput eorum esset et pater, vendicaret sibi pertinere et de rei familiaris cognicione merito debere certificari, contradicebant ei monachi in faciem, constanter appellantes ne in preiudicium eorum et approbatam ecclesie antiquam consuetudinem aliquid novum attemptaret. Credebant enim quam plures confidenter et indubitanter ipsas libertates sibi specialiter pertinere, super quo cartas ostendebant et privilegia. Quorum unum quod, ut asserebant, ex diligencia beati Thome martiris fuerat optentum, secus quam deceret

---

[1] archiepiscopo *cod*

[a] Cf. *Vita S. Thomae* auct. *Joanne Saresberiensi, Materials*, ii. 309.

[b] Cf. the almost identical words used by Matthew to describe the conduct of the monks in *Hist. Angl.* ii. 411.

suspectum erat et videbatur adulteratum, et iccirco aliquorum fratrum consilio combustum est. Unde non minimum ortum est scisma in conventu. Eo | autem tempore Otto cardinalis, (fo. 139ʳ) Romane Sedis legatus existens in Anglia, ut tante perturbacionis dampnosum ac probrosum[1] tumultum et discordiam pacificaret, Cantuariam adiit, quia scandalum iam super hoc exortum per totam ventilatum regionem fetorem exalavit. Intransque monachorum capitulum, facta diligenti inquisicione, dixit conventui,

'Fratres karissimi, qui monachi venerabiles huius estis nobilissime metropolitane ecclesie, qua non maior est in Anglia immo nec ei par, infirma est pars vestra, nec vos unitatis iungit conformitas. Humiliamini sub potenti manu.[a] Obediant membra capiti suo. Obedite pastori ac patri vestro sanctissimo archipresuli. Et antequam amplius scandalum oriatur quod famam vestram indelebili nota possit obfuscare, hec contagio sepeliatur.'

Cui sic peroranti pars conventus benignius adquievit. Et cum post non multos dies rediens, archiepiscopus intrasset capitulum, intellexit illico quod orto scismate non omnes idem senciebant. Volentibus enim aliquibus humiliari et cedere, alii credentes ecclesiam super hoc enormem subire lesionem, reclamabant, appellantes. Pro qua discordia dispersus est grex dominicus, et multi, ut in pace dies suos residuos ducerent, fratrum Cartusiensium[2] vel alium ordinem sibi eligentes, irremeabiliter recesserunt.[b] Porro insurrexerunt aliqui monachorum pertinaces et eorum amici seculares improperantes archiepiscopo quod ecclesie et conventus sui non tantum esset perturbator, set manifestus impugnator, nimisque indecenter in ipsos proterviret qui eum, spretis eciam nobilissimis, contra

---

[1] probosum *cod*   [2] Cartusiensem *cod*

[a] Humiliamini &c.: *1 Pet.* v. 6.

[b] In fact, as can be seen from Gervase, ii. 133-4, the prior was removed to a Carthusian monastery for his part in the forgery of a privilege. That Matthew knew the true facts, which he has glossed over, is evident from his account of the same incident in *Chron. Maiora*, iii. 492.

regis et aliorum multorum peticionem, in tante dignitatis apicem de humillimo eligentes, sullevarunt.

XXVIII. Archiepiscopus misertus condescendit in multis voluntati conventus sui

Archiepiscopus igitur perturbacioni conventus et ecclesie condolens, non mediocriter ab alto ducens suspiria, usque ad amaritudinem spiritus angebatur. Una igitur dierum ut imminenti scandalo obviaret, capitulum cum summa humilitate intravit, statera racionis et modestie motam perturbacionem prudenter compescens ne beneficiorum sibi impensorum[1] a monachis immemor videretur. Formidabat enim vehementer ne nota ingratitudinis colore ei posset obici qualicumque. Voluntati igitur in tantum eorum condescendit ut, omni sopita lite, pax tam decenter quam gaudenter reformaretur, quam omnes et singuli monachorum benigne concesserunt, gracias[2] super hoc Deo et archipresuli referentes. Archiepiscopus itaque ut ipsius pacis formam apostolica confirmaret auctoritate et quamdam aliam controversiam inter ecclesiam suam et ecclesiam cathedralem Londonie, tempore pie recordacionis Rogeri episcopi motam, et ut quedam alia ardua negocia ecclesiam et officium suum contingencia expediendo determinari procuraret, Romam se protestatus est aditurum. Qui quam tempestive potuit, dispositis necessariis, transalpinavit.[a] Et ecce cum iam Romam pervenisset, prima die quosdam de monachis Cantuarie, suorum causidicorum fallacibus promissis inherentes, invenit, qui raptim et cum indecenti festinacione ipsum archiepiscopum prevenerant. Ipsi igitur contra pacem memoratam quam proposuit archiepiscopus feliciter confirmare,

---

[1] impensorum: *add* ei *cod*   [2] grates *cod*

[a] In the margin of the *Chronica Maiora* Matthew noted that the archbishop departed for Rome during the week before Christmas, 1237: *Chron. Maiora*, iii. 470. An act of the archbishop's referring to the composition with the convent is dated at Canterbury on 19 Dec. 1237: Lambeth MS. 582, fo. 58. This fixes St. Edmund's departure between the 19th and 24th.

Vita S. Edmundi auctore Matthaeo Parisiensi

inopinabiliter et non sine maxima admiracione ipsius et suorum, procaciter appellarunt. Et cum, super hoc nimis confusus, archiepiscopus asseruisset hoc in contumeliam | sui et sue dam- (fo. 140ʳ) pnum ecclesie et scandalum redundare, animabant advocati, qui tantum munera sequuntur et retribuciones, ipsos monachos ut in faciem archiepiscopi starent contradicentes. Quibus ait archiepiscopus, nimis detestans supinam monachorum simplicitatem,

'Non est pax impiis, dicit Dominus.'[a]

Quid plura? Tandem obstinatis monachis nec volentibus quomodolibet a conducticiorum causidicorum suorum consiliis recedere, in omnes pacis perturbatores archiepiscopus sentenciam tulit excommunicacionis. Et ex tunc inposterum diatim crevit concepta indignacio inter ipsum archiepiscopum et sibi singulos adversantes.

XXIX. Multiplicantur undique adversarii archiepiscopi

Verum preter omnes istos qui videbantur esse sue filii ecclesie, insurrexerunt in ipsum archiepiscopum, graves et arduas moventes questiones, episcopus Londoniensis Rogerus, conventus Rofensis, comes Harundelie Hugo, Iusticiarius Anglie Hubertus, comes Legecestrie Simon. Quorum impetus, quos videbantur racionibus suffulcire,[1] cum molestia et expensis non minimis sustinuit archiepiscopus. Cum ipsis enim insurgentibus qui maiores videbantur, levaverunt et minores in ipsum calcaneum. Tandem habito cum domino Papa tractatu secreto super hiis negociis, ad iudices in Angliam destinatur super hiis questionibus predictis quod ius dictaret reportaturus. Postea vero *convenientibus suffraganeis ex mandato regis*[2] *ad excipiendas ecclesie necessitates, orta est contencio inter regem et ecclesiam que*

---

[1] suffulsire *cod*
[2] *Eustace habet* archiepiscopi et proceribus ex mandato regis *quod forte per errorem excidit*

[a] *Is.* xlviii. 22.

instigante diabolo magis ac magis indies augebatur. Reformande quidem paci constituti sunt dies plurimi, set stimulante *dissencionis auctore, post prorogaciones* | frustratorias, *discordes ab invicem* recesserunt. *Tunc archiepiscopus securus ascendens ex adverso, opponensque se murum pro domo Israel, post renovatas vexaciones et* multiplicatas *iniurias de consilio suffraganeorum suorum in pacis ecclesiastice perturbatores sentenciam* anathematis iterando, renovando, et ampliando, fulminavit. Porro *vir Dei fundatus* super *petram* que Christus est *et solidatus nec blandiciis emolliri potuit nec minis terreri ut a cultu iusticie deviaret* enervatus.

Otto vero legatus placere regi cupiens, postquam vidit cor ipsius regis iam penitus aversum[1] ab ipso archiepiscopo et undique sibi adversarios multiplicari, multitudini studuit complacere. Auctoritate igitur qua fungebatur facta archiepiscopi cassavit, absolvens quos specialiter excommunicaverat et eos, quos aliquando archiepiscopus absolveret, anathematis vel suspensionis vinculis innodavit. Quid multa? Omnia eius facta nugatoria censuit et reputavit. Monachi insuper Cantuarie post obitum eius, iuvantibus eos rege et legato, impetrata Rome sine difficultate et more dispendio absolucione, absolvendi destinati sunt in Angliam ad priorem Dunstaplie, Ricardum, et archidiaconum Sancti Albani, Iohannem, qui protinus auctoritate apostolica ipsos absolvebant.[a] Monachi hoc non optinuerunt beneficium sine multa pecunie effusione. Data est insuper sentencia eadem auctoritate contra eum pro conventu Rofensi.[b] Comes insuper Legecestrie, Simon, permissus est sponsam suam in pace retinere licet ipse archiepiscopus rei veritatem domino pape super voto suo in presencia sua solempniter facto plenius | intimasset. In aliis quoque causis usque ad thesauri exquisiti

---

[1] adversum *cod*

[a] Cf. the parallel phrasing of *Chron. Maiora*, iv. 103, and Richard of Morins' own account in *Ann. Mon.* iii. 156. The papal mandate was dated 6 Mar. 1241: *CPL* i. 194.

[b] Cf. the wording of *Hist. Angl.* ii. 411. Matthew's account ignores the chronology: the judgement in the Rochester case was given in 1238, see Auvray, 4197, and that in Montfort's case similarly, see *CPL.* i. 172.

Vita S. Edmundi auctore Matthaeo Parisiensi 259

exinanicionem[1] miserabiliter fatigatus dampnificabatur et multipliciter gravabatur.

XXX. Omnia sinistre archiepiscopo acciderunt et male interpretantur actus eius.[2]

Hanc[a] itaque mutacionem dextere Excelsi[b] maligna interpretacione conati sunt impii obfuscare, supersticioni ascribentes quod vitam duceret altiorem, zelum iusticie crudelitatem asserentes, affabilitatem suam scurilem garrulitatem esse certius asserebant. Quod ecclesie procurabat utilitates avaricie attribuebant. Contemptum[3] mundani favoris veneracionem vane glorie menciebantur. Curialis quoque *magnificencia fingebatur elacio. Quod divinitus edoctam voluntatem sequebatur in plurimis nota supercilii dicebatur.* Hec rei summa: *nichil iam ab eo dici vel fieri poterat quod non* a malicia sinistre interpretacionis obfuscaretur. Et si multa eum moverent et commovere merito deberent et offendere, super hoc precordialius[4] conquestus est in secreto. Quando baptizabatur domini nostri regis Anglie primogenitus et universorum heres, preelectus fuit ad ipsum baptizandum Otto tunc legatus qui eciam ad hoc se ingessit, ordine diaconus, nacione alienigena, moribus inferior, sciencia theologica satis supinus, postposito archiepiscopo Cantuariensi, tocius Anglie primate, quem constat fuisse presbiterum nacione indigenam, moribus immo omni sanctitate perspicuum, sciencia multiplici doctorem et lectorem celeberrimum.[c] Qui tunc profecto presens extiterat, principale autem officium legato peragente, Karleolensis infantem baptizandum inmersit. Verumtamen ipsum baptizatum permissus est confirmare. Ex quo | igitur omnes eum inutilem censuerunt (fo. 141ᵛ

[1] exumacionem *cod*
[2] interpretantur actus: interpretativos actuum *cod*
[3] contempnum *cod*
[4] precordalius *cod*

[a] Hanc &c. *Vita S. Thomae, Materials*, p. 309; see Eustace.
[b] Hanc mutacionem &c. Cf. *Ps.* lxxvi. 11.
[c] Cf. Matthew's progressive development of this antithesis in *Chron. Maiora*, iii. 539 and *Hist. Angl.* ii. 422. His animosity towards the legate is here given fullest expression.

et omnibus contemptui habitus vilius. Set quid aliud superfuit quam ipsi omnia relinquere?

XXXI. Cessio

Videns igitur vir Dei quia cedere oportuit et sese absentare secundum illud poeticum,

Dum furor in cursu est, currenti cede furori,[a]

quadam nocte oravit propensius ut magni consilii angelus vias suas dirigeret, cordique suo revelaret quid melius, quid decencius, quidve anime sue salubrius in hoc articulo sibi foret faciendum. Et ecce inter orandum cum vehementer formidaret recedendo recedere, revelatum est ei desuper quid agendum hoc modo, voce desuper elapsa:

'Crede minoris sigilli tui circumscriptioni et sequere illum cuius in medio martirium figuratur.'

Erat autem sigilli sui secrecioris epigramma hic versus, 'Edmundum doceat mors mea ne timeat', et in medio beatus Thomas martir et milites eum excerebrantes eleganter insculpti.[b]

XXXII. Consilium beati Thome

Certificatus igitur archiepiscopus celitus quid agendum, conabatur ex tunc beati Thome martiris sequi vestigia pedetentim. Datum est enim ei in spiritu nosse hanc fuisse beati Thome predecessoris sui vocem, consilium, et consolacionem. Et quamvis moris id habuisset ipsum martirem in pressuris crebro, solempniter, et devote invocare, ex tunc crebrius, solempnius, ac devocius venerando deprecabatur, ut sicut et ipse erumpnas et tribulaciones huius mundi fortiter tolerando ad quietem eternam gloriose migravit, ita et ipse seculi et secularium pressuras viriliter paciendo tandem ad Deum tocius consolacionis et quietis eo iuvante avolaret. Confortabatur igitur archiepi- (fo. 142ʳ) scopus in Domino et | sollicitudinem precordialem vultu sereno

---

[a] Ovid, *Remed. Amoris*, 119.

[b] Matthew noted the details of the archbishop's seal in the margin of fo. 88ᵛ of his Liber Additamentorum: *Chron. Maiora*, vi. 124 n.

palliavit. O mira viri Dei paciencia et per secula recitabilis! Quocienscunque cause vel causidici ipsum (superaverunt),[1] memorans que adversus eum finem adversum sorciebantur, iunctis manibus et oculis in celum intensis, oravit alacriter dicens,

'Domine Ihesu qui orans dixisti, "pater, non mea set tua voluntas fiat"[a] eodem precor scemate, non ut ego set ut tu vis, fiat, et sicut fuerit voluntas in celo sic eveniat. Optineat utinam tantummodo ecclesia mea quod iure dictante[2] suum esse debet, et alia licet videatur adversari, quod suum est feliciter adquirat et possideat.'

Et cum audisset pluries plures adversarios suos optinere postulata—quid mirum? Otto legatus immo alter papa eidem potenter adversabatur—in nullo mota est viri sancti constancia ut saltem in aspera verba resolverentur labia sua nec sunt in diversa mutati aliquatenus vultus eius, set sancti Iob formam induens, ait,

'Sicut Domino placuit, sic factum est. Sit nomen Domini benedictum.[b] Sic decreverunt cum deliberacione iuris periti. Presumendum est tot et tantos viros discretos non errasse vel decipi potuisse.'

XXXIII. Multiplicatis pressuris exulat[3] archiepiscopus

Tandem cum tribulaciones multiplicarentur per potenciores regni quos redarguere nominatim tum propter papalem tum regalem reverenciam decens vel tutum non arbitror, cogitavit archiepiscopus illud Evangelicum adimplere, 'Si persecucionem patimini in una civitate, fugite in aliam.'[c] Et *cum pastoralis cure* sibi commisse *officium libere non* valuit cum voluit *exercere, cedendum censuit,* discedendo actus et | consilium beati Thome, (fo. 142ᵛ) ut prelibatum est, prosequendo.

[1] super *cod. Sed aliquid in textu deesse videtur* [2] dictacte *cod*
[3] exultat *cod*

[a] *Luc.* xxii. 41.   [b] Sicut &c. *Iob* i. 21.   [c] *Matth.* x. 23.

XXXIV. Transfretat

In orientali igitur parte Anglie que extenditur insula dicta Thanetos,[a] *navigio clam* et repente *preparato*, prospero cursu in partem portus ultramarini transfretatus[1] est, *se suosque ecclesie quoque sue causam Deo et gloriose Virgini* domine ac sponse *et beato* Thome predecessori ac duci suo *commendans*. Familiam suam, *quia alieno ere* non modicum obligabatur, abbreviavit. Et ut beati Thome actus conformiter imitaretur et vestigia sine errore sequeretur, versus Pontiniacum gressus maturavit ut ibidem in pace secrecius commorans, oracionibus et contemplacioni vacando donec visitaret ipsum et regnum Anglie oriens ex alto[b] et debitis quibus onerabatur alleviaretur, aliquot diebus prestolaretur.

XXXV. De honore quem ei exhibuit Blanchia regina Francorum

Cum autem in Franciam pervenisset archiepiscopus, apud Silvanectem habuit familiare colloquium et prolixum cum domina Blanchia, domini regis Francorum genetrice, quam constat esse[c] mulierem consilii magni et non muliebris. Que adducens filios suos secum in presencia sua se et ipsos precibus suis commendavit et ut benediccionem suam eis daret postulavit. Instantissime quoque iunctis manibus deprecabatur ut pro statu regni Francorum et regis incolumitate iugiter Deo funderet cum devocione preces indefessas. Quod et ipse cum certa affirmacione concessit et indubitanter adimplevit. Hinc est quod credimus, quod et credere pium arbitror, ipsam suam benediccionem vitam et sanitatem regi, postea gravissime infirmato et secundum multorum assercionem exanimato,[2] contulisse et postea honorem cum prosperitate, quod futura

[1] transfretus *cod*   [2] exanimato *add* vitam et sospitem *cod*

[a] que dicitur Sandwicus: Eustace.   [b] oriens ex alto: *Luc.* i. 78.
[c] Blanche of Castile died in 1253.
[d] Cf. the parallel wording in *Chron. Maiora*, iv. 397. Louis IX's illness occurred in Dec. 1244; see Guillaume de Nangis in *Recueil*, xx. 344.

successio veraciter | comprobavit. Hoc autem memorata regina (fo. 143ʳ) eo instancius supplicavit quod multa sanctitatis insignia in eo audierat choruscasse, ipsumque beati Thome martiris vestigia sequi non erronee pedetentim. Exposuit igitur nutui suo regnum Francorum ut eidem cum honore maximo ad sumptus domini regis filii[1] sui foret pacis et quietis refugium speciale. Quod et ipse rex et fratres sui devote precabantur. Archiepiscopus vero, qui moram nectere recusavit, gracias eisdem solvit multiplicatas. Licencia igitur optenta et vale dicto, versus Pontiniacum iter maturavit, ubi cum summo ut decuit honore et condigna reverencia susceptus est, assignata eidem domo quadam cum cameris honestis et archanis non procul a claustro et ecclesia, quam domum vel domus locum asserebant monachi fuisse beati Thome exulantis[2] secretum domicilium. Quod et archiepiscopus gratanter, immo gaudenter, acceptavit.

XXXVI. Quomodo se habuit apud Pontiniacum

Commorans ibidem pacifice aliquot diebus, oracionibus, contemplacionibus, confessionibus, predicacionibus, et aliis piis operibus adeo diligenter intendebat, ut omnium ibidem degencium religionem augeret, informaret, et ad augmentum feliciter provocaret. Mirabantur utique tantam in seculari vigere religionem. Et cum nimis et plus forte solito dietam suam attenuasset in escis quadragesimalibus, licet ab aliquibus fratrum pie corriperetur, perstitit in inceptis. Dicebant enim,

'Pater sancte, dicit unus doctorum nostrorum, videlicet beatus Bernardus abbas Clarevallensis, "corpus tuum restringe non extingue, reprime non opprime."[a] Et usus ecclesiasticus orans nos edocet, "racionabile fiat obsequium | vestrum."[b] Et (fo. 143ᵛ) ut illud magistrale, "iumento, hoc est corpori, escam provide, onus et virgam."'[c]

Dictis igitur eorum persuasibilibus adquiescens, archiepi-

---

[1] filii *bis in cod*   [2] exulanti *cod*

[a] I have been unable to trace this quotation.
[b] *Rom.* xii. 1.   [c] Apparently from a gloss on *Eccli.* xxxiii. 25.

scopus rigorem abstinencie in multis mitigavit, set penitus peticionibus eorum non satisfecit. Erubuerunt igitur cucullati, suam imbecillitatem et desidiam, licet severam vitam Cisterciensium[1] ducerent, condempnantes.

XXXVII. Quomodo fraternitatem in capitulo eorum accepit

Una igitur dierum ad peticionem abbatis et conventus intravit archiepiscopus capitulum et, sermonem faciens eis, omnium corda et moribus informavit et sciencia efficaciter erudivit. Habuit sermonem ignitum vehementer multa sentencia impregnatum et brevitate succincta castigatum in Latino retoricum et in communi, scilicet Franco[2] tamquam Gallicano.[3] Et post sermonem petiit et optinuit unius monachi sortem in spiritualibus et ut optineret tocius domus consorcium speciale. Ex tunc autem factus est inter eos quasi unus monachorum ipsius cenobii, licet non cucullatus, ita ut eorum confratrem se esse confiteretur. Ipsos quoque in refeccionibus, quas pitancias dicimus, gratanter recreavit.

XXXVIII. Quomodo infirmatus se contra mortem preparavit

Cum autem apud *Pontiniacum* parvo tempore moram continuasset, *quadam infirmitate corripitur que,*[4] *licet dolorem ingereret* non minimum, *minus tamen sensum eius vel racionis vigorem pristinum immutavit.* Ut igitur puriorem aëra et suo naturali similiorem hauriens respiraret, consilium suorum accepit medicorum ut a Pontiniaco ad horam recederet, ut sibi restitutus sanior remearet. Et cum suorum persuasionibus | adquiescens, erat enim supra id quod dici potest tractabilis, et in itineris procinctu (esset)[5] recessurus, fratres Pontiniaci eiulando et flendo dixerunt,

[1] Cistercium *cod*   [2] francto *cod*   [3] Gallicanum *cod*
[4] qui *cod*   [5] esset *supplevi*

'Cur nos, pater, deseris, aut cui nos desolatos relinquis? Cur a nobis tibi devotis et subiectis tam propere recedis? Quanto de tua venerabili presencia consolabamur, tanto de tuo recessu nunc contristamur. Ecce nobis tantummodo de tua dulcedine concessum est modicum pregustare, de qua, heu, heu, non meruimus plenius satiari. O quantum formidandum est ne hanc nobis peccata nostra penam preparaverint.'

XXXIX. Nota quod habuit spiritum prophecie

Hiis igitur lacrimis et eiulatui condolens, beatus archiepiscopus consolando dixit eis,

'Nolite fratres, de recessu meo contristari, quia in festo sancti Edmundi regis et martiris, per Dei graciam, ad vos revertar.' Quod et ita factum est. Eadem siquidem die beati confessoris corpus Pontiniacum constat esse delatum, sicut sequens sermo plenius suo loco declarabit. *Cum* autem memoratus sanctus, crebro ab immo[1] trahens suspiria cum gemitibus, *ad Soysi*,[a] domum videlicet Canonicorum Regularium, non sine difficultate *pervenisset*, contra spem et iudicium phisicorum *infirmitas eius* magis ac magis sensim *ingravescebat in dies. Quadam* vero *die,* cum in spiritu precognosceret diem sue dissolucionis imminere, *Eucaristiam cum debita veneracione* sibi *fecit deferri. Ante cuius percepcionem proposuit omnes articulos fidei. Et ex fervore fidei* et devocionis *loquebatur et ita se habebat* in gestu, in lacrimarum effusione, ut *suis et aliis astantibus et videntibus* certissime videretur *presencialiter in carne Dominicam* representari *passionem. Cuius fidei fervor et* intense *devocionis affectus multo maior fuit quam* | dici valeat nedum scribi. *Inter cetera* vero que *proposuit hec et hiis similia dixit*,

'*Tu es Domine, in quem credidi, quem dilexi, quem amavi, quem*

---

[1] immo: uno *cod*

[a] Soisy-en-Brie (Seine-et-Marne). The priory was dependent on the Augustinian abbey of St. Jacques at Provins: Cottineau, *Répertoire topo-bibliographique*, ii. 2369.

predicavi, quem docui. Et Tu michi testis es quod non quesivi in terra nisi Te.'

Que verba nonnulli sapientes admirabantur. Constat autem ipsum hec verba instinctu Spiritus Sancti pronunciasse, ut sic videlicet tanti dignitas sacramenti in cordibus fidelium solidius firmaretur. Ipse enim Altissimus qui postea sanctum suum virtutibus innumerabilibus illustravit, hec verba cum eorum omnimoda assercione reddit sub sigillo veritatis irrefragabilis cerciora. Qua propter restoratur[1] decencius fides catholica, confunditur Iudeorum pertinacia, hereticorum repellitur versucia, paganorum cecitas expavescit, pusillanimorum peccatorum spes respirat, ecclesia universalis honoris suscepit incrementum.

XL. Quedam mirabilia que dixit et fecit cum iam ad ipsam mortem vergeret

Postquam autem viatico salutari muniretur, cepit meliuscule se habere et quasi celesti convivio saginatus ac refectus, exhilaratus est. Et quodam pulvinari suffultus ut erectius sederet, dixit quasi iocose sereno vultu circumstantibus lingua Anglicana hoc eulogium proverbiale,

'Men seth gamen gooth on wombe. Ac ich segge, gamen gooth on herte.' *Quod est dictum: ludus ut dicitur, vadit in ventrem. At ego dico nunc ludus intrat cor.*

Cuius apologi hec est sentencialis intencio: vulgariter dicitur quod venter repletus pronus est ad ludum et gaudium generat. Set mea est nunc sentencia quod cor spirituali convivio saginatum pocius generat consciencie serenitatem, securitatem, et leticiam. *Et re vera tantam pretendebat hilaritatem et iocunditatem quod* hii qui cum | eo fuerant, *non modicum admirarentur. Cuius hilaritatis* modum *qui* plane ac *veraciter vellet depromere* quoddam celeste ac spirituale gaudium verbis appropriatis conaretur describere vel *metas excederet veritatis*. Iocundus enim ille fletus vel flebilis iocunditas, risus lugubris vel luctus risibilis, tristis

---

[1] restoret *cod*

hilaritas vel hilaris tristicia, in quasdam graciarum actiones que humanam naturam transvolarunt, iam iam resolvuntur, ut videretur gaudiis paradisi cercius subarrari. Et ne aliquatenus negligencie argui valeam, immensitatem pietatis eius, qua super omnes quos vidimus, affluebat, reticendo et scripturis commendare omittendo, quoddam misericordie opus huic libello dignum arbitror inserendum. Cum viderent eum ministri eius quos omnes habuit honestos, positos et sub arta custodia disciplinatos, iam ad portas mortis declinare, ceperunt lacrimabiliter lamentari, dicentes

'O Deus, quid de nobis erit? Mortuo karissimo domino nostro, quo deveniemus? Nos regio[1] longinqua detinet exules et egenos et omni eciam genere victualium destitutos. Redditus multiplices hos clericos ditant curiales, set nos dominus noster deserit penitus mendicantes. Heu! heu! mendicare erubescimus, fodere nescimus,[a] negociari non consuevimus, nec permittit penuria. Repatriantes, regi vel magnatibus pro domino nostro illis exoso, erimus onerosi. Quid nobis nisi mors restat miserabilis?'

Hec cum audisset archiepiscopus ineffabili motus est pietate, et advocans unum eorum qui miserabilior videbatur, ait

'Amice, scribam cuidam fideli amico meo pro te. Qui nec michi scribenti, nec tibi deerit indigenti.'

Et postulans que ad scribendum | sunt necessaria, (scripsit (fo. 145ᵛ) hec verba:)[2]

Litere Archiepiscopi ultime

Edmundus Dei gracia Cantuariensis archiepiscopus tocius Anglie primas venerabili in Christo fratri W.[b] eadem gracia Norwycensi episcopo, salutem et sinceram in Domino dilectionem. Licet a quibusdam vulgariter dicatur quod mors omnia tollat, verumptamen illam dilectionem que in radice caritatis fundata est nec adversitas frangit nec casus mortis disiungit, quia caritas nunquam excidit. Huius igitur dilectionis affectione a longo tempore fraternitatis

---

[1] regia *cod* [2] scripsit hec verba *supplevi*

[a] *mendicare* &c. Cf. *Luc.* xvi. 3. [b] William de Ralegh.

vestre fidelitatem totis viribus amplectentes ac personam nostram a vestra benignitate amplecti per experienciam scientes, gravissima infirmitate corporis afflicti ac quasi in articulo mortis positi, indefesse dilectionis vestre constanciam interpellare non cessamus, pietatis intuitu humiliter petentes et devote quatinus anime nostre memoriam cordi vestro imprimentes, pro nobis orare dignemini ac per vestram diocesim faciatis orari. Insuper eciam vobis supplicantes quatinus dilectissimum nostrum Robertum de Essex latorem presencium quem coram Deo et hominibus credimus et experti sumus commendacione dignum in moribus fidelitate et honesto servicio, munificencia vestra in obsequio velitis retinere, ut per ipsum, quem cordis nostri vere dilectioni a longo tempore meritis suis exigentibus inpressimus, ad nostri memoriam vestra frequencius excitetur devocio. Ceterum quia mortui raros et paucos invenire solent amicos, et maxime in regno Anglie, testamentum nostrum a nobis ordinatum et signo nostro signatum ac executores nostros in eodem nominatos, (fo. 146ʳ) vestre perfecte dilectioni recommendamus. Ob amorem | ipsius qui bonorum omnium est remunerator magnificus rogantes quatinus memoratis executoribus consilium vestrum et auxilium impendatis. Datum apud Soysi xviii Kalendas Decembris. Pontificatus nostri anno viii°.[1]

XLI. Quam certe precognovit mortem suam

Et cum similiter quibusdam aliis simile fecisset tante humanitatis beneficium, tradidit suas singulas quas scripserat epistolas que gracia Dei omnes effectum habuerunt gratissimum. Dixerat insuper ipsis,

'Hec mea litera et manus, quam ipsi amici mei fidelissimi, quibus pro vestra commoditate scribo, cognoscunt, omni sigillo prestancior est et efficacior.'

Et sic quievit multorum egenorum sollicitudo. Hec iccirco dixerim, ut sciat quisque huius lector opusculi quantus in beatissimo Edmundo Cantuariensi archiepiscopo fervor caritatis estuabat.[2] Penset autem lector huius litere quam pagine huic duxi conglutinandam, quam certus fuit memoratus sanctus pater noster Edmundus quod a carnis sue tunc migraret

---

[1] *sic in codice, sed legendum* vii°   [2] estuebat *cod*

domicilio, quia ipsum amicum suum cui scribit de testamenti sui execucione fideliter ac diligenter prosequenda obnixius[1] deprecatur.

XLII. De gestu et devocione in extrema inunctione

Succumbente igitur vigore naturali et invalescente morbi gravitate, unctionis extreme[2] sacramentum postulabat quod ex sacra institucione beati Iacobi Apostoli[a] constat exordium et consuetudinem documento Sancti Spiritus assumpsisse. Quod cum rite sacerdos officium peragendo competenter exequeretur, quis inuncti[3] vel inungendi[4] sancti Dei lacrimas, quis gemitus, fremitus, scribendo vel | eciam enarrando plenius explicaret? (fo. 146ᵛ) Oculis namque ac manibus in celum semper intentis, corpore exausto, videbatur iam spiritus ad supera transvolare et grave reputare ei in carnis carcere amplius detineri. Ipso igitur sacramento venerabiliter ut decuit celebrato, vir sanctus ex manu ministrantis *crucem* arripiens, *mira devocione loca clavorum* sanguineo colore rubricata ori et oculis imprimens, *frequenter et morose deosculabatur* et lacrimis uberrimis irrigavit. Maxime tamen *vulnus lateris lanceati diu suggens* et lambens hiatum vulneris, suspiriis sermonem prorumpentibus, ait

'Haurietis aquas de fontibus salvatoris' etcetera.[b] *Cuius devocio et devocionis modus sensibus astancium* non minimam de novitate generarunt, nam merito generare poterant, admiracionem.

XLIII. Quod spiritus prophecie in ipso erat

Cum autem ad instanciam circumastancium omnibus monachis Cantuarie omnem rancorem animi remisisset et sentenciam relaxasset volentibus humiliari et satisfacere, et ab omnibus ibi

[1] obnoxius *cod* [2] extremo *cod* [3] iniuncti *cod*
[4] iniungendi *cod*

[a] Cf. *Iac.* v. 14. [b] Haurietis &c. *Is.* xii. 3.

existentibus veniam iunctis manibus quoquo modo postulasset, corpus suum domui Pontiniaci delegavit. Hec autem verba cum nec adhuc bene finierat, prior domus archiepiscopo carissimus, qui tunc presens erat, ait,

'Heu! heu! siccine, sic nos penitus deseris et a nobis recedis?' At ille,

'Nequaquam. Meum cor et dilectio vobiscum semper est.' Et non intellexerunt verbum. Set post obitum eius facta anathomia de corpore eius, sepulta sunt ibidem cor et viscera eius. Et tunc aperti sunt oculi eorum, et intellexerunt verbum.[a] Hoc autem factum est quia deferendum fuit corpus usque Pontiniacum quod distat a Soysi, ubi obiit, circiter xx leucis, id (est),[1] duabus ad minus dietis.

XLIV. De pallio et tabula

Set nec sanctarum duarum sororum suarum pius frater obliviscitur, | sanctimonialium scilicet apud Katebyam commorancium, in extremis licet agens. Pallium namque suum coloris cinerei, de panno videlicet qui vulgariter dicitur 'camelot', cum penula agnina et quandam tabellam argenteam in qua insculpta sunt ymago beate Marie filium foventis in gremio et Christi passio et martirium beati Thome, transmisit.[b] Pro quibus usque in presentem diem apud Katebyam, ubi tunc veneranter reservantur, Dominus miracula eterna condigna memoria operatur.

XLV. Qualiter in sacratissimam mortem resolutus sit

Et cum iam hiis laboribus vexatus fatigaretur, siluit. *Sompno autem deinde ultimo exceptus, in mortis quietem sub quiete* et specie

---

[1] est *supplevi*

[a] Cf. *Luc.* xxiv. 31. Cf. the whole paragraph with the identical passage in the margin of *Chron. Maiora*, iv. 73.

[b] Cf. the parallel passage in *Hist. Angl.* ii. 448.

Vita S. Edmundi auctore Matthaeo Parisiensi

dormientis resolutus et *sine ullo*, ut solet morituro vel morienti evenire, gutturis murmure, letali indicio, vel *luctamine* expirans, fratribus et seculo valefecit. Et sic dormiens, in Domino lenius obdormivit, *nullius difficilis obitus mora*[1] vel agone pregravatus. Sicque qui semper pacificus extiterat, pacifice ad pacem eternam transmigravit. Similium enim transitus facilis esse perhibetur. Sic igitur beatissimus Edmundus Cantuariensis archiepiscopus et confessor Domini gloriosus a carnis domicilio ad celi palacium, ab exilio ad patriam, a caligine mundi huius ad polorum claritatem septimo[2] *decimo Kalendas Decembris* feliciter advolavit. *Undecimo* vero *Kalendas eiusdem mensis, corpus eius in ecclesia beate Marie* apud *Pontiniacum humane condicionis lege sepultum est.* Quo in loco memoratus sanctus *se vere in Christo vivere* manifeste *demonstrat*, et in *frequentissima vivencium consolacione* se probat expressius gloriosum. Nam signorum frequencia, que perlongum est enumerare, et miraculorum numerositas nobis videntur apostolorum tempora renovare. Gaudeat igitur Anglia talem ac tantum | patronum ex sinu (fo. 147ᵛ) Abendonie originaliter produxisse.[a] Exultet[3] Pontiniacum tanti presulis exuvias in gremio suo suscepisse. Gratuletur Francia que exulanti[4] ianuas refugii patefecit. Iocundetur insuper qui aliquod[5] ministerii vel societatis solacium eidem aliquando impenderunt. Convertantur autem et conversi peniteant qui aliquando molestie, perturbacionis, aut detractionis eidem intulerunt, et triumphantem nunc saltem honorent qui iniurias tollerantem ignoranter vel procaciter persequebantur. Venient quidem ad eum, Deo vindice, qui detrahebant eidem, ut *adorent vestigia pedum eius.*[b] Vincunt enim denique milites tui, Christe, qui pro iusticie dimicant veritate, et subtractis adversariis, triumpho perpetuo gloriantur.

[1] nullas difficilis obitus moras sensit *Eustace*
[2] *sic in codice, sed legendum* sexto
[3] Exultat *cod*   [4] exultanti *cod*   [5] aliquam *cod*

[a] The passage appears to be suggested by the bull of canonization.
[b] *Venient* &c. Cf. *Is*. lx. 14.

XLVI. De hiis que post mortem facta recenter fuerunt

Cum igitur prima die post dormicionem suam ille qui cancellarii fungebatur officio[a] literas memoratas, que ultimo sigillo suo consignabantur, consignaverat, tradidit eas in crastino mane ipsis quibus sanctus eas concesserat amicis suis deferendas. Quibus optentis, statim cum lacrimis et crebris singultibus famuli, valedicto clericis qui cum corpore remanserant, recesserunt. Confractum igitur est sigillum coram omnibus convocatis, ut moris est, propter adulterancium fraudem et cavillaciones, in quo, ut prelibatum est,[b] effigies predecessoris sui, beati scilicet Thome, insculta fuit excerebrati. Cuius et ipse beatus Edmundus sequens vestigia, consorcium promeruit in celestibus. Eademque die *de Soysi apud Triangulum Pagum* cum corpus deportaretur pontificalibus honorifice redimitum,[1] sequebatur | illud *agminibus* ordinatis longe lateque *distentis*, cum maxima *fidei devocione* et laudum veneracione, fidelium innumerabilis multitudo. Et quanto remocius ferebatur, tanto, ad instar fluvii qui ex torrentibus pluvialibus suscipit incrementum, magis ac magis turbarum crescebat multitudo numerosa subsequencium. *Omnes delectantur aspectu,* ad quem pedetentim consequendum sanctum sese comprimunt.[d] Et iam arta via ministris vix circumstrepentibus castigantur et cohibentur, et dum alter alterum preire contendit, ruunt catervatim, et seipsos conglomerantes impediuntur et retardantur. Beatos namque et a peccatis expiatos se reputant quicunque sanctum corpus se iactitant tetigisse. Nec inmerito vel sine causa, cum quamplurimi de suis angustiis levamen acceperunt et iuvamen.

---

[1] redemitum *cod*

[a] i.e. Richard Wych. The oblique reference to the chancellor suggests that this passage constitutes Richard Wych's own contribution to the narrative, cf. *Chron. Maiora,* v. 369, and p. 78 above. Matthew's repeated use of the first person plural below indicates that he is using another document, containing first-hand testimony, to fill out the narrative of Eustace.

[b] Above, p. 260.   [c] Trainel (Aube).

[d] This and the following passage is a paraphrase of a similar passage in Eustace. Cf. *Chron. Maiora,* iv. 74.

Vita S. Edmundi auctore Matthaeo Parisiensi 273

Hinc mulieres pueros egros apportantes, hinc alii varie laborantes, valide clamitant,

'O baiuli, quid properatis? Quare non sinitis nos saltem per modicum istius sancti corporis presencia gratulari? Etsi peccatores sumus ut tanto indigni habeamur beneficio, non qui bene set qui male se habent, medico indigere noscuntur.'

Neque enim ullus indempnis sibi videbatur qui feretrum, manus, aut pedes osculo vel manu tetigisse se non arbitrabatur,[1] si conspectu sacri corporis caruit, si aliquam reverenciam tantis exequiis non exhibuisset. Eramus[a] autem sub numerosa multitudine clerici ac religiosi, sacerdotes[2] in divinis, videlicet superpelliciis, albis et capis, ordinate secundum ordinem processionis, castigate ac mature incedentes. | Inter nos quoque multi fuerunt (fo. 148ᵛ) cucullati, quorum habitus pro ornatu reputabatur,[b] ubi eciam *abbas* erat, qui nobis obviam venerat, *Pontiniacensis. Qui cum vidisset populi concursum et cleri ac populi supra humanam opinionem admirabilem devocionem et reverenciam corpori exhibitam, amotis prius extraneis, in hunc modum* sanctum Dei quasi vivum al*locutus est dicens,*

'*Bone pater, in eo quod es frater ecclesie Pontiniacensis, teneris michi obedire.* Confidenter loquor tibi. Ego abbas tuus sum, tu vero monachus meus. Presum non tamen tibi archiepiscopo set monacho. Obedi et exaudi preces meas. Obsecro *nulla facias* amplius qualia fecisti *signa,* donec *pervenias ad locum requiescionis tue,* videlicet *Pontiniacum.*'

Verum abbas vehementer formidabat propter signa aliqua iam facta et notoria, *ne corpus* eiusdem gloriosi confessoris violenter ablatum raperetur vel furto subriperetur. *Signavit* igitur *feretrum sigillo suo, presente*[3] *illo et vidente qui scripsit hec, et aliis pluribus.*

---

[1] arbitrabantur *cod* [2] sacerdotes: sacris *cod*
[3] presento *cod*

[a] On Matthew's use of the first person in this passage, see note a on p. 272 above.

[b] i.e. whose habit was thought to add distinction to the procession: this is a typical 'improvement' of Matthew's on his document.

XLVII. Quid secunda die de sacro corpore factum sit

Vendicabat autem iccirco specialius et confidencius sanctum corpus abbas memoratus, quia dum archiepiscopus Pontiniaci morabatur, intravit una dierum capitulum ut faceret sermonem conventui. Quo consummato devotissime petiit fraternitatis fedus et participacionem sibi fieri caritative. Quod et concessum est ei. Unde abbas frequenter iocose[1] secularibus dixit 'Quid vobis de monachi mei exuviis?' et ad efficaciorem racionem divertens, subiunxit

'Certe non valet quis adversarius ordinacioni beati Thome, de qua nobis dudum prophetavit, contradicendo obviare. Iste enim, iste est quem nobis aliquando promisit. Iste solvet omnia in quibus pauperi domui Pontiniaci martir ille debitor | tenebatur. Habetis vos Anglici martirem. Nos nostrum monachum retinemus et confessorem.'

Hec inter nos nocte illa, cum de corporis possessione iustiori contenderemus, verba recitata revolvebantur. Apposita vero diligenti custodia atque valida, dispositis excubitoribus vigili(as)[2] noctis, timentes ne quid sinistri, peccatis nostris exigentibus, nobis de corpore accidisset, cum sollicitudine peregimus. Mane vero secunda die cum sacrum corpus deferentes transitum *faceremus per Villam Novam archiepiscopi,*[a] *occurrit ei multitudo virorum ac mulierum letabundis acclamacionibus* et *devotissimis vociferacionibus applaudencium, et feretrum mira veneracione deosculancium inter agminum* compressionem *detentum. Et licet hoc moleste acciperemus, nulla tamen pronos et devotos racione compescere, nulla interdictione potuimus repellere, quin vi et virium suarum* robusta *violencia corpus ad ecclesiam deportarent, illud maiori altari imponentes. Irruunt alii in ecclesiam. Alii propter magnum* et densum *populi concursum, donec corpus* asportaretur, *prestolantur,* ut mirabile presagium glorificacionis censeretur.

---

[1] iacose *cod*
[2] *post* vigili *in codice est spatium vacuum; forte legendum* vigilias

---

[a] Villeneuve-l'Archevêque (Yonne).

Vita S. Edmundi auctore Matthaeo Parisiensi

Tandem maiores de villa, post diutinam expectacionem ad instanciam quarundam personarum notarum, cum fustibus populum abscedere compulerunt. Accepimus igitur corpus et, precedentibus multis *et subsequentibus, delatum est eadem die usque ad domum Templariorum*[1] *de Colors,*[a] *per quam in recessu suo a Pontiniaco cum transitum fecisset vir sanctus, et domum illam vidisset, quesivit cuius*nam *illa domus esset. Cui* responsum est,
'Templariorum'.
At ille,
'In domo illa iacebo in reditu meo.'
Et ita factum est. In domo enim *superius memorata cum corpore sancto* in continua psalmodia *pernoctavimus.* Ubi, cum suborto murmure consiliarentur inter se fratres domus illius, non minimum | formidabamus ne corpus a nobis auferrent violenter. Dicebant enim quod ipse sanctus dixerat, spiritu prophetico celitus eruditus, quod ibidem vellet requiescere. Nos tamen constanter eisdem contradicentes, propositum ipsius sancti expressum et verbis et literis determinatum ostendendo, vix spiritum improbitatis eorum compescuimus. Comminabamur etenim asserentes in spiritu amaritudinis quod si vim inferrent, Dei et sancti gravamen sentirent (ac)[2] ulcionem. Non enim hoc sanctus dicebat nisi de ipsius noctis quiete. Et sic dimissum est nobis licet cum magnatum difficultate.

XLVIII. Quid tercia die de sancto corpore factum sit

Tercia vero cum inde progrederemur die, sicut pridie et nudius tercius, *occurrerunt nobis utriusque sexus populi innumerabiles clamantes et* clamando *ingeminantes*
'Ubi est sanctum corpus? Ubi est corpus?'

[1] contemplariorum *cod*   [2] ac *supplevi*

[a] Coulours (Aube), see T. Boutiot and E. Socard, *Dictionnaire topographique du Département de l'Aube* (Paris, 1874), p. 51. I have not been able to find any reference to a house of the Templars at this place. The Order had a commandery at Provins: V. Carrière, *Histoire et cartulaire des Templiers de Provins* (Paris, 1919).

Hinc psalmicines clericorum phalanges, illinc religiosorum processiones ordinate, hinc cruciferi et sacris induviis vestiti exequialiter canentes, *hinc ruricole ex agris,* qui eciam boves in aratris coniunctos quasi stupidi reliquerant, accurrentes, innumerabilem concursum populorum quasi exercitum copiosum conflaverunt ex agris, villis, *castellis, et vicis,* congregati. *Tunc duo ex nostratibus admirantibus* vehementer de *populi concursu* insolito et de populorum turmis stupefacti, *dixerunt ad invicem*

'Quid sibi vult hec novitas inaudita?' Excessit enim, ut eis videbatur, tam mensuram quam racionem. Et dixit unus alteri, quo animo Deus scit,

'Videtur quod monachi Pontiniaci, ut sibi sanctum fingant et oblacionum emolumenta recipiant, nova super terram de corpore hoc magnalia predicaverint. Dicit enim populus clamitando, "obviam occurramus, precurramus, sequamur, videamus, tangamus, et | sanctissimum corpus omnibus quibus possumus modis veneremur," et certatim sese festinant et comprimunt. Nichil tamen de sanctitate eius constat hominibus, videtur, vel scribitur.'

Respondit alter alteri colloquencium vel pocius obloquencium,

'Si sanctus esset et inter sanctos autenticos computandus, non curaret in Cisterciensium[1] domo sepeliri et quiescere tumulatus. Omnes fere sancti gloriosi in domibus iacent nigri ordinis monachorum, pauci vel nulli in Cisterciensium domiciliis.'

Ad quem sermonem confirmandum, domum Cantuarie, Sancti Albani, Sancti Edmundi, Dunelmi, et multas alias in regno Francorum quam Anglorum recitando[2] exempli gracia dinumeravit. Et ortum est scisma et sentenciarum diversitas inter eos et multos alios secundum illud Ysaie, 'Deducam cecos in viam quam nesciunt, et in semitis quas ignoraverunt

---

[1] Cistercium *cod*
[2] recitanda *cod*

[a] Thus far Matthew paraphrases a similar conversation in Eustace. What follows, however, is his own.

ambulare eos faciam.'ª Set post signorum claritatem infra paucos dies, illud quod sequitur propheticum choruscabat manifestum, 'Ponam tenebras coram eis in lucem et prava in directa.'ª

XLIX. Quomodo aliqui de nostris clericis et laicis adhuc de sanctitate eiusdem sancti non crediderunt

Affuerunt autem aliqui aliorum quorundam clericorum nostrorum et laicorum, videlicet ministrorum, qui, in hoc vere Didimi, sanctitatis eius immensitatem, quamvis in vita ipsius sancti frequenter vidissent, non crediderunt. Nec credentes asserere voluerunt quod tam specialis Altissimi fuisset amicus, qualiter sequencia Dei testimonia manifeste comprobarunt, inexcusabiliter redarguendi ad credendum tardi cordes. Quibus addendi sunt eciam quidam cucullati conventus Cantuarie. Absit tamen quod aliquorum reatus in universitatem conventualem valeat redundare, prout satis civiliter edocet poeta dicens,

Parcite paucorum | diffundere crimen in omnes.[b]

Sicuti non decet in totam sancti familiam quorundam obloquencium incredulitatem retorqueri. Porro[1] autem patet quod hominibus[2] quos secula parturiunt presencia igniculus caritatis refrigescit, incineratur. Et quid mirum? De discipulis quidem Salvatoris, qui de scola ipsiusmet,[3] magistrorum optimi, fidei exhauserant rudimenta, scriptum reperitur 'Apparuit eis' Ihesus 'et exprobravit incredulitatem et duriciam cordis quia hiis qui viderant eum surrexisse a mortuis non crediderunt.'[c] Quanto forcius presentes, quos lutea secula parturiunt inquinatos, obcecantur indurati! Nos quidem bubonibus et vespertilionibus assimilamur, quibus diurnum lumen non conceditur intueri. O quam difficile est hiis temporibus ypocritam a sancto discernere, verum Dei amatorem a dissimulatore sequestrare!

---

[1] Per *cod*   [2] homini *cod*   [3] ipsummet *cod*

[a] Is. xlii. 16.   [b] Ovid, *Ars Amat.* iii. 9.   [c] Cf. *Marc.* xvi. 14.

Hec iccirco dixerim quia multipliciter eciam a viris discretis in hoc mundo (non)[1] iudicabatur beatus Dei confessor Edmundus. Set 'homo videt faciem, Deus autem cor intuetur.'[a] Sanum igitur et salubre arbitror esse consilium ut, quem Deus clarificat et clarificando manifestat, homo deinceps veneretur, a Deo correptus et eruditus.

L. De venerabili sepultura eiusdem

Elapsis igitur post hec quatuor diebus quibus tanta hominum frequencia congregata est, quantam solet publice negociacionis indigencia ad nundinas convocare, die sancti Clementis, videlicet (nono)[2] Kalendas Decembris, sepultum est corpus beati ac gloriosi patris nostri Edmundi Cantuariensis archiepiscopi et confessoris in ecclesia beate Dei genetricis et virginis Marie in domo Ordinis Cisterciensis Pontiniaci, cum assistencium prelatorum, monachorum, clericorum, et nobilium numerosa multitudine secularium | laicorum. Cuius exequiis assistebant viri graves et autentici, videlicet pontifices, abbates, priores, monachi, et magnates, cum classicorum, luminum, vestimentorum, et multiplicis obsequii divini devotissima celebritate. In quo loco, et in aliis ubi eiusdem sancti agitur in honore Dei dulcis memoria, ad fidei Christiane robur et confirmacionem, miracula eterna recordacione condigna et nostris temporibus[3] nec visa nec audita eminus ac manifeste celebrantur.

LI. De miraculis apud Kateby celebratis

Et ut lacius beati Edmundi beneficia odore suavissimo multarum regionum repleant latitudines, in Anglia quoque que tanti pontificis meruit esse genitrix et nutrix, videlicet apud Kateby, domum sanctimonialium, miracula choruscant inaudita.[b] Ibi nempe due sorores eiusdem pontificis Edmundi,

[1] non *supplevi sicut requirit sensus*   [2] undecimo *cod*   [3] tempori *cod*

[a] Cf. *1 Reg.* xvi. 7.
[b] Cf. this and the following passage with *Chron. Maiora*, iv. 102 and *Hist. Angl.* ii. 448.

Vita S. Edmundi auctore Matthaeo Parisiensi

eximie religionis mulieres, velum susceperant perpetui celibatus. Ipsis profecto tum propter sanguinis propinquitatem, tum propter sanctam earum innocenciam, quas tanquam sorores non degeneres precordialiter diligebat, in signum caritatis pallium suum et quandam tabellam pictam vel insculptam, ubi passio Christi figurabatur, ab hoc mundo migraturus, delegavit. Que hucusque in presentem diem in sepe dicti sancti memoriam in ecclesia de Kateby reservantur. Et domicilium illud, quod exile fuerat, ditarunt et venustarunt, multiplicatis miraculis et beneficiis cismarinis et partibus transmarinis ad honorem et gloriam regnorum Anglie et Francie, largiente eo qui vivit et regnat per omnia secula.

LII. Qualiter per invidiam dilata fuit eiusdem canonizacio

Gloriose recordacionis beatum Edmundum proposuerunt maxime auctoritatis viri, | videlicet primus, dominus papa (fo. 151ᵛ) et alii graves dignitate et sanctitate prelati, procuraverantque quod in concilio Lugdunensi sollempniter valde canonizaretur. Set invidorum, quos non est tutum nominare, morsibus ipsius honor impediebatur terrenus.[a] Qui ipsum eciam post mortem, sicut Iudei Christum, oblocucionibus dilacerare et virtutibus quas mundus vidit detrahere conabantur. Qui tamen honor eidem collatus est tempore celitus opportuno. Quod sic disposuit[1] qui, 'attingens a fine usque ad finem fortiter, disponit omnia suaviter',[b] ut civitas in monte posita nullatenus abscondi poterat.[c] Et qui ipsum inexorabili odio persequebantur, ex quo signis perpenderent irrefragabilibus quod Dei amicus manifeste factus est, eundem sanctum propensiori veneracionis officio persequebantur, de ignorancia propria fructuose postea penitentes.

---

[1] disposuit *add* quod *cod*

[a] Cf. *Chron. Maiora*, iv. 336-7.
[b] *Sap.* viii. 1.   [c] Cf. *Matt.* v. 14.

LIII. Incipit autenticum canonizacionis
beati Edmundi confessoris[a]

INNOCENTIUS servus servorum Dei episcopus venerabilibus fratribus archiepiscopis, episcopis, et dilectis filiis abbatibus, prioribus, decanis, archidiaconis, prepositis, archipresbyteris, et aliis ecclesiarum prelatis ad quos litere iste pervenerint, salutem et apostolicam benedictionem. Novum matris ecclesie gaudium, novi sancti celebritate, iocunde leti referimus. Grande a celesti collegio[1] agi festum exultanti animo nunciamus. Gaudet quidem ecclesia se talem ac tantum produxisse filium, qui alios et sacre conversacionis exemplo dirigat, et, percepto iam beatitudinis premio, firmam spem eis tribuat de salute. Letatur nimirum se tam preclara sobole illustratam que digno ab omnibus attollenda preconio,[2] et devota veneracione colenda, manifeste declarat ad hereditatis eterne participium admittendos qui ecclesiam ipsam matrem fide et opere profitentur, et nullos in supernam posse gloriam, nisi per eam, tanquam regni celorum | clavigeram, introire. Gaudet celestis patria nobilis habitatoris adventu, expertumque colonum fidei suis incolis noviter adunari. Exultant cives celibes[3] de celebris[4] aggregacione concivis, de condigno celi consorte nuper ipsis adhibito, psallunt sancti. Exurgite igitur, et vos fidei zelatores, et una cum ecclesia, matre vestra, letamini de magnificencia et exaltacione confratris. Affluite gaudio et spem tutam assumite de condigena terrenorum facto compatriota celestium. Exultate ingenti leticia quod novellus vobis apud Dominum

---

[1] collegio *add* de college novi consortio Chron. Maiora; Bullarium
[2] premio *cod, sed correxi iuxta text. cit.*
[3] celestes Bullarium, *et inseritur in margine* Chron. Maiorum, vi. 120
[4] cebris *cod*

---

[a] Matthew refers to this copy of the bull in Hist. Angl. iii. 135. He kept a copy of it in his Liber Additamentorum, Chron. Maiora, vi. 120–5. Originals of the bull, addressed to the church of Lyons and to the English baronage, are in the muniments of Sens cathedral, nos. 31, 32. Copies are very numerous, see Potthast, ii. 12392. Printed texts in Wilkins, i. 694; Bullarium Romanum (editio Taurinensis) (1858), iii. 522.

patronus accrevit, quod adest coram ipso pro salute nostra placidus intercessor. En, siquidem beatus Edmundus archiepiscopus Cantuariensis salubriter pensans ad factorem suum facturam affectu dirigi naturali, naturamque collapsam reparatorem debere recognoscere, proprium creatorem ac redemptorem suum affectuose ac studiose quesivit. Recte namque intencionis lumen baiulans, ad Christum[1] perfectorem[2] operum processit gressibus, salutis semitam aliis et splendore vite ac doctrine claritate demonstrans. Unde horum trium, intencionis pure, perfecti operis, et recti sermonis, dulci concordia, velud delectabili psallens tripudio, tribus hostibus, carne, mundo, demone, virtute perseverancie superatis, digne meruit, vere fidei, secure spei, et fervide caritatis ternario insignitus summe Trinitatis arce, trino electorum, virginum scilicet, continencium, et coniugatorum ordine, preparata palma victorie honorari. Etenim ut de suis actibus aliquid referamus: licet ipsius vita, quo plenius exponitur, eo relatoris gustui plus dulcescat, magisque delectet animos auditorum; ab annis teneris Dei filium tenere diligens, eum postmodum tenere corde non desiit, quia ipsum tenelle mentis tabule stilo recte | consideracionis inscripsit. Quinimmo quanto maiori profecit (fo. 152ᵛ) etate, tanto pleniori cognicione in amorem eius exarsit. Et ne fervor spiritus sue carnis extingueretur ardore, set mortificacione pocius accenderetur ipsius, assidui eam asperitate cilicii edomans, eius libitum arcte abstinencie nexibus alligavit, ut non suo ducta voto set spiritus voluntate, ad licita tute pergeret et provide ab illicitis declinaret. Nam districtis corpus maceravit ieiuniis, antiquorum observancie novorum austeritatem que sibimet ipsi idem indixerat superaddens, dum deliciosorum ciborum oblectacione despecta, refectione contentus humilium, communium ieiuniorum temporibus a permissis eciam elegit ieiunare cibariis et ceteris insuper in ebdomada diebus amplius abstinere. Sompni quoque prolixitatem odiens, diuturnis vacabat vigiliis et, excusso corpore, oracioni sedulo insistebat.

[1] Christum: ipsum *Chron. Maiora; Bullarium*
[2] perfectorum *cod*

Cubilis enim spreta mollicie, ne requie delicata lentesceret, illam membris indulgebat iacendo quietem, ut sopore brevissimo refectus, protinus[1] surgeret, seque genuflexionibus et oracionibus diucius deputaret. Ab inicio autem viarum suarum sic munde usque in finem incedere studuit, quod mundi vitato[2] lubrico, in lutum non defluens voluptatis, mundicie nitore prefulsit. Quid amplius? Contrivit fragile carnis vasculum, ut in eo thesaurum anime sibi creditum caucius conservaret. Doctor vero preclarus ac predicator eximius et auditorum mentibus sciencie lumen infudit, et pectoribus fidelium, avulsis viciorum tribulis, semina virtutum iniecit. Humilitate quippe sublimis, mansuetudine placidus, paciencia fortis, benignitate affabilis, pietate condolens, misericordia ignoscens, et multiplici elemosinarum irriguo in subvencionem affluens egenorum. Et ut gestorum suorum multitudinem succincta relacione texamus, |
(fo. 153ʳ) sic Ihesum firma credulitate cognovit et cognitum sincero corde dilexit, ac dilectum totis votis concupivit,[3] quod mundo et eis que in mundo sunt penitus vilipensis, ad celestia cunctis studiis inhiavit, satagens se suo nomini actibus coaptare; ut, sicut vocabatur Edmundus, sic se vel a criminum labe mundum, vel e mundo abductum, seu extra mundi amplexus positum, operum testificacione probaret. Unde tamquam spiritualis omnino Edmundus,[4] a carnis contagiis in extremis agens, et corpus Christi sibi delatum reverenter adorans, hec verba omni attencione notanda mira protulisse compunctione aperte monstratur, 'Tu es in quem credidi, quem predicavi, quem docui. Et tu testis es[5] michi quia nichil aliud, nisi te Domine, in terra quesivi. Sicut tu scis quod nichil volo nisi quod tu vis, fiat voluntas tua.' Verum cum vivens Dei ecclesiam preclaris illuminasset meritis, mortuus sue sibi claritatis radios non subtraxit. Set cum functus hac vita verius viveret quam vixisset, eam postmodum illustravit fulgore luminis plenioris. Non enim

[1] protinus: *bis in cod*
[2] vitato: *puncto subscripto, scriptor ab* in tanto *correxit*
[3] concupivit: ambivit *Chron. Maiora; Bullarium; add* et *cod*
[4] omnino et mundus: homo et mundus *Bullarium*
[5] es: eis *cod*

Vita S. Edmundi auctore Matthaeo Parisiensi

voluit Dominus sanctitatem mundo supprimi tanti viri, quin, sicut pluralitate innotuerat meritorum, sic miraculorum diversitate pateret. Ut qui tota ipsum devocione in terra[1] coluerat, iam secum regnans venerabiliter coleretur. Nam cecis lumen restituit, et, quod est gloriosus, de cuiusdam oculis innate cecitatis tenebras infusi visus perspicuitate fugavit. Alii, cuius linguam natura diutina taciturnitate ligaverat, liberam loquendi tribuit, soluto silencio, facultatem. Leprosam quandam squamis lepre mox decidentibus, subita et mirabili abstersione mundavit. Tremula paralitici membra firmavit consolidacione nervorum. | Contractis artuum extensione subvenit. Tumentem ydropicum (fo. 153ᵛ) corporis extenuacione curavit, et quandam senilis etatis veteri gibbo imis inflexam restituit, erecta sursum eius facie, sanitati. Hiis et aliis quampluribus choruscavit miraculis manifestis, quorum seriem non duximus presentibus inserendam. Convalescit ex ipsis fides catholica, Iudeorum pertinacia erubescit, confunditur hereticorum fallacia, et obstupescit ignorancia paganorum. Cantet itaque Cantuariensis ecclesia laudis divine canticum, quod inter alias modernis temporibus venerabilibus est decorata patronis, unius quidem rubricata martirio, et confessione alterius candidata. Exultet pleno gaudio fertilis Cantuaria, quod ab ecclesie sue area tam purum granum transmisit ad horrea summi regis. Letetur Pontiniacense monasterium, quod talium ac tantorum patrum meruit honorari presencia, dum unus diu ibi degens, illud sue vite nobilitavit moribus, et alter illuc accedens, ipsum, reddita celo anima, sui corporis thesauro ditavit. Ut quasi adimpleretur quod ipse gloriosus martir, Thomas videlicet, post longam moram quam exilii sui tempore in eodem continuavit monasterio, cum ipsis monachis de multa honorificencia caritative[2] sibi ab eis exhibita respondere iuxta sui voti plenitudinem non valeret, dixisse asseritur quod esset sibi aliquis successurus qui dignam ipsis retribucionem rependeret pro eodem. Porro quia quos omnipotens Deus perpetue corona glorie in celum manifestat,[3] summe

---

[1] in terra: *om Bullarium et Chron. Maiora*   [2] caritate *cod*
[3] magnificat *Chron. Maiora; Bullarium*

devocionis studio ab hominibus in terris convenit venerari, ut quo sollempnius fideles sanctorum memoriam agunt,[1] eo dignius ipsorum patrocinium promerentur, nos de sanctitate vite ac veritate miraculorum eiusdem sancti Edmundi curiose (fo. 154ʳ) inquisicionis | sollempnitate ac districti examinis discussione premissis, plenariam certitudinem optinentes, ipsum de communi fratrum nostrorum et prelatorum omnium tunc apud Sedem Apostolicam existencium consilio et assensu, in dominica de Adventu qua cantatur *Gaudete in Domino semper*,[a] sanctorum cathalogo ascribendum, vel[2] ascriptum pocius (duximus) nunciandum. Ideoque universitatem vestram monemus et exhortamur attente, per apostolica scripta precipiendo mandantes, quatinus (sexto decimo)[3] Kalendas Decembris, cum tunc felix ipsius anima de carnis liberata carcere, ad astra conscendens, aulam celestem adiverat[4] paradisi deliciis fruitura, festum eiusdem devote ac sollempniter celebretis. Et faciatis vos, fratres archiepiscopi et episcopi, per vestras civitates et dioceses a Christifidelibus congrua veneracione celebrari, ut pio eius interventu, et hic et ab imminentibus possitis periculis erui, et in futuro salutis premium consequi sempiterne. Ceterum ut ad venerabile eius sepulcrum fervencius et copiosius Christiani populi confluat multitudo, ac celebrius eiusdem sancti agatur sollempnitas, omnibus vere penitentibus (et)[5] confessis, qui cum reverencia illuc in eodem festo annuatim accesserint, ipsius suffragia petituri, de omnipotentis Dei misericordia et beatorum Petri et Pauli apostolorum eius auctoritate confisi, unum annum et quadraginta dies, accedentibus vero annis singulis ad predictum sepulcrum infra eiusdem festi octavas, quadraginta dies de iniuncta sibi penitencia

---

[1] agimus *in codice et sic quoque in* Chron. Maioribus *sed sensus requirit* agunt. *Habet textus Bullarii* recolunt
[2] vel *add* iam *Chron.* Maiora; *Bullarium*
[3] septimo decimo *cod. Sed correxi iuxta Bullarium et Chron. Maiora*
[4] adiverit *Chron.* Maiora; *Bullarium*
[5] et *supplevi iuxta Bullarium et Chron.* Maiora

[a] Introit of the 3rd Sunday in Advent: in 1246, 16 Dec.

misericorditer relaxamus. Datum Lugduni iii° Idus Ianuarii pontificatus nostri anno iiii°.[a]

LIV. Evidens testimonium quale inventum est corpus eius quando translatum est[b]

R(icardus) Dei gracia Cicestrensis episcopus venerabili amico suo R(oberto) abbati de Begeham, salutem. Ut de elevacione et statu sanctissimi corporis beati Edmundi | efficiamini cerciores, noveritis quod in crastino sancte Trinitatis proximo preterito, anno videlicet gracie MCCXL septimo, mense (Maio),[1] xv Kalendas Iunii,[c] cum monumentum dicti[d] patris nostri Edmundi primo, paucis in sero presentibus, fuisset apertum, statum[2] corporis eiusdem suavissimo redolentis odore plenum et integrum invenimus, caput quidem cum capillis et facie prefulgida, corpusque cum membris aliis plenarium, integrum, et supra balsamum et omnia thimiata celitus odoriferum, solo tamen naso per lamine contingentis et comprimentis pondera iniuriam passo modice lesionis. Totumque corpus, maximeque facies, quasi oleo perfusum repertum est et illesum. Et ex hoc merito quia per integritatem virginalem, quam anulo suo beate Virginis subarrando ymagini spopondit et conservavit, interpretamur. Per oleum vero olei similitudinem significare competenter possumus qua prefulsit graciam tam morum quam doctrine atque excellentis sciencie. Quia 'diffusa fuit gracia in labiis suis'[e] legendo, disputando, predicando vel docendo, 'propterea unxit eum Dominus oleo leticie pre omnibus'[f] lectoribus et doctoribus sui temporis. Reperimus eciam quedam alia virtutum insignia que, nacta temporis opportunitate,

(fo. 154ᵛ)

[1] Iunio *cod*   [2] statim *cod*

[a] 11 Jan. 1247: thus in Potthast and *Bullarium*. The two bulls in the Sens muniments are, however, dated 10 Jan.

[b] Cf. the text of this letter in *Chron. Maiora*, vi. 128–9.

[c] The clause *anno videlicet*, &c. is omitted in the *Liber Additamentorum* and was evidently inserted by Matthew when he copied the letter into the *Vita*. Either his memory or his calendar was at fault, for in 1247 Trinity Sunday fell on 26 May, so the morrow of Trinity would be *vi Kal. Iunii*.

[d] sancti: *Liber Additamentorum*.   [e] *Ps*. xliv. 3.   [f] *Ps*. xliv. 8.

vobis secretius et plenius referamus,[1] que in scriptis redigi prolixitas eventuum non permittit. De memoratis autem non dubitet discrecio vestra, quia quod scimus loquimur et quod videmus testamur, et de scribendis indubitanter certificamur. Manibus quoque propriis contrectavimus ipsius sanctum corpus, caputque cum capillis firmis et illesis pectine diligenter ac reverenter necnon et gaudenter pectinebamus et composuimus. Dominica vero proxima ante festum beati (Barnabe),[2][a] domino (fo. 155ʳ) rege Francorum et | matre et fratribus suis, comitibus et multis magnis presentibus, preterea duobus cardinalibus, Albanensi videlicet et legato Francie, cum archiepiscopis, episcopis, abbatibus, prioribus, et aliis prelatis venerabilibus quampluribus assistentibus, quorum numerum scire non potuimus, apud Pontiniacum, voluntate divina cum exultacione et gloria ineffabili et Dei laudibus magnificis, celebrata est translacio beatissimi patris nostri Cantuariensis archiepiscopi et confessoris, necnon ad augmentum honoris nostre nacionis non modicum. Valeat sanctitas vestra cum sospite desiderata per tempora diuturna.[b]

LV. Sermo quem beatus Edmundus in capitulo Pontiniacensi fecit conventui post quem societatem domus peciit et optinuit et specialitatem beneficii spiritualis quantum contigit monachum unum

'Qui est ex Deo verba Dei audit.'[c] Set omnes sunt ex Deo, ergo audiunt. Quod non est verum. Sciendum est quod aliquid

---

[1] reformemus *cod*, *sed correxit scriptor* [2] Bernarde *cod*

[a] In 1247 this would be the 9 June. The medieval English Church kept the feast of the translation on this date. In the chronicles, however, Matthew gives the 7 June as the date of the solemn translation of the relics: *Chron. Maiora*, iv. 631; *Hist. Angl.* iii. 26–27. In the *Historia* too he has made the error of writing *vii Id. Iulii* instead of *vii Id. Iunii*.
[b] The valediction is omitted in the *Liber Additamentorum* text.
[c] *Ioh.* viii. 47.

est ex aliquo tanquam a causa efficienti, et sic omnia sunt a Deo. Aliquid est ab alio tanquam a causa materiali, sic nichil est a Deo, quia Deus non est materia alicuius. Item aliquid est ab alio tanquam a causa formali, ut forma cere a sigillo; sic tantum boni sunt a Deo, quia informat eos gracia et virtutibus. Isti audiunt verba Dei, scilicet vii verba in cruce, tanquam sonum septem cordarum in cithara David magni. In cithara extenduntur corde a ligno in lignum, et Dominus extensus fuit in duobus lignis ipsius crucis, scilicet in stipite et transtro. Septem sunt dona Spiritus Sancti, scilicet donum timoris, pietatis, sciencie, fortitudinis, consili, intellectus, et sapiencie. Prima corda dedit melodiam, scilicet 'Eloy labazatani', hoc est, 'Quare me | Deus dereliquisti?'[a] Iste sonus incutit nobis timorem, quia si Dominus vidit[1] se fuisse a patre derelictum, multo forcius formidare possumus et debemus ne derelinquamur. Hanc cordamru perunt Iudei, sublato timore, dicentes, 'Non habemus regem nisi Cesarem',[b] quasi dicerent, 'neminem timemus nos imperiales.' Secunda corda pietatis, scilicet, 'Pater ignosce eis, quia nesciunt quid faciunt.'[c] Hanc cordam ruperunt Iudei dicentes, 'Crucifige eum.'[d] Hic fuit crudelitas. Tercia corda dedit melodiam sciencie, scilicet, 'Ecce filius tuus.'[e] Dominus scivit Iohannem virginem, ideo virginem virgini commendavit. Hanc cordam ruperunt Iudei dicentes, 'Quis est qui te percussit?'[f] quasi dicerent[2] 'nescit'. Quarta corda dedit melodiam fortitudinis, scilicet, 'Hodie eris mecum in paradiso.'[g] Hic fuit fortitudo et promissio confidencie. Unde Abacuc, 'Ibi abscondita est fortitudo eius.'[h] Hanc cordam ruperunt Iudei dicentes, 'Seipsum non potest salvum facere',[i] quasi dicerent[2] 'impotens est'. Quinta corda dedit melodiam consilii, scilicet, 'Sicio.'[j] Consilium enim succurrit in adversis, et Dominus voluit ibi succurrere, set ipsi optulerunt ei acetum,

---

[1] vivit *cod* [2] diceret *cod*

[a] *Matth.* xxvii. 46; *Ps.* xxi. 2. [b] *Ioh.* xix. 15.
[c] Cf. *Luc.* xxiii. 34. [d] *Marc.* xxv. 13. [e] *Ioh.* xix. 26.
[f] *Matth.* xxvi. 68. [g] *Luc.* xxiii. 43. [h] *Hab.* iii. 4.
[i] *Matth.* xxvii. 42. [j] *Ioh.* xix. 28.

vinum mirratum vel venenum, quod est potus corruptus et letifer. Que omnia insipida sunt. Insipiens non sapit, sicut nec insulsus. Hanc cordam ruperunt Iudei, scilicet gens sine consilio, quia et ideo perdiderunt locum et gentem, quia crucifixerunt Ihesum, scilicet per Titum et Vespasianum. Sexta corda dedit melodiam intellectus, cum dixit 'Consummatum est',[a] quasi diceret 'Scriptura consummata est et aperta est intelligencia sacre Scripture'. Hanc cordam ruperunt Iudei messiam expectando, et heretici male exponendo, et Christiani male vivendo. Septima corda dedit melodiam sapiencie, scilicet, (fo. 156r) 'Pater, in manus tuas | commendo spiritum meum.'[b] Sapiencia dicitur a sapore. Lingua congruit in duo opera nature, gustum scilicet, et loquelam. Set et hanc ruperunt Iudei nescientes discernere Deum ab homine, ignorantes et ignorare volentes verbum Patris, hoc est Filium, per saporem, omnia confundentes tanquam insipientes. Summus vero sapor et summa delectacio est esse cum Deo: 'Gustate et videte quoniam suavis est.'[c] Insuper hanc rumpendo insipientes decipiebant, dicentes 'Mori debet, quia Filium Dei se fecit',[d] imponentes ei quod se fecerit quod non erat. Utinam superbi attenderent melodiam timoris, quia timor humiliat hominem et mentem ad se revocat. Utinam invidi attenderent melodiam pietatis. Pietas gaudet de alieno bono, invidus dolet. Utinam iracundi attenderent melodiam sciencie, quia ira impedit animum, ne possit cernere verum, et sciencia illuminat, datque tempus et locum deliberacionis et que agenda sunt ostendit. Utinam accidiosi attenderent melodiam fortitudinis. Accidia est tedium vite spiritualis quando tedet hominem legere, orare, immo eciam vivere, proveniens ex pusillanimitate cordis. Utinam avari attenderent melodiam consilii, quia supremum consilium est, si quis misericordiam consequi voluerit, illam indigentibus impendat.[1] Avari autem opera misericordie non impendunt,[2] ut est, pascere esurientem etcetera. Utinam gulosi audirent sonum

---

[1] impendant *cod* [2] impendet *cod*

[a] *Ioh*. xix. 30. [b] *Luc*. xxiii. 46. [c] *Ps*. xxxiii. 9.
[d] *Ioh*. xix. 7.

Vita S. Edmundi auctore Matthaeo Parisiensi

intellectus, quia 'vinum et ebrietas auferunt cor',[a] id est, intellectum, 'sobrietas autem sanitas anime et corporis'.[b] Utinam luxuriosi audirent sonum sapiencie et sentirent saporem et dulcedinem sive dilectionem in spiritualibus et non fetorem in stercoribus. Unde Ioel, 'Computruerunt iumenta in stercore suo.'[c] Saul | audiebat citharam David et levibus se habebat.[d] (fo. 156ᵛ) Utinam et nos audiamus citharam istam, ut possimus alleviari ab onere dolenti, ut cum eo conregnemus.[1] Qui vivis et regnas Deus . . . .

[1] congregemus *cod, sed scriptor punctis subscriptis correxit*

[a] *Os.* iv. 11.   [b] *Eccli.* xxxi. 37.   [c] *Ioel* i. 17.
[d] See *1 Reg.* xvi. 23.

APPENDIX A

LETTERS OF POSTULATION

Letter of Postulation Addressed to the Pope by Oxford University (Jan.–Sept. 1241)

Original MSS.: Sens archives nos. 5 and 6.
Copies: (1) Auxerre, Bibl. Mun. MS. 123, fo. 60; (2) BM Add. MS. 46352, fo. 48: St. Augustine's cartulary; (3) Bodleian, Rawlinson MS. B 254, fo. 86: Hearne's transcript of (2).
Printed: MD. Thes. iii, cols. 1839-41; A. B. Emden, *An Oxford Hall in Medieval Times* (1927), pp. 267-70.

quarta
CLEMENTISSIMO patri suo et domino GG. dei gracia summo pontifici sue sanctitatis grex humilis, universitas magistrorum et scolarium Oxonie commorancium, cum universa multitudine Fratrum Predicatorum et Minorum ceterorumque religiosorum ibidem habitancium, devota pedum oscula cum obediencie humili famulatu. Quod scimus loquimur et quod vidimus testamur de conversacione venerabilis patris nostri E. bone memorie, nuper Cantuariensis archiepiscopi, qui in nostra fuit universitate non modico tempore discipulus et magister. Fuit igitur dictus pater *ex piis parentibus* genitus et a puericia tam *religiose nutritus*[a] ut, docente eum Christianissima matre sua quam florem postea fuisse viduarum et vita sua clamat et fama, ieiunare inciperet et orare *cum adhuc esset puerulus*.[a] Adolescens autem factus, cum iam esset liberalibus studiis traditus, via qua prius ducebatur, incedebat spontaneus. Nam ex tunc voluntarie Deo sacrificare cepit, ecclesie limina sponte frequentans, vana et *frivola*,[b] *quibus adolescencior habundat etas*, devitans, *erudicioni sue diligenter intendens*, carnis delicias non solum fugiens, sed et crucis Christi mortificacionem iugiter in suo corpore portans,[c] toto mentis studio vite requisivit auctorem. *Videbatur*[b] enim *iam illud quod nondum legerat intellexisse proverbium*, '*Adolescens iuxta viam suam, eciam cum senuerit, non recedet ab ea*',[d] quod in eo vere invenitur completum esse. Nam ieiunare et vigilare, sed et cetera penitencie

[a] *Legenda S. Dominici* auct. Petro Ferrandi, MOFPH xvi. 211-12.
[b] Ibid., p. 212.
[c] crucis Christi &c. Cf. 2 Cor. iv. 10.
[d] Adolescens &c. Prov. xxii. 6.

gravia opera *ex tunc*[a] tam *duxit in consuetudinem* facere, quod postmodum, ut ipsemet perhibebat, non tam facilia quam eciam delectabilia ei fuerant in proveciori etate. Verum quia corporalis exercitacio ad modicum utilis est, pietas autem ad omnia, iam qualiter etate crescente crevit et gracia, paciencer audire dignetur sanctitas vestra. Factus itaque magister arcium, nondum ad sacros ordines promotus, nec adhuc racione alicuius adepti beneficii ecclesiastici compulsus, sed solo Dei instinctu et studio pietatis ductus, supra morem tunc legencium singulis diebus priusquam legeret missam suam audire consuevit. Quod ut devocius faceret, de collectis in scolis suis et de aliis quibus poterat, capellam de beata virgine, quam speciali quodam privilegio amoris semper dilexit, in parochia in qua tunc habitabat construxit, ubi adhuc solempnes misse non desinunt celebrari ad laudem et gloriam ipsius. Cetera vero sive de predictis collectis sive de aliis que ei superfuerant pauperibus et egenis maxime autem scolaribus largissime erogabat. Porro transactis fere sex annis quibus in artibus rexerat, cum iam placuisset ei qui eum segregavit ex utero matris sue ut in eo et per eum revelaret Filium suum[b] fieretque vas electionis,[c] ipso adhuc cursim legente arismeticam quibusdam sociis suis, apparuit ei in sompnis pia mater eius paulo ante defuncta dicens, 'Fili, quid legis? Que sunt ille figure quibus tam studiose intendis?' Quo respondente, 'Talia lego', ostensis protractionibus que in illa solent fieri facultate, illa mox dextram manum eius arripuit, et in ea tres circulos depinxit in quibus hec tria nomina per ordinem inscripsit: 'Pater, Filius, Spiritus Sanctus'. Et hoc facto sic ait, 'Fili karissime, talibus figuris et non aliis de cetero intende.' Quo sompnio quasi per revelacionem edoctus, statim *ad studium theologie se* transtulit,[d] in quo tam mirabiliter in brevi profecit quod cito post paucos annos suadentibus multis cathedram magistralem ascendit. Nimirum[e] *tanta diligencia tantaque discendi aviditate sacris literis prius inheserat quod pene noctes ducebat insompnes et videbantur ei dies pauci pre amoris magnitudine* quo *ad speciose Rachelis castos anelabat amplexus. Nec est fraudatus a desiderio suo*.[f] Nam *iuxta estimacionem* suam modicum *in opere* eius *laboravit et cito de generacionibus illius percepit. Etenim divini verbi*

---

[a] *Legenda S. Dominici*, op. cit., p. 212.
[b] cum iam &c. Cf. *Galat.* i. 15–16.   [c] fieretque vas: *Act.* ix. 15.
[d] *Legenda S. Dominici*, op. cit., p. 213.
[e] tanta . . . producebat: ibid.   [f] nec est fraudatus &c. *Ps.* lxxvii. 30.

semina intenta cordis aure suscipiens, tanquam terre celesti rore perfusa, non solum sanctarum meditacionum et affectionum segetes sed[1] *eciam bonorum operum fructus uberrimos* ex se *producebat.* Verum eciam legendo et disputando necnon et predicando eiusdem verbi strenuus et egregius seminator ad aliorum edificacionem tanquam imbres eloquia divine sapiencie mittebat.[a] Erat enim in lectione sedulus, in disputacione acutus, in predicacione ferventissimus, unde et effectus est clericis gratus, laicis acceptus, ipsis eciam principibus reverendus. Cumque sederet inter primos erat tamen merencium consolator. *Ab*[b] *infancia quippe cum eo creverat miseracio*[c] *que aliorum sibi coacervans miserias, nullius afflictionis aspecte permittebat eum non esse participem. Talibus*[d] igitur *virtutum floribus in beato viro gratissima venustate vernantibus, cepit odor* honestatis necnon et *sanctitatis eius circumquaque diffundi.* Et quia talis decebat ut nobis esset pontifex, sanctus, innocens, inpollutus, et segregatus a peccatoribus,[e] vacante postmodum sede Cantuariensi divine inspirante gracia in archipresulem est electus. Pastor autem et dux inclitus in populo Dei factus, priorem humilitatem non deposuit, sed in abstinencia iugi, in vestis asperitate, in vigiliis multis, carnem spiritui et sensualitatem racioni servire coegit. Sane sunt quidam inter nos qui eius lateri dum viveret longo tempore adheserunt, videlicet frater Robertus Bacun, rector in theologia Oxonie, et frater Ricardus de Drinstapele, prior Fratrum Predicatorum ibidem, quorum relatu, cum aliis multis que premisimus, hoc eciam didicimus, quod dictus vir sanctus a tempore quo rexerat in artibus nunquam vel raro lectum intraverat, sed vestitus et cinctus, iacens ante lectum, corpus sompno modico refovebat. Reliquum vero noctis in meditacionibus et oracionibus expendebat. Erat enim in oracione continuus, in lacrimarum effusione profluus, in animarum zelo fervidus, ad prospera non remissus, ad adversa securus. Quid plura? In omnibus exhibuit semetipsum tanquam Dei ministrum, probabilem in moribus, operarium inconfusibilem in actibus et recte tractantem verbum Dei in sermonibus. Erat enim quasi sol refulgens in doctrina, et quasi thus redolens in

---

[1] seu MS

[a] Cf. *Eccli.* xxxix. 9.
[b] Ab ... participem: *Legenda S. Dominici,* op. cit., p. 214.
[c] Ab infancia &c. *Iob* xxxi. 18.
[d] Talibus ... diffundi: *Legenda S. Dominici,* op. cit., p. 215.
[e] talis decebat &c. Cf. *Heb.* vii. 26.

operacione, implens illud Apostoli, *sic loquimini et sic facite*.[a] Denique laudabilis vita laudabilem exitum est sortita. Nam ut *condempnet vivos impios iustus mortuus*,[b] et ut gloriosus appareat in sanctis suis sanctorum auctor et remunerator Deus, quos prius instituerat meritis, informaverat exemplis, tam miraculis confirmat evidentibus et probatis. Etenim preter opera sanctitatis et signa virtutis quibus in carne positus claruit, multorum et diversorum iam curatis languoribus et pristine sanitati restitutis, aperte patet qualis spiritus in eius sanctissimi gleba corporis habitaverit. Totam eciam ecclesiam, que tenebris tribulacionum et peccatorum videbatur obducta temporibus nostris, quasi infuso respectu novi luminis prefatis illustravit Dominus miraculis ad conversionem infidelium, ad repressionem hostium, ad solacium electorum. Cum igitur tot constent sanctitatis eius argumenta et insignis vite eius testimonia, ad sanctitatis vestre genua provoluti suppliciter exoramus quatinus quem Deus glorificavit in celis et mirificavit in terris, ascribi sanctorum cathalogo iubere velitis, ut per multorum ora Dominus, in eius memoriam invocatus, succurrat ecclesie laboranti in multis, et plebs Christiana proficiat ipsius meritis et exemplis. Conservet vos Dominus ecclesie sue per tempora diuturna.

(Tags and fragments of seals attached.)

Letter of Postulation from Bishop Robert Bingham and the Dean and Chapter of Salisbury (Jan.-Sept. 1241)

Original MS.: Sens archives no. 12.
Copies: (1) BM Add. MS. 46352, fo. 49: St. Augustine's cartulary; (2) Salisbury D. and C. mun., Liber Evidentiarum C. 457; (3) Bodl. Rawlinson MS. B. 254, fo. 88ᵛ: Hearne's transcript of (2).
Printed: *M.D. Thes.* iii, col. 1900; W. R. Jones and W. D. Macray, *Sarum Charters* (RS), pp. 272-3.

SANCTISSIMO patri et domino reverendo . . . Dei gracia summo pontifici sue sanctitatis servi, R. divina miseracione Saresbiriensis ecclesie episcopus et eiusdem loci decanus et humile capitulum tanto patri (cum omni subiectione et reverencia devota) pedum oscula. Ea que audivimus et nos capitulum vidimus et quasi manibus attrectavimus de E. venerabili olim archipresule Cantuariensi qui a gremio ecclesie nostre ad archipresulatus dignitatem est translatus (vestre precellencie humili sermone vero et plano) significamus.

[a] *Iac.* ii. 2.   [b] *Sap.* iv. 16.

Appendix A

Sciat igitur, si placet, vestre paternitatis preeminencia quod in ecclesia nostra inter nos fere per decem annos egregie et laudabiliter conversatus, imitator fuit illius de quo scriptum est (Erat Iohannes *lucerna ardens et lucens.*[a] Arsit) quidem illo igne de quo Veritas dicit *Ignem veni mittere in terram.*[b] In omnibus enim operibus suis secundum possibilitatem suam relucebat zelus animarum, fervor caritatis (et affectus pietatis. Contemptor eciam erat seculi, legendo et predicando) opus faciens evangeliste. Cuius doctrina ita erat catholica et lucida ut de eo per totam regionem Anglicanam passim ab hominibus diceretur *lingua eius calamus (scribe velociter scribentis.*[c] Scivit eciam iuxta humanam capacitatem) quodam modo excellentissimo de thesauro sacre Scripture proferre nova et vetera, ita quod cum legeret vel predicaret visum esset auditoribus suis quod digitus (Dei scribebat in corde suo verba vite que procedebant de ore eius. Et) quasi alter Iohannes Baptista in deserto Anglie factus generalis predicator turbis et publicanis et militibus, magnis et parvis utriusque sexus, religiosis et clericis, (verba sancte predicacionis et exhortacionis, cum affectu et effectu, lucide et) salubriter et incessanter proposuit. Erat enim emulator precursoris Domini in mira abstinencia cibi et potus, in asperitate vestitus cilicini, in modicitate sompni, (nunquam vel raro in lecto membra sua quieti subiciens, qui iugiter in suo) corpore crucis mortificacionem portavit. Sublimatus autem divina disposicione ad apicem pontificalem in priori humilitate et benignitate perseverans (omnem excellenciam oculorum abiecit, omnibus se affabilem exhibuit, super) afflictos piissima gestans viscera. Et ne longo sermone vestram sanctissimam serenitatem tot et tantis negociis occupatam tedio afficiamus, videtur nobis quod (erat veracissimus Dei cultor, potens in opere et sermone, in vinea Domini laborans) assidue, vigilans et expectans beatam Domini vocacionem. Cum igitur a Domino iam sit vocatus, et quanti meriti fuerit in hac vita divina clemencia mirifice ostendat (per crebra miracula ad tumbam eius et alias ad invocacionem nominis) sui facta, vestre sanctissime paternitatis pedibus provoluti, humiliter et devote supplicamus quatinus tantam lucernam super candelabrum iubeatis poni et in sanctorum (catalogo annumerari. Vitam et incolumitatem vestram nobis et) ecclesie sue conservet Altissimus per tempora diuturna.

[a] *Ioh.* v. 35.   [b] *Luc.* xii. 49.   [c] *Ps.* xliv. 2.

Letters of Postulation

(Endorsed faintly, in a thirteenth-century hand, 'Id. Augusti xli'. Seal of Robert Bingham, in green wax, and fragments of two others attached. Rats have gnawed a large hole in the parchment, which is responsible for the lacunae. These have been filled from the text of the letter reproduced in *Sarum Charters*.)

Letter of Postulation from Abbot John and the Convent of Abingdon (Sept. 1241–Aug. 1243)

Original MS.: an *inspeximus* in Sens archives no. 16.
Copies: BM Add. MS. 46352, fo. 50–50ᵛ; Bodl. Rawlinson MS. B. 254, fo. 90ᵛ: Hearne's transcript.
Printed: *MD. Thes.* iii, col. 1908.

SANCTISSIMO patri et domino reverendo . . . Dei gracia summo pontifici sue sanctitatis servi I. divina permissione abbas Abbendonie et eiusdem loci conventus humiliter cum omni subiectione et reverencia devota pedum oscula beatorum. Oriens sol iusticie Christus Ihesus dignatus est illustrare per ministros lucis sue cunctos fines orbis terre. Ipsi laus qui dedit nobis lucernam nostre salutis Edmundum archipresulem super astra refulgentem, cuius ipse summus rerum arbiter testis est in celo fidelis, qui eum tam sublimiter honorat in terris renovans ad sepulcrum eius et alibi per eius merita antiqua sua miracula. Unde *repletum est gaudio os nostrum et lingua nostra exultacione.*[a] *Facti sumus letantes* videntes nostris diebus quia magnificavit Dominus facere cum servis suis.[b] Cum igitur dies boni nuncii sit, ne sceleris arguamur[c] si de tot bonis nichil nunciaverimus cum fuerimus eius affines et vicini, huius laudabilis viri ortum felicem, processum prosperum et finem gloriosum vestre sanctitati qualicunque sermone intimare curavimus. Extitit igitur Abendonie oriundus parentibus Christianissimis moribus honestis, operibus bonis et elemosinis plenis. Cuius mater tam sancte vivebat ut loricam ferream sue carni innexam finetenus portaret. Hec dulci puero cum lactis dulcedine lacte dulcius Christi nomen indidit, amorem inmisit, timorem incussit, crescentem et proficientem suo exemplo informavit. Ad quantam vero messem materna, immo divina, in eo convaluerunt semina innumera pietatis opera, quibus tota vita sua strenuus insudabat, manifeste preconatur. Nam a puericia semper

[a] *Ps.* cxxv. 2.
[b] Cf. ibid.
[c] dies boni &c. Cf. *4 Reg.* vii. 9.

cilicio utebatur. Litteris traditus, vigiliis, ieiuniis et oracionibus carnem edomans, iam tunc spiritui servire cogebat, semper nitens in carne preter carnem vivere, hostiam[a] vivam, sanctam, Deo placentem seipsum offerre, optinere per graciam quod non habuit per naturam, scilicet quam modo invenit celestem vitam. Beati itaque Iohannis Evangeliste imitator existens, virginitatem perpetuam in carne observavit, quod firmiter asserunt qui eius confessionem audierunt et qui ipsum ex familiari cum ipso conversacione ab annis puerilibus noverunt. Crescens igitur et etate sapienciaque proficiens, liberalibus disciplinis iam sufficienter imbutus, ad sacre Scripture audienciam se contulit, in qua demum tantum profecit ut quod omnium sanctorum pace dixerimus nulli Anglicane ecclesie doctori fuit secundus et sicut augebatur et multiplicabatur in eo interius divine lumen sapiencie, sic multipliciter refulsit exterius divinissimorum operum claritate. Erat enim predicator eximius, doctor egregius, ignitum in predicacione et doctrina habens eloquium mentes auditorum ad veritatis cognicionem illuminans, et affectus ad bonitatem accendens ut effectu verbi in auditoribus luce clarius pateret quod ipse in eo et per eum loquebatur de quo scriptum est *Deus noster ignis consumens est.*[b] Hec de processu. Finem vero illius ut supradictum est, glorificavit ipse de cuius munere venit ut sibi digne et laudabiliter deserviret. Qui enim dudum animam suam ad celestia desideranda sustulit, ipse eandem ad diu desiderata gaudia sublimavit. Unde nos tante glorie quondam vicini, hoc autem tempore patris nostri tanquam filii devoti illacrimando congaudentes, ad pedes vestre sanctitatis devotissime et humillime inclinati, obsecramus quatinus tantam tamque splendidam lucernam sub modio latere non permittat, sed super candelabrum ponere dignetur sancta paternitas vestra et in sanctorum cathalogo annumerare, ut ei orando dicere possimus 'O magne presul Edmunde, cui Christus fuit vivere, cui mori lucrum perenne,[c] dum post mortem vivis vere, signis divinis inclite, languidos sanans a labe, hoc rogamus pauperes, tu pro nobis intercede.' Vitam et incolumitatem vestram ecclesie sue conservet Altissimus per tempora diuturna.

[a] hostiam vivam &c. Cf. *Rom.* xii. 1.
[b] *Heb.* xii. 29.
[c] Christus fuit &c. Cf. *Phil.* i. 21.

Letter of Postulation from Robert, Prior, and the Brethren of Merton (27 Feb. 1242)

Original MS.: Sens archives no. 9.
Copy: (extract) Cambridge, Trinity College MS. R. 5.40, fo. 58ʳ.
Printed: *MD. Thes.* iii, col. 1899–1900.

PATRI suo clementissimo et domino semper reverendo... Dei gracia summo pontifici fratrum monasterii de Mertona Ordinis Sancti Augustini Robertus humilis minister ac eiusdem loci conventus sibi semper humilis et devotus devota pedum oscula beatorum. Quamvis sanctitatem vestram felicis recordacionis venerabilis patris Eadmundi quondam Cantuariensis archiepiscopi universa fidelium plebe proclamante, vita beata, finis beatior, ac eiusdem actus et merita non credimus latere, qui vere lucerna erat non absconsa modio set super candelabrum posita omnibus qui in domo erant luce claruit prefulgenti. Verum quia scriptum est *clama, ne cesses*,[a] non sufficientes ipsum ad plenum commendare quem suorum commendant premia meritorum, tamen ut eum qui fide et opere gloriosus extitit, gloriosius veneremur in terris quem, ut credimus, Dominus noster inter sanctos suos gloriosissime collocare dignatus est in celis, non solum diversa miraculorum genera que postquam (migravit a seculo) Dominum audivimus et firmiter credimus pro eo fecisse set quod de facto scimus et oculata fide vidimus, testamur. Nam idem venerabilis pater (antequam theologie publicus) rector existeret, per annum et amplius in domo nostra iugiter morabatur et postea per longum tempus quasi unus ex nostris sepius intravit et exiit, quia quidam fratrum (nostrorum in) ipsius sanctis valde delectabantur colloquiis et fovebantur consiliis, conversacionem ipsius ineffabiliter admirantes. Nam in mundo conversans mundum conculcaverat et etate iuvenis quosque senes fide, doctrina, sciencia, consilio excedebat et quod mirabile dictu inter seculares gradiens non solum religiosus, set eciam forma tocius religionis inter nos videbatur. Erat enim in lectionibus et meditacionibus assiduus, in oracione devotissimus, semper in ieiuniis et vigiliis continuus, horam nullam matutinarum dormiendo preteriens set ad omnes, nobiscum quasi deditus esset, accedens. Nec solum gestus exteriores religionis gerebat set eciam secretissimos quos Spiritu Sancto didiscerat, pretendebat, clavem scilicet tocius religionis habens, quia fedus in tantum cum oculis pepigerat[b] ut quendam fratrem per annum ei in mensa ministrantem

[a] *Is.* lviii. 1.   [b] fedus &c. Cf. *Iob* xxxi. 1.

minime cognosceret. Equidem qualiter de virtute in virtutem celitus creverit ut Deum deorum in Syon videret non solum nobis set omnibus innotuit. (Ideo breviter de sancta ipsius conversacione) diximus, omittendo ineffabilis bonitates eius quas multi fratrum ab eodem oculte viderunt et perceperunt et qualiter Dominus meritis ipsius quem amavimus in terris post mortem operatus sit, brevi stilo perstringimus. Accidit enim postquam idem sanctus carnis ergastulum est egressus quod quidam canonicus (ex fratribus nostris) quinquagenarius cui nomen Iohannes morbo paralitico graviter percussus virtute membrorum et actu penitus destitutus ita quod quidam medici qui ad eum accesserant curandi causa incurabilem eum credebant. Cumque quidam ex fratribus nostris qui cum eo erant in domo infirmorum audientes qualiter Dominus sanctum suum (glorificavit) in celis et mirificavit in terris pro eo Deum meritis iam dicti gloriosi archipresulis deprecabantur. Et quia desiderium pauperum suorum exaudit Deus, *a desiderio suo (non sunt) fraudati*,[a] nam post paucos dies integram idem frater assecutus est sanitatem. Cum igitur predictus sanctus inter nos in vita sua honestissime et sanctissime conversacionis (existens), tanti miraculi ac aliorum plurium virtute refulgentibus in se meritis, moribus, ac vita choruscaverit, sanctitati vestre placeat ad honorem et gloriam ecclesie (sancte Dei) et gloriose virginis Marie eundem in sanctorum cathalogo connumerare, ut quem Deus glorificavit in celis venerari debeamus in terris ad eiusdem Domini nostri ac universalis ecclesie gloriam et honorem. Ecclesie sue sancte pastorem conservet vos omnipotens per tempora longa. Datum anno gracie Millesimo Ducentesimo Quadragesimo Primo, die Iovis proxima post festum sancti Mathie.

(Conventual seal of Merton priory in brown wax attached. Lacunae caused in the text by rats have been filled from the text reproduced by Martène and Durand.)

Letter of Postulation from Abbot R. and the Convent of Reading (Sept. 1241–Aug. 1243)

Original MS.: Sens archives no. 13.
Printed: MD. Thes. iii, col. 1909.

SANCTISSIMO patri et domino reverentissimo . . . divina prudencia universalis ecclesie pontifici summo devotus filius suus frater R.

[a] *Ps.* lxxvii. 30.

Letters of Postulation

dictus abbas Rading' et eiusdem loci conventus unanimis tam devotam quam debitam in omnibus obedienciam et reverenciam cum devotissimis sanctorum pedum osculis. Virorum plurium fide dignissimorum inspeximus scripta, vive vocis audivimus testimonia sanctitati vite venerabilis patris nostri Edmundi quondam Cantuariensis archiepiscopi irrefragabiliter attestancia. Ideoque *tantam habentes impositam nubem testium*[a] quorum *testimonia credibilia facta sunt nimis*,[b] de sanctitate eiusdem viri non habemus hesitare, precipue cum non sit qui audeat vel possit contrahiscere vel se tot et tantis testimoniis opponere, nisi si forte, quod absit, sint aliqui veritatis inimici qui non formident tangere Christos Dei et in prophetis eius malignari. Verumptamen quia segnius irritant animos demissa per aures quam que sunt oculis subiecta fidelibus, testimonium perhibemus veritati et nos testes super hiis que de viro memorato oculata fide cognovimus. Cum aliquando ab Oxon', ubi scolas theologie regebat, vocatus ad cenobium nostrum tempore vacacionis in festo[1] dominice Nativitatis penes nos perhendinaret. Cum enim tunc temporis indulgencius habere se solent homines ex more, ipse nichil omnino de solito rigore omisit, continuans abstinenciam victualium, laborem vigiliarum, frequenciam sanctarum meditacionum, instanciam oracionum, profluvium lacrimarum, infinitatem quamdam genuflexionum, doctrine salutaris infatigabilem usum, necnon et interule cilicine asperitatem, quam tamen quantum potuit, occultavit. Unde factum est ut ob tantam edificacionem tam in maturitate sermonum quam in exhibicione salubrium exemplorum multi fratrum nostrorum, quorum corda tetigerat Deus, tanta et talia perpendentes in eo sanctitatis indicia, se in comparacione ipsius, in habitu seculari constituti, tepidos arbitrantes et desides, cum haberentur religiosi, iuxta illud vaticinium Ysaie, *Erubesce Sydon ait mare*,[c] de tepore suo ceperint erubescere et ad talis et tanti viri imitacionem vitam ducere solito correctiorem. Hec et alia huiusmodi digna memoria pro certo circa ipsum cognovimus, quod et confidenter testamur, scientes quia verum est testimonium nostrum.[d] Asserunt eciam eius quondam secretarii et collaterales quod, cum promotus esset in Cantuar' archipresulem,

---

[1] festo: *post habet MS.* videlicet *sed deletum*

[a] *Hebr.* xii. 1.   [b] *Ps.* xcii. 5.   [c] *Is.* xxiii. 4.
[d] Cf. *Ioh.* xxi. 24.

nichil sibi de dicta austeritate indulserit, immo de die in diem ut filius accrescens rigorem ampliaverit, adeo ut clerici quidam super hoc fastiditi ab eo recesserint, occasionem sibi confingentes et querentes ut ab amico diverterent, rigorem tantum abhorrentes et odorem bonum minime sustinentes. Hiis et aliis testimoniis eius religiositati attestantibus, accedunt post eius obitum ad tumbam eius et alias creberrima miracula omni testimonio maiora, tam merita vivi quam premia defuncti preconancia, ac si confractis lagunculis ad nutum Gedeonis lampades emicent,[a] ac si multiplicentur fulgura que hostes et emulos eius conturbent. Vestigiis igitur vestre sanctitatis provoluti, omni qua possumus affectione supplicamus quatinus si vobis dignum videatur et iustum, memoratum virum asscribi iubeatis in sanctorum cathalogo, nec tantam lucernam sinatis abscondi sub modio sed poni faciatis super candelabrum ut luceat omnibus qui sunt in domo. Valeat sancta paternitas vestra per tempora longa.

(Silk tag att. Seal missing.)

Letter of Postulation from Ralph, Bishop of Chichester (Sept. 1241– Aug. 1243)

The original of this letter has disappeared since Viole made his transcripts of the Pontigny archives. It is not in the Sens collection, but, as will be seen from the list in App. E, the documents numbered 49 and 81 are missing, and Bishop Ralph's letter may have been one of these. The text given here is taken from MD. Thes. iii, cols. 1905–6.

SANCTISSIMO patri in Christo et domino reverendo . . . Dei gratia summo pontifici eius devotus R. Cicestrensis episcopus cum omni subjectione et reverentia devotissima pedum oscula beatorum. Odor famae miraculorum quae Dominus ad memoriam felicissimae recordationis Edmundi quondam archiepiscopi Cantuar' operari dignatus est, longe lateque spirans et Gallicanae atque Anglicanae ecclesiae totam domum replens, cogit me vestrae sanctitati scribere pauca de dicti archipraesulis sanctissima conversatione. Noverit ergo vestrae paternitatis sanctitas quod dictus Dei cultor, Johannis imitator evangelistae, virginitatem perpetuam creditur in carne servasse, quod et firmiter asserunt qui ipsius confessionem audierunt. Dum in annis juvenilibus liberalibus intenderet disciplinis, nondum

[a] See *Iud.* vii.

sacrae Scripturae auditor effectus, honesta, matura et sancta conversatione doctor esse videbatur Scripturae, non solum prius incipiens facere quam docere. Deinde ipso effecto sacrae paginae auditore et postea doctore, sicut augebatur et multiplicabatur in eo interius divinae lumen sapientiae, sic multipliciter refulsit exterius divinissimorum operum claritate. Erat enim praedicator eximius, doctor egregius, ignitum in praedicatione et doctrina habens eloquium, mentes auditorum ad veritatis cognitionem illuminans, et affectus ad bonitatem accendens, ut ex effectu verbi in auditoribus luce clarius pateret quod ipse in eo et per eum loquebatur, de quo scriptum est, *Deus noster ignis consumens est*,[a] pauper et dives, subjectus et praelatus, ut esset vere beatus, manus suas excussit ab omni munere, habens victum et vestitum, novit iis contentus esse. Indefessus operator omnium operum misericordiae, et ad imitationem Praecursoris Domini vir mirae et velut singularis abstinentiae, carnem edomans cilicii asperitate, somni modicitate, in lecto non recubans, sed ante lectum jacens vel sedens somnum brevissimum capiebat, residuum noctis in lectione seu oratione cum gemitibus et lacrimis, et in divinis obsequiis peragebat. Omnia ipsius tam verba quam opera quasi cujusdam latentis energiae voce in mentibus omnium clamabant quod operator eorum non quae sua sunt, sed quae Jesu Christi, per ista veraciter quaerebat. Ad pedes igitur vestrae sanctitatis devotissime et humillime inclinati obsecramus, quatenus tantae tamque eximiae sanctitatis archipraesulem, vestra dignetur sanctitas in sanctorum catalogo connumerare, cum evidentissime et irrefragabiliter ipsius probent sanctitatem miracula quae per ipsum operator Dominus ad sanctitatis ejus ostensionem. Incolumitatem vestram conservet Dominus ecclesiae suae per tempora longissima.

Letter of Postulation from Walter, Archbishop of York (c. 1243)

Copies: an *inspeximus*, Sens archives no. 15; extract in Trinity Coll. MS. R. 5.40, fo. 59ᵛ.
Printed: *MD. Thes.* iii, col. 1838.

SANCTISSIMO patri et domino Innocencio Dei gracia summo pontifici eius devotus G. miseracione divina Eboracensis ecclesie minister humilis cum omni subiectione devota pedum oscula beatorum.

[a] *Heb.* xii. 29.

Appendix A

Inter ea que de felicis memorie Edmundo Cantuariensi archipresule sanctitati vestre a prelatis et viris fide dignis tam Anglie quam Francie referuntur, silere non sinit devocio quin vobis insinuem aliqua de vita ipsius, quem olim existens eius auditor in artibus et postmodum, regimen ecclesie Eboracensis adeptus, in partem sollicitudinis mee assumpsi, vidi specialiter, et agnovi. Fuit itaque ut credo firmiter a lapsu carnis omnino immunis, fide firmus, spe robustus, caritate ferventissimus, lingua facundus, abstinencie plurimum deditus, in oracionibus sedulus, in vigiliis creber, strenuus in disciplinis, doctor egregius, predicator eximius, confessor discretus, cilicio ad carnem indutus, in lecto vix aut nunquam quietis gracia recubans, in adversis fortissimus, in prosperis mansuetus, affabilis omnibus, verbo pius, cum debita maturitate semper gaudens et hilaris, compaciens miseris, elemosinarum largitor largissimus, merencium consolator, usque adeo quod tanquam alter Iob dicere potuit, *Pes fui claudo, oculus ceco, pater pauperum,*[a] solacium miserorum. Et ut breviter dicam, ita se universis exemplar bonitatis exhibuit ut eius merita paternitati vestre vix humana lingua sufficeret enarrare. Cum igitur miraculorum frequencia que ad tumbam eius et alibi Dominus operatur, prout littere quorumdam prelatorum Francie vobis transmisse testantur, claret in terris quanta gloria tam gloriosus Christi confessor fruetur in celis, provolutus sanctitatis vestre pedibus instanter peto quatinus tantum lumen vestris temporibus revelatum poni super candelabrum et annumerari in sanctorum catalogo faciatis, ad Dei et universalis ecclesie gloriam et honorem. Conservet vos etc.

[a] *Iob* xxix. 15.

APPENDIX B

NOTE

The *acta* of St. Edmund form the basis for a chronology of his pontificate and for the reconstruction of his *familia*. The following list is the outcome of a systematic but limited search. It makes no claim to be exhaustive. I am indebted to Miss Kathleen Major for the reference to No. 31 and for the references to the Leeds cartulary of which she kindly lent me her photostats. I owe Nos. 17 and 44 to Professor C. R. Cheney, No. 12 to Miss Jane Sayers, and No. 43 to the Hon. Rosemary Barnes.

A LIST OF THE *ACTA* OF ARCHBISHOP EDMUND OF ABINGDON

1. Confirmation of an agreement between the prior and convent of Lewes and the dean and chapter of South Malling concerning the chapel of Shotenbury.
    South Malling. January 1234.
    (Copy: BM Cott. MS. Vesp. F xv, fo. 311; transl. by L. F. Salzman, *The Chartulary of the Priory of St. Pancras of Lewes*, Sussex Rec. Soc. xl (1932–8), p. 128.)

2. Confirmation of a grant of the church of Eye made to the abbot and convent of Reading by H., bishop of Hereford.
    Leominster. 13 May 1234.
    (Copy: BM Cott. MS. Domit. A iii, fo. 70.)

3. Letters of Indulgence granting twenty days' relaxation of canonical penance to all who contribute to the hospital for the poor at Hereford.
    Hereford. 15 May 1234.
    (Original: Hereford, D. & C. mun. record 2036; sealed *en double queue* with a good specimen of the archbishop's seal and counterseal.)

4. Mandate to archdeacons, deans, and rectors in the dioceses of St. David's and St. Asaph's to excommunicate all those who disturb the possessions of Leominster priory.
    Leominster. 26 June 1234.
    (Copy: BM Cott. MS. Domit. A iii, fo. 71^v.)

Appendix B

5. *Inspeximus* for Lanthony-by-Gloucester of charters relating to the appropriation of the church of Wick.
   Undated. ? May–June 1234.
   (Copy: PRO Chancery Masters' Exhibits, C 115/A 1, section xvi, fo. 1^v.)

6. Grant to the abbot and convent of Walden of the manors of Walden and Depden, saving the advowsons of Walden abbey and Depden church to the Countess Maud de Mandeville. Witnessed by Reginald, abbot of Bayham; Richard, prior of Holy Trinity, London; Masters Elyas de Dereham, John de Offenton, Robert de Stafford; Dns. Aaron, parson of Wimbledon; Richard Reynger; Geoffrey de Essendon; William de Thorleya; William Flambard; Peter Cardun; Roger Galiun.
   London. 30 September 1234.
   (Copy: PRO Charter Roll 19 Henry III, m. 13; cal. in *CCR* i. 196–7.)

7. Confirmation to the prior and convent of Christ Church, Canterbury, of a rent of eight pounds annually from the archbishop's manor of Reculver.
   January 1235.
   (Copy: Canterbury, D. & C. mun. Reg. A, fo. 147; printed by Wallace, p. 487.)

8. *Cautio* that the consecration of Robert Grosseteste at Reading shall not prejudice the rights of Christ Church, Canterbury.
   Undated. 17 June 1235.
   (Original: Canterbury, D. & C. mun. Chartae Antiquae C. 120. Copy: Lambeth Palace MS. 585, p. 37.)

9. Confirmation to the prioress and nuns of Wintney of all their possessions.
   Farnham. 23 June 1235.
   (Copy: PRO Charter Roll 11 Edward III, m. 31; printed in *CCR* iv. 395.)

10. Confirmation to the prior and convent of St. Martin's, Dover, of the appropriation of the church of St. Laurence, Hougham.
    Aldington. 24 November 1235.
    (Copy: Lambeth Palace MS. 241, fo. 190^v.)

The Acta of Archbishop Edmund of Abingdon

11. Grant to the prior and convent of Leeds of forty shillings annually from the church of Ham, and eight shillings annually from the church of Chillenden, for the infirmary.

    Aldington. 10 December 1235.
    (Copy: Maidstone Rec. Office, Leeds Cartulary fo. 7^v; printed in *CCR* v. 201.)

12. Letter appointing the prior of Dunstable sub-delegate, in pursuance of a papal mandate (dated 22 November 1234) appointing Archbishop Edmund judge-delegate in a case concerning the alienated property of the abbey of Bec.

    Undated. 1235.
    (Copy: St. George's Chapel, Windsor, D. & C. mun. IV.B.1. (Arundel White Book), p. 231.)

13. Mandate to the dean and chaplains of Dover to enforce the payment of tithes to the monks of St. Martin's, Dover, by canonical penalties.

    South Malling. 21 February 1236.
    (Copy: Lambeth Palace MS. 241, fo. 41.)

14. Grant to the prior and convent of Boxgrove of ten marks annually from the church of Bilsington, with the advowson thereof.

    South Malling. 5 March 1236.
    (Copy: BM Cott. MS. Claudius A vi, fo. 117; printed from an *inspeximus* by C. E. Woodruff, 'Notes on Some Early Documents relating to the Priory of Bilsington', *Arch. Cant.* xli (1929), pp. 22–23.)

15. Appointment of the priors of Kirkby and Combe as the archbishop's officials in a tuitory appeal made by the abbot and convent of Sulby against a citation before the archdeacon of Leicester.

    Croydon. 4 April, 1236.
    (Original: BM Add. Charter 21, 289; fragment of seal.)

16. Grant to the prior and convent of Leeds of ten marks annually from the church of Stokenbury.

    Slindon. 19 May 1236.
    (Copy: Maidstone Record Office, Leeds cartulary, fo. 7.)

17. Confirmation to the prior and convent of Sele of the churches and other possessions confirmed to them by T., archbishop of

Canterbury, and of the tithe agreement between them and the church of West Tarring.
>   Slindon. 1 June 1236.
>   (Original: Oxford, Magdalen College, Durrington Charter 2; sealed *en double queue* with a perfect impression of the archbishop's seal and counterseal.)

18. Letter to W(illiam), bishop of Worcester. The archbishop had proposed to visit the monastery of Worcester on Tuesday next, the feast of St. Mary Magdalen (i.e. 22 July 1236), but, at the bishop's request, postpones his visit.
>   Undated. July 1236.
>   (Copy: Cambridge, Clare College MS. Kk. 5. 6, fly-leaf.)

19. Appropriation to the prior and convent of Dover of the church of Guston, reserving eight marks to be paid to a perpetual vicar.
>   Wingham. 22 April 1237.
>   (Copy: Lambeth Palace MS. 241, fo. 118.)

20. Grant to the prior and convent of St. Martin's, Dover, of the church of Hougham, saving a sufficient vicarage to be ordained therein.
>   Maidstone. 4 May 1237.
>   (Copy: Lambeth Palace MS. 241, fo. 190^v.)

21. Confirmation to the prior and convent of Leeds of the church of Goudhurst, saving a vicarage of fifteen marks to be ordained therein.
>   Canterbury. 18 December 1237.
>   (Copy: Maidstone Rec. Office, Leeds Cartulary fo. 4.)

22. Agreement between the archbishop and Prior John and the convent of Christ Church, Canterbury, concerning the advowsons of churches and the *exennia* on the conventual manors, the appointment of obedientiaries, and other matters.
>   Canterbury. 18 December 1237.
>   (Original cyrograph: Canterbury, D. & C. mun. Chartae Antiquae C. 34. Copies: BM Cott. MS. Vitell. A viii, fo. 101^v; Lambeth Palace MS. 582, p. 58; printed in Wallace, pp. 495–8.)

23. Notification that an agreement (i.e. No. 22) between the archbishop and Prior John and the convent of Christ Church, Canter-

bury, conferred on the archbishop no right to retain the priorate on its falling vacant.

> Canterbury. 19 December 1237.
> (Original: Canterbury, D. & C. mun. Chartae Antiquae C. 36, sealed *en simple queue* with the archbishop's seal attached. Copy: Lambeth Palace MS. 582, p. 58.)

24. Agreement between Archbishop Edmund and Archdeacon Simon Langton on the one part, and Abbot Robert and the convent of St. Augustine's, Canterbury, on the other, concerning the church of Chislet, the ordination of vicarages in the chapels pertaining to the church of Minster, the churches of Middleton and Faversham, and other matters. Witnessed by Anger, abbot of Dereham; Masters Robert de Abingdon, Thomas de Frakenham, Robert de Stafford, Richard de Langdon, Nicholas de Burford, then Official, Richard de Wich, then chancellor of the archbishop, Richard, rector of Hollingbourne, Walter de Somercote, William, rector of Bekesbourne; Henry de Welles and Robert de Dorking, clerks of the archbishop.

> 1237.
> (Original: Canterbury, D. & C. mun. Chartae Antiquae C. 257, Copies: BM Cott. MS. Claudius D x, fo. 271^v; Cott. MS. Julius D ii, fo. 83; PRO Misc. Books E 164, vol. 27, fo. 93; Lambeth Palace MS. 1212, fos. 132-4; cal. in *CPL* i. 171-2, and in *CChR* i. 238-40.)

25. Notification that on the composition of a dispute between the prior and convent of Boxgrove and the earl of Hereford, Thomas de Gosebech has been admitted to the church of Bilsington on the presentation of Boxgrove.

> Canterbury. April-December 1237.
> (Copy: printed by C. E. Woodruff, 'Notes on Some Early Documents relating to the Priory of Bilsington', *Arch. Cant.* xli (1929), pp. 22-23.)

26. Institution of Thomas de Gosebech, chaplain, to the vicarage of Bilsington, on presentation of Boxgrove priory.

> Undated. April-December 1237.
> (Copy: BM Cott. MS. Claudius A vi, fo. 117^v.)

27. Grant to the sacrist of Christ Church, Canterbury, of six marks annually from the church of St. Mary, Aldermary, with the

advowson thereof. Witnessed by Master Nicholas de Burford, Official; Master John de Offinton; Master Robert de Stafford; Master Aaron; Henry de Welles, clerk.
> Undated. 1234–7.
> (Original: Canterbury, D. & C. mun. Chartae Antiquae L. 7. Copy: Lambeth Palace MS. 582, p. 48.)

28. *Inspeximus* of a tithe agreement between the prior and convent of St. Gregory's, Canterbury, and Master Robert, rector of Chart. Witnessed by Master William, archdeacon of Berkshire; Master R. de Hereford, Official of Canterbury; Master Robert de Stafford; G. de Stapelherst, Aaron, clerks; Eudo, dean of Burn'; Master John de Walemere.
> Undated. 1234–7.
> (Copy: Cambridge Univ. MS. Ll.ii.15, fo. 61ᵛ; printed A. M. Woodcock, *Cartulary of the Priory of St. Gregory* (CS 3rd ser.) lxxxviii (1956), p. 139.)

29. Appropriation to the abbey of St. Mary, Anagni, of the church of Leeds, saving a perpetual vicarage to be ordained therein.
> Undated. April–May 1238.
> (Copy: Reg. Gregorii IX; printed: Auvray, 4381.)

30. *Inspeximus* of an agreement between the prior and convent of St. Martin's, Dover, and Master John, rector of Sibertswold, concerning tithes.
> Undated. After July 1238.
> (Copy: Lambeth Palace MS. 241, fo. 176ᵛ.)

31. Mandate to Master Nicholas de Burford, the archbishop's Official, to admit the prior and convent of Christ Church, Canterbury, to the church of Seasalter.
> Undated. 1237–8.
> (Copy: Canterbury, D. & C. mun. Reg. A, fo. 320.)

32. Notification that the archbishop's residence at St. Augustine's, Canterbury, occasioned by the visit to Canterbury of the cardinal legate, is not to prejudice the abbey's rights of exemption.
> Undated. August–November 1238.
> (BM Cott. MS. Claudius D x, fo. 276ᵛ; printed from Thorne's chronicle in Twysden, *Scriptores X* (1652), 1884–5.)

33. Letter to the monks of Christ Church, Canterbury, warning those who have been suspended to desist from the celebration of divine service.
    Canterbury. 20 November 1238.
    (Printed: Gervase, ii. 135.)

34. Letter to the monks of Christ Church, containing a third admonition in the same terms as the previous one.
    Canterbury. 21 November 1238.
    (Printed: Gervase, ii. 137.)

35. Letters of credence for the archbishop's representatives, Bishop John, Master R., the archbishop's chancellor, and Master H. de Bissopstone, in the election of a prior of Christ Church.
    Canterbury. 11 December 1238.
    (Printed: Gervase, ii. 139.)

36. An admonition to the monks of Christ Church to regularize their position so that the archbishop can proceed to the appointment of a prior.
    Canterbury. 13 December 1238.
    (Printed: Gervase, ii. 140.)

37. A second admonition to the same effect as the previous.
    Canterbury. 14 December 1238.
    (Printed: Gervase, ii. 140.)

38. A third admonition to the same effect as the previous.
    Canterbury. 15 December 1238.
    (Printed: Gervase, ii. 140-1.)

39. Judgement in an action between Alice, countess of Eu, and the abbot and convent of St. Radegund's, in which the advowson of the church is awarded to the countess, saving an annual pension of 20 marks to St. Radegund's. Witnessed by R., abbot of Bayham; Master Nicholas de Burford, Official; Master Richard, chancellor; Master John de Offinton; Master Roger de Leicester; Sir Aaron, rector of Wimbledon; Sir R. de Dorking.
    Undated. 1234-8.
    (Original: Oxford, Merton Coll. record 957)

40. Letter announcing the suspension of the monks of Christ Church

ab ingressu ecclesie and citing the instigators of rebellion before the archbishop.
>Canterbury. 4 January 1239.
>(Printed: Gervase, ii. 144.)

41. Relaxation of the archbishop's sentence in favour of four monks deputed to receive pilgrims and to keep the relics.
>Canterbury. 5 January 1239.
>(Printed: Gervase, ii. 145.)

42. Letter of the archbishop to the monks of Christ Church, excusing Eustace his chaplain from answering the summons to attend the chapter.
>Teynham. 6 January 1239.
>(Printed: Gervase, ii. 146.)

43. *Inspeximus* and confirmation of a composition between the prior and convent of Leeds and the prior and convent of Combwell.
>Hadlow. 10 January 1239.
>(Copy: Register of Archbishop Warham, fo. 138.)

44. Sentence of excommunication against the electors of Roger de la Lege as prior.
>Hadlow. 15 January 1239.
>(Printed: Gervase, ii. 151.)

45. Appointment of the prior and sacrist of Southwark as the archbishop's judges to hear the appeal of the prior and convent of Stoke against the archdeacon of Sudbury.
>Lambeth. 20 January 1239.
>(Copy: BM Cott. Appendix xxi, fo. 62^v.)

46. Letter to the monks of Christ Church, citing the leaders of rebellion (named) and requesting Roger de la Lege to say whether or not he accepts election as prior.
>Undated. *c.* 1 February 1239.
>(Printed: Gervase, ii. 153.)

47. Letter to the monks of Christ Church, repeating the citation of those named and ordering Roger de la Lege to repudiate his election to the office of prior.
>Undated. *c.* 22 February 1239.
>(Printed: Gervase, ii. 156–7.)

The Acta of Archbishop Edmund of Abingdon

48. Letters of credence to Albert, archbishop elect of Armagh, Master Robert de Abingdon, and Master Richard de Langdon, to discuss terms of agreement with the monks of Christ Church.
   South Malling. 12 April 1239.
   (Printed: Gervase, ii. 165.)

49. Mandate to W., rector of St. Martin's, Canterbury, the archbishop's penitentiary, to excommunicate those who take bodies to Christ Church for burial.
   Wingham. 27 April 1239.
   (Printed: Gervase, ii. 169.)

50. Mandate to Master Richard de Langdon, the archbishop's Official, to publish the excommunication of the chapter throughout the diocese of Canterbury.
   Wingham. 26 April 1239.
   (Printed: Gervase, ii. 170–1.)

51. Mandate to Master John de London, the archdeacon's Official, to publish the excommunication of the chapter throughout the archdeaconry of Canterbury.
   Wingham. 27 April 1239.
   (Printed: Gervase, ii. 167–8).

52. Mandate to the prior and monks of St. Martin's, Dover, not to communicate with the monks of Christ Church.
   Wingham. 5 October 1239.
   (Copy: Lambeth Palace MS. 241, fo. 23^v.)

53. Mandate to the bishop of London and other suffragans of the Canterbury province to publish the excommunication of the monks of Christ Church in their dioceses.
   Teynham. 16 November 1239.
   (Printed: Gervase, ii. 175.)

54. Mandate to the dean of Dover concerning processions and the payment of pensions to St. Martin's priory.
   Lyminge. 2 January 1240.
   (Copy: Lambeth Palace MS. 241, fo. 50.)

55. Injunction to the sheriff and people of Kent not to communicate with the monks of Christ Church. Jordan, the archbishop's clerk, is being sent to explain the position more fully.
   Undated. *c.* 4 March 1240.
   (Printed: Gervase, ii. 176.)

56. Mandate to R., the archbishop's official, to publish the excommunication of those who have entered the fiefs of the monks of Christ Church on the occasion of return of writ.

S. Malling. 4 March 1240.

(Printed: Gervase, ii. 177.)

57. Letters to the subprior and monks of St. Martin's, Dover, on the death of their prior, appointing Eustace, the archbishop's chaplain, to be their prior.

South Malling. 7 March 1240.

(Original: Canterbury D. & C. mun. Chartae Antiquae D. 76.)

58. Letter to the monks of Christ Church, warning them against alienating the property of the church of Canterbury and forbidding them to hear confessions.

South Malling. 15 March 1240.

(Printed: Gervase, ii. 177-8.)

59. Notification of the grant of the church of Elmstead to the priory of St. Gregory, Canterbury. Witnessed by Master (Robert) de Abingdon, rector of Wingham; Master Richard de Wich, archbishop's chancellor; Master Nicholas de Burford; Master Roger de Burewarecote; Master John de Wich; Master Roger de Leicester; Master Geoffrey de Ferring; Dns. Henry de Wintreselle and Dns. William Taleboth, knights; Jordan the clerk.

Aldington. 9 July 1240.

(Copy: Cambridge Univ. MS. Ll.ii.15, fo. 66; printed in *Cartulary of St. Gregory*, p. 156.)

60. Appropriation to the priory of St. Gregory, Canterbury, of the church of Bekesbourne, saving a vicarage of ten marks therein. Witnessed by Master Robert de Abingdon, the archbishop's brother, rector of Wingham; Master Elyas de Dereham; Master Richard de Wich, the archbishop's chancellor; Master Nicholas de Burford; Master Reginald de London; Master Roger de Leicester; Master John de Wich; Eustace the monk; Jordan the clerk.

Wingham. 23 July 1240.

(Copy: Cambridge Univ. MS. Ll.ii.15, fo. 66^v; printed in *Cartulary of St. Gregory*, p. 157.)

61. *Inspeximus* of an agreement between Roger, rector of Lenham,

The Acta of Archbishop Edmund of Abingdon

and the prior and convent of St. Gregory, Canterbury, concerning tithes.

Wingham. 23 July 1240.

(Copy: Cambridge Univ. MS. Ll.ii.15, fo. 67: printed in *Cartulary of St. Gregory*, p. 159.)

62. *Inspeximus* of an agreement between Master Luke, rector of Harbledown, and the prior and convent of St. Gregory, Canterbury, concerning tithes.

Undated. July–September 1240.

(Copy: Cambridge Univ. MS. Ll.ii.15, fo. 66^v; printed in *Cartulary of St. Gregory*, p. 158.)

63. Agreement between the archbishop and Abbot Robert and the convent of St. Augustine's, Canterbury, concerning the moor of Shirley, and the construction of a ditch to be maintained by the bailiffs of Aldington and Snave. Witnessed by the Lord Bishop John; the Lord R., abbot of Bayham; Master R. de Abingdon, rector of Wingham; Master Richard de Wich, the chancellor; Master Walter de Somercote; Master Nicholas de Burford.

1240.

(Copy: Lambeth Palace MS. 1212, fo. 135; Cott. MS. Faust. A i, fo. 336; printed in *The Register of St. Augustine's Abbey*, ed. G. J. Turner and H. E. Salter (Brit. Acad. Records 1924), p. 538.)

64. Letter testimonial on behalf of Eustace, monk of Christ Church, the archbishop's chaplain, secretary, and chamberlain, indemnifying him in advance against any action which the monks of Christ Church may take against him.

Soisy. 13 November, 1240.

(*Inspeximus*: Sens cathedral archives, no. 3.)

65. Letter testimonial addressed to William, bishop of Norwich, on behalf of Robert of Essex, a servant of the archbishop's.

Soisy. 14 November, 1240.

(Copy: BM. Cott. MS. Jul. D vi, fo. 145^v; printed above, p. 267.)

66. *Inspeximus* and confirmation of charters appropriating the church of Wye to Battle Abbey. Witnessed by Master Richard de Wich, the archbishop's chancellor; Master Geoffrey de Ferring;

Master Roger de Leicester; Master Richard de Hollingbourne; Master Aaron, parson of Wimbledon; Robert de Dorking; Henry de Bech'.
Undated.
(Original: PRO E 315/45 (Chartae Miscellaneae), No. 139.)

67. *Inspeximus* of a privilege of Pope Gregory, granting exemption from episcopal synods to the abbot of Cluny and the monks of the Cluniac order.
Undated.
(Original: PRO Anc. Deeds A 15420.)

68. The same as above, but in favour of the prior and convent of St. Pancras, Lewes.
Undated.
(Original: PRO Anc. Deeds A 15421.)

69. Sentence of excommunication against those who unjustly retain the property of St. Augustine's, Canterbury.
Undated.
(Copy: BM Cott. MS. Claud. D x, fo. 277.)

70. Agreement between the archbishop and Earl William de Warenne to the effect that the archbishop may have free access to the fisheries of Lewes while he is staying at Malling.
Undated.
Copies: Lambeth Palace MS. 1212, fo. 137; Bodl. Tanner MS. 223, fo. 96.

71. Letters of Indulgence granting forty days' relaxation of canonical penance to those who contribute to the completion of Salisbury cathedral.
Undated.
(Original: Salisbury, D. & C. mun. Press IV, Indulgentiae; printed in *H.MSS.C. rep. Various Collections*, i. 377–8.)

72. Confirmation to the prior and brethren of the hospital of St. Laurence, Canterbury, of the demesne tithes of Langport and of their other possessions.
Undated.
(Copies: Bodl. MS. Top. Kent D 3, fo. 7; Canterbury, D. & C. library, MS. C 20, fo. 12.)

APPENDIX C

SOME ABINGDON DEEDS RELATING TO THE PROPERTY OF SAINT EDMUND'S FAMILY

Grant by Master Edmund of Abingdon to the Hospital of St. John the Baptist, Oxford, of the house of Reginald Rich in West Street, Abingdon

Text: Bodl. Lyell MS. 15, fo. 92^v.[1]

De mesuagio quod fuit Reginaldi Divitis in Vico West: Omnibus sancte matris ecclesie filiis ad quos presens scriptum pervenerit magister Eadmundus de Abbendonia salutem in Domino. Noverit universitas vestra me concessisse et dedisse et hac presenti carta mea confirmasse Deo et hospitali sancti Iohannis de Oxonia ad portam orientalem et fratribus ibidem commorantibus domum cum omnibus pertinenciis que fuit Reginaldi Divitis in vico West in villa de Abbendonia, que sita est inter domum Thurberni Manegod ex una parte et domum Gunivilde Ater ex alia parte. Habendam et tenendam libere, quiete, honorifice, pacifice, in puram et perpetuam elemosinam. Salvis Aldithe de Abbendonia et heredibus suis ii solidis annuatim inde percipiendis ad duos terminos anni, videlicet duodecim[2] denarios ad festum Annunciacionis beate Marie in

---

[1] This cartulary of Abingdon is written in different hands of the thirteenth and fifteenth centuries. The contents are divided into six *particulae*, preceded by an index, as follows:

  (i) fos. 12–27 (papal privileges; 47 entries);
  (ii) fos. 32–50 (royal charters);
  (iii) fos. 52–70 (episcopal charters; 36 entries);
  (iv) fos. 74–82 (abbatial agreements with convent; 40 entries);
  (v) fos. 86–144 (private deeds; 266 entries);
  (vi) fos. 145–204 (miscellaneous later deeds).

The index (fos. 1–5^v) and *particulae* 1–5 are all in a single hand of *c.* 1300. The contents of *particula* 1 are printed in *Chronicon Monasterii de Abingdon*, ed. J. Stevenson (RS 1858). Before the cartulary was recovered, H. E. Salter drew attention to it and to the deed of St. Edmund in 'A Lost Cartulary of Abingdon Abbey', *Berks. Bucks. and Oxon. Arch. Journal*, xxiv. 1918, p. 28, and in his preface to *The Cartulary of the Hospital of St. John the Baptist, Oxford*, vol. iii (OHS 1916), p. lii.

[2] duos sol. *MS.* sol. *has been expuncted.*

Marcio, et xii denarios ad festum sancti Michelis. Et ut hec mea donacio firma et inconcussa permaneat eam sigilli mei munimine roboravi. Hiis testibus.

Grant by Andrew Halegod of a rent of three shillings from the tenement in Abingdon which Master Edmund gave to the Hospital of St. John the Baptist, and which Andrew has acquired by an exchange

Text: ibid., fo. 92^v.

Item de predicto mesuagio:

Sciant presentes et futuri quod ego Andreas Halegod de Oxon' dedi et concessi et hac presenti carta mea confirmavi domino Luce abbati de Abbendonia et eiusdem loci conventui et eorum successoribus ad exhibicionem pauperum pro salute anime mee et animabus antecessorum meorum tres solidos de annuali redditu in Abbendonia quos habui per escambium de fratribus sancti Iohannis de Oxon', scilicet quod predictus Lucas abbas et sui successores et conventus Abbendonie percipient illos iii solidos de annuali redditu de illo tenemento quod magister Eadmundus Abbend' antequam esset archiepiscopus Cantuariensis dedit et incartavit domui sancti Iohannis Oxon' ad terminos consuetos. Predicto eciam Luce abbati et suis successoribus et conventui Abbendonie pro me et heredibus meis dedi potestatem ad distringendum et namiandum in predicto tenemento si redditus ille in aliquo tempore fuerit aretro. Et ego Andreas Aligod et heredes mei predictum redditum predicto Luce abbati et suis successoribus et conventui Abbendon' sicut liberam elemosinam nostram contra omnes homines et feminas warentizabimus. Et in huius rei testimonium et securitatem hanc presentem cartam sigillo meo confirmavi. Hiis testibus.

Grant to St. Mary's, Catesby, by Edmund of Abingdon, of a house in Abingdon with a garden

Text: original, PRO Anc. Deeds E 326 B 4.

Sciant presentes et futuri quod ego Eadmundus de Abbendun' dedi et concessi et hac presenti carta mea confirmavi Deo et ecclesie beate Marie de Katesbi unam domum cum orto ad eandem pertinente in Abbendun'. Illam scilicet que sita est inter domum Symonis cisoris et domum Radulfi bolter, tenendam et habendam libere et quiete reddendo inde annuatim coquinario de Abbendun' duos denarios ad festum sancti Michaelis pro omni servicio. Concessi eciam eidem ecclesie unam croftam in Abbendun' fossis inclusam, illam scilicet que iacet inter terram Philippi Gule ad orientem et Petri de Coles ad occidentem. Tenendam et habendam libere et quiete reddendo inde annuatim Reginaldo de pistrino et heredibus suis duos capones ad natale Domini pro omni servicio. Et ut hec datio mea et concessio firma et inconcussa permaneret hoc scriptum sigilli mei apposicione roboravi. Hiis testibus: Briano de Sarum, Radulfo de Wikes, Hugone de Wutheham, Hugone de Ledebir', et multis aliis.

(Sealed *en double queue*; seal missing. Endorsed in a thirteenth-century hand: 'Carta sancti Eadmundi de mesagio in Abendon''.)

Grant by William, son of Reginald of Abingdon, to the nuns of St. Mary's, Catesby, of a rent of twelve pence in Abingdon

Text: original, PRO Anc. Deeds E 326 B 5.

Sciant presentes et futuri quod ego Willelmus filius Reginaldi de Abendon' dedi et concessi et hac presenti carta mea confirmavi Deo et beate Marie de Catesbi et monialibus ibidem Deo servientibus pro animabus patris mei et matris mee et antecessorum et successotum meorum, redditus duodecim denariorum annuatim ad festum sancti Michaelis, in villa de Abendon' de Rondulfo cementario vel de heredibus suis percipiendorum in puram et perpetuam elemosinam. Ut autem hec mea donacio, concessio, et contra omnes homines et feminas warantizacio firma sit et stabilis in perpetuum, presenti scripto sigillum meum apposui. Hiis testibus: Domino Thoma de Abendon', Hugone filio Henrici eiusdem ville, Domino Mathia de Abendon', Willelmo filio Iohannis, Roberto fratre suo, Rogero filio Reginaldi, Petro de Coles, et multis aliis.

(Sealed *en double queue* with small seal of yellow wax. Endorsed in a thirteenth-century hand: 'Reginaldus de Abendon' de xii d.')

APPENDIX D

TWO *ACTA* OF ARCHBISHOP EDMUND CONCERNING EUSTACE OF FAVERSHAM

Letter of Archbishop of Edmund to the subprior and convent of Dover, appointing Eustace his chaplain to be prior (7 March 1240)

Text: original, Canterbury D. and C. mun. Chartae Antiquae D 76.

Edmundus Dei gracia Cantuariensis archiepiscopus tocius Anglie primas dilectis in Christo filiis subpriori et conventui Dovor' salutem graciam et benedictionem. Audito nuper de morte cari nostri R. quondam prioris vestri, cupientes vobis tanquam filiis nostris specialibus salubriter providere, habito sollicito vobiscum tractatu tandem dilectum in Christo filium E. monachum ecclesie Christi Cantuariensis, capellanum nostrum virumque litteratum, providum et benignum, morum honestate preclarum et, ne ulterius eius laudibus insistamus, quem credimus secundum cor Dei, vobis prefecimus in priorem, credentes ex eius prefectione restauratam vobis ruinam que domui vestre per mortem alterius imminebat, attendentes eciam eius scienciam vobis sufficere ad doctrinam, et conversacionem eius laudabilem ad exemplum. Quo circa discretioni vestre mandamus firmiter iniungentes quatinus dicto E. priori vestro reverenciam et obedienciam tam devotam quam debitam impendentes eidem in spiritualibus et temporalibus sic affectuose ac efficaciter intendatis ut in vobis appareat filialis devocio per effectum, nosque id gratum habentes et acceptum ad vestrum commodum et honorem forcius animemus. Datum apud Sumalling' Nonas Marcii, pontificatus nostri anno sexto.

(Sealed *en queue simple*, the archbishop's seal att. in fragmentary state. Endorsed: 'De subiectione ecclesie Dovor'' and in another hand: 'Qualiter sanctus E. archiepiscopus ibi fecit priorem capellanum suum et monachum nostrum.')

Appendix D

Inspeximus by the bishops of Exeter, Worcester, and Norwich, of a letter of protection, dated 13 November 1240, granted by Archbishop Edmund to Eustace his chaplain

Text: original, Sens archives no. 3.

Omnibus Christi fidelibus presentes litteras inspecturis . . . miseracione divina Exon' . . . Wigorn' et . . . Norwicens' episcopi salutem eternam in Domino. Noverit universitas vestra nos litteras recolende sanctitatis beati Edmundi quondam Cantuariensis archiepiscopi patris nostri inspexisse quarum tenor talis est:

Omnibus Christi fidelibus ad quos presentes littere pervenerint E. permissione divina Cantuariensis archiepiscopus et tocius Anglie primas salutem eternam in Domino. Quod scimus loquimur et quod vidimus hoc testamur et, eo teste qui[1] vere veritas est, verum est testimonium nostrum. Ad hec sciatis quod dilectus in Christo filius, frater Eustachius, ecclesie nostre monachus, de precepto nostro circa nos ac nobiscum officium capellani, secretarii, ac cubicularii gerens, ordinate et religiose vivendo in hiis que obediencie ac observancie regularis existunt, prout perpendere potuimus, per omnia se nobis commendabilem ostendit. Unde eius conversacionem[2] non immerito approbantes et paci, tranquillitati, necnon et indempnitati eiusdem quantum possumus secundum Deum prospicere cupientes, ad vestram volumus pervenire noticiam quod si monachi Cantuarie ob multiplicatam eorundem contumaciam et manifestam offensam merito a nobis sentencia excommunicacionis innodati, contra ipsum eis communicare vel obedire nolentem aliquid statuere vel attemptare presumpserint, illud irritum decernimus et inane et eundem auctoritate ordinaria ab omnibus sentenciis suspensionis et excommunicacionis ab eisdem forsan latis in eum sive quibuscumque aliis sentenciis, quantum in nobis est, denunciavimus et denunciamus non ligatum. In cuius rei testimonium has litteras sigillo nostro signatas eidem duximus concedendas. Datum apud Soysy. Idus Novembris, pontificatus nostri anno septimo.

Nos igitur in testimonium inspectionis predictarum litterarum has litteras nostras fecimus fieri et sigillis nostris signari. Datum apud Pontiniacum.

[1] que MS   [2] comiseracionem MS

APPENDIX E

THE MUNIMENTS IN THE TRÉSOR OF SENS CATHEDRAL

THE canonization archives and other documents, which were presented to the cathedral in the nineteenth century, are in the charge of the Conservateur du Trésor, the Very Rev. Canon R. Fourrey. They are kept in a specially constructed wooden case, with sliding trays, and are generally in a fair state of preservation. But some of the documents bear traces of earlier neglect and a few have been severely damaged by damp and vermin. The documents have been numbered by an eighteenth-century hand in brown ink.

1. Letter of postulation from Guy, abbot of Provins. December 1240.
2. Notification by Master Richard de Wych of Archbishop Edmund's will to be buried at Pontigny. Dated at Orleans, 20 April 1242.
3. *Inspeximus* by the bishops of Exeter, Worcester, and Norwich, of letters of protection granted by Archbishop Edmund to Eustace his chaplain, at Soisy, 13 November 1240. Given at Pontigny. Undated. (Fragments of three seals attached.)
4. Letter of postulation from Abbot J. and convent of Pontigny. Undated.
5. Letter of postulation from the University of Oxford. Undated. (Seal tags and fragments of seals attached. Endorsed in a thirteenth-century hand: 'Quarta. Universitas Oxon.' Text slightly damaged by rats.)
6. Another copy of the above. Undated. (Rats have eroded a large hole extending from the fourth to the twelfth line.)
7. Letter of postulation from Abbot B. of La Ferté and the Cistercian General Chapter. 1241.
8. Letter of postulation from Abbot G. and convent of Eynsham. Undated.
9. Letter of postulation from Prior R. and convent of Merton. 27 February 1242. (Conventual seal attached.)

The Muniments in the Trésor of Sens Cathedral

10. Letter of postulation from R., Bishop of Nevers. Undated.
11. Letter of postulation from W., bishop of Exeter. Undated.
12. Letter of postulation from Bishop R. and chapter of Salisbury. Undated, but faintly endorsed in a thirteenth-century hand: 'Id. Augusti xli'. (Bishop's seal, and fragments of two others attached. There are many lacunae in the text caused by rats.)
13. Letter of postulation from Abbot R. and convent of Reading. Undated.
14. Letter of postulation from Abbot R. and convent of Westminster. Undated.
15. *Inspeximus* by four Cistercian abbots of letters of postulation from (i) the archbishops of Bourges and Tours, (ii) W., archbishop of York, (iii) the bishops of Meaux and Nevers, (iv) the bishop of Senlis, (v) the bishop of Auxerre. Undated.
16. *Inspeximus* by the same of letters from the bishops of Bangor and Bath, and the abbot and convent of Abingdon. Undated.
17. Bull of Innocent IV addressed to the archbishop of Armagh, the bishop of Senlis, and the dean of Paris, ordering them to convene an inquiry into the merits of St. Edmund. 23 April 1244. (Leaden bulla attached.)
18. Another copy of the above.
19. The same, addressed to the bishops of London and Lincoln. Dated as above.
20. Mandate of A., archbishop of Armagh, and the dean of Paris addressed to the ordinaries of the provinces of Rheims, Sens, and Lyons, convoking witnesses to the inquiry. 15 July 1244. (Fragments of two seals attached.)
21. Letters of F., bishop of London, and R., bishop of Lincoln, submitting to the Pope their report on the inquiry. Undated. (Seal of Bishop Robert Grosseteste attached.)
22. Parchment roll of six membranes containing fragment of the procès-verbal taken at Pontigny. Undated.
23. Letters of A., archbishop of Armagh, and the abbot of St. Marien, Auxerre, submitting their report on the second inquiry to the Pope. May 1245.

24. Another copy of the above (with seals of the archbishop and the abbot attached. This copy is endorsed in a thirteenth-century hand: 'Ultima relatio de Francia').
25. Letters of R., bishop of Chichester, the prior of Canons Ashby, and Master R. Bacon, O.P., submitting to the Pope their report on the second inquiry. November 1245. (Fragment of a seal attached.)
26. *Inspeximus* by W., bishop of Norwich, and R., bishop of Chichester, of a grant of 50 marks out of the church of New Romney made to Pontigny by Archbishop Stephen Langton in 1222, and of a grant of 10 marks out of the same church made by Archbishop Edmund in 1238. September 1245.
27. Apostolic mandate from I., cardinal-priest of St. Laurence in Lucina, and H., cardinal-priest of Santa Sabina, to the bishop of Lincoln, to procure witnesses to go to the papal court. 9 April 1246.
28. The same to the abbot of Bayham.
29. Letters of Archdeacon Simon Langton to I., cardinal-priest of St. Laurence in Lucina, and H., cardinal-priest of Santa Sabina, concerning his difficulties in procuring witnesses to go to the papal court. Hackington. 6 June 1246.
30. Letters of G., abbot of Provins, to the same, concerning the procuring of witnesses. June 1246.
31. Bull *Novum matris ecclesie* announcing the canonization of St. Edmund to the province of Lyons. 10 January 1247. (Leaden bulla attached.)
32. The same to the lay barons of England.
33. Letters of Archbishop Boniface to the suffragans of the Canterbury province, ordering the celebration of the feast of St. Edmund in the province. 1247.
34. Letter of cardinals to the church of Lyons, ordering the celebration of the feast of St. Edmund. 9 February 1247.
35. Bull of canonization. 29 March 1247 (Leaden bulla attached.)
36. Bull of Innocent IV confirming licence granted to Pontigny by the cardinal legate of Albano to decorate the reliquary of St. Edmund, notwithstanding statutes to the contrary. 10 December 1250.

The Muniments in the Trésor of Sens Cathedral

37. Another copy of the same.
38. *Inspeximus* by G., bishop of Auxerre, and the dean of Auxerre of a grant of 20 marks annually made by Henry III to maintain candles at the shrine of St. Edmund, dated 6 March 1251. August 1251. (The bishop's seal attached.)
39. Letters of credence by Archbishop A. of Livonia for those collecting for the reliquary of St. Edmund. Undated.
40. The same, addressed to the province of Dublin.
41. Bull of Alexander IV, ordering the celebration of the feast of St. Edmund by the church of Lyons. 4 February 1261.
42. Letters of Indulgence by Y., bishop of Connor, for those visiting the shrine of St. Edmund. 1245.
43. Letters of Indulgence by —, bishop of Liège. 1245.
44. Letters of Indulgence by A., bishop of Semgallen. 1246.
45. Letters of Indulgence by W., archbishop of York. 1246.
46. Letters of Indulgence by P., bishop of Hereford. 1246.
47. Letters of Indulgence by Boniface, archbishop of Canterbury.
48. Bull of Innocent IV, granting an Indulgence to all who visit Pontigny within a year of the canonization. 13 January 1247. (Leaden bulla attached.)
49. Missing.
50. Letters of Indulgence by W., bishop of Winchester. April 1247.
51. Letters of Indulgence by —, bishop of Carinola. 1248.
52. Bull of Innocent IV, authorizing women to enter the precinct of Pontigny on the anniversary of St. Edmund's canonization. 5 February 1248. (Leaden bulla attached.)
53. Letters of Indulgence by William, bishop of Bath and Wells. 18 February 1249.
54. Letters of Indulgence by Peter, bishop of Aberdeen. 1249.
55. Letters of Indulgence by E., bishop of Constance. 1250.
56. Letters of Indulgence by —, bishop of Tortosa. 1250.
57. Letters of Indulgence by Albert, archbishop of Livonia and Estonia. July 1250.
58. Letters of Indulgence by William, bishop of Le Puy. 1250.

Appendix E

59. Letters of Indulgence by B., bishop of Cahors. 1250.
60. Letters of Indulgence by Philip, archbishop of Bourges. 1250.
61. Letters of Indulgence by Henry of Segusia, bishop of Sisteron. 1250.
62. *Inspeximus* by J., cardinal-priest of St. Laurence in Lucina, of Indulgence granted by W., bishop of Bath and Wells. 27 December 1250.
63. Another copy of the same.
64. *Inspeximus* by abbots of the Cistercian Order at Pontigny of the letters of cardinals, authorizing the ornamentation of the reliquary of St. Edmund. 1251.
65. Letters of Indulgence by —, bishop of Culm. 1251.
66. Letters of Indulgence by John, archbishop of Genoa. 1251.
67. Letters of Indulgence by R., bishop of Rieti. 1251.
68. Letters of Indulgence by —, bishop of (?) Narni. 1251.
69. Letters of Indulgence by —, bishop of Noli. 1251.
70. Letters of Indulgence by S., bishop of Kilmore. 1251.
71. Letters of Indulgence by Clement, bishop of Dunblane. 1251.
72. Letters of Indulgence by G., bishop of Lacedaemon. 1251.
73. Letters of Indulgence by —, bishop of Brescia. 1251.
74. *Inspeximus* of Indulgences by the papal legate, Peter, bishop of Paneas. 1252.
75. Letters of Indulgence by —, bishop of St. David's. 1252.
75 bis. *Inspeximus* of Indulgences by the papal legate, Peter, bishop of Paneas. 1252.
76. Another copy of the same.
77. *Inspeximus* of Indulgences by Richard, bishop of Chichester. September 1252.
78. Letters of Indulgence by R., bishop of Dunkeld. June 1252.
79. Missing.
80. Letters of Indulgence by R., bishop of Venafro. 1250.
81. Missing.
82. Letters of Indulgence by Luke, bishop of Sora. 1254.
83. Letters of Indulgence by P., bishop of Todi. 1254.

The Muniments in the Trésor of Sens Cathedral 325

84. Letters of Indulgence by T., bishop of Samland. 1255.
85. Bull of Alexander IV, granting Indulgences on the anniversary of the translation of St. Edmund. 5 April 1255. (Leaden bulla attached.)
86. Bull of Alexander IV, authorizing English women to enter the precinct of Pontigny for the feast of the translation. 13 April 1255. (Leaden bulla attached.)
87. Bull of Alexander IV, confirming all Indulgences granted to contributors to the shrine. 16 April 1255. (Leaden bulla attached.)
88. Bull of Alexander IV, confirming the privilege granted to English women to enter the precinct of Pontigny. 22 April 1255.
89. Letters of Indulgence by John, bishop of Lübeck. 1255.
90. Letters of Indulgence by Peter, bishop of Nola. 1255.
91. Letters of Indulgence by Robert, bishop of Ross. 1255.
92. Letters of Indulgence by —, archbishop of Salerno. 1255.
93. Letters of Indulgence by T., bishop of Verona. 1255.
94. Letters of Indulgence by James, bishop of Bologna. 1255.
95. An *inspeximus* of Indulgences: sender and date obscured. Badly damaged by damp and vermin.
96. Letters of Indulgence by —, archbishop of Santa Severina. 1255.
97. Letters of Indulgence by John, archbishop of Messina. 1257.
98. Letters of Indulgence by Ithier, bishop of Laon. 1257.
99. Letters of Indulgence by Bartholomew (title omitted). 1260.
100. Letters of Indulgence by Hugh of Balsham, bishop of Ely. 1261.
101. Bull of Innocent IV, granting the Queen of France the privilege of burial at Pontigny. 24 April 1250. (Leaden bulla attached.)
102. A letter dated 1622, requesting the abbot of Pontigny for relics. Signature illegible.

APPENDIX F

LIST OF MANUSCRIPTS CITED

Auxerre
    Bibliothèque et Musée, MS. 123.

Cambridge
    Clare College MS. Kk.5.6.
    St. John's College, MS. c.12.
    Trinity College, MS. R.5.40.
    University Library, MS. LL.2.15.
                  MS. MM.4.6.

Canterbury
  Dean and Chapter muniments:
    Register A.
    Chartae Antiquae, C 35.
                   C 36.
                   C 120.
                   C 257.
                   D 76.
                   L 7.
    Literary manuscript C 20.

Dijon
    Bibliothèque municipale, MS. 646.

Douai
    Bibliothèque municipale, MS. 843.

Dublin
    Trinity College, MS. C.3.19.

Hereford
    D. & C. record 2036.

Leipzig
    Universitäts-Bibliothek, MS. 590.
                         MS. 633.

Lille
   Bibliothèque municipale, MS. 761.

London
  British Museum:
    Addit. Charter 21, 289.
    Addit. MS. 46352.
    Arundel MS. 68.
    Cotton MS. Claudius A vi.
              Claudius D x.
              Cleopatra B i.
              Domitian A iii.
              Faustina B i.
              Julius D ii.
              Julius D v.
              Julius D vi.
              Nero C iii.
              Nero D i.
              Vespasian F xv.
              Vitellius A viii.
              Vitellius C xii.
              Appendix xxi.
    Cotton Roll xiii. 27.
    Egerton MS. 3031.
    Harley MS. 2.
    Harley MS. 325.
    Royal MS. 2 D vi.
              8 F xiv.
              14 C vii.
    Stowe MS. 925.

  Inner Temple Library:
    Petyt MS. 538.

  Lambeth Palace:
    MS. 135.
    MS. 241.
    MS. 582.
    MS. 585.
    MS. 1212.

Public Record Office:
    Ancient Correspondence xi. 159.
    Ancient Deeds A 15420.
                    B 4.
                    B 5.
                    E 315/45, No. 139.
    K.R. Misc. Books E 164/27.
    Chancery Masters' Exhibit C 115/A 1.

Maidstone
    County Record Office: The Leeds cartulary.

Munich
    Bayerische Staatsbibliothek MS. lat. 2689.

Namur
    Bibliothèque du Musée archéologique, MS. 73.

Oxford
    Balliol College, MS. 226.
    Bodleian Library, Fell MS. 2.
                     Lyell MS. 15.
                     Rawlinson MS. B 254.
                     Tanner MS. 223.
                     Top. Kent MS. D 3.
    Corpus Christi College, MS. 154.
    Magdalen College, Durrington Charter 2.
    Merton College record 957.

Sens
    Trésor de la cathédrale, see app. E.

Windsor
    St. George's Chapel, D. & C. mun. IV.B.1.

INDEX

Aaron, archbishop's clerk, parson of Wimbledon, 142, 152, 154, 304, 308, 309, 313.
Abbeville, Master John of, 119, 121 n.
Aberdeen, bishop of, see Ramsey.
Abingdon, town of, 68, 100, 108–10, 315; abbey of 34, 295; abbots of, see John, Luke; cartulary of, 108 & n., 315 n.; church of St. Helen at, 110; church of St. Nicholas at, 109–10; hospital of, 77, 109.
— Aldithe of, 315.
— Alice of, sister of St. Edmund, 83, 101, 107–8, 222, 270, 279.
— St. Edmund of, his family, 106–10, 222–3, 250; his studies at Paris, 117, 122, 223, 248; his regency in Arts at Oxford, 110–17, 249; his regency in theology, 117–20, 234, 251; his pupils, 115–16, 118–19; Treasurer of Salisbury, 122–4, 237; his *Speculum Ecclesie*, 121–2; his gloss on the Psalms, 120–1; lectures at Salisbury, 123–4; preaches the Crusade, 53, 123, 236, 251; elected archbishop, 124–9, 210, 237–9; his character, 129, 131–2; his asceticism, 113–14, 129, 187–202 *passim*; mediates in the Marshal's war, 132–8, 240–2; *familia*, 138–55; visitations, 156–7; dispute over law of bastardy, 158–60; project for a collegiate church, 165–7; relations with papal legate, 162–4, 199, 258, 259; relations with the king, 161–2, 171–2, 199, 216–17, 258–60; visits Rome, 141, 163, 170; dispute with the chapter of Rochester, 170; struggle with his chapter, 164–8, 199, 216, 254–8; alleged exile, 168–81, 200, 217, 261–3; Itinerary 183–5; Canonization Process of, 1–2, 4, 7–9, 14–30, 240, 279, 280–5 (bull of canonization); Translation of, 285–6; Office of, 48, 60 & n., 63; Lives of, *see* Anonymous 'A', Anonymous 'B', Anonymous 'C', Faversham, Matthew Paris, Pontigny Life, Quadrilogus.
— Hugh, son of Henry of, 317.
— Mabel of, mother of St. Edmund, 68, 83, 100–1, 195, 203, 222–3, 250, 290, 291, 295; apparition of, 69, 206–7, 229, 250–1.
— Margery of, sister of St. Edmund, prioress of Catesby, 83, 101, 107–8, 222, 270, 279.
— Sir Mathias of, 317.
— Nicholas of, brother of St. Edmund, 83, 106, 222.
— Reginald of, father of St. Edmund, 55–56, 77 n., 83, 106–10, 222, 315.
— Robert of, brother of St. Edmund, rector of Wingham, 6, 37–38, 39, 45–46, 61, 83, 106, 111, 144–6, 147 & n., 152, 154, 163, 203, 222, 307, 310, 312, 313.
— Rondulf the mason of, 107, 109.
— Roger, son of Reginald of, 317.
— Simon of, 316.
— Sir Thomas of, 317.
—William, son of John of, 317.
Abraham, treasurer of Salisbury cathedral, 122 n.
Achab, 131.
Ad limina, 175.
Aigueblanche, Peter d', bishop of Hereford, 323.
Alagno, Caesare di, archbishop of Salerno, 325.
Alban, St., Life of, 70–71.
Albeney, Hugh of, *see* Arundel.
Albert, archbishop of Armagh, archbishop of Livonia, 8, 14–18, 23, 46, 59–60, 104, 310, 321, 323.
Alconbury, 12.
Aldersbach, abbey of, 48.
Aldington, archbishop's manor of, 156 & n., 183, 184, 185, 304, 305, 312; bailiff of, 313.
Alexander III, Pope, 10, 72 n., 158.
Alexander IV, Pope, 323, 325.

Index

Alpine passes, 177.
Altzelle, abbey of, 48.
Amphibalus, St., Life of, *see* St. Alban.
Anagni, abbey of St. Mary at, 308.
Andres, William of, chronicler, 127.
Andrew, servant of Sir Robert Asthall, 22.
Anonymous 'A', Life of St. Edmund by, 4, 29–30, 49–61, 100–5, 106–7, 169, 179.
Anonymous 'B', Life of St. Edmund by, 4, 5, 61–63, 100–5.
Anonymous 'C', Life of St. Edmund by, 4, 5, 64–70, 100–5.
Anselm, St., archbishop of Canterbury, 177.
Arden, Master Philip of, 124 n.
Arderne, Simon of, 156.
Ardfert, bishop of, *see* John.
Arezzo, Rainaldus of, bishop of Rieti, 324.
Aristotle, reception of, 112–13; New Logic of, 1, 112, 116; *libri naturales* of, 113.
Armagh, bishop of, *see* Albert.
Arnold, bishop of Semgallen, 323.
Ars dictaminis, 236 & n.
Arundel, Thomas, archbishop of Canterbury, 5.
— Hugh, Earl of, 84, 172, 257.
— Isabella, Countess of, 75, 76 n.
Asthall, Sir Robert of, 22, 189; his servants, *see* Andrew, Walter.
Ater, Gunivilde, 108, 315.
Attenborough, Ralph of, 12.
Auvergne, William of, bishop of Paris, 127.
Auxerre, bishops of, *see* Sully, Mello.
— dean of, 323.
— abbey of St. Germain, 9.
— abbot of St. Marien at, 321.
Avranches, Master Henry of, 127, 128.

Bacon, Peter, 155 n.
Bacon, Master Robert, O.P., 6, 17, 28, 64, 73–74, 76, 84, 96, 103, 111, 113–14, 117, 119, 121 n., 131, 153, 292, 321; deposition of, 248–53.
Bacon, Roger, 1, 112 & n.
Baker, A. T., 74–76.

Baldwin, archbishop of Canterbury, 166.
Bale, John, 28, 37.
Balsham, Hugh of, bishop of Ely, 325.
Bangor, bishop of, *see* Richard.
Bar-sur-Seine, 177.
Bartholomew, bishop of Cahors, 324.
Basset, Fulk, bishop of London, 16, 321, 323.
Basset, Gilbert, 134, 241.
Bastardy, law of, 158–60.
Bath (& Wells), bishops of, *see* Wells, Button; archdeacons of, 140 n.
— Robert of, 154.
Battle, abbey of, 313.
Bayham, abbot of, *see* Reginald.
Bazoches, Guy of, 113 n.
Beauvais, Vincent of, 48.
Beaune, 177.
Bec, abbey of, 305.
Bech, Henry of, 154, 313.
Becket, St. Thomas, archbishop of Canterbury, 168, 169, 178, 179, 254, 260; Life of by John of Salisbury, 2, 34, 35–38, 44, 49, 70–73, 217; promise of, 8, 105, 274, 283; charter of, 88; St. Edmund's vision of, 104.
Bekesbourne, rectory of, 142, 144, 312; rector of, *see* William.
Benedict, St., 224.
Beoli, Anclina, of 21.
Berkshire, archdeacon of, *see* William.
Bernard, St. of Clairvaux, 31, 263.
Berruyer, Philip, archbishop of Bourges, 321, 324.
Bertrand, prior of Pontigny, alleged author of the Life of St. Edmund, 46, 48, 49.
Beverley, St. John of, 32.
— minster, provost of, 150.
Bexley, manor of, 155 n.
Bilsington, church of, 305, 307; vicar of, *see* Gosebech.
Bingham, Robert, bishop of Salisbury, 293, 295, 321.
Bishopstone, Master Henry of, canon of Salisbury, 154, 309.
Blanche of Castile, Queen Regent of France, 84, 104, 262, 286.
Blois, William of, bishop of Worcester, 157 n., 306.

Index

Blund, Master John, 83, 125–7, 128, 164, 239.
Bocking, rectory of, 144, 152; rector of, *see* Abingdon, Master Robert of.
— Ralph of, 131 n., 148 n.
Bologna, bishop of, *see* Buoncambio.
Bourges, archbishop of, *see* Berruyer.
Boxgrove, prior and convent of, 305, 307.
Boxley, abbey of, 83, 100, 106, 222; abbot of, 165.
Bracton, Henry, 159 & n.
Bradeley, church of, 150 n.
Bradsole, St. Radegunde's, abbot of, 165; abbot and convent of, 309.
Braose, lands of, 137.
Bredon, Brother A. of, 50.
Brescia, bishop of, *see* Torbiato.
Brewer, William, bishop of Exeter, 320, 321.
Bridport, Giles of, bishop of Salisbury, 64.
Brockton, truce of, 132, 136, 137.
Bruno, abbot of La Ferté, 15, 320.
Buckland, abbey of, 53 & n.; vision of the nun of, 102.
Bullok, William, bailiff of Bexley, &c., 155 n.
Buoncambio, James, bishop of Bologna, 325.
Buoni, St. John, canonization of, 12, 25–26.
Burford, Master Nicholas of, archbishop's Official, 143, 144, 147 n., 154, 307, 308, 309, 312, 313.
Burgh, Hubert de, earl of Kent, Justiciar, 84, 87, 103, 125, 130, 134, 241 & n., 257.
Burn, Eudo dean of, 308.
Burne, William of, 154.
Burton, annalist of, 161 & n.
Burwardiscote, Master Roger of, 151, 154, 312.
Bury, Richard of, 31.
Bury, St. Edmund's abbey, 31, 276.
Button, William, bishop of Bath & Wells, 323, 324.

Cahors, bishop of, *see* Bartholomew.
Calne, prebendal church of, 58, 103, 122, 124, 129, 237 n.
Cambrai, bishop of, *see* Laudano.
Canonization, 1, 10; reservation of, 10; process of, 7, 10–14, 25–27, 30; of St. Edmund, *see* Abingdon.
Canons Ashby, prior of, 17, 322.
Canterbury, archbishops of, *see* Anselm, Becket, Dover, Baldwin, Walter, Langton, Grand, Abingdon, Savoy, Pecham, Arundel; archdeacon of, *see* Langton; chancellors of, *see* Reginald, Wich; council of, 147 & n.; collegiate church of, 165–7; Officials of, *see* Frekenham, Burford, Langdon; seal of, 143, 147; diocese of, 311; Christ Church cathedral priory, 39, 63, 82, 84, 89, 276, 304, 307, 308, 309; prior of, *see* Chetham; subprior of, 167; monks of, 124, 148–9, 163, 164–8, 172, 254–5, 258, 269, 277, 309, 310, 311, 312, 313; Liberty of, 164, 171; Gervase, chronicler of, 161, 165, 173; St. Augustine's abbey at 16, 50, 61, 140, 308, 314; abbot and convent of, 307, 313; St. Gregory's priory at, 144, 308, 312, 313; St. Laurence's Hospital at, 314; St. Martin's church, rector of, 311; town of, 4, 306, 307, 309, 310.
Cantilupe, Walter of, bishop of Worcester, 184.
Cantimpré, Thomas of, 127.
Cardun, Peter, 304.
Carinola, bishop of, 323.
Carlisle, bishop of, *see* Mauclerc.
Carsing, Peter of, 154.
Carthusian Order, 88, 103, 163, 255.
Catesby, priory of, 83, 85, 101, 104, 105, 107–8, 222, 250, 270, 278–9, 316, 317; prioress of, *see* Abingdon, Margery of.
Chalgrove, 53, 55, 101.
Châlis, abbey of, 49.
Châlons-sur-Saône, 177.
Chambly, Adam de, bishop of Senlis, 321.
Chanter, Peter the, 121, 251 n.
Chardonnet, College of the Cistercians, 118 & n.
Chart, rector of, *see* Robert.
Chartres, Theodoric of, 122.
Cheshunt, 12.

Index

Chetham, John of, prior of Christ Church, 83, 87, 163, 239, 255, 306.
Chichester, bishops of, *see* Neville, Wich; precentor of, 150 n.
Chillenden, church of, 305.
Chislet, church of, 307.
Cistercian Order, 48, 118–19; General Chapter of, 15, 320; *see also* Chardonnet, Cîteaux.
Cirencester, annals of, 174 n.
Cîteaux, abbey of, 48; abbot of, 15, 104.
Clarendon, Constitutions of, 72 n.
Clement, bishop of Dunblane, 15 n., 324.
Cluny, Order of, 313.
Cogorno, John of, archbishop of Genoa, 324.
Colonna, John, archbishop of Messina, 325.
Combe, prior of, 305.
Combwell, prior and convent of, 310.
Connor, bishop of, *see* Isaac.
Conrad, bishop of Noli, 324.
Constance, bishop of, *see* Walburg.
Cornut, Robert, bishop of Nevers, 321.
Cortiniaco, Robin of, 20.
Cotton, Sir Robert, 37.
Coulours, The Templars at, 104, 220, 275.
Courçon, Robert, Cardinal priest of St. Stephen on the Coelian Hill, 116.
Coventry (& Lichfield), bishops of, *see* Stavensby, Pateshull.
Cremona, Sicard of, 9 & n.
Croydon, manor of, 155 n., 156 n., 183, 305.
Crusade, preached by St. Edmund, 53, 102, 123.
Crutch, 53, 102.
Cuisy, Peter de, bishop of Meaux, 321.
Culm, bishop of, *see* Heidenreich.
Curragh, the, 135.

Davis, H. W. C. 53, 55.
Denham, rectory of, 150 n.
Depden, manor and church of, 304.
Dereham, abbot of, 307.
— Master Elias of, canon of Salisbury, 141–2, 144, 147, 148, 152, 154, 167, 304, 312.
Dominic, St., 13, 25–26, 27, 86.
Dominicans (Friars Preachers), 152–3, 243, 290; General Chapter of, 243 n.
Dorking, Robert of, 154, 307, 309, 313.
Dover, 177, 183; dean and chaplains of, 305, 311; St. Martins priory, 41; prior of, 149, *and see* Faversham, Olecumbe; convent of, 304, 305, 306, 308, 311, 312.
— Richard of, archbishop of Canterbury, 166.
Dublin, citizens of, 133 n.
Dunblane, bishop of, *see* Clement.
Dunkeld, bishop of, *see* Inverkeithing.
Dunstable, annalist of, prior of, *see* Morins.
— Master Richard of, O.P., 21, 22–24, 111, 114, 153, 187, 292.
Durand, Dom. U., 8, 47.
Durham, cathedral priory of, 276.
— Richard of, 111 n.

Eccleston, Thomas of, 132 n.
Ednevet, Howell-ap, bishop of St. Asaph's, 176 n.
Edward the Confessor, 10, 71.
Edward, Prince, son of Henry III, 90, 104, 170, 259.
Eleanor, Countess of Leicester, sister of Henry III, 170.
Elham, church of, 150 n., 152.
Elizabeth, St., of Hungary, 26–27.
Ellesmere, 137.
Elmstead, church of, 312.
Ely, bishop of, *see* Balsham, Gray.
Emden, A. B., 6 & n., 116 n.
Essendon, Geoffrey of, 304.
Essex, Robert of, 77, 85, 268, 313.
Eu, Alice Countess of, 309.
Evesham, battle of, 181.
Exeter, bishop of, *see* Brewer; Breviary of, 63.
Eye, church of, 303.
Eynsham, abbey of, 83, 100, 106–7, 222; abbot of, 320.

Fairford, Richard of, 155 n.

Index

Farnham, 183, 304.
Faversham, church of, 307.
— Eustace of, chaplain and hagiographer of St. Edmund, 2–3, 19, 21, 25, 58, 114, 144, 148–9, 154, 310, 312, 313, 318, 319, 320; Life of St. Edmund by, 30–47, 178–81, **203–21**; Deposition of, 120, 178–81, **195–202**.
Ferriby, Brother Walter of, archbishop's steward, 148, 151 n., 154.
Ferring, Master Geoffrey of, 150, 152, 154, 312, 313.
FitzBernard, Ralph, fees of, 171.
FitzGerald, Maurice, Justiciar of Ireland, 134.
Flambard, William, 304.
Fleta, 146 n.
Folcard, 32.
Foliot, Gilbert, bishop of London, 72 n., 139 n.
Francis, St. of Assisi, Life of, 50; testament of, 50.
Freckenham, Master Thomas of, Official of Canterbury, 141, 147, 154, 307.
Frederick II, Emperor, 126, 177.

G., bishop of Lacedaemon, 324.
Gaëtano, Peter, bishop of Todi, 324.
Galiun, Roger, 304.
Garland, John of, 236 n.
Gascony, 5.
Genoa, archbishop of, see Cogorno.
Gilbert, *de camera*, 155.
Glorieux P., 117 n., 123 n.
Gloucester, 53, 102; council at, 133–4, 183.
Gosebech, Thomas of, vicar of Bilsington, 307.
Goudhurst, church of, 306.
Grand, Richard le, archbishop of Canterbury, 124, 125, 140, 141, 147.
Gravelines, 173, 177, 185.
Gray, Hawysia de, 115 n.
— John de, bishop of Norwich, 115.
— Walter de, Chancellor, bishop of Worcester, archbishop of York, 34, 43, 76, 77, 101, 103, 115–16, 214, 247, 252, 301, 321, 323.
— William, bishop of Ely, 50.

Great Seal, The, 116, 180 n.
Gregory, St., 210; Dialogues of, 31, 35, 189, 238.
Gregory IX, Pope, 16, 27, 103, 125, 126, 128, 129, 212, 239 & n., 244, 257, 290, 313.
Grosseteste, Robert, bishop of Lincoln, 1, 108, 121 n., 146, 163, 181; consecration of, 304; *familiares* of, 151, 152–3; dispute with his chapter, 156–7; his relations with St. Edmund, 158 & n., 159 & n., 160 & n., 162, 171; member of the canonization commission, 16, 18, 19, 321, 322.
Guala, James, cardinal priest of St. Martin, papal legate, 144.
Guston, church of, 306.
Guy, abbot of Provins, 19, 320, 322.

Hackington, 322.
Hadlow, manor of, 184, 310.
Halegod, Andrew, 109, 316.
Hailes, annals of, 173, 174.
Hales, Master Alexander of, 18, 121 n.
Ham, church of, 305.
Harbledown, rector of, see Luke.
Hardy, Sir Thomas Duffus, 34.
Harrow, rectory of, 152; manor of, 155 n.
Heidenreich, bishop of Culm, 324.
Henry III, king, 4, 103, 130–8, 158, 159, 160, 171, 199, 216, 239, 257–8, 323.
Henschenius, the Bollandist, 8.
Heptateuchon, the, of Theodoric of Chartres, 112.
Hereford, 53, 102, 183, 303; bishops of, see Aigueblanche; bishopric of, 171; hospital of, 303.
— Master R. of, archdeacon of Middlesex, 143, 153, 308.
Hermagnus, Brother, monk of Pontigny, 105.
Higden, Ranulph, chronicle of, 60.
Hildegarde, St., canonization of, 26.
Historia Canonizationis, the, by Albert archbishop of Armagh, 8, 15, 46.
Hollingbourne, rector of, see Richard.
Homobonus, St., canonization of, 11 n.

Index

Honorius III, Pope, 11–12.
Hook, Dean, *Lives of the Archbishops* by, 5 & n.
Hostiensis, *see* Segusia, Henry of.
Hougham, church of St. Laurence of, 304, 306.
Hugh, bishop of St. Asaph's, 176.
Hugh, Master, regent at Oxford, 112.
Hugh, St., of Lincoln, 12–13, 27; Life of, 86.
Hugh of St. Cher, cardinal priest of S. Sabina, 17, 19, 322.

Indulgence, letters of, 323–5.
Innocent III, Pope, 10, 11, 17, 125.
Innocent IV, Pope, 16, 18, 27, 240, 279, 321, 322, 323, 325.
Inverkeithing, Richard of, bishop of Dunkeld, 324.
Ireland, Estates of Marshal in, 132–3; war in, 133–4; Justiciar of, 134, 136.
Isaac, bishop of Connor, 323.

James, M. R., 71 & n.
Jardinet, Le, abbey of, 48.
John, king, 116, 125.
John (Tolet), cardinal priest of S. Lorenzo-in-Lucina, 15, 17–18, 46, 322, 324.
John, bishop of Ardfert, 149, 309, 313.
John, bishop of Lübeck, 325.
John, archdeacon of St. Albans, 258.
John, the archbishop's almoner, 154.
John the chaplain, 38.
John, Master, rector of Sibertswold, 308.
Jordan, clerk of the archbishop, 144, 154, 311, 312.
Judges delegate, 165, 173, 257, 305, 310.

Kenilworth, siege of, 181.
Kent, sheriff of, 167, 311.
Kilkenny, church of the Franciscans at, 135.
Kilmore, bishop of, *see* O'Ruark.
Kirby, prior of, 305.
Kirkestede, Brother Henry of, 31.
Kunegunde, St., canonization of, 11 n.

Lacedaemon, bishop of, *see* G.
Lacock, abbey of, 58; abbess of, *see* Salisbury, Ela Countess of.
Lacy, Irish lands of, 134.
La Ferté, abbot of, *see* Bruno.
Lambeth, manor of, 155 n., 184, 310; bailiff of, 140 n.
Lanercost, chronicle of, 111 & n., 224 n.
Langdon, Master Richard of, archbishop's Official, 143, 154, 307, 310, 311.
Langport, church of, 314.
Langton, Master Simon, archdeacon of Canterbury, 19, 40, 125, 127, 129, 140–1, 307.
—— Stephen, cardinal, archbishop of Canterbury, 1, 12, 121, 123 n., 141, 142, 149, 152, 157, 168, 169, 181, 252–3, 322; Life of, 71, 73.
Laon, bishop of, *see* Mauny.
Lateran, Councils of, 107 n.
Laudano, Guido de, bishop of Cambrai, 18.
Laurence, St., of Dublin, canonization of, 11.
Ledebir, Hugh of, 317.
Leeds, prior and convent of, 305, 306, 310; church of, 308.
Lege, Roger de la, prior-elect of Christ Church, 167, 310.
Leicester, archdeacon of, 305.
—— Master Roger of, 144, 154, 309, 312, 313.
—— Simon of, monk of Christ Church, 89 & n.
Leinster, earldom of, 133, 134.
Leland, John, 28, 37–38.
Lenham, rector of, *see* Roger.
Leominster, 53, 102, 183, 303.
Le Puy, bishop of, *see* Murat.
Lewes, prior and convent of, 53, 104, 303, 314; fisheries of, 314.
Lewknor, 55.
Lexington, Henry of, bishop of Lincoln, 118.
—— Master Stephen of, 58, 101, 118, 251; abbot of Stanley, 102, 118, 123; abbot of Savigny, 118; abbot of Clairvaux, 59, 118.
Libellus Quatuor Ancillarum, 26.
Liber Sancti Edmundi, 8, 15, 47.

Liebermann, Felix, 73.
Liège, bishop of, see Thorete.
Ligny, 54, 104.
— Margaret of, 21.
Lincoln, bishops of, see Hugh, Grosseteste, Lexington; chapter of, 156.
Livonia, archbishop of, see Albert.
Llanthony by Gloucester, priory of, 9, 304.
Llewelyn-ap-Gryfedd, prince of Snowdon, 132, 137-8, 157.
London, bishops of, see Foliot, Niger, Basset; St. Paul's cathedral, 176; chancellor of, 150; dean of, see Ferring; Holy Trinity, prior of, see Richard; St. Mary Aldermary, 307.
— Master John of, 311.
— Master Reginald of, 144, 312.
Loos, abbey of, 48.
Louis IX, king of France, 262 & n., 286.
Louis St., of Toulouse, 42 n.
Lübeck, bishop of, see John.
Luke, bishop of Sora, 324.
Luke, Master, rector of Harbledown, 313.
Lumley, Lord, books of, 31, 49.
Luvel, Henry, 154.
Lyminge, manor of, 156 n., 185, 311.
Lyons, 85, 177, 285; Council of, 176, 279.

Mâcon, 177.
Maidstone, 156 n., 183, 306; collegiate church at, 166-7.
Malmesbury, William of, 31, 33.
Mandeville, Countess Maud de, 304.
Manegod, Thurbern, 108, 315.
Mansueti, James, bishop of Narni, 324.
Margam, abbey of, 132.
Margaret, St., Life of, 50.
Margaret of Provence, Queen of France, 325.
Marsh, Adam, O.F.M., 145.
Marshal, earl Richard the, 1, 84, 91-92, 129, 130-7, 240.
— earl Gilbert the, 84, 87, 92, 103, 133-4, 136, 137, 180 n., 240-41.
Martène, Dom E., 8-9, 47.

Martin, St., of Tours, Life of, 18, 34, 35-36, 47, 103, 212, 244, 245.
Mathefelon, Juhellus de, archbishop of Tours, 321.
Mauclerc, Walter, bishop of Carlisle, 259.
Mauny, Ithier de, bishop of Laon, 325.
Maurice, abbot of Quimper, canonization of, 12.
Meath, 133.
Meaux, bishop of, see Cuisy.
Mello, Guy de, bishop of Auxerre, 323.
Merton, priory of, 34, 43, 83, 101, 111, 119-20, 207, 230, 234, 297, 320; prior of, see Robert; Council of, 160, 183.
Messina, archbishop of, see Colonna.
Meyer, Paul, 71.
Middle, truce of, 137-8, 183.
Middlesex, archdeacon of, see Reginald.
Middleton, church of, 307.
Minster, church of, 307.
Montfort, Simon de, earl of Leicester, 84, 104, 169, 257, 258.
Montmirail, Master John of, O.P., 21 & n., 189.
Moralitates, of St. Edmund, 120-1.
More, John, bishop of Norwich, 50.
Morins, Richard of, prior of Dunstable, annalist, 119, 172-3, 258 & n., 305.
Morley, Master Daniel, 113.
Mt. Cenis pass, 177.
Murat, Guillaume de, bishop of Le Puy, 323.

Narni, bishop of, see Mansueti.
Nequam, Alexander, 113.
Nevers, bishop of, see Cornut.
Neville, Ralph, bishop of Chichester, Chancellor, 34, 80, 83, 124, 148 & n., 180 n., 239, 300.
— Thomas, dean of Canterbury, book owner, 34.
Newark, 176, 185.
New Logic, see Aristotle.
New Romney, church of, 322.
Nicholas, St., Life of, 224.

Index

Niger, Roger, bishop of London, 76–77, 83, 84, 89–90, 103, 130, 157, 174 n., 238 & n., 256, 257, 311.
Nogent, 177.
Nola, bishop of, *see* Peter.
Noli, bishop of, *see* Conrad.
Northampton, schools at, 53, 101.
Northfleet, manor of, 145 n., 155 n.
Norwich, bishops of, *see* Ralegh, Suffield, Gray, More.
North Luffenham, rectory of, 22 n.
North Stoke, rectory of, 22 n.

Offington, Master John of, 39 n., 150–1, 154, 304, 308, 309.
Olecumbe, Robert of, prior of Dover, 41.
Orleans, 320.
Orpington, Ralph of, monk of Christ Church, 163.
Orta, John of, 42 n.
O'Ruark, Simon, bishop of Kilmore, 324.
Oseney, abbey of, 162; annalist of, 173, 176.
Otford, 103, 216, 248.
Otto Candidus, cardinal deacon of St. Nicholas in carcere Tulliano, papal legate, 139 n., 147 n., 161, 166; his visitation of Christ Church, 84, 88, 103, 255, 308; relations with archbishop Edmund, 44, 104, 162–4, 169–70, 199, 258, 259, 261; Matthew Paris's hostile portrait of, 87, 90–91, 162; his character, 162, 164; statutes of, 156 n., 162.
Oxford, University of, 1, 7, 16, 22, 34, 66, 83, 111–20, 126, 234 & n., 290–3, 320; chancellor's commissary, 151; St. Edmund Hall, 6, 116 n.; Dominican priory at, 22, 29; St. Peter's-in-the-East, 116 n.; All Saints churchyard, 53, 102; St. John's churchyard, 53–54, 102; Hospital of St. John the Baptist, 108, 315, 316; the King's Hall, 54, 102.

Pallium, the, 128, 143, 175, 239.
Paneas, bishop of, *see* Peter.
Papebroch the Bollandist, 8.
Paravicini, Baroness de, 6 & n.

Paris, bishops of, *see* Auvergne; dean of, 16–17, 321; University of, 83, 101, 111–13, 117, 126, 127, 248; Dominican priory at, 21, 189; church of S. Merri, 117.
— Matthew, 124, 126, 128, 147, 162, 164, 165; Life of St. Edmund by, 2–3, 4, 5–6, 28, 34–35, 47, 62, 70–100, 100–5 (synopsis), 106, 107, 108 n., 109, 114, 124, 145, 147, 169–70, 179–80, **222–89**; *Chronica Maiora* of, 72–73, 95–100, 131, 179–80; *Historia Anglorum* of, 89–92, 95–100, 177, 179–80; *Liber Additamentorum* of, 94, 97–100.
Pateshull, Hugh, bishop of Coventry, 176, 185.
Pecham, John, archbishop of Canterbury, 148 & n.
Perrons, Bernard of, 21.
Peter, bishop of Nola, 325.
Peter, bishop of Paneas, 324.
Peter, the Chancellor of Paris, 127.
Peter, the sacrist of Pontigny, 105.
Pisa, Agnellus of, O.F.M., 132 & n.
Pitseus, 29, 37.
Pluralities, 127–8, 152.
Pontigny, abbey of, 7–20 *passim*, 35, 85, 104, 168, 173, 177, 178 n., 180, 200, 217, 263, 270, 271, 278, 286, 320, 322, 325; abbot of, 14, 39, 57, 78, 220, 273–4, 320; shrine of St. Edmund at, 4, 219, 322, 323, 324.
Pontigny Life of St. Edmund, 4, 8, 47–49, 51–61, 100–5 (synopsis), 106, 169, 179.
Poore, Richard le, bishop of Salisbury, 68, 102, 122.
Posterior Analytics of Aristotle, 112.
Powicke, F. M. 97–98.
Precentor, John the, of St. Edmund's, 29.
Privy Seal, the, 130, 132, 134.
Provins, 177; abbey of St. Jacques, 15, 104, 178, 200 n.; abbot of, *see* Guy; the Templars at, 220 n.

Quadrilogus, the, by St. Edmund's *familiares*, 2, 3, 4, 9–10, 21–30, 41, 42–45, 50, 57, **187–202**.
Quarr, abbey of, 101; abbot of, 65, 118, 251.

Index

Quimper, abbot of, see Maurice.

Rainaldus, bishop of Venafro, 324.
Ralegh, William, royal judge, bishop of Norwich, 59–60, 104, 150, 158, 160 n., 185, 267 & n., 313, bishop of Winchester, 59, 323; Official of, 150.
Ramsey, Peter of, bishop of Aberdeen, 323.
Reading, abbey of, 34, 80, 82, 113 n.; abbot and convent of, 298, 303, 321.
Reculver, manor of, 304.
Reginald, abbot of Bayham, 19, 78, 85, 100, 148, 285, 304, 309, 313, 322.
Reginald, Master, archdeacon of Middlesex, 146.
Reynger, Richard, 304.
Rhône, the, 177.
Richard, bishop of Bangor, 115, 321.
Richard, earl of Cornwall, 22–23, 98 n.
Richard, Master, rector of Hollingbourne, 152, 154.
Richard, prior of Holy Trinity, London, 304.
Rieti, bishop of, see Arezzo.
Rievaulx, Ailred of, 71.
Rievaux, Peter des, Keeper of the Wardrobe, 125, 130, 132, 133.
Risborough, rectory of, 145.
Robert, bishop of Ross, 325.
Robert, prior of Merton, 297, 320.
Robert, Master, rector of Chart, 308.
Robert, *cubicularius* of Archbishop Edmund, 21, 24, 155; deposition of, 191–5.
Roches, Peter des, bishop of Winchester, 125, 126, 128, 130, 131 n., 132, 133.
Rochester, bishops of, see Sandford, Wendene; cathedral priory of, 30–31, 82, 103, 170, 172, 175; chapter of, 84, 169, 257, 258; annalist of, 172.
Roger, rector of Lenham, 312.
Ross, bishop of, see Robert.
Royaumont, abbey of, 47.

St. Albans, abbey of, 88, 115, 149, 276; chronicles of, see Paris, Matthew; Wendover, Roger; archdeacon of, see John.
— Benedict of, 72.
— William of, 71.
St. Asaph's, bishops of, see Ednevet, Hugh.
St. Bertin, abbey of, 163, 177, 184.
St. David, bishop of, see Waleys.
St. Edmund, William of, 142.
S. Germano, Nicholas de, archbishop of S. Severina, 325.
St. Giles, Master John of, O.P., 127 n.
S. Lorenzo-in-Lucina, cardinal priest of, see John.
S. Merri, church of, 101.
S. Sabina, cardinal priest of, see Hugh.
S. Severina, archbishop of, see S. Germano.
St. Valery, honour of, 22.
St. Victor, Hugh of, 122.
Salerno, archbishop of, see Alagno.
Salisbury, bishops of, see Poore, Bingham, Bridport; cathedral church of, 123 & n., 190, 192, 314; chapter of, 34, 68, 112, 122–4, 191, 293; dean of, 58; treasurer of, see Abraham, Abingdon.
— Ela, Countess of, 53, 55, 58 & n., 102; abbess of Lacock, 102.
— Brian of, 317.
— John of, 35–36, 169.
Samland, bishop of, see T.
Sandford, Henry, bishop of Rochester, 132, 137.
Sandwich, 177, 217.
Savoy, Boniface of, archbishop of Canterbury, 147 n., 322, 323.
Saxony, Jordan of, O.P., 86.
Seasalter, church of, 143, 308.
Segrave, Stephen, 241.
Segusia, Master Henry of, bishop of Sisteron, cardinal bishop of Ostia (Hostiensis), 14 n., 324.
Seinliz, Simon of, 148 & n., 154.
Sele, prior and convent of, 305.
Semgallen, bishop of, see Arnold.
Sempringham, St. Gilbert of, canonization of, 11–12, 16, 32 n.
Senlis, bishop of, see Chambly.

Sens, archbishop of, *see* Walter; cathedral of, 7, 15.
Shalmsford, 184.
Shirley, moor of, 313.
Shotenbury, chapel of, 303.
Shrewsbury, 132, 183.
Sibertswold, rector of, *see* John.
Sisteron, bishop of, *see* Segusia.
Sittingbourne, John of, prior of Christ Church, 125.
Siward, Richard, 134.
Slindon, manor of, 156 n., 183, 305, 306.
Snave, bailiff of, 313.
Soisy, 14, 38, 40, 54, 104, 173, 178 & n., 185, 200, 217, 219, 265 & n., 270, 313; prior of, 85, 93, 95, 270.
Somercote, Walter of, 142, 154, 307, 313.
Sophistici Elenchi, 112.
Sora, bishop of, *see* Luke.
South English Legendary, 60 & n.
South Malling, manor of, 155 n., 156 & n., 183, 184, 185, 303, 305, 310, 311, 312, 314, 318; dean and chapter of, 303.
Southwark, manor of, 155 n.; prior of, 310.
Speculum Historiale, 48.
Stafford, Master Robert of, archbishop's clerk, archdeacon of Stafford, 140 n., 143 n., 149–50 & n., 152, 154, 304, 307, 308.
Stanley, abbey of, 58, 123; abbot of, *see* Lexington.
Stapelhurst, Geoffrey of, archbishop's clerk, 154, 308.
Stavensby, Alexander of, bishop of Coventry, 132, 137.
Stephen, archdeacon of Wiltshire, 119.
Stephen, subdeacon, *cubicularius* of archbishop Edmund, 21, 24–25, 155; deposition of, 189–91.
Stoke, prior and convent of, 310.
Stokenbury, church of, 305.
Stoneton, chapel of, 50.
Stratford, 53, 102.
Striguil, castle of, 137.
Sudbury, archdeacon of, 310.
Suffield, Walter, bishop of Norwich, 320, 322.

Sulby, abbot and convent of, 305.
Sully, Bernard de, bishop of Auxerre, 16, 321.
Sulpicius Severus, 18 & n., 35.
Surius, 37, 61–62.
Swinfield, Master Richard, 124.

T. bishop of Samland, 325.
T. (?), bishop of Verona, 325.
Talbot, Sir William, 155, 312.
Tanner, Thomas, 38.
Tewkesbury, 157, 183; annalist of, 173, 174–5, 176.
Teynham, manor of, 40, 149, 156 n., 184, 185, 310, 311.
Thanet, Isle of, 262.
Thetford, priory of, 37.
Thorete, Robert of, bishop of Liège, 323.
Thorley, William, 304.
Thornton-on-Humber, abbey of, 31.
Todi, bishop of, *see* Gaëtano.
Toledo, school of, 112.
Tonnerre, 177.
Torbiato, Azzo de, bishop of Brescia, 324.
Tournai, Stephen of, 230 n.
Tours, archbishop of, *see* Mathefelon.
Trainel, 14, 57, 104, 219, 272.
Trivet, Nicholas, 153.
Troyes, 177.
Tunbridge, manor of, 184.
Twelve Apostles, cardinal priest of, *see* William.

Urban II, Pope, 10.
Usk, siege of, 131.

Vaughan, R. 73 n.
Venafro, bishop of, *see* Rainaldus.
Verona, bishop of, *see* ? T.
Villeneuve l'archevêque, 104, 220, 274.
Vincentius Hispanus, 18.
Viole, Dom George, 8–9.
Visch, Charles de, 49 & n.
Visitations, episcopal, 156–7.
Vitry, Jacques de, 230 n.

Walburg, Eberhard of, bishop of Constance, 323.

Index

Walden, abbot and convent of, church of, 304.
Walemere, Master John de, 308.
Wales, Marches of, 130–33.
Waleys, Thomas le, bishop of St. David's, 324.
Wallace, Dom Wilfrid, 3 & n., 5–6, 61–62.
Walsingham, Thomas of, chronicler of St. Albans, 70.
Walter, servant of Sir Robert Asthall, 22.
Walter, archbishop of Sens, 105.
Walter, Hubert, archbishop of Canterbury, 16, 116, 141, 142, 157, 159 n., 166 & n.
Waltham, abbey of, 74.
Warenne, Earl William of, 314.
Welbeck abbey, Legendary of, 74.
Wells, Henry of, archbishop's clerk, 154, 307, 308.
— Jocelin of, bishop of Bath & Wells, 321.
Wendene, Richard of, bishop of Rochester, 170, 184.
Wendover, Roger of, 70, 82, 91, 124, 126, 128, 132, 135–6.
Westminster, abbot and convent of, 321; council at, 183.
West Tarring, church of, 306.
Wich, Master John of, 144, 151, 154, 250 & n., 312.
— Master Richard of, chancellor of the archbishop, 85, 94, 100, 131 n., 144, 146–7, 153, 245 n., 272 & n., 285, 307, 309, 312, 313, 320; bishop of Chichester, 17, 73–74, 78, 96, 105, 322, 324.
Wick, church of, 304.
Wikes, Ralph of, 317.
William, cardinal priest of the Twelve Apostles, 18.
William, Master, archdeacon of Berkshire, 308.
William, rector of Bekesbourne, archbishop's clerk, 154, 307.
William Longspée, earl of Salisbury, 53, 55, 58, 102.
Wiltshire, archdeacon of, see Stephen.
Wimbledon, manor of, 155 n.; rector of, see Aaron; church of, 142 & n., 152.
Winchelsea, Master Robert, 124.
Winchester, bishops of, see Roches, Ralegh; bishopric of, 171; cathedral priory of, 306; chapter of, 171 & n., annals of, 174 n.
Wingham, manor of, 147 n., 155 n., 156, 176, 183, 184, 185, 306, 311, 312; rector of, see Abingdon, Master Robert of; rectory of, 144, 145, 152.
Wintney, prioress and convent of, 304.
Wintreselle, Henry of, 155, 312.
Wissant, 177.
Wood, Anthony, 3, 9, 116 n.
Woodstock, royal palace of, 84, 133, 136, 183, 240.
Worcester, 53, 102, 184; bishops of, see Gray, Blois, Cantilupe; cathedral priory of, 157; annals of, 174 & n.
Writs of prohibition, 161, 165.
Writ, return of, 311.
Wrotham, vision of St. Edmund at, 103, 216, 248.
Wulfstan, St., of Worcester, canonization of, 11.
Wutheham, Hugh of, 317.
Wye, church of, 313.
Wymondham, priory of, 75.
Wykes, Thomas, annalist, 176.

OTHER TITLES IN THIS HARDBACK REPRINT PROGRAMME FROM SANDPIPER BOOKS LTD (LONDON) AND POWELLS BOOKS (CHICAGO)

ISBN 0–19–	Author	Title
8143567	ALFÖLDI A.	The Conversion of Constantine and Pagan Rome
6286409	ANDERSON George K.	The Literature of the Anglo-Saxons
8219601	ARNOLD Benjamin	German Knighthood
8208618	ARNOLD T.W.	The Caliphate
8228813	BARTLETT & MacKAY	Medieval Frontier Societies
8219733	BARTLETT Robert	Trial by Fire and Water
8111010	BETHURUM Dorothy	Homilies of Wulfstan
8142765	BOLLING G. M.	External Evidence for Interpolation in Homer
814332X	BOLTON J.D.P.	Aristeas of Proconnesus
9240132	BOYLAN Patrick	Thoth, the Hermes of Egypt
8114222	BROOKS Kenneth R.	Andreas and the Fates of the Apostles
8203543	BULL Marcus	Knightly Piety & Lay Response to the First Crusade
8216785	BUTLER Alfred J.	Arab Conquest of Egypt
8148046	CAMERON Alan	Circus Factions
8148054	CAMERON Alan	Porphyrius the Charioteer
8148348	CAMPBELL J.B.	The Emperor and the Roman Army 31 BC to 235
826643X	CHADWICK Henry	Priscillian of Avila
826447X	CHADWICK Henry	Boethius
8222025	COLGRAVE B. & MYNORS R.A.B.	Bede's Ecclesiastical History of the English People
8131658	COOK J.M.	The Troad
8219393	COWDREY H.E.J.	The Age of Abbot Desiderius
8644043	CRUM W.E.	Coptic Dictionary
8148992	DAVIES M.	Sophocles: Trachiniae
825301X	DOWNER L.	Leges Henrici Primi
814346X	DRONKE Peter	Medieval Latin and the Rise of European Love-Lyric
8142749	DUNBABIN T.J.	The Western Greeks
8154372	FAULKNER R.O.	The Ancient Egyptian Pyramid Texts
8221541	FLANAGAN Marie Therese	Irish Society, Anglo-Norman Settlers, Angevin Kingship
8143109	FRAENKEL Edward	Horace
8201540	GOLDBERG P.J.P.	Women, Work and Life Cycle in a Medieval Economy
8140215	GOTTSCHALK H.B.	Heraclides of Pontus
8266162	HANSON R.P.C.	Saint Patrick
8224354	HARRISS G.L.	King, Parliament and Public Finance in Medieval England to 1369
8581114	HEATH Sir Thomas	Aristarchus of Samos
8140444	HOLLIS A.S.	Callimachus: Hecale
8212968	HOLLISTER C. Warren	Anglo-Saxon Military Institutions
8226470	HOULDING J.A.	Fit for Service
2115480	HENRY Blanche	British Botanical and Horticultural Literature before 1800
8219533	HOUSLEY Norman	The Italian Crusades
8223129	HURNARD Naomi	The King's Pardon for Homicide – before AD 1307
8140401	HUTCHINSON G.O.	Hellenistic Poetry
9240140	JOACHIM H.H.	Aristotle: On Coming-to-be and Passing-away
9240094	JONES A.H.M	Cities of the Eastern Roman Provinces
8142560	JONES A.H.M.	The Greek City
8218354	JONES Michael	Ducal Brittany 1364–1399
8271484	KNOX & PELCZYNSKI	Hegel's Political Writings
8212755	LAWRENCE C.H.	St Edmund of Abingdon
8225253	LE PATOUREL John	The Norman Empire
8212720	LENNARD Reginald	Rural England 1086–1135
8212321	LEVISON W.	England and the Continent in the 8th century
8148224	LIEBESCHUETZ J.H.W.G.	Continuity and Change in Roman Religion
8143486	LINDSAY W.M.	Early Latin Verse
8141378	LOBEL Edgar & PAGE Sir Denys	Poetarum Lesbiorum Fragmenta
9240159	LOEW E.A.	The Beneventan Script
8241445	LUKASIEWICZ, Jan	Aristotle's Syllogistic
8152442	MAAS P. & TRYPANIS C.A.	Sancti Romani Melodi Cantica
8142684	MARSDEN E.W.	Greek and Roman Artillery—Historical
8142692	MARSDEN E.W.	Greek and Roman Artillery—Technical
8148178	MATTHEWS John	Western Aristocracies and Imperial Court AD 364–425
9240205	MAVROGORDATO John	Digenes Akrites
8223447	McFARLANE K.B.	Lancastrian Kings and Lollard Knights
8226578	McFARLANE K.B.	The Nobility of Later Medieval England
814296X	MEIGGS Russell	The Athenian Empire
8148100	MEIGGS Russell	Roman Ostia
8148402	MEIGGS Russell	Trees and Timber in the Ancient Mediterranean World
8141718	MERKELBACH R. & WEST M.L.	Fragmenta Hesiodea

8143362	MILLAR F.G.B.	Casssius Dio
8142641	MILLER J. Innes	The Spice Trade of the Roman Empire
8147813	MOORHEAD John	Theoderic in Italy
8264259	MOORMAN John	A History of the Franciscan Order
8181469	MORISON Stanley	Politics and Script
9240582	MUSURILLO H.	Acts of the Pagan Martyrs & Christian Martyrs (2 vols)
9240213	MYRES J.L.	Herodotus The Father of History
8219512	OBOLENSKY Dimitri	Six Byzantine Portraits
8270259	O'DONNELL J.J.	Augustine: Confessions (3 vols)
8116020	OWEN A.L.	The Famous Druids
8131445	PALMER, L.R.	The Interpretation of Mycenaean Greek Texts
8143427	PFEIFFER R.	History of Classical Scholarship (vol 1)
8143648	PFEIFFER Rudolf	History of Classical Scholarship 1300–1850
8111649	PHEIFER J.D.	Old English Glosses in the Epinal-Erfurt Glossary
8142277	PICKARD–CAMBRIDGE A.W.	Dithyramb Tragedy and Comedy
8269765	PLATER & WHITE	Grammar of the Vulgate
8213891	PLUMMER Charles	Lives of Irish Saints (2 vols)
820695X	POWICKE Michael	Military Obligation in Medieval England
8269684	POWICKE Sir Maurice	Stephen Langton
821460X	POWICKE Sir Maurice	The Christian Life in the Middle Ages
8225369	PRAWER Joshua	Crusader Institutions
8225571	PRAWER Joshua	The History of The Jews in the Latin Kingdom of Jerusalem
8143249	RABY F.J.E.	A History of Christian Latin Poetry
8143257	RABY F.J.E.	A History of Secular Latin Poetry in the Middle Ages (2 vols)
8214316	RASHDALL & POWICKE	The Universities of Europe in the Middle Ages (3 vols)
8154488	REYMOND E.A.E & BARNS J.W.B.	Four Martyrdoms from the Pierpont Morgan Coptic Codices
8148380	RICKMAN Geoffrey	The Corn Supply of Ancient Rome
8141556	ROSS Sir David	Aristotle: De Anima
8141076	ROSS Sir David	Aristotle: Metaphysics (2 vols)
8141092	ROSS Sir David	Aristotle: Physics
8142307	ROSTOVTZEFF M.	Social and Economic History of the Hellenistic World, 3 vols.
8142315	ROSTOVTZEFF M.	Social and Economic History of the Roman Empire, 2 vols.
8264178	RUNCIMAN Sir Steven	The Eastern Schism
814833X	SALMON J.B.	Wealthy Corinth
8171587	SALZMAN L.F.	Building in England Down to 1540
8218362	SAYERS Jane E.	Papal Judges Delegate in the Province of Canterbury 1198–1254
8221657	SCHEIN Sylvia	Fideles Crucis
8148135	SHERWIN WHITE A.N.	The Roman Citizenship
9240167	SINGER Charles	Galen: On Anatomical Procedures
8113927	SISAM, Kenneth	Studies in the History of Old English Literature
8642040	SOUTER Alexander	A Glossary of Later Latin to 600 AD
8270011	SOUTER Alexander	Earliest Latin Commentaries on the Epistles of St Paul
8222254	SOUTHERN R.W.	Eadmer: Life of St. Anselm
8251408	SQUIBB G.	The High Court of Chivalry
8212011	STEVENSON & WHITELOCK	Asser's Life of King Alfred
8212011	SWEET Henry	A Second Anglo-Saxon Reader—Archaic and Dialectical
8148259	SYME Sir Ronald	History in Ovid
8143273	SYME Sir Ronald	Tacitus (2 vols)
8200951	THOMPSON Sally	Women Religious
924023X	WALBANK F.W.	Historical Commentary on Polybius (3 vols)
8201745	WALKER Simon	The Lancastrian Affinity 1361–1399
8161115	WELLESZ Egon	A History of Byzantine Music and Hymnography
8140185	WEST M.L.	Greek Metre
8141696	WEST M.L.	Hesiod: Theogony
8148542	WEST M.L.	The Orphic Poems
8140053	WEST M.L.	Hesiod: Works & Days
8152663	WEST M.L.	Iambi et Elegi Graeci
9240221	WHEELWRIGHT Philip	Heraclitus
822799X	WHITBY M. & M.	The History of Theophylact Simocatta
8206186	WILLIAMSON, E.W.	Letters of Osbert of Clare
8208103	WILSON F.P.	Plague in Shakespeare's London
8247672	WOODHOUSE C.M.	Gemistos Plethon
8114877	WOOLF Rosemary	The English Religious Lyric in the Middle Ages
8119224	WRIGHT Joseph	Grammar of the Gothic Language